# Lecture Notes in Computer Science     **15499**

Founding Editors

Gerhard Goos
Juris Hartmanis

The series Lecture Notes in Computer Science (LNCS), including its subseries Lecture Notes in Artificial Intelligence (LNAI) and Lecture Notes in Bioinformatics (LNBI), has established itself as a medium for the publication of new developments in computer science and information technology research, teaching, and education.

LNCS enjoys close cooperation with the computer science R & D community, the series counts many renowned academics among its volume editors and paper authors, and collaborates with prestigious societies. Its mission is to serve this international community by providing an invaluable service, mainly focused on the publication of conference and workshop proceedings and postproceedings. LNCS commenced publication in 1973.

Jong-Hyouk Lee · Keita Emura · Sokjoon Lee
Editors

# Information Security Applications

25th International Conference, WISA 2024
Jeju Island, South Korea, August 21–23, 2024
Revised Selected Papers

 Springer

*Editors*
Jong-Hyouk Lee 🆔
Sejong University
Seoul, Korea (Republic of)

Keita Emura 🆔
Kanazawa University
Kanazawa, Japan

Sokjoon Lee 🆔
Gachon University
Seongnam, Korea (Republic of)

ISSN 0302-9743          ISSN 1611-3349 (electronic)
Lecture Notes in Computer Science
ISBN 978-981-96-1623-7          ISBN 978-981-96-1624-4 (eBook)
https://doi.org/10.1007/978-981-96-1624-4

This Springer imprint is published by the registered company Springer Nature Singapore Pte Ltd.
The registered company address is: 152 Beach Road, #21-01/04 Gateway East, Singapore 189721, Singapore

If disposing of this product, please recycle the paper.

# Preface

Artificial Intelligence, cloud computing, and a myriad of other innovative IT technologies are profoundly transforming and enriching our lives. In today's rapidly evolving digital landscape, cybersecurity transcends the realm of mere technicality; it emerges as a paramount challenge that demands collective societal responsibility and collaborative effort. Addressing this critical issue necessitates vibrant dialogue and rigorous discourse grounded in the profound insights of leading researchers, ultimately propelling the advancement of groundbreaking innovations and technological progress.

The World Conference on Information Security Applications (WISA) stands as a premier platform in the field of security research, jointly organized by the Korea Institute of Information Security and Cryptology (KIISC) and the Electronics & Telecommunications Research Institute (ETRI), with the esteemed support of co-sponsors such as the National Intelligence Service (NIS), the Ministry of Science and ICT (MSIT), the Korea Internet and Security Agency (KISA), the National Security Research Institute (NSR), and the Korea Institute of Science and Technology Information (KISTI).

This year, WISA delved into the transformative potential of diverse cutting-edge technologies to enhance cybersecurity. The conference addressed both theoretical and practical dimensions of topics such as artificial intelligence-driven security, 5G/6G security, supply chain security, and other emerging applications.

This volume features 28 distinguished papers selected from the proceedings of WISA 2024, held from August 21 to 23 on the picturesque Jeju Island, South Korea. These contributions were meticulously curated from a total of 87 submissions spanning a broad array of subjects, with a rigorous peer-review process conducted by 44 Program Committee members, resulting in a competitive acceptance rate of 32.2%. We express our heartfelt gratitude to the authors for their exemplary submissions and their willingness to engage with the constructive feedback offered by editors and reviewers, as well as for their cooperation throughout the revision process.

We were particularly honored to feature two keynote addresses of profound significance: Koji Nakao from the National Institute of Information and Communications Technology, Japan explored "Proactive Cybersecurity Measures and Response through Passive Monitoring Technology," while Sal Francomacaro from the National Institute of Standards and Technology, USA illuminated "Information Security and Standards: Common Goals and Synergies." Furthermore, we were delighted to feature an invited talk by Junji Shikata of Yokohama National University, Japan who discussed "Advanced Cryptography Based on Post-Quantum Cryptography for Future Communication Services."

The success of WISA 2024 is a testament to the unwavering dedication and collective efforts of the General Chairs, Advisory and Steering Committees, Organizing Committee, and reviewers. It is also a reflection of the generous support provided by our sponsors and co-sponsors, and the enthusiastic engagement of all participants. We extend our deepest appreciation to the Program Committee members for their diligent contributions, to the authors for their scholarly excellence, and to the attendees for their active participation. Lastly, we wish to express our sincere gratitude to the Springer team for their invaluable assistance in producing the LNCS proceedings.

November 2024

Jong-Hyouk Lee
Keita Emura
Sokjoon Lee

# Organization

## General Co-chairs

Jaecheol Ha      Hoseo University, South Korea
Seung Chan Bang      ETRI, South Korea

## Advisory Committee

Dong-Hoon Lee      Korea University, South Korea
Heekuck Oh      Hanyang University, South Korea
Jaecheol Ryou      Chungnam National University, South Korea
Kyung-Hyune Rhee      Pukyong National University, South Korea
Okyeon Yi      Kookmin University, South Korea
Souhwan Jung      Soongsil University, South Korea
Yoojae Won      Chungnam National University, South Korea

## Steering Committee

Dooho Choi      Korea University, South Korea
Ho-Won Kim      Pusan National University, South Korea
Ilsun You      Kookmin University, South Korea
Jeong-Nyeo Kim      ETRI, South Korea
Jin Kwak      Ajou University, South Korea

## Program Committee Co-chairs

Jong-Hyouk Lee      Sejong University, South Korea
Keita Emura      Kanazawa University, Japan
Sokjoon Lee      Gachon University, South Korea

## Organizing Committee Co-chairs

Manhee Lee      Hannam University, South Korea
Yousung Kang      ETRI, South Korea

## Program Committee

| | |
|---|---|
| Byoungyoung Lee | Seoul National University, South Korea |
| Cheng-Chi Lee | Fu Jen Catholic University, Taiwan |
| Chun-Wei Tsai | National Sun Yat-sen University, Taiwan |
| Daiki Miyahara | University of Electro-Communications, Japan |
| Deok-Gyu Lee | Seowon University, South Korea |
| Gunhee Lee | NSR, South Korea |
| Hikaru Tsuchida | Saitama Institute of Technology, Japan |
| Hiroaki Kikuchi | Meiji University, Japan |
| Hyoungshick Kim | Sungkyunkwan University, South Korea |
| Hyung Chan Kim | NSR, South Korea |
| Ijaz Ahmad | VTT - Technical Research Centre of Finland, Finland |
| Il-Gu Lee | Sungshin Women's University, South Korea |
| JaeSeung Song | Sejong University, South Korea |
| Ji Sun Shin | Sejong University, South Korea |
| Jong Hwan Park | Sangmyung University, South Korea |
| Jongsung Kim | Kookmin University, South Korea |
| Joobeom Yun | Sejong University, South Korea |
| Jun Lee | KISTI, South Korea |
| Kaisei Kajita | Japan Broadcasting Corporation, Japan |
| Kamal Singh | Jean Monnet University, France |
| Keisuke Hara | AIST, Japan |
| Ki-Woong Park | Sejong University, South Korea |
| Kouichi Sakurai | Kyushu University, Japan |
| Kwangsu Lee | Sejong University, South Korea |
| Kyosuke Yamashita | Osaka University, Japan |
| Madhusanka Liyanage | University College Dublin, Ireland |
| Manabu Tsukada | University of Tokyo, Japan |
| Masayuki Fukumitsu | University of Nagasaki, Japan |
| Mika Ylianttila | University of Oulu, Finland |
| Mun-Kyu Lee | Inha University, South Korea |
| Naveen Chilamkurti | La Trobe University, Australia |
| Neeraj Kumar | Thapar Institute of Engineering and Technology, India |
| Nobuyuki Sugio | Hokkaido University of Science, Japan |
| Pawani Porambage | VTT - Technical Research Centre of Finland, Finland |
| Pham Van Huy | Ton Duc Thang University, Vietnam |
| SeogChung Seo | Kookmin University, South Korea |
| Shingo Sato | Yokohama National University, Japan |

Taisei Takahashi            Tsukuba University, Japan
Tetsushi Ohki               Shizuoka University, Japan
Young-Gab Kim               Sejong University, South Korea
Yuseok Jeon                 Ulsan National Institute of Science and
                            Technology, South Korea

## Organizing Committee

Changhoon Kim               Daegu University, South Korea
Daesun Choi                 Soongsil University, South Korea
Dongho Kang                 ETRI, South Korea
Eunjoong Kim                Igloo Security, South Korea
Haehyun Cho                 Soongsil University, South Korea
Jaedeok Lim                 ETRI, South Korea
Jinyoung Oh                 KISA, South Korea
Jonghee Youn                Yeungnam University, South Korea
Jungtaek Seo                Gachon University, South Korea
Junghee Kim                 KISA, South Korea
Junghoon Lee                Somansa, South Korea
Jungseok Song               KISTI, South Korea
Jungsoo Park                Kangnam University, South Korea
Myoungho Kim                Coontec, South Korea
Wonho Kim                   NSR, South Korea
Wonhyouk Lee                KISTI, South Korea
Woonyeon Kim                NSR, South Korea
Youngcheol Cho              Piolink, South Korea

# Invited Talk and Keynotes

# Advanced Cryptography Based on PQC for Future Communication Services (Invited Talk)

Junji Shikata

Yokohama National University, Japan

**Abstract.** By Advanced Cryptography, we mean cryptographic schemes that claim superiority over conventional cryptographic primitives in terms of added or improved functionality, or new functionality, such as being able to solve problems that were difficult to solve with the conventional ones. For example, advanced cryptography includes ID-based encryption, attribute-based encryption, broadcast encryption, homomorphic encryption; and ID-based signature, aggregate signature, attribute-based signature, ring signature. This talk explains advanced cryptography based on PQC for their utilization under future emerging environments such as Beyond 5G (B5G). In addition, Japanese research projects on advanced cryptography based on PQC for secure wireless communication and their activities are introduced and explained.

# Proactive Cybersecurity Measures and Response through Passive Monitoring Technology (Keynote)

Koji Nakao

National Institute of Information and Communications
Technology (NICT), Japan

**Abstract.** Due to the diversification and sophistication of cyber attacks in recent years, there has been no end to the number of serious attacks on organizations, and the damage (impact) to organizations is increasing. As a countermeasure, I will provide more proactive cyber security measures and methods for responding to cyber attacks by observing and capturing cyber attacks using passive monitoring methods such as darknet and honeypots to capture signs of attacks, etc.

# Information Security and Standards: Common Goals and Synergies (Keynote)

Sal Francomacaro

National Institute of Standards and Technology (NIST), USA

**Abstract.** Information security and standards are critical components in safeguarding digital information and ensuring consistent, reliable, and secure operations across various industries. This presentation explores the common goals and synergies between information security practices (and Cryptography) and established standards. By examining the intersection of these domains, we identify how standards can facilitate the implementation of robust security measures, enhance interoperability, and promote a unified approach to risk management. Furthermore, this presentation discusses best practice in information security standardization and the role of standards in fostering global collaboration, streamlining compliance efforts, and driving continuous improvement in information security. The findings highlight the importance of aligning security initiatives with standard frameworks to achieve comprehensive protection and operational excellence.

# Contents

**Malware**

**Software Security**

**Emerging Topic**

# Cryptography

# ECPM Cryptanalysis Resource Estimation

Dedy Septono Catur Putranto[1,2] , Rini Wisnu Wardhani[3] , Jaehan Cho[3] ,
and Howon Kim[3(✉)] 

[1] IoT Research Center, Pusan National University, Busan 609735, South Korea
[2] Blockchain Platform Research Center, Pusan National University, Busan 609735,
South Korea
[3] South Korea School of Computer Science and Engineering,
Pusan National University, Busan 609735, South Korea
howonkim@pusan.ac.kr

**Abstract.** Elliptic Curve Point Multiplication (ECPM) is a key component of the Elliptic Curve Cryptography (ECC) hierarchy protocol. However, the specific estimation of resources required for this process remains underexplored despite its significance in the cryptanalysis of ECC algorithms, particularly binary ECC in GF $(2^m)$. Given the extensive use of ECC algorithms in various security protocols and devices, it is essential to conduct this examination to gain valuable insights into its cryptanalysis, specifically in terms of providing precise resource estimations, which serve as a solid basis for further investigation in solving the Elliptic Curve Discrete Logarithm Problem. Expanding on several significant prior research, in this work, we refer to as ECPM cryptanalysis, we estimate quantum resources, including qubits, gates, and circuit depth, by integrating point addition (PA) and point-doubling (PD) into the ECPM scheme, culminating in a Shor's algorithm-based binary ECC cryptanalysis circuit. Focusing on optimizing depth, we elaborate on and implement the most efficient PD circuit and incorporate optimized Karatsuba multiplication and FLT-based inversion algorithms for PA and PD operations. Compared to the latest PA-only circuits, our preliminary results showcase significant resource optimization for various ECPM implementations, including single-step ECPM, ECPM with combined or selective PA/PD utilization, and total−step ECPM ($2n$ PD +2 PA).

**Keywords:** ECC · ECPM · Point Addition · Point Doubling ·
Quantum Cryptanalysis

D. S. C. Putranto—This research was supported by the MSIT (Ministry of Science and ICT), Korea, under the Convergence security core talent training business (Pusan National University) support program (RS-2022-II221201) supervised by the IITP (Institute for Information & Communications Technology Planning & Evaluation).

J.-H. Lee et al. (Eds.): WISA 2024, LNCS 15499, pp. 3–15, 2025.
https://doi.org/10.1007/978-981-96-1624-4_1

# 1    Introduction

Elliptic-curve cryptography (ECC), introduced by Koblitz and Miller in 1985, has become a cornerstone of modern cryptography due to its ability to achieve equivalent security levels with significantly smaller key sizes than traditional cryptosystems. This efficiency has led to widespread adoption in various applications, including Transport Layer Security (TLS) 1.3 [13] and cryptographic standards set by the National Institute of Standards and Technology (NIST) [2]. However, the security of ECC hinges on the difficulty of the elliptic curve discrete logarithm problem (ECDLP). While ECC offers advantages in key size, Shor's algorithm [15], proposed in 1994, poses a significant threat to its long-term security. Extensive research has focused on the practical implementation of Shor's algorithm for ECDLP on quantum computers, particularly targeting superconducting qubit architectures. These studies have explored both prime and binary elliptic curves, leading to significant advancements in optimizing quantum circuits for ECDLP solving (e.g., [4,14]).

Building upon this prior work, this research delves deeper into the resource estimation of elliptic curve point multiplication (ECPM), a critical operation within ECC protocols (as depicted in Level 3 of Fig. 1). While classical implementations of ECPM have explored optimized architectures utilizing Montgomery modular multiplication (e.g., [10]), our focus lies on building optimum depth and estimating resource requirements for ECPM in a quantum context. Notably, this research aims to estimate resources for ECPM as a building block for binary ECC cryptanalysis circuits based on Shor's algorithm, drawing inspiration from established works such as [1,12,14].

Specifically, we elaborate on depth optimization within the first and second levels of the ECC hierarchy by analyzing existing constructions in finite field arithmetic operations in $GF(2^m)$ for binary ECC circuits. These optimized operations are then employed in both point addition (PA) and point doubling (PD) to construct a resource-efficient ECPM scheme (as the third level) that can be integrated into a binary ECC cryptanalysis circuit. We propose and compare optimized quantum circuit designs for these operations, focusing on a detailed comparative analysis of circuit depth. The key contributions of this research include:

- We leverage recent advancements in finite field arithmetic for $GF(2^m)$. Specifically, we incorporate the improved Karatsuba multiplication algorithm proposed by Putaranto et al. [12] and the FLT-based inversion algorithm from Larasati et al. [9] (or incorporation research in [12]) into our quantum circuits for PA and PD. Additionally, we identify improved PA algorithm from existing research [12] and integrate it into the ECPM circuit construction.
- We analyze three PD circuit versions from Larasati et al. [8] and select the most depth-efficient model for inclusion within our ECPM scheme for binary ECC cryptanalysis based on Shor's algorithm. This choice deviates from the PD circuits employed in previous works by Roetteler et al. [14], Banegas et al. [1], and Putranto et al. [12], prioritizing circuit depth optimization.

- We construct an ECPM circuit within a quantum environment and perform a comprehensive resource estimation, including the number of qubits, gates, and circuit depth. Notably, we compare our findings with concrete binary ECC cryptanalysis previous studies that solely utilize PA circuits (e.g., [1, 12]). This comparison highlights the depth optimization achieved through our work.
- We report our preliminary results, based on comparisons with the most recent PA-only circuit from [12], demonstrating the resource efficiency achieved through our approach. These comparisons encompass single-step ECPM, ECPM with combined or selective PA/PD utilization, and total-step ECPM ($2n$ PD $+2$ PA).

## 2    Related Works

Shor's groundbreaking in 1994 addressed two fundamental problems: integer factorization and computing discrete logarithms in finite fields [15]. Building on this foundation, Proos and Zalka made significant strides by translating Shor's high-level ECDLP algorithm into a format suitable for quantum circuit implementation for specific elliptic curve groups [11]. This paved the way for a surge of research on the practical application of Shor's algorithm for ECDLP in quantum cryptanalysis.

Pioneering work by Roetteler et al. [14] and Haner et al. [4] refined quantum cryptanalysis techniques for ECC over prime fields. More recently, Banegas et al. [1] directed their efforts towards optimizing Shor's algorithm for binary elliptic curves in a concrete quantum cryptanalysis circuit. Their work centered on optimizing the algorithm's critical multiplication and division circuits, proposing space-efficient techniques like Van Hoof's Karatsuba multiplication to reduce the required qubits and Toffoli gates [5]. The performance of two inversion circuits (GCD-based and FLT-based) was compared to calculate the resource cost of PA. Their primary objective was to minimize the number of qubits and Toffoli gates needed [1]. Complementing these binary field studies, Putranto et al. [12] and Larasati et al. [9] investigated depth-reduction techniques for implementing Shor's algorithm on quantum cryptanalysis binary elliptic curves. This focus on efficiency reflects the ongoing quest to improve the practicality of quantum cryptanalysis for ECC.

Figure 1 illustrates a widely adopted hierarchy for ECC implementations. The base layer (Level 1) comprises finite field arithmetic operations in either prime or binary fields ($GF(p)$ or $GF(2^m)$), including addition, subtraction, multiplication, and division. These operations serve as building blocks for higher-level ECC functionalities. Level 2 utilizes these operations to construct PA and PD circuits. Finally, Level 3 achieves elliptic curve point multiplication, refer as ECPM in this study. Optimization of the underlying quantum arithmetic circuits is crucial for the efficient execution of quantum algorithms like Shor's [12]. This optimization primarily focuses on minimizing circuit width or depth, especially for computationally expensive operations like multiplication and inversion. This becomes particularly critical for intricate circuits like PA, which forms the foundation

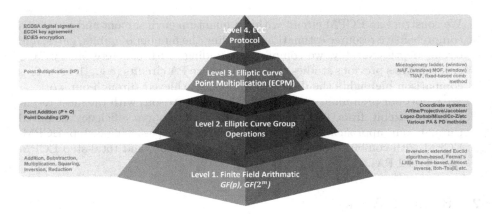

**Fig. 1. General Hierarchy of ECC Protocol Implementation.** We illustrate levels 1 through 4 as detailed in prior works [9,12], and [8]. Specifically, this research focuses on levels 1 through 3 to construct the Elliptic Curve Point Multiplication (ECPM) based on several notable prior works

of scalar multiplication as ECPM- the most resource-intensive step in circuits designed.

This study leverages efficient finite field arithmetic operations in GF($2^m$) for binary ECC. Specifically, we examine the improved Karatsuba multiplication algorithm from Putranto et al. [12], and the FLT-based inversion technique from Larasati et al. [9,12] for constructing second-level quantum circuits for PA and PD scheme. These choices aim to minimize the resource requirements of the circuits. PA and PD's fundamental operations in ECC are crucial, as is scalar multiplication ECPM construction. Scalar multiplication, in turn, is essential for various cryptographic tasks such as generating public and private keys, encrypting and decrypting data, and verifying digital signatures.

## 3 Finite Field Arithmetic in GF ($2^m$) Binary ECC Operations

Elliptic curves defined over a binary field, denoted as $\mathbb{F}_{2^n}$, are a specific type of elliptic curve used in cryptography. Figure 1 depicts a wide hierarchy for implementing finite field arithmetic in ECC. This hierarchy highlights the importance of underlying field operations like modular addition, subtraction, multiplication, squaring, and inversion for optimal ECC implementations, regardless of whether the field is prime ($\mathbb{F}_p$) or binary ($\mathbb{F}_{2^n}$) [1]. This subsection provides a brief introduction to binary elliptic curve cryptography.

This experimental study adopts a polynomial representation for $\mathbb{F}_{2^n}$ similar to Banegas et al. [1] and Putranto et al. [12]. Elements are represented as polynomials of degree less than $n$ with coefficients in $\mathbb{F}_2$. Computations leverage the isomorphism $\mathbb{F}_{2^n} \cong \mathbb{F}_2[z]/m(z)$, where $m(z)$ is an irreducible polynomial of degree $n$ in $\mathbb{F}_2[z]$ in all computations are done modulo $m(z)$ [1]. For defining polynomial $m(z)$ used, Table 1 shows a list of irreducible polynomials in a curve over binary fields that are standardized in [6].

**Table 1. List of standardized irreducible polynomials** suitable for defining the binary field $\mathbb{F}_{2^n}$ used in elliptic curve cryptography (ECC) implementations. These polynomials are referenced in prior works by Banegas et al. [1], Putranto et al. [12], and are also employed in this study.

| Degree (n) | Irreducible polynomial | Source |
|:---:|:---:|:---:|
| 8 | $x^8 + x^4 + x^3 + x + 1$ | [3] |
| 16 | $x^{16} + x^5 + x^3 + x + 1$ | [3] |
| 127 | $x^{127} + x + 1$ | [3] |
| 163 | $z^{163} + z^7 + z^6 + x^3 + 1$ | [6] |
| 233 | $z^{233} + z^{74} + 1$ | [6] |
| 283 | $z^{283} + z^{12} + z^7 + z^5 + 1$ | [6] |
| 409 | $z^{409} + z^{87} + 1$ | [12] |
| 571 | $z^{571} + z^{10} + z^5 + z^2 + 1$ | [6] |

A binary elliptic curve is defined by the equation $y^2 + xy = x^3 + ax^2 + b$, where $a \in \mathbb{F}_2$ and $b \in \mathbb{F}_{2^n}^*$. Points on this curve are represented as tuples $P = (x, y) \in \mathbb{F}_{2^n}^2$ that satisfy the curve equation. Additionally, a special point denoted by $O$ serves as the "point at infinity" and acts as the neutral element for PA. The negative of a point $P_1 = (x_1, y_1)$ is defined as $-P_1 = (x_1, y_1 + x_1)$, such that $P_1 + (-P_1) = O$.

PA on the curve is defined as follows. For two distinct points $P_1 = (x_1, y_1)$ and $P_2 = (x_2, y_2)$, their sum, $P_1 + P_2 = P_3 = (x_3, y_3)$, is calculated using specific formulas: $x_3 = \lambda^2 + \lambda + x_1 + x_2 + a$ and $y_3 = (x_2 + x_3)\lambda + x_3 + y_2$ where $\lambda = \frac{y_1 + y_2}{x_1 + x_2}$. Similarly, PD, denoted as $[2]P_1$, where $P_1 \neq -P_1$, is achieved using: $x_3 = \lambda^2 + \lambda + a$ and $y_3 = x_1^2 + (\lambda + 1)x_3$ with $\lambda = x_1 + \frac{y_1}{x_1}$.

Elliptic Curve Diffie-Hellman (ECDH) is a key exchange protocol based on elliptic curves. The sender and receiver agree on a public curve with a secret point $P$ (having a large prime order) in this protocol. Each party then chooses a secret integer, $\alpha$ for the sender and $\beta$ for the receiver. The shared secret key is established by calculating shared points $P_{\alpha\beta}$. These shared points can be computed in two equivalent ways: $P_{\alpha\beta} = [\alpha\beta]P = [\alpha]P_\beta = [\beta]P_\alpha$ where $P_\alpha = [\alpha]P$ and $P_\beta = [\beta]P$ each shared chosen by the sender and the recipient. The security of ECDH relies on the difficulty of the ECDLP. Given a point $P_\alpha$ and the public base point $P$, the ECDLP problem asks for the secret integer $\alpha$ used to compute $P_\alpha$. The complexity of finding or computing $\alpha$ from $P_\alpha$ and P is the basic concept of the ECDLP, which Peter Shor addressed to compute $\alpha$ in time polynomial in $ord(P)$ in his major work in [15].

## 3.1  Improved Karatsuba Multiplication

Putranto et al. [12] proposes modifying the Karatsuba multiplication algorithm used in prior work by Banegas et al. [1]. Their key improvement lies in eliminating the CONSTMODMULT$^{-1}$ function, which relies heavily on Linear Universal Problem (LUP) decompositions and a high number of CNOT gates. This modification also involves restructuring the function within the algorithm, leading to a reduction in circuit depth, CNOT gates, and Toffoli gates compared to Banegas et al.'s approach. The core idea of Putranto et al.'s [12] improvement involves achieving the same Karatsuba multiplication result with fewer resources by utilizing more efficient operations like MODSHIFT$^{-1}$, a binary shift function, and free swap/relabeling functions. These functions rely on the irreducible polynomial defining the field rather than the field extension degree ($n$). The details of enhanced Karatsuba base algorithm are provided below [12]:

- Three calls to KMULT$_n$: two for multiplying $k-$by$-k$, and one for multiplying $(n - k)-$by$-(n - k)$.
- $2k$ calls to MODSHIFT$_{m(x)}$ for multiplication by $x^k$, once in reverse.
- One call to CONSTMODMULT$_{f(x),m(x)}$, with the same polynomial $1 + x^k$ being multiplied each time.
- $4\,(n-k)$ CNOT gates, with the ability to execute half of them simultaneously.

## 3.2  Improved FLT-Based Inversion with Improved Karatsuba Multiplication

Larasati et al. [9] present a depth-reduction technique for the existing quantum circuit implementing Fermat's Little Theorem (FLT)$-$based inversion in the binary finite field. Their approach revolves around a "complete waterfall" strategy for translating Itoh$-$Tsujii's variant of FLT into the corresponding quantum circuit. This eliminates the need for inverse squaring operations in Banegas et al.'s work [1]. As detailed in [9], this modification significantly reduces the number of CNOT gates (CNOT count) and slightly decreases the circuit's T-depth. Consequently, the overall circuit depth and gate count are reduced, improving efficiency. This optimization complements adopting the enhanced Karatsuba multiplication algorithm proposed by Putranto et al. [12]. Their work, explained in detail within [12], demonstrates how these combined optimizations significantly reduce the overall resource requirements for quantum cryptanalysis circuits used in binary ECC. This study utilizes the work of Putranto et al. [12] on reconstructing improved FLT-based inversion with improved Karatsuba multiplication to develop an efficient circuit for binary elliptic curve cryptanalysis.

# 4   ECPM

This research builds upon established methodologies for quantum cryptanalysis of binary elliptic curves within the framework of Shor's algorithm. These methodologies draw inspiration from foundational works by Proos and Zalka [11],

Roetteler et al. [14], Banegas et al. [1], and Putranto et al. [12]. Besides elaborating on improved level 1–2 operations, the main contribution of this research is to integrate the most efficient variant of the PD design from previous work by [8] to quantum cryptanalysis of binary elliptic curves, which are currently only based on PA in [1,14], and [12]. Figure 2 illustrates PD incorporation within a SHOR-based binary ECC cryptanalysis circuit in this study, which was previously explored without the application of PD. This modification is hypothesized to reduce the required quantum resource depth, thereby enhancing computational capabilities. As noted in [8]'s research, quantum computers are susceptible to various sources of error, including gate errors, decoherence, and crosstalk. Reducing circuit depth correlates with fewer gates and operations, minimizing the potential for error accumulation. Minimizing error rates is crucial in the context of error-corrected quantum computing.

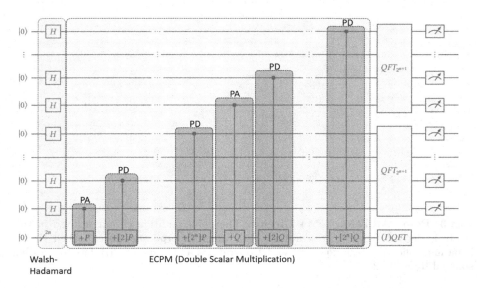

**Fig. 2. The Quantum Circuit for Binary Elliptic Curve Cryptanalysis** utilizes the Shor Approach and integrates Point Doubling (PD) for Elliptic Curve Point Multiplication (ECPM). We developed a quantum circuit for binary ECC cryptanalysis using a Shor-based approach, modified to include PD. This work builds on the original research by Roetteler et al. [14] and Banegas et al. [1] and incorporates additional PD optimizations as utilized in the study by Putranto et al. [12].

## 4.1 Point Addition

For PA operation, our circuit construction employed an optimized Karatsuba multiplication algorithm (level 1) from Putranto et al. [12] and an improved FLT-based inversion technique (level 1) for efficiency. Putranto et al. evaluated

**Fig. 3. Point Addition (PA) Circuit.** The point addition circuit utilized in this study is derived from the research on [12], which incorporates an enhanced Karatsuba multiplication technique for level 1 operations and employs FLT-based inversion sourced from [9,12].

these optimizations in Qiskit for $n = 8$ due to the lengthy output generated by Qiskit simulations for larger values of $n$ [12]. In contrast, resource estimations for larger circuits (up to $n = 512$) were performed using simulation capabilities. This study elaborates on the integration of PA within binary ECC cryptanalysis circuit; we reconstruct prior work [12] to optimum PA in the Qiskit environment, as depicted in Fig. 3 with specifications, utilizing an x64-based desktop PC (Intel i7-8700, six-core CPU) running Windows 10 Pro with 64GB of RAM. Our software environment includes Python 3.9.7 and Qiskit version 0.30.0. The resulting gate resource estimation data is presented in a benchmarking table due to the significant size of the simulated circuits for single-step and total-step PA in Table 4.

## 4.2    Point Doubling

Recent research by Larasati et al. [8] emphasizes the significance of PD, particularly when the scalar $k$ leads to $P = R$ (point coincidence). Unlike PA, which combines two distinct points on the elliptic curve, PD adds a point to itself $(P + P)$ to yield a new point $(2P)$. This operation plays a crucial role in scalar multiplication $(kP)$, which necessitates a series of PA, as exemplified in the binary elliptic curve cryptanalysis circuit (Fig. 2) [1,12,14]. This work delves into the analysis of PD operations presented by Larasati et al. [8] to establish the foundation for the ECPM circuit model that utilizes PD along with PA. We utilize Qiskit to simulate three model PD circuits on an x64-based desktop PC with an Intel i7-8700 six-core CPU running Windows 10 Pro, 64GB of RAM, Python 3.9.7, and Qiskit version 0.30.0.

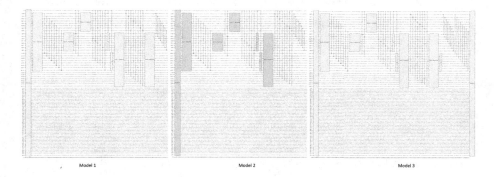

Model 1                         Model 2                         Model 3

**Fig. 4. Three-Model Point-Double (PD) Circuit.** The circuits utilized in this study are based on the research presented in [7], which proposed three versions of PD circuit designs. This paper refers to these designs as Models 1 through 3. Model 1 features a design with one cleared ancilla register; Model 2 omits the uncomputation process; and Model 3 incorporates a complete uncomputation process.

We compared the design circuit proposed by Larasati et al. [8] regarding resource requirements and performance relative to existing PA-only-based circuits. Figure 4 depicts the Larasati et al. model implemented in our Qiskit environment. We comprehensively compared resource requirements for optimal PA and the three PD versions (number of qubits, depth, width, size, CCX (Toffoli) count, and CX (CNOT count) in Table 2.

Regarding formula complexity comparison, depicted in Table 3 Model 3 requires computations up to formula line 15, while Models 1 and 2 conclude at lines 12 and 10, respectively. In this work, we decompose the Point Addition (PA) step based on the foundational work of Banegas et al. [1] on reversible PAs, as the basis in [12]. Conversely, for Point-Doubling (PD), we present a high-level overview of the steps involved in the approach proposed by Larasati et al. [7]. This analysis facilitates a comparison of the complexity of each method for elliptic curve points. An elliptic curve point $P_1$ is represented as two binary

**Table 2. Resource Estimation for Point Addition (PA) and Three Models of Point Doubling (PD):** Quantification of quantum resources required for a single operation of PA and each PD version, including Depth (number of sequential operations), Width (number of qubits involved), Size (number of quantum states), CCX (Toffoli) gates, and CX (CNOT) gates.

| Group Operation | | $n$ | Qubit Counts | OverallDepth | ToffoliDepth | OverallGate Count | ToffoliCount | CNOTCount |
|---|---|---|---|---|---|---|---|---|
| Point Addition | | 8 | 81 | 2,853 | 33 | 3,326 | 348 | 2968 |
| | | 16 | 209 | 6,372 | 57 | 18,514 | 1,344 | 17,160 |
| | | 127 | 2,668 | 9,672 | 498 | 1,624,081 | 57,143 | 1,566,928 |
| | | 163 | 3,261 | 218,114 | 498 | 2,391,927 | 96,363 | 2,295,554 |
| | | 233 | 4,894 | 1,259,306 | 708 | 4,961,503 | 152,099 | 4,809,394 |
| | | 283 | 6,510 | 734,129 | 858 | 8,123,381 | 267,179 | 7,856,092 |
| | | 409 | 9,408 | 293,0002 | 1,236 | 16,011,803 | 445,085 | 15,566,708 |
| | | 571 | 14,847 | 1,716,035 | 1,722 | 35,775,039 | 935,947 | 34.839.082 |
| point Doubling | Model 1 | 8 | 89 | 1,235 | 24 | 2,224 | 232 | 1992 |
| | | 16 | 225 | 4,262 | 40 | 11,536 | 842 | 10,694 |
| | | 127 | 2,795 | 59,769 | 262 | 947,250 | 33,029 | 914,221 |
| | | 163 | 3,424 | 134,043 | 334 | 1,419,228 | 57,357 | 1,361,871 |
| | | 233 | 5,127 | 784,917 | 474 | 2,907,971 | 88,988 | 2,818,983 |
| | | 283 | 6,793 | 427,698 | 574 | 4,691,980 | 154,661 | 4,537,319 |
| | | 409 | 9,817 | 1,791,019 | 826 | 9,261,328 | 257,333 | 9,003,995 |
| | | 571 | 15,418 | 9,988,487 | 1,150 | 20,287,244 | 531,049 | 19,756,195 |
| | Model 2 | 8 | 89 | 1,089 | 23 | 1,969 | 205 | 1,764 |
| | | 16 | 225 | 3,845 | 39 | 10,449 | 761 | 9,688 |
| | | 127 | 2,795 | 146,313 | 261 | 2,465,023 | 85,469 | 2,379,554 |
| | | 163 | 3,424 | 124,226 | 333 | 1,313,879 | 52,970 | 1,260,909 |
| | | 233 | 5.127 | 724,650 | 473 | 2,703,752 | 82,665 | 2,621,087 |
| | | 283 | 6,793 | 402,941 | 573 | 4,388,894 | 144,388 | 4,244,506 |
| | | 409 | 9,817 | 1,663,168 | 825 | 8,651,040 | 240,232 | 8,410,808 |
| | | 571 | 15,418 | 939,686 | 1,149 | 19,114,233 | 499,878 | 18,614,355 |
| | Model 3 | 8 | 89 | 2,561 | 26 | 4,988 | 502 | 4,486 |
| | | 16 | 225 | 9,296 | 42 | 27,772 | 1,976 | 25,796 |
| | | 127 | 2,795 | 55,772 | 264 | 884,740 | 33,029 | 853,896 |
| | | 163 | 3,424 | 340,122 | 336 | 3,622,619 | 145,097 | 3,477,522 |
| | | 233 | 5,127 | 1,905,876 | 476 | 7,495,234 | 228,094 | 7,267,140 |
| | | 283 | 6,793 | 1,101,299 | 576 | 12,252,297 | 401,213 | 11,851,084 |
| | | 409 | 9,817 | 4,422,595 | 828 | 24,116,751 | 667,757 | 23,448,994 |
| | | 571 | 15,418 | 2,512,026 | 1,149 | 53,815,007 | 1,403,837 | 52,411,170 |

polynomials $x_1, y_1$ stored in $x, y$ of size $n$ (where $q$ denotes qubit control, $\lambda$ array calculation with initialization state $|0\rangle$ and $anc$ refer to ancillary qubit).

Based on those analyses, including visualized the depth comparison of PA and PD circuits (in Fig. 5), in this study, we chose version 2 (lowest depth) for integration into the ECPM circuit to achieve optimal depth efficiency.

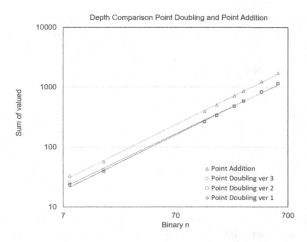

**Fig. 5. Comparative Analysis of the Depth of Operations for Point Addition and three variations of Point Doubling.** We calculate the interpolation of the value $n$ and the sum value depth required for estimating the resource.

**Table 3.** Comparative analysis of formula complexity for point addition and three variations of point doubling

| Step | Point Addition | | Point Doubling model 1 | | Point Doubling model 2 | | Point Doubling model 3 | |
|---|---|---|---|---|---|---|---|---|
| | $q=1$ | $q=0$ | $q=1$ | $q=0$ | $q=1$ | $q=0$ | $q=1$ | $q=0$ |
| 1 | $x = x_1 + x_2$ | $x = x_1 + x_2$ | $anc_1 = \frac{y_1}{x_1}$ | $anc_1 = \frac{y_1}{x_1}$ | $anc_1 = \frac{y_1}{x_1}$ | $anc_1 = \frac{y_1}{x_1}$ | $anc_1 = \frac{y_1}{x_1}$ | $anc_1 = \frac{y_1}{x_1}$ |
| 2 | $y = y_1 + y_2$ | $y = y_1$ | $y = 0$ | $y = y_1$ | $y = 0$ | $y = y_1$ | $y = 0$ | $y = y_1$ |
| 3 | $\lambda = \frac{y_1+y_2}{x_1+x_2}$ | $\lambda = \frac{y_1}{x_1+x_2}$ | $anc_1 = \frac{y_1}{x_1} + x_1 = \lambda$ | $anc_1 = \frac{y_1}{x_1} + x_1 = \lambda$ | $anc_1 = \frac{y_1}{x_1} + x_1 = \lambda$ | $anc_1 = \frac{y_1}{x_1} + x_1 = \lambda$ | $anc_1 = \frac{y_1}{x_1} + x_1 = \lambda$ | $anc_1 = \frac{y_1}{x_1} + x_1 = \lambda$ |
| 4 | $y = 0$ | $y = 0$ | $y = \lambda^2$ | $y = y_1$ | $y = \lambda^2$ | $y = y_1$ | $y = \lambda^2$ | $y = y_1$ |
| 5 | $y = \lambda^2$ | $y = \lambda^2$ | $y = \lambda^2 + \lambda$ | $y = y_1$ | $y = \lambda^2 + \lambda$ | $y = y_1$ | $y = \lambda^2 + \lambda$ | $y = y_1$ |
| 6 | $x = x_2 + x_3$ | $x = x_1 + x_2$ | $y = \lambda^2 + \lambda + a = x_3$ | $y = y_1$ | $y = \lambda^2 + \lambda + a = x_3$ | $y = y_1$ | $y = \lambda^2 + \lambda + a = x_3$ | $y = y_1$ |
| 7 | $x = x_2 + x_3$ | $x = x_1 + x_2$ | $anc_1 = \lambda + 1$ | $anc_1 = \lambda + 1$ | $anc_1 = \lambda + 1$ | $anc_1 = \lambda + 1$ | $anc_1 = \lambda + 1$ | $anc_1 = \lambda + 1$ |
| 8 | $x = x_2 + x_3$ | $x = x_1 + x_2$ | $anc_2 = (\lambda + 1)x_3$ | $anc_2 = (\lambda+1)y_1$ | $anc_2 = (\lambda + 1)x_3$ | $anc_2 = (\lambda+1)y_1$ | $anc_2 = (\lambda + 1)x_3$ | $anc_2 = (\lambda+1)y_1$ |
| 9 | $y = 0$ | $y = y_1$ | $x = x_1^2$ | $x = x_1$ | $x = x_1^2$ | $x = x_1$ | $x = x_1^2$ | $x = x_1$ |
| 10 | $y = (x_1 + x_2) + \lambda$ | $y = y_1$ | $x = x_1^2 + (\lambda+1)x_3 = y_3$ | $x = x_1$ | $x = x_1^2 + (\lambda+1)x_3 = y_3$ | $x = x_1$ | $x = x_1^2 + (\lambda+1)x_3 = y_3$ | $x = x_1$ |
| 11 | $\lambda = 0$ | $\lambda = 0$ | $anc_2 = 0$ | $anc_2 = 0$ | – | – | $anc_2 = 0$ | $anc_2 = 0$ |
| 12 | $x = x_3$ | $x = x_1$ | $swap : x = x_3.y_3$ | $none : x = x_1.y_1$ | – | – | $swap : x = x_3.y_3$ | $none : x = x_1.y_1$ |
| 13 | $y = y_2$ | $y = y_1$ | – | – | – | – | $anc_1 = (\lambda+1) - 1 = \lambda$ | $anc_1 = \lambda$ |
| 14 | – | – | – | – | – | – | $anc_1 = \lambda$ | $anc_1 = \lambda - x_1 = \frac{y_1}{x_1}$ |
| 15 | – | – | – | – | – | – | $anc_1 = \lambda$ | $anc_1 = 0$ |

## 4.3  ECPM Results

By utilizing recent developments in finite field arithmetic for $GF(2^m)$, specifically optimized algorithms for Karatsuba multiplication [12] and FLT-based inversion (Larasati et al. [9] or an alternative approach in [12]), we have incorporated these advancements into our quantum circuits for PA and PD. This integration results in an improved PA and model 2 of PD, with depth optimization. This study performed a comprehensive resource estimation, including qubits, gates, and circuit depth, comparing these findings with existing concrete binary ECC cryptanalysis studies that solely utilize PA circuits [12].

Table 4 presents a comprehensive comparison of the resource required for different ECPM implementations. This table compares our work, based on Qiskit simulations and resource estimation, and the work conducted by Putranto et al.

**Table 4. Comparison of Resource Analysis of Single Step ECPM (PA or PD) and Point Addition (1 PA) and in Total Step ECPM($2n$ PD $+2$ PA) Point Addition ($2n+2$ PA) for n bit ECC with Previous Work.** In both Toffoli and CNOT gates, qubit and Depth, This Work Based on Qiskit Simulation Result. Note that, PUT (Point Addition algorithm by Putranto et al. [12]).

| n | Ours qubits | PUT qubits | Toffoli | Ours (1 ECPM (PA or PD)) CNOT | depth | Toffoli | PUT (1 PA) CNOT | depth | Ours ($2n$PD + 2PA) Toffoli | PUT ($2n$ + 2 PA) Toffoli |
|---|---|---|---|---|---|---|---|---|---|---|
| i | ii | iii | | v | | | vi | | vii | viii |
| 8 | 89 | 74 | 205 | 1,764 | 23 | 348 | 2,734 | 210 | 3,976 | 6,264 |
| 16 | 225 | 194 | 761 | 9,688 | 39 | 1,344 | 15,924 | 623 | 27,040 | 45,696 |
| 127 | 2,795 | 2,320 | 85,469 | 2,379,554 | 261 | 52,773 | 1,352,497 | 7,010 | 21,823,412 | 13,509,888 |
| 163 | 3,424 | 2,805 | 52,970 | 1,260,909 | 333 | 96,299 | 2,137,063 | 14,632 | 17,460,946 | 31,586,072 |
| 233 | 5,127 | 4,228 | 82,665 | 2,621,087 | 473 | 152,067 | 4,480,745 | 46,702 | 38,826,088 | 71,167,356 |
| 283 | 6,793 | 5,694 | 144,388 | 4,244,506 | 573 | 267,115 | 7,376,571 | 34,792 | 82,257,966 | 151,721,320 |
| 409 | 9,817 | 8,214 | 240,232 | 18,410,808 | 825 | 445,021 | 14,565,173 | 111,858 | 197,399,946 | 364,917,220 |
| 571 | 15,418 | 13,167 | 499,878 | 18,614,355 | 1,149 | 935,883 | 32,888,178 | 93,142 | 572,732,570 | 1,070,650,152 |

[12] for $n-$bit ECC. The comparison specifically examines the qubits in columns ii and iii. The single-step ECPM comparison is presented in columns v and vi, where ECPM with combined PA or PD is compared against the single-step PA algorithm (from PUT). The result from our recent study on total-step ECPM ($2n$ PD + 2 PA) revealed reduced quantum resource usage in column vii, and we compared it to recent PUT results in column viii in scenarios that exclusively utilize point addition ($2n + 2$ PA).

## 5    Conclusion

This work advances resource estimation for Elliptic Curve Point Multiplication (ECPM) in the context of quantum cryptanalysis of binary ECC. We leveraged recent advancements in finite field arithmetic for $GF(2^m)$ by incorporating the improved Karatsuba multiplication algorithm from Putaranto et al. [12] and the FLT-based inversion algorithm from Larasati et al. [9] (or the combination approach presented in [12]) into our quantum circuits for both point addition (PA) and point doubling (PD). Additionally, we integrate an optimized PA algorithm from prior research [12] into the ECPM construction. Furthermore, we analyzed three PD circuit versions by Larasati et al. [8] and selected Model 2 as the most depth-efficient model for our binary ECC cryptanalysis scheme based on Shor's algorithm. Finally, we performed a comprehensive resource estimation, including qubits, gates, and circuit depth. In the final comparisons, we compared ECPM as single-step, ECPM with combination or selection in PA/PD utilization, and total-step ECPM ($2n$ PD $+2$ PA). We compare these findings with existing concrete binary ECC cryptanalysis studies that solely utilize PA circuits [12], highlighting the depth optimization achieved through the proposed approach.

## References

1.  Banegas, G., Bernstein, D.J., van Hoof, I., Lange, T.: Concrete quantum cryptanalysis of binary elliptic curves. IACR Tran. Cryptogr. Hardw. Embed. Syst. 451–472 (2021)

2. Chen, L., Moody, D., Regenscheid, A., Randall, K.: Recommendations for discrete logarithm-based cryptography: elliptic curve domain parameters. Technical report, National Institute of Standards and Technology (2019)
3. Cohen, H., et al.: Handbook of Elliptic and Hyperelliptic Curve Cryptography. CRC Press (2005)
4. Häner, T., Jaques, S., Naehrig, M., Roetteler, M., Soeken, M.: Improved quantum circuits for elliptic curve discrete logarithms. In: Post-Quantum Cryptography: 11th International Conference, PQCrypto 2020, Paris, France, 15–17 April 2020, pp. 425–444. Springer (2020)
5. van Hoof, I.: Space-efficient quantum multiplication of polynomials for binary finite fields with sub-quadratic Toffoli gate count. arXiv preprint arXiv:1910.02849 (2019)
6. Kerry, C.F., Gallagher, P.D.: Digital signature standard (DSS). FIPS PUB, pp. 186–4 (2013)
7. Larasati, H.T., Kim, H.: Quantum cryptanalysis landscape of Shor's algorithm for elliptic curve discrete logarithm problem. In: Information Security Applications: 22nd International Conference, WISA 2021, Jeju Island, South Korea, 11–13 August 2021, Revised Selected Papers 22, pp. 91–104. Springer (2021)
8. Larasati, H.T., Kim, H.: Quantum circuit designs of point doubling operation for binary elliptic curves. In: International Conference on Information Security Applications, pp. 297–309. Springer (2023)
9. Larasati, H.T., Putranto, D.S.C., Wardhani, R.W., Park, J., Kim, H.: Depth optimization of FLT-based quantum inversion circuit. IEEE Access (2023)
10. Mohammadi, M., Molahosseini, A.S.: Efficient design of elliptic curve point multiplication based on fast montgomery modular multiplication. In: ICCKE 2013, pp. 424–429. IEEE (2013)
11. Proos, J., Zalka, C.: Shor's discrete logarithm quantum algorithm for elliptic curves. arXiv preprint quant-ph/0301141 (2003)
12. Putranto, D.S.C., Wardhani, R.W., Larasati, H.T., Ji, J., Kim, H.: Depth-optimization of quantum cryptanalysis on binary elliptic curves. IEEE Access (2023)
13. Rescorla, E.: The transport layer security (TLS) protocol version 1.3. RFC 8446, RFC Editor (2018)
14. Roetteler, M., Naehrig, M., Svore, K.M., Lauter, K.: Quantum resource estimates for computing elliptic curve discrete logarithms. In: Advances in Cryptology–AsiaCrypt 2017: 23rd International Conference on the Theory and Applications of Cryptology and Information Security, Hong Kong, China, 3–7 December 2017, Part II, pp. 241–270. Springer (2017)
15. Shor, P.W.: Algorithms for quantum computation: discrete logarithms and factoring. In: Proceedings 35th Annual Symposium on Foundations of Computer Science, pp. 124–134. IEEE (1994)

# Integral Attack with Bit-Based Division Property on the Lightweight Block Cipher LBC

Naoki Shibayama[✉] and Yasutaka Igarashi

Tokyo University of Science, 2641 Yamazaki, Noda, Chiba 278-8510, Japan
7323703@ed.tus.ac.jp, yasutaka@rs.tus.ac.jp

**Abstract.** LBC is the lightweight block cipher proposed by Kapalova *et al.* in 2023. The block size is 64 bits, the secret key size is 80 bits, and the number of rounds is 20, respectively. The designer analyzed the avalanche effect and evaluated the security against differential and linear cryptanalysis. On the other hand, the security against integral cryptanalysis, one of the most powerful cryptanalyses on block cipher, has yet to be evaluated. In this paper, we evaluated the security of LBC by applying integral cryptanalysis. We investigated the integral characteristics with the bit-based division property using Mixed Integer Linear Programming (MILP). Consequently, we found that LBC has the 18-round integral characteristic using the 60-th order differential. Exploiting the discovered 16-round integral characteristic using the 48-th order differential, the integral attack on the full-round LBC can be efficiently performed with $2^{50.8}$ blocks of chosen plaintext and $2^{51.4}$ times of encryption operation. Then, we improve the round function of LBC and discuss its security against integral attack.

**Keywords:** Cryptanalysis · Integral attack · Bit-based division property · Block cipher · LBC

## 1 Introduction

Information and communication technology has developed remarkably in recent years, including the Internet of Things (IoT) system, in which everything is connected. A lightweight block cipher is an effective solution to provide security in resource-constrained environments, such as low power consumption, small footprint, and low computational complexity.

LBC [1] is a 64-bit block cipher with an 80-bit secret key designed by Kapalova *et al.* in 2023. The recommended number of rounds is 20. In [1], the avalanche effect of LBC was investigated, and its properties were described as similar to random numbers. Then, the security against differential and linear attacks were evaluated, and LBC was reported to resist these attacks. Meanwhile, the security against integral attack has not been evaluated. The integral attack [2] is cryptanalysis proposed by Knudsen *et al.*, which focuses on the

© The Author(s), under exclusive license to Springer Nature Singapore Pte Ltd. 2025
J.-H. Lee et al. (Eds.): WISA 2024, LNCS 15499, pp. 16–28, 2025.
https://doi.org/10.1007/978-981-96-1624-4_2

XOR sum property of a data set and can be widely applied to symmetric key cryptographic algorithms. Todo *et al.* [3,4] proposed a method for finding better integral characteristics: division property (DP), which enables the use of algebraic degrees, and bit-based division property (BDP). Subsequently, Xiang *et al.* [5] proposed an efficient method for searching integral characteristics by BDP using MILP.

In this paper, we evaluate the security of LBC against integral attack. We explored the integral characteristics by BDP using MILP and found that LBC has 18-round integral characteristics. Moreover, exploiting the 16-round integral characteristic using the 48-th order differential, an integral attack can be efficiently performed on the full-round LBC with $2^{50.8}$ blocks of chosen plaintext and $2^{51.4}$ times of encryption operation. In order to overcome this weakness, we attempt to improve the round function of LBC. Specifically, we added a linear layer to the original one. As a result, the length of the integral characteristic was reduced to 8 rounds in the improved LBC, which strengthens the original LBC algorithm.

The remainder of this paper is organized as follows. Section 2 explains the algorithm of LBC. Section 3 gives an overview of the integral attack. Section 4 explains the division property and the method for searching the integral characteristic using MILP. Section 5 shows the results of the integral characteristics of LBC. Then, we perform the integral attack to full-round LBC in Sect. 6. Section 7 presents the improved LBC and describes its security against integral attack. Section 8 finally concludes the paper.

## 2 The Algorithm of LBC

This section briefly describes the structure of LBC. LBC has a 64-bit block size and an 80-bit secret key size. Encryption iterations are performed for 20 rounds. It consists of the key addition, the nonlinear transformation, and the left cyclic shift. Figure 1 shows the data processing part of LBC. In the figure, the symbol $\oplus$ represents an Exclusive-OR (XOR) operation, and the symbol S denotes four parallel 4-bit S-boxes, which are bijective and nonlinear. The 4-bit S-box $s_4$ is shown in Table 1 in hexadecimal format. Also, RL is a linear function given by

$$\mathrm{RL}(X) = X \oplus (X \lll 7) \oplus (X \lll 10), \qquad (1)$$

where $X \in \mathrm{GF}(2)^{16}$, $\lll \ell$ is a left cyclic shift by $\ell$ bits. Let $\mathbf{X}^{(i)} = (X_1^{(i)}, X_2^{(i)}, X_3^{(i)}, X_4^{(i)})$, $X_j^{(i)} = (x_{j,1}^{(i)}, x_{j,2}^{(i)}, x_{j,3}^{(i)}, x_{j,4}^{(i)})$, $x_{j,\ell}^{(i)} \in \mathrm{GF}(2)^4$ be the input of the $i$-th round, and $\mathbf{C}^{(i)} = (C_1^{(i)}, C_2^{(i)}, C_3^{(i)}, C_4^{(i)})$, $C_j^{(i)} = (c_{j,1}^{(i)}, c_{j,2}^{(i)}, c_{j,3}^{(i)}, c_{j,4}^{(i)})$, $c_{j,\ell}^{(i)} \in \mathrm{GF}(2)^4$ be the output. Note that $1 \le i \le 20$, $1 \le j \le 4$, and $1 \le \ell \le 4$. The data processing part generates 64-bit ciphertext $\mathbf{C}^{(20)}$ from 64-bit plaintext $\mathbf{X}^{(1)}$, 64-bit whitening key $\mathbf{WK} = (WK_1, WK_2, WK_3, WK_4)$, $WK_j \in \mathrm{GF}(2)^{16}$, and twenty 64-bit round keys $\mathbf{RK}^{(i)} = (RK_1^{(i)}, RK_2^{(i)}, RK_3^{(i)}, RK_4^{(i)})$, $RK_j^{(i)} = (rk_{j,1}^{(i)}, rk_{j,2}^{(i)}, rk_{j,3}^{(i)}, rk_{j,4}^{(i)})$, $rk_{j,\ell}^{(i)} \in \mathrm{GF}(2)^4$.

Since our attack does not use the relationship between the round keys, we omit a description of the key schedule. Please refer to [1] for detailed specifications.

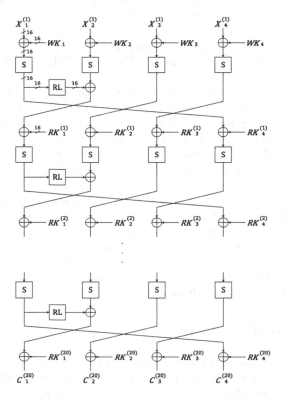

**Fig. 1.** Data processing part of LBC.

**Table 1.** S-box $s_4$.

| $x$ | 0 | 1 | 2 | 3 | 4 | 5 | 6 | 7 | 8 | 9 | A | B | C | D | E | F |
|---|---|---|---|---|---|---|---|---|---|---|---|---|---|---|---|---|
| $s_4(x)$ | 9 | 2 | A | 4 | 0 | 6 | 7 | D | 5 | 1 | 8 | 3 | E | F | B | C |

## 3   Integral Attack

The integral attack [2] is a cryptanalysis proposed by Knudsen and Wagner in 2002. We describe the definition of integral properties related to this paper.

**Integral Property.** We define the following four properties of the set $\{X_i | X_i \in \{0,1\}^\ell, 0 \le i < 2^\ell\}$ of $\ell$-bit data $X$.

$$\textbf{Constant}\,(\,\text{C}\,) \ : \ \text{if } \forall i, j \ X_i = X_j,$$
$$\textbf{All}\,(\,\text{A}\,) \ : \ \text{if } \forall i, j \,(i \ne j) \ X_i \ne X_j,$$
$$\textbf{Balance}\,(\,\text{B}\,) \ : \ \text{if } \bigoplus_i X_i = 0,$$
$$\textbf{Unknown}\,(\,\text{U}\,) \ : \ \text{Others.}$$

In this paper, for example, if the integral property of 1-nibble data $x_{j,\ell}^{(i)}$ is B, we denote this as $\{x_{j,\ell}^{(i)}\} = \text{B}$, where $1 \le i \le 20$, $1 \le j \le 4$, and $1 \le \ell \le 4$. In addition, as an example, if the integral property of 4-nibble data $(x_{j,1}^{(i)}, x_{j,2}^{(i)}, x_{j,3}^{(i)}, x_{j,4}^{(i)})$ is (B B B U), then we represent this as $\{(x_{j,1}^{(i)}, x_{j,2}^{(i)}, x_{j,3}^{(i)}, x_{j,4}^{(i)})\} = (\text{B B B U})$. Furthermore, if the integral property of each nibble data is the same, for example, $\{(x_{j,1}^{(i)}, x_{j,2}^{(i)}, x_{j,3}^{(i)}, x_{j,4}^{(i)})\} = (\text{B B B B})$, this can be expressed as $\{X_j^{(i)}\} = \textbf{B}$.

The attacker encrypts a set of chosen plaintexts and investigates the propagation of the integral property. Suppose $2^\ell$ chosen plaintexts are input, and the integral property of the output from a reduced $r$-round cipher is All, Balance, or Constant. Then, we say the cipher has an $r$-round integral characteristic using the $\ell$-th order differential. By exploiting the characteristic that the XOR sum is 0, the attacker derives an attack equation to estimate and determine the key by solving it.

## 4 MILP-Aided Bit-Based Division Property

Todo *et al.* [3,4] generalized the integral property and proposed the division property (DP), which can utilize algebraic degrees. Then, the bit-based division property (BDP) was devised to enable the bitwise operation of DP.

### 4.1 Bit Product Function and BDP

This subsection presents definitions of the bit product function and BDP.

**Bit Product Function.** For any $a \in \text{GF}(2)^n$, let $a[i]$ be the $i$-th bit of $a$, and the Hamming weight of $a$ is calculated as $w(a) = \sum_{i=1}^{n} a[i]$. For any $n$-bit variable $u \in \text{GF}(2)^n$ and input variable $x \in \text{GF}(2)^n$, the bit product function $\pi_u(x)$ is defined by

$$\pi_u(x) := \prod_{i=1}^{n} x[i]^{u[i]}, \tag{2}$$

where $x[i]^0 = 1$ and $x[i]^1 = x[i]$.

Next, for an arbitrary $m$-dimensional vector $\boldsymbol{u} = (u_1, u_2, \cdots, u_m)$, $u_i \in$ GF(2), an input vector $\boldsymbol{x} = (x_1, x_2, \cdots, x_m)$, a bit product function $\pi_{\boldsymbol{u}}(\boldsymbol{x})$ for $x_i \in$ GF(2) is defined as follows.

$$\pi_{\boldsymbol{u}}(\boldsymbol{x}) := \prod_{i=1}^{m} \pi_{u_i}(x_i) \tag{3}$$

**BDP.** Let $\mathbb{X}$ be a multiset whose elements are $m$-dimensional vectors $\boldsymbol{x}$, and we call $\mathbb{X}$ has BDP $D_{\mathbb{K}}^{1^m}$ if the set $\mathbb{X}$ satisfies the following equation.

$$\bigoplus_{\boldsymbol{x} \in \mathbb{X}} \pi_{\boldsymbol{u}}(\boldsymbol{x}) = \begin{cases} \text{Unknown} & \text{, if there is } \boldsymbol{k} \in \mathbb{K} \text{ s.t. } W(\boldsymbol{u}) \succeq \boldsymbol{k}, \\ 0 & \text{, otherwise,} \end{cases}$$

where $W(\boldsymbol{u}) = (w(u_1), w(u_2), \cdots, w(u_m))$, and we denote $\boldsymbol{k'} \succeq \boldsymbol{k}$ if $k_i' \geq k_i$ for all $i$. Note that $n_1, n_2, \cdots, n_m$ are restricted to 1 when we consider BDP $D_{\mathbb{K}}^{1^m}$.

### 4.2 Division Trail

Consider an $n$-bit BDP passing through the round function until the $r$-th round, which changes as shown in the following equation.

$$D_{\mathbb{K}_0}^{1^n} \rightarrow D_{\mathbb{K}_1}^{1^n} \rightarrow \cdots \rightarrow D_{\mathbb{K}_r}^{1^n} \tag{4}$$

At this point, for any $\overrightarrow{k_i^*} \in \mathbb{K}_i$ in $\mathbb{K}_i$ $(1 \leq i \leq r)$, a propagation vector $\overrightarrow{k_{i-1}^*}$ in $\mathbb{K}_{i-1}$ exists. Therefore, the propagation of $\overrightarrow{k_i^*}$ can be expressed as in Eq. (5), called the division trail.

$$\overrightarrow{k_0^*} \rightarrow \overrightarrow{k_1^*} \rightarrow \cdots \rightarrow \overrightarrow{k_r^*} \tag{5}$$

### 4.3 MILP-Aided Bit-Based Division Property

In 2016, Xiang *et al.* [5] proposed a technique that combines the BDP and searches for the division trails by employing the MILP. We use it to search for the integral characteristics of LBC.

**Constraints for Copy, XOR and AND.** We denote a bit-wise linear inequalities model of Copy, XOR and AND, and show how to model BDP propagations of S-box by linear inequalities. For more details, please refer to [5].

**Model 1 (Copy).** Let $(a) \xrightarrow{\text{Copy}} (b_1, b_2)$ be a division trail of Copy. The following inequalities are sufficient to describe the propagation of the division property for Copy.

$$\begin{cases} a - b_1 - b_2 = 0, \\ a, b_1, b_2 \text{ are binaries.} \end{cases}$$

**Model 2 (XOR).** Let $(a_1, a_2) \xrightarrow{\text{XOR}} (b)$ be a division trail or XOR. The following inequalities are sufficient to describe the propagation of the division property for XOR.

$$\begin{cases} a_1 + a_2 - b = 0, \\ a_1, a_2, b \text{ are binaries.} \end{cases}$$

**Model 3 (AND).** Let $(a_1, a_2) \xrightarrow{\text{AND}} (b)$ be a division trail of AND. The following inequalities are sufficient to describe the propagation of the division property for AND.

$$\begin{cases} b - a_1 \geq 0, \\ b - a_2 \geq 0, \\ b - a_1 - a_2 \leq 0, \\ a_1, a_2, b \text{ are binaries.} \end{cases}$$

**Model 4 (S-box).** Each division trail of an $n$-bit S-box can be viewed as a $2n$-dimensional vector in $\{0,1\}^{2n} \subset \mathbb{R}^{2n}$ where $\mathbb{R}$ is the real number field. Thus, all division trails form a subset $P$ of $\{0,1\}^{2n}$. Next, we compute the H-representation of $\text{Conv}(P)$ using the *inequality_generator*() function Sagemath [6], which returns a set of linear inequalities $\mathcal{L}$.

**Objective Function.** The vector $\overrightarrow{k_r^*}$ in the $r$-th round of the division trail can be expressed as Eq. (6).

$$\overrightarrow{k_r^*} = (a_0^r, a_1^r, \cdots, a_{n-1}^r) \tag{6}$$

The objective function is then given by Eq. (7).

$$obj = Min\{a_0^r + a_1^r + \cdots + a_{n-1}^r\} \tag{7}$$

Here, when the value of the objective function is 1, a unit vector is in the set $\mathbb{K}_r$ of the $r$-th round. It means that the bitwise integral property 'U' exists.

## 5 Integral Characteristics of LBC

The results of the BDP investigation are shown in Table 2 using Gurobi [7], one of the MILP solvers. In the table, note that $d$ represents the order of differential, and $r$ denotes the number of rounds of the integral characteristic. However, for the $d (1 \leq d \leq 63)$-th order differential, the bits from the right to the $d$-th of the plaintext are set to All. A comprehensive examination using the 63-rd order differential revealed that the 19-round integral characteristic was not found, so the 18-round integral characteristic using the 60-th order differential, the longest with the lowest order of differential, was the best.

## 6    Integral Attack on the Full-Round LBC

By exploiting the 16-round integral characteristic of LBC using the 48-th order differential, the integral attack on the full-round LBC is possible efficiently. This section estimates the number of chosen plaintexts and the computational complexity required for the attack.

### 6.1    Attack Equation

Figure 2 shows the equivalent circuit from the 20-th round output $(C_1^{(20)}, C_2^{(20)}, C_4^{(20)})$ to the 16-th round output $C_2^{(16)}$. The $S^{-1}$ in the figure shows four inverse functions of S-box $s_4$ in parallel. RL is a linear operation, and the 16-bit round key $RK_4^{(i)}$ of the $i$-th round can be moved to directly after the S-box, which is a nonlinear operation. In addition, the round key $RK_1^{(17)}$, $RK_4^{(17)}$, $RK_1^{(20)}$, and $RK_4^{(20)}$ are moved equivalently, as shown in Fig. 2, to reduce the attack cost. Note that $RK'_1^{(i)} = RK_1^{(i)} \oplus RL(RK_4^{(i)})$. Let $H^{(i)} = (h_1^{(i)}, h_2^{(i)}, h_3^{(i)}, h_4^{(i)})$, $h_\ell^{(i)} \in GF(2)^4$ represents the data after adding the key $RK'_1^{(i)}$ of the $i$-th round as the intermediate variable, and $Z^{(i)} = (z_1^{(i)}, z_2^{(i)}, z_3^{(i)}, z_4^{(i)})$, $z_\ell^{(i)} \in GF(2)^4$ denotes the data after the output of RL. Furthermore, RL is expressed as follows.

$$RL = \begin{bmatrix} m_1 & m_2 & m_3 & m_4 \\ m_4 & m_1 & m_2 & m_3 \\ m_3 & m_4 & m_1 & m_2 \\ m_2 & m_3 & m_4 & m_1 \end{bmatrix}, \tag{8}$$

**Table 2.** $r$-round integral characteristics of LBC using $d$-th order differential.

| $d$ | $r$ | Integral property of $\mathbf{C}^{(r)}$ |
|---|---|---|
| 1−3 | 6 | $\mathbf{U}\,(\mathbf{B}\,\mathbf{B}\,\mathbf{B}\,\mathbf{U})\,\mathbf{U}\,\mathbf{U}$ |
| 4−11 | 7 | |
| 12−15 | 8 | |
| 16−19 | 9 | |
| 20−23 | 10 | |
| 24−27 | 11 | |
| 28−35 | 12 | $\mathbf{U}\,\mathbf{B}\,\mathbf{U}\,\mathbf{U}$ |
| 36−39 | 13 | |
| 40−43 | 14 | |
| 44−47 | 15 | |
| 48−55 | 16 | |
| 56−59 | 17 | |
| 60−63 | 18 | |

$$m_1 = \begin{bmatrix} 1 & 0 & 0 & 0 \\ 0 & 1 & 0 & 0 \\ 0 & 0 & 1 & 0 \\ 0 & 0 & 0 & 1 \end{bmatrix}, \; m_2 = \begin{bmatrix} 0 & 0 & 0 & 1 \\ 0 & 0 & 0 & 0 \\ 0 & 0 & 0 & 0 \\ 0 & 0 & 0 & 0 \end{bmatrix}, \; m_3 = \begin{bmatrix} 0 & 0 & 1 & 0 \\ 1 & 0 & 0 & 1 \\ 0 & 1 & 0 & 0 \\ 0 & 0 & 1 & 0 \end{bmatrix}, \; m_4 = \begin{bmatrix} 0 & 0 & 0 & 0 \\ 0 & 0 & 0 & 0 \\ 1 & 0 & 0 & 0 \\ 0 & 1 & 0 & 0 \end{bmatrix}.$$

Examining the subsequent change in the integral property 'B' which appears in $c_{2,\ell}^{(16)}$ ($1 \le \ell \le 4$) in the 16-round integral characteristic using the 48-th order differential, we find that this passes through the S-box $s_4$ in the 17-th round. Then, the key $rk'^{(17)}_{1,\ell}$ is added, and the following integral property holds for the intermediate variable $h_\ell^{(17)}$.

$$\{h_\ell^{(17)}\} = \mathrm{B}$$

Therefore, from its XOR sum property, by applying the meet-in-the-middle technique [8], the attack equation is given by

$$\bigoplus z_\ell^{(17)} = \bigoplus c_{1,\ell}^{(17)}, \tag{9}$$

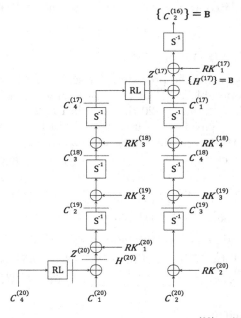

**Fig. 2.** Equivalent circuit from the 20-th round output $(C_1^{(20)}, C_2^{(20)}, C_4^{(20)})$ to the 16-th round output $C_2^{(16)}$.

where

$$^{\mathrm{T}}(z_1^{(17)}, z_2^{(17)}, z_3^{(17)}, z_4^{(17)}) = \mathrm{RL}\ ^{\mathrm{T}}(c_{4,1}^{(17)}, c_{4,2}^{(17)}, c_{4,3}^{(17)}, c_{4,4}^{(17)}),\ c_{4,\ell}^{(17)} = s_4^{-1}(c_{3,\ell}^{(18)} \oplus rk_{3,\ell}^{(18)}),$$

$$c_{1,\ell}^{(17)} = s_4^{-1}(c_{4,\ell}^{(18)} \oplus rk_{4,\ell}^{(18)}),\ c_{3,\ell}^{(18)} = s_4^{-1}(c_{2,\ell}^{(19)} \oplus rk_{2,\ell}^{(19)}),\ c_{4,\ell}^{(18)} = s_4^{-1}(c_{3,\ell}^{(19)} \oplus rk_{3,\ell}^{(19)}),$$

$$c_{2,\ell}^{(19)} = s_4^{-1}(h_\ell^{(20)} \oplus rk'^{(20)}_{1,\ell}),\ c_{3,\ell}^{(19)} = s_4^{-1}(c_{2,\ell}^{(20)} \oplus rk_{2,\ell}^{(20)}),\ h_\ell^{(20)} = z_\ell^{(20)} \oplus c_{1,\ell}^{(20)},$$

$$^{\mathrm{T}}(z_1^{(20)}, z_2^{(20)}, z_3^{(20)}, z_4^{(20)}) = \mathrm{RL}\ ^{\mathrm{T}}(c_{4,1}^{(20)}, c_{4,2}^{(20)}, c_{4,3}^{(20)}, c_{4,4}^{(20)}).$$

Note that $s_4^{-1}$ is the inverse function of S-box $s_4$, and T is the transposition of a vector or matrix. To compute the attack equation in Eq. (9), we need the output of 32-bit $(C_1^{(20)}, C_4^{(20)})$ on the left side and 16-bit $C_2^{(20)}$ on the right side. Here, the keys to be identified are the six 16-bit keys $RK_3^{(18)}$, $RK_4^{(18)}$, $RK_2^{(19)}$, $RK_3^{(19)}$, $RK'^{(20)}_1$, and $RK_2^{(20)}$ located in the equivalent circuit from $(C_1^{(20)}, C_2^{(20)}, C_4^{(20)})$ to $H^{(17)}$ in Fig. 2, i.e., 96-bit keys in total.

In this paper, to improve the efficiency of the attack, we use the Mod2 Frequency Distribution Table (MFDT) of $z_\ell^{(17)}$ and $c_{1,\ell}^{(17)}$, which are derived sequentially by the partial sum technique [9] proposed by Ferguson *et al.*, and $\bigoplus z_\ell^{(17)}$ and $\bigoplus c_{1,\ell}^{(17)}$ are calculated, respectively. Then, the true key is identified by examining Eq. (9).

## 6.2   Derivation of MFDT of $Z^{(17)}$

In this subsection, we show the procedure for sequentially deriving the MFDT of the intermediate variable $Z^{(17)}$ of the 17-th round from the MFDT of the intermediate variable $H^{(20)}$ of the 20-th round in Fig. 2.

Figure 3 shows the equivalent circuit from $H^{(20)}$ to $Z^{(17)}$ expressed in nibble values. As shown in the figure, the nibble variables after the XOR operation at the two locations directly before $z_\ell^{(17)}$ ($1 \leq \ell \leq 4$) are $v_\ell$ and $w_\ell$ from the left. First, the MFDT of $z_\ell^{(17)}$ can be derived from the 8-bit MFDT of $(w_\ell, h_4^{(20)})$ by assuming the 12-bit key $rk'^{(20)}_{1,4}, rk_{2,4}^{(19)}$, and $rk_{3,4}^{(18)}$. The MFDT of $(w_\ell, h_4^{(20)})$ can also be derived from the 12-bit MFDT of $(v_\ell, h_3^{(20)}, h_4^{(20)})$ by assuming the 12-bit key $rk'^{(20)}_{1,3}, rk_{2,3}^{(19)}$, and $rk_{3,3}^{(18)}$. Furthermore, the MFDT of $(v_\ell, h_3^{(20)}, h_4^{(20)})$ can be derived from the total 16-bit MFDT of $(h_1^{(20)}, h_2^{(20)}, h_3^{(20)}, h_4^{(20)})$ by assuming the 24-bit key $rk'^{(20)}_{1,1}, rk_{2,1}^{(19)}, rk_{3,1}^{(18)}, rk'^{(20)}_{1,2}, rk_{2,2}^{(19)}$, and $rk_{3,2}^{(18)}$.

## 6.3   Attack Algorithm

The attacker recovers the 96-bit round keys according to the following procedure.

*Step1.* Encrypt $2^{48}$ plaintexts of 48-bit data $(X_2^{(1)}, X_3^{(1)}, X_4^{(1)})$ whose integral property is All.

*Step2.* From the ciphertext corresponding to the plaintext above, the 16-bit MFDT (MFDT($H^{(20)}$)) of $H^{(20)}(= C_1^{(20)} \oplus \mathrm{RL}(C_4^{(20)}))$ and the four 4-bit MFDTs (MFDT($c_{2,\ell}^{(20)}$)) of $c_{2,\ell}^{(20)}$ ($1 \leq \ell \leq 4$) are derived.

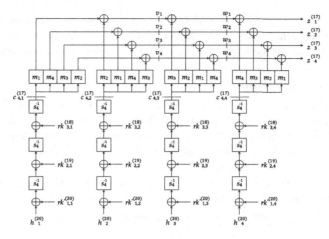

**Fig. 3.** Equivalent circuit from the 20-th round intermediate variable $h_\ell^{(20)}$ $(1 \le \ell \le 4)$ to the 17-round intermediate variable $z_\ell^{(17)}$.

*Step3.* By assuming the 24-bit key $rk'^{(20)}_{1,1}, rk^{(19)}_{2,1}, rk^{(18)}_{3,1}, rk'^{(20)}_{1,2}, rk^{(19)}_{2,2},$ and $rk^{(18)}_{3,2}$, the 16-bit MFDT $(\mathrm{MFDT}(c^{(17)}_{4,1}, c^{(17)}_{4,2}, h^{(20)}_3, h^{(20)}_4))$ of $(c^{(17)}_{4,1}, c^{(17)}_{4,2}, h^{(20)}_3, h^{(20)}_4)$ can calculate from $\mathrm{MFDT}(H^{(20)})$.

*Step4.* Using $\mathrm{MFDT}(c^{(17)}_{4,1}, c^{(17)}_{4,2}, h^{(20)}_3, h^{(20)}_4)$ and the linear operations $m_\ell$, calculate the four 12-bit MFDTs $(\mathrm{MFDT}(v_\ell, h^{(20)}_3, h^{(20)}_4))$ of $(v_\ell, h^{(20)}_3, h^{(20)}_4)$.

*Step5.* By assuming the 12-bit key $rk'^{(20)}_{1,3}, rk^{(19)}_{2,3}$, and $rk^{(18)}_{3,3}$, the four 12-bit MFDTs $(\mathrm{MFDT}(v_\ell, c^{(17)}_{4,3}, h^{(20)}_4))$ of $(v_\ell, c^{(17)}_{4,3}, h^{(20)}_4)$ can calculate from $\mathrm{MFDT}(v_\ell, h^{(20)}_3, h^{(20)}_4)$.

*Step6.* Using $\mathrm{MFDT}(v_\ell, c^{(17)}_{4,3}, h^{(20)}_4)$ and the linear operations $m_\ell$, calculate the four 8-bit MFDTs $(\mathrm{MFDT}(w_\ell, h^{(20)}_4))$ of $(w_\ell, h^{(20)}_4)$.

*Step7.* By assuming the 12-bit key $rk'^{(20)}_{1,4}, rk^{(19)}_{2,4}$, and $rk^{(18)}_{3,4}$, the four 8-bit MFDTs $(\mathrm{MFDT}(w_\ell, c^{(17)}_{4,4}))$ of $(w_\ell, c^{(17)}_{4,4})$ can calculate from $\mathrm{MFDT}(w_\ell, h^{(20)}_4)$.

*Step8.* Using $\mathrm{MFDT}(w_\ell, c^{(17)}_{4,4})$ and the linear operations $m_\ell$, calculate the four 4-bit MFDTs $(\mathrm{MFDT}(z_\ell^{(17)}))$ of $z_\ell^{(17)}$.

*Step9.* By assuming the four 12-bit keys $rk^{(20)}_{2,\ell}, rk^{(19)}_{3,\ell}$, and $rk^{(18)}_{4,\ell}$, the four 4-bit MFDTs $(\mathrm{MFDT}(c^{(17)}_{1,\ell}))$ of $c^{(17)}_{1,\ell}$ can calculate from $\mathrm{MFDT}(c^{(20)}_{2,\ell})$.

*Step10.* From $\mathrm{MFDT}(z_\ell^{(17)})$ and $\mathrm{MFDT}(c^{(17)}_{1,\ell})$, calculate the value of $\bigoplus z_\ell^{(17)}$ and $\bigoplus c^{(17)}_{1,\ell}$, respectively. Then, an attacker can judge whether the key is correct by examining Eq. (9) holds.

*Step 11.* The 32-bit key $RK_3^{(18)}$ and $RK_4^{(18)}$ in the 18-th round has been determined so far; the remaining $48\,(= 80 - 32)$ bits key in the 80-bit key register of the 18-th round of the key schedule is identified by an exhaustive key search.

### 6.4   Complexity Estimation

Since Eqs. (9) are four 4-bit attack equations, the probability that it is satisfied for a false key is $(2^{-4})^4 = 2^{-16}$. Thus, to reduce the number of $2^{96}$ candidate keys to the true key, it is sufficient to have $7\,(> \frac{96}{16})$ sets of 48-th order differential. Therefore, the number of chosen plaintexts required for the attack is $7 \cdot 2^{48} \approx 2^{50.8}$.

Next, we consider the computational complexity of recovering all keys. From the attack algorithm, the overall computational complexity **T** is given by

$$\mathbf{T} = T_1 + T_2 + T_3 \approx 2^{50.8} + 2^{49.3} + 2^{48} \approx 2^{51.4},$$
$$T_1 = 2^{50.8},$$
$$T_2 = 2^{24}(2^{16} \cdot 6 + 2^{12}(2^{12} \cdot 3 + 2^{12}(2^8 \cdot 3))) + (2^{12} \cdot 2^4 \cdot 3) \cdot 4 \approx 2^{57.6} \text{ (S-box)},$$
$$T_3 = 2^{48},$$

where $T_1$ is the computational complexity of 7 sets of 48-th order differential, $T_2$ and $T_3$ are the computational complexity required to determine the 96-bit key by solving the attack equation and exhaustive key search for the remaining 48-bit key, respectively. Because the full-round LBC consists of $320\,(= 16 \times 20)$ S-boxes, the computational complexity of $T_2$ is equivalent to $2^{57.6}/320 \approx 2^{49.3}$ times of encryption operation.

Table 3 shows the results of applying an integral attack on the full-round LBC exploiting different integral characteristics. Moreover, the attack exploiting the 15-round or less characteristic is ineffective because the computational complexity required for the attack exceeds $2^{80}$, and the attack exploiting the 16-round integral characteristic is the best from the table.

**Table 3.** Results of integral attacks on the full-round LBC.

| $d$ | $r$ | Guess Keys | Data Complexity | Time Complexity |
|-----|-----|-----------|-----------------|-----------------|
| 60 | 18 | 32 | $2^{61.6}$ | $2^{61.6}$ |
| 56 | 17 | 64 | $2^{58.3}$ | $2^{58.3}$ |
| 48 | 16 | 96 | $2^{50.8}$ | $2^{51.4}$ |

## 7   Improvement of LBC

Due to the low diffusion property, LBC has more than 16-round integral characteristics, and these can be exploited for the integral attack on the full-round LBC. This section attempts to strengthen the LBC algorithm and discusses its security against integral attack.

## 7.1   The Algorithm

Figure 4 shows the improved LBC's round function. To introduce the better diffusion property, an XOR operation from the third 16-bit data, which applied the linear function RL, to the fourth 16-bit data (in the red-colored part of Fig. 4) is added after the S-boxes.

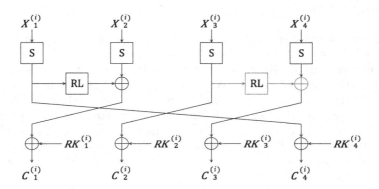

**Fig. 4.** Round function of the improved LBC.

## 7.2   Security Against Integral Attack

In this subsection, we evaluate the security of the improved LBC against integral attack.

The integral characteristics of the improved LBC were investigated using the search method shown in Sect. 5. As a result, we found the 8-round integral characteristics shown in Table 4 to be the longest. In the table, $d$ denotes the order of differential. Since the 9-round integral characteristic was not confirmed in the comprehensive search using the 63-rd order differential, it was revealed that the 8-round integral characteristic using the 52-nd order differential was the best in terms of efficient attack. Thus, its length is reduced to 8 rounds compared to the 18-round integral characteristic discovered in LBC so that the algorithm of the improved LBC is confirmed to be stronger than the original one.

**Table 4.** 8-round integral characteristics using $d$-th order differential of the improved LBC.

| $d$ | Integral property of $\mathbf{C}^{(8)}$ |
|---|---|
| 52−59 | **U B B U** |
| 60−63 | **B B B B** |

We apply the integral attack on the improved LBC by exploiting the 8-round integral characteristic using the 52-nd order differential. Although the details of the attack algorithm are omitted here due to the space limit, its key recovery is executed similarly, as shown in Sect. 6. We confirmed that the improved 11-round LBC can be attacked more efficiently than an exhaustive key search.

## 8   Conclusion

In this paper, we evaluated the security against integral attack on the block cipher LBC. First, we searched for integral characteristics with the bit-based division property using MILP and found the 18-round integral characteristic using the 60-th order differential. We also showed the 16-round integral characteristic using the 48-th order differential, which can efficiently be exploited for an integral attack on the full-round LBC with $2^{50.8}$ blocks of chosen plaintext and $2^{51.4}$ times of encryption operation. Furthermore, we tried to improve the round function of LBC. Then, we confirmed that the improved LBC strengthens the original one because the length of the integral characteristic is reduced to 8 rounds.

In future work, we will analyze the key scheduling part and consider the attack that exploits its property.

## References

1. Kapalova, N., Algazy, K., Haumen, A.: Development of A New Lightweight Encryption Algorithm. Eastern-Eur. J. Enterp. Technol. 6–19 (2023). ISSN 1729-3774
2. Knudsen, L., Wagner, D.: Integral cryptanalysis. In: FSE 2002. LNCS, vol. 2365, pp. 112–127, Springer, Heidelberg (2002)
3. Todo, Y.: Structural evaluation by generalized integral property. In: EUROCRYPT 2015. LNCS, vol. 9056, pp. 287–314. Springer (2015)
4. Todo, Y., Morii, M.: Bit-based division property and application to SIMON family. In: FSE 2016, LNCS, vol. 9783, pp. 375–377. Springer (2016)
5. Xiang, Z., Zhang, W., Bao, Z., Lin, D.: Applying MILP method to searching integral distinguishers based on division property for 6 lightweight block ciphers. In: ASIACRYPT 2016. LNCS, vol. 10031, pp. 648–678. Springer (2016)
6. SageMathCell. https://sagecell.sagemath.org/
7. Gurobi Optimization, LCC Gurobi Optimizer Reference Manual (2023). https://www.gurobi.com
8. Sasaki, Y., Wang, L.: Meet-in-the-middle technique for integral attacks against feistel ciphers. In: SAC 2012. LNCS, vol. 7707, pp. 234–251. Springer (2013)
9. Ferguson, N., et al.: Improved Cryptanalysis of Rijndael. In: FSE 2000. LNCS, vol. 1978, pp. 213–230. Springer (2001)

# Network Security

# ARP Spoofing Mitigation for the E2 Interface in Open RAN: An xApp Approach

Jihye Kim[1], Jaehyoung Park[2], and Jong-Hyouk Lee[2(✉)] (iD)

[1] Department of Computer and Information Security, Sejong University,
Seoul 05006, Republic of Korea
jihye@pel.sejong.ac.kr
[2] Department of Computer and Information Security and Convergence Engineering
for Intelligent Drone, Sejong University, Seoul 05006, Republic of Korea
jaehyoung@pel.sejong.ac.kr, jonghyouk@sejong.ac.kr

**Abstract.** In the 5G-Advanced and 6G era, the Open Radio Access Network (Open RAN) will support hardware and software interoperability between different vendors. The O-RAN Alliance, which leads the Open RAN initiative, has released standards addressing potential threats and mitigation requirements to the framework. While the standards specify Man-in-the-Middle (MitM) attacks on the E2 interface and recommend using IPsec, a Layer 3 security protocol, they do not cover defenses against Layer 2 attacks, such as Address Resolution Protocol (ARP) spoofing. This paper proposes an xApp with preventive and reactive mechanisms to protect the E2 interface from ARP spoofing in Open RAN. The xApp proactively prevents attacks through a static ARP table and continuously monitors the E2 interface to detect and react to the ARP spoofing, offering better network resilience than existing methods.

**Keywords:** Open RAN · E2 interface · xApp · MitM

## 1 Introduction

In anticipation of the 5G-Advanced and 6G era, Open Radio Access Network (Open RAN) has emerged as the next-generation RAN technology to rapidly process the massive amounts of data generated by an increasing number of mobile devices and applications in the existing RAN. Open RAN incorporates new components and interfaces into the NG-RAN as defined by the 3rd Generation Partnership Project (3GPP). Open RAN, which aims to enhance the flexibility and interoperability of networks, emphasizes the openness and intelligence of RAN. Open RAN disaggregates functions of the base station to improve data processing in the traditional RAN, providing a distributed deployment. And software-based components are interconnected through open interfaces. Various equipment suppliers enable interoperability between different vendors by flexibly deploying virtualized software. This allows multiple enterprises and individual

J.-H. Lee et al. (Eds.): WISA 2024, LNCS 15499, pp. 31–43, 2025.
https://doi.org/10.1007/978-981-96-1624-4_3

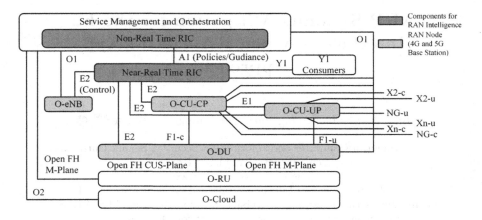

**Fig. 1.** Open RAN architecture by the O-RAN Alliance

users to leverage the RAN ecosystem. Furthermore, Artificial Intelligence (AI) models are employed to maintain the RAN's optimal state in Open RAN. AI models are integrated into the RAN Intelligent Controller (RIC) in Open RAN to automate network operations and provide efficient performance [1].

The O-RAN Alliance takes a leading role in addressing security standards for the advancement of Open RAN. Figure 1 illustrates the Open RAN architecture provided by the O-RAN Alliance. Non-Real-Time (Non-RT) RICs and Near-Real-Time (Near-RT) RICs are key to the intelligence of the RAN. The Non-RT RIC utilizes advanced AI models to predict and analyze network traffic and Quality of Service (QoS). The Near-RT RIC leverages the AI models deployed by the Non-RT RIC to monitor and dynamically control the state of the RAN. The A1 interface connecting two RICs and the E2 interface connecting the Near-RT RIC with RAN nodes (i.e., gNBs) contribute to the automation and optimization of RAN, enhancing its intelligence [2].

While commercialization of Open RAN is still in its early stages, recent research and documents have also focused on security aspects to complement Open RAN. The O-RAN Alliance defines potential security threats and requirements for each component and interface from the Open RAN framework [3]. Recently, new releases of Open RAN have been published approximately yearly, aiming to reinforce the components necessary to prepare for Open RAN deployment. We have referenced the standards published by the O-RAN Alliance to identify threats and requirements for the E2 interface, which is utilized for the intelligence of RAN. The O-RAN Alliance identifies Man-in-the-Middle (MitM) attacks as potential threats to the E2 interface. Furthermore, to enhance the security of the E2 interface, the O-RAN Alliance proposes utilizing the IPsec, the Layer 3 security protocol. MitM attacks include not only Layer 3 attacks like IP spoofing and ICMP redirect but also Layer 2 attacks like ARP spoofing. However, since the published standards only address Layer 3 security, this paper proposes functionalities to protect the E2 interface from Layer 2 attacks. The contribution of this paper is threefold:

- By proposing protective functionalities for Layer 2 of the E2 interface, we emphasize the necessity of Layer 2 security for the E2 interface.
- We provide advanced functionalities beyond existing research by proposing both preventive and reactive measures to prevent ARP spoofing.
- Our research establishes a foundation for security-related studies and standardization efforts aimed at advancing the next-generation RANs.

The structure of this paper is as follows. Section 2 analyzes existing research on security for the E2 interface of Open RAN, specifically existing mechanisms aimed at preventing and mitigating Layer 2 attacks. Section 3 proposes an ARP spoofing mitigation xApp to protect the E2 interface. Section 4 evaluates the proposed xApp for ARP spoofing mitigation by comparing it with existing research. Section 5 discusses the result and limitation of the proposed xApp, and finally, Sect. 6 concludes this paper.

## 2   Related Work

### 2.1   Security Threat and Requirements on the E2 Interface

The E2 interface connects the Near-RT RIC with RAN nodes and serves as a crucial interface in Open RAN for RAN intelligence and optimization. The Near-RT RIC collects the status information from RAN nodes via the E2 interface to assess their optimization status, predicts future status, and controls the RAN in Near-RT (e.g., 0.01 s to 1 s). If attacks occur on the E2 interface, it can lead to system errors such as RAN being paused or performance degradation. This emphasizes the critical importance of securing the E2 interface in maintaining the operational integrity and performance of the RAN. Therefore, the E2 interface security must be considered mandatory.

The O-RAN Alliance WG11 provides security standards for components and interfaces. According to the O-RAN security threat modeling and risk assessment published by WG11, Open RAN systems can be vulnerable to attackers who may exploit the E2 interface to compromise the system. Furthermore, data transmitted through the E2 interface can be maliciously manipulated by malicious xApps. In the E2 interface, if an untrusted Near-RT RIC or E2 node communicates with other components through the E2 interface, it is vulnerable to mutual authentication issues. Furthermore, attackers can access the E2 interface via MitM attacks, allowing them to read, manipulate, and insert messages. As a result, the Near-RT RIC or the E2 nodes can receive malicious messages [3]. Table 1 lists security threats related to the E2 interface referencing the threat IDs defined by the O-RAN Alliance.

According to the security requirements and controls specification published by WG11, the E2 interface must support confidentiality, integrity, replay protection, and data origin authentication. Furthermore, for the IP layer protection of

**Table 1.** Security threats on the E2 interface by the O-RAN Alliance

| ID | Title |
|---|---|
| T-O-RAN-05 | Attacker penetrates and compromises the O-RAN system through the O-RAN's Fronthaul, O1, O2, A1, and E2 |
| T-xApp-01 | Attacker exploits xApps vulnerabilities and misconfiguration |
| T-E2-01 | Untrusted Near-RT-RIC and E2 Nodes |
| T-E2-02 | Malicious actor monitors messaging across the E2 interface |

**Table 2.** Security requirements and controls on the E2 interface by the O-RAN Alliance

| ID | Description |
|---|---|
| REQ-SEC-E2-1 | E2 interface shall support confidentiality, integrity, replay protection and data origin authentication |
| SEC-CTL-E2 | For the security protection at the IP layer on E2 interface, IPsec shall be supported as specified in O-RAN Security Protocols Specifications |

the E2 interface, it should support IPsec [3]. Table 2 lists security requirements related to the E2 interface referencing the IDs defined by the O-RAN Alliance.

According to the standards of the O-RAN Alliance, the E2 interface is susceptible to MitM attacks, where attackers can intercept messages transmitted through the E2 interface by performing MitM attacks. This exposes the E2 interface to secondary threats such as message manipulation. To protect the E2 interface from such threats, it should support functionalities that ensure confidentiality and integrity. Additionally, support for IPsec is necessary to safeguard communications at the IP layer. However, the IPsec, the Layer 3 security protocol, provided in the standards by the O-RAN Alliance can only address Layer 3 attacks such as IP spoofing and ICMP redirect. Therefore, there is a need for functionalities to prevent Layer 2 attacks, such as ARP spoofing.

## 2.2 Literature Review of the E2 Interface Security

This section presents existing research to identify and mitigate security threats to the E2 interface above the Open RAN environment.

Hung et al. [4] provide insights into threats discovered from O-RAN A-Release to H-Release, the open-source of Open RAN. The author emphasizes the necessity of detecting malicious xApps. In the open-source environment discussed, the lack of specific access control privilege for xApps allows malicious attackers to potentially disrupt the RAN by attacking legitimate the xApps and the E2 nodes. The author demonstrates privilege management threats, E2 subscription issues, and Denial of Service (DoS) attacks through experiments.

Djuitcheu et al. [5] analyze threats related to complex services and functionalities on the E2 interface. The author analyzes threats posed by agents such as malicious xApps, compromised xApps, malicious E2 nodes, and terminations of interfaces. The study focuses on threats related to the E2 interface, including DoS attacks, MitM attacks, protocol exploitation, replay attacks, unauthorized access, manipulation and tampering of E2 data, and malware deployment. In response to these threats, mitigation strategies proposed theoretically include applying IPsec, leveraging xApps and Machine Learning (ML), and utilizing a new security design incorporating zero trust architecture.

Radhakrishnan et al. [6] provide use cases involving communication between the Near-RT RIC and the E2 interface, as well as controlling the RAN through multi-xApps. Following this, the author explains the security of the E2 interface for the Near-RT RIC. The author provides scenarios of resource exhaustion and signaling storm DoS attacks on the E2 interface and presents the results of designing and developing xApp-based latency monitoring to detect and mitigate these attacks.

Table 3 compares security threats or potential attacks on the E2 interface across existing studies and outlines mitigation strategies. We denoted with "-", which papers do not provide mitigation strategies.

**Table 3.** Comparison of related works for the E2 interface security

| Ref. | Security threats and attacks | Mitigation strategies |
|------|------------------------------|------------------------|
| [4] | Privilege management, E2 subscription issue, DoS attack | – |
| [5] | DoS attack, MitM attack, Protocol exploitation, Replay attack, Unauthorized access, Manipulation and tampering of E2 data, Malware deployment | IPsec, xApp, Machine Learning, Zero trust architecture |
| [6] | DoS attack | Latency monitoring xApp |

According to existing research, there is a lack of research solely focused on protecting the E2 interface and developing security mechanisms specifically for the E2 interface. Also, the protection of the E2 interface can be achieved by designing xApps effectively. Additionally, applying security protocols like IPsec and leveraging AI can help mitigate attacks effectively.

### 2.3    Literature Review on Mitigation Strategies of Layer 2 Attacks

Continuous research is essential to safeguard the E2 interface in Open RAN, against Layer 2 attacks like ARP spoofing that are not covered in current Open RAN literature. This paper introduces existing research focused on preventing and mitigating traditional Layer 2 attacks in similar network environments.

**Static ARP Cache.** ARP spoofing is when an attacker alters a node's MAC address to impersonate it, tricking others into thinking the attacker's device is the real node. This manipulation affects ARP tables of other Local Area Network (LAN) nodes, displaying the attacker's MAC as the legitimate one. Setting static ARP mappings on each LAN host can prevent unauthorized network access [7].

**Duplicated MAC Address.** ARP spoofing involves an attacker changing a node's MAC address to their own, causing the ARP table to associate the attacker's MAC address with the victim node. Therefore, duplicate MAC addresses in the ARP table can be detected as an ARP spoofing attempt [8,9].

**Delete the Attacker's ARP Cache.** ARP spoofing involves an attacker attacking the interface between two legitimate nodes on a network. Therefore, if the attacker attempts to attack the interface, their cache in the ARP table can be cleared to remove their presence and block them [10,11].

**MAC Address Blocking Rule.** ARP spoofing involves an attacker attacking the connection between nodes, which can lead to secondary threats such as packet manipulation. Therefore, when detecting the attacker, setting a rule to block the attacker's MAC address prevents them from attempting further attacks [12].

**Restore the Original ARP Table.** ARP spoofing is when an attacker manipulates a node's MAC address. After detecting and blocking the attack, it's crucial to restore the affected node's connection by updating the ARP table with its original MAC address using functions [9].

# 3   Proposed ARP Spoofing Mitigation xApp

## 3.1   System Architecture

This section describes the ARP spoofing mitigation xApp proposed to protect the E2 interface from ARP spoofing, which is a potential MitM attack specific to Layer 2. A typical xApp is an application utilized by the Near-RT RIC to provide specific services. The Near-RT RIC utilizes multi-xApps to provide various services. Additionally, users can design, develop, and utilize xApps to provide the services they need. The proposed xApp includes both preventive and post-event response functions for ARP spoofing prevention on the E2 interface, shown by the gray part in Fig. 2. The proposed xApp can be utilized alongside various other xApps within Near-RT RIC, serving as an application and service that contributes to the overall functionality and optimization of the network. The notations within this xApp are described in Table 4.

The preventive function utilized in the proposed xApp manages the ARP table, while the post-event response function detects and responds to ARP spoofing. ARP spoofing can be prevented in advance by statically setting the MAC

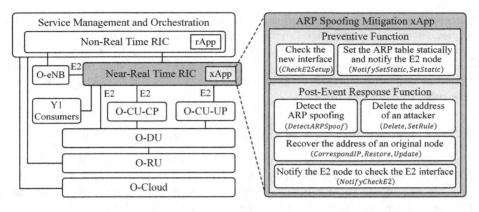

**Fig. 2.** System architecture containing the proposed xApp for the E2 interface security

**Table 4.** Notation of the proposed xApp

| Notation | Description |
|---|---|
| $MAC_{NearRTRIC}$ | MAC address of a Near-RT RIC |
| $MAC_{E2node}$ | MAC address of an original E2 node |
| $MAC_{attacker}$ | MAC address suspected by an ARP spoofing attacker |
| $IP_{NearRTRIC}$ | IP address of the Near-RT RIC |
| $IP_{E2node}$ | IP address of the original E2 node |
| $IP_{attacker}$ | IP address suspected by the ARP spoofing attacker |
| $ARP_{table}$ | ARP table of the Near-RT RIC |
| $CheckE2Setup(x)$ | Check the setting of the new E2 interface with $x$ |
| $NotifySetStatic(x,y)$ | Notify the E2 node to set the ARP cache statically corresponding to $x$ and $y$ |
| $DetectARPSpoof(x)$ | Detect the ARP spoofing on the E2 interface with $x$ |
| $Delete(x,y)$ | Delete $y$ from $x$ |
| $SetStatic(x,y)$ | Set the ARP cache statically corresponding to $x$ and $y$ |
| $SetRule(x,y)$ | Set a rule to block $x$ and $y$ |
| $CorrespondIP(x)$ | IP address corresponding to $x$ |
| $Restore(x)$ | Restore the MAC address of the original node with $x$ |
| $Update(x,y,z)$ | Update $y$ to $z$ from $x$ |
| $NotifyCheckE2(x)$ | Notify the E2 node to check the E2 interface connectivity and verify that the MAC address of the Near-RT RIC is $x$ |

addresses of the nodes connected through the E2 interface. However, despite the implementation of preventive functions, ARP spoofing can still occur when performing tasks such as the RAN status measurement through the E2 interface. To address this attack, the proposed xApp provides the post-event response function that deletes the attacker's traces from the Near-RT RIC's ARP table and sets rules to block the attacker.

## 3.2   Prevention Function of the ARP Spoofing Mitigation xApp

The proposed xApp statically manages the ARP table of Near-RT RIC to prevent ARP spoofing on the E2 interface. ARP spoofing targets interfaces, so it is possible only when the E2 interface exists between the Near-RT RIC and the E2 node. Therefore, the principle of this function is for the Near-RT RIC to statically set the MAC address of the newly connected E2 node when setting the E2 interface. Furthermore, ARP spoofing involves an attacker falsifying the MAC address of the node. By statically managing the ARP table, the attacker is prevented from manipulating MAC addresses.

The proposed xApp can verify the setting of E2 interfaces by monitoring packets related to the E2 interface. The setting of E2 interfaces refers to the E2 setup procedure provided by the O-RAN Alliance. As depicted in Fig. 3, the E2 interface is established when the Near-RT RIC receives an E2 SETUP REQUEST from the E2 node and subsequently sends an E2 SETUP RESPONSE to the E2 node [3]. Using this procedure, you can monitor the setting of the E2 interface and statically configure the MAC address of the E2 node as soon as it is established.

**Fig. 3.** E2 setup procedure by the O-RAN Alliance [3]

Algorithm 1 is the first function of the proposed xApp, which aims to prevent ARP spoofing proactively by statically managing the ARP table of the Near-RT RIC. Lines 2 to 3 monitor packets transmitted over the E2 interface, checking the setting of the E2 interface by observing the process where the Near-RT RIC receives the E2 SETUP REQUEST from an E2 node and sends the E2 SETUP RESPONSE to that node. If confirmed, it saves the MAC address of the E2 node connecting to the new E2 interface as $MAC_{E2node}$ and stores the corresponding IP address as $IP_{E2node}$. Lines 4 to 7 are executed if $IP_{E2node}$ and $MAC_{E2node}$ is found in $ARP_{table}$. In this case, we can see that the E2 node connected to the new E2 interface is successfully connected, so we notify the E2 node to set the ARP cache for $IP_{NearRTRIC}$ and $MAC_{NearRTRIC}$ statically in ARP table of it, by transmitting those addresses. Later, statically set the ARP cache corresponding to $IP_{E2node}$ and $MAC_{E2node}$ in $ARP_{table}$. This prevents ARP spoofing by making it difficult to manipulate the MAC address of the E2 node in the ARP table.

---

**Algorithm 1.** Preventive Function: ARP table management

---

1: begin
2: **for** each *packet* in *packets* **do**
3:     $IP_{E2node}, MAC_{E2node} \leftarrow CheckE2Setup(packet)$
4:     **if** $IP_{E2node}, MAC_{E2node}$ in $ARP_{table}$ **then**
5:         $NotifySetStatic(IP_{NearRTRIC}, MAC_{NearRTRIC})$
6:         $SetStatic(IP_{E2node}, MAC_{E2node})$
7:     **end if**
8: **end for**
9: end

---

### 3.3   Post-event Function of the ARP Spoofing Mitigation xApp

In the proposed xApp, ARP spoofing prevention for the E2 interface is achieved by continuously detecting and responding to ARP spoofing after the attack event. This function operates after performing the preemptive prevention measures for the E2 interface. ARP spoofing involves an attacker falsifying the MAC address of an E2 node connected to the Near-RT RIC via the E2 interface. Consequently, the MAC addresses of nodes stored in the Near-RT RIC's ARP table are also altered to reflect the attacker's MAC address. Therefore, the principle of the post-event response function is to detect ARP spoofing attempts on the E2 interface, block the attacker, and restore the ARP table with the original E2 node's MAC address. Furthermore, it prevents potential reattacks during the restoration process by immediately blocking the attacker upon detecting the attack and restoring the original address.

The proposed xApp enables ARP spoofing detection through packets received by the Near-RT RIC. An ARP REPLY follows the format shown in Fig. 4, and an attacker exploits this to attempt ARP spoofing. The attacker continuously sends the ARP REPLY to the Near-RT RIC, where the target protocol address is the IP address of a legitimate E2 node connected to the E2 interface, and the target hardware address is the MAC address of the attacker. Furthermore, the attacker continuously sends the ARP REPLY to the E2 node, where the target protocol address is the IP address of the Near-RT RIC, and the target hardware address is the MAC address of the attacker itself. Therefore, the Near-RT RIC and the E2 node each received the ARP REPLY will think that the attacker is each other's counterpart node. By continuously monitoring the transmission of numerous ARP REPLY, it is possible to detect ARP spoofing. The node sending these packets can be identified as the attacker attempting ARP spoofing.

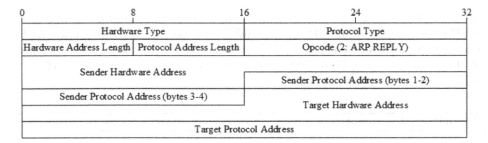

**Fig. 4.** ARP REPLY packet format

Algorithm 2 is the second function of the proposed xApp, which detects and responds to ARP spoofing on the E2 interface. Lines 2 to 3 monitor packets transmitted over the E2 interface and, upon detecting an attack through the Near-RT RIC continuously receiving an ARP REPLY, consider the node responsible for the attack as the attacker. It then stores the IP address of the node suspected to be the attacker as $IP_{attacker}$ and its MAC address as $MAC_{attacker}$. Lines 4 to 11 are executed if $IP_{attacker}$ and $MAC_{attacker}$ is found in $ARP_{table}$. In this case, two IP addresses associated with $MAC_{attacker}$ is checked. The IP address is found to be different from the attacker's IP address, $IP_{attacker}$. A different IP address corresponds to the original E2 node previously connected to the E2 interface, and this address is saved as $IP_{E2node}$. Afterward, the ARP cache corresponding to $IP_{attacker}$ and $MAC_{attacker}$ in the $ARP_{table}$ is deleted. The process involves verifying and removing duplicate MAC addresses. And setting network rules to block the $IP_{attacker}$ and $MAC_{attacker}$ which is a suspected attacker. Since the attacker has been blocked, retrieve the original MAC address corresponding to the $IP_{E2node}$ of the original E2 node and store it in $MAC_{E2node}$. Finally, update $ARP_{table}$ by replacing $MAC_{attacker}$ with $MAC_{E2node}$ to restore it to its origi-

---

**Algorithm 2.** Post-Event Response Function: ARP spoofing detection and response

---

1: begin
2: **for** each *packet* in *packets* **do**
3:         $IP_{attacker}, MAC_{attacker} \leftarrow DetectARPSpoof(packet)$
4:     **if** $IP_{attacker}, MAC_{attacker}$ in $ARP_{table}$ **then**
5:             $IP_{E2node} \leftarrow CorrespondIP(IP_{attacker}, MAC_{attacker})$
6:             $Delete(ARP_{table}, IP_{attacker}, MAC_{attacker})$
7:             $SetRule(IP_{attakcker}, MAC_{attacker})$
8:             $MAC_{E2node} \leftarrow Restore(IP_{E2node})$
9:             $Update(ARP_{table}, MAC_{attacker}, MAC_{E2node})$
10:            $NotifyCheckE2(IP_{NearRTRIC}, MAC_{NearRTRIC})$
11:        **end if**
12: **end for**
13: end

---

nal state. This enables detection and response against ARP spoofing on the E2 interface. The Near-RT RIC notifies the E2 node to check the E2 interface ARP spoofing is attempted and set up a new E2 interface connection, by transmitting $IP_{NearRTRIC}$ and $MAC_{NearRTRIC}$.

# 4   Comparison

The proposed xApp provides functions to prevent and respond to Layer 2 attacks such as ARP spoofing on the E2 interface. There are no mechanisms or solutions currently available to prevent attacks in Open RAN. Therefore, by comparing the existing ARP spoofing prevention mechanisms introduced in Sect. 2 with the proposed xApp in Table 5, we demonstrate the superiority of our system.

The existing research involves setting a static ARP table and deleting the attacker's cache. Furthermore, it sets up rules to block the attacker and restores the original ARP table to detect and respond to ARP spoofing. The proposed xApp adheres to all five functionalities in existing research. To prevent intrusions by attackers proactively, the xApp manages the ARP table by statically setting the MAC address of the E2 node. However, despite these proactive measures, considering the possibility of advanced and sophisticated attacks, the xApp also monitors duplicate MAC addresses in the ARP table and removes the cache of attackers with those addresses. Additionally, the xApp sets up rules to block the identified attackers, making it difficult for them to attempt further attacks. It then verifies the original MAC address of the E2 node and updates the ARP table to ensure uninterrupted connectivity.

**Table 5.** Comparison between the proposal xApp and the existing defense mechanisms

| Defense mechanism | Static ARP table | Duplicated MAC address | Delete the attacker's ARP cache | Attacker blocking rule | Restore the original ARP table |
|---|---|---|---|---|---|
| Galal et al. [8] | X | O | X | X | X |
| Prasad et al. [9] | X | O | X | X | O |
| Hou et al. [10] | O | X | O | X | X |
| Hijazi et al. [11] | O | X | O | X | O |
| Ortega et al. [12] | X | X | X | O | X |
| Proposal xApp | O | O | O | O | O |

## 5   Discussion

Since Open RAN allows implementation using publicly available software, including interfaces such as E2 and A1, there is a possibility of attacks like MitM attacks [13]. If a Layer 2 attack like ARP spoofing occurs on the E2 interface, the attacker can eavesdrop on the status information of RAN nodes. By manipulating this information, they can potentially induce pause states in the RAN, thereby delaying its operations. As a result, if the Near-RT RIC fails to monitor the RAN due to such attacks, it can lead to errors in RAN management.

Therefore, the proposed xApp provides preventive and post-event response functions within the Near-RT RIC to prevent and mitigate the ARP spoofing on the E2 interface. Due to the nature of ARP spoofing, where attackers falsify MAC addresses of legitimate nodes to impersonate them, utilizing preventive measures ensures an environment where attackers cannot manipulate MAC addresses. However, this xApp sets the MAC address of an E2 node statically as soon as it connects to the E2 interface, without distinguishing whether the node is legitimate or an attacker. Therefore, it is necessary to verify whether the node is trusted or not, and this verification process should be expanded in future research to focus on developing secure security functions and mechanisms.

Existing studies suggest static ARP table configuration to prevent ARP spoofing. However, concerns remain about ARP spoofing attempts due to system failures, mismanagement, or sophisticated attacks. To prepare for such worst-case scenarios, continuous monitoring of the E2 interface is essential even after managing the ARP table statically.

## 6   Conclusion

Open RAN has emerged as a new paradigm for next-generation RAN, particularly towards 5G-Advanced and 6G. It is being researched to overcome the limitations of traditional RAN, with ongoing studies focused on security to facilitate its future commercialization. This paper investigates the protection of the E2 interface, which is crucial for the intelligence of RAN. According to the O-RAN Alliance, MitM attacks are possible on the E2 interface, necessitating the implementation of IPsec. However, MitM attacks include not only Layer 3 attacks but also Layer 2 attacks such as ARP spoofing. Thus, despite IPsec implementation, bypassing attacks can still occur. To address this, we have presented the proposed xApp, which protects the E2 interface from Layer 2 attacks, specifically ARP spoofing. The xApp prevents attacks proactively through static ARP table management and continuously monitors the E2 interface to detect attacks, block attackers, and restore the ARP table, providing better network resilience compared to existing research. For future research, we aim to enhance the preventive function of the xApp to develop a superior ARP spoofing mitigation mechanism. Furthermore, through the xApp, we emphasize the necessity of Layer 2 security for the E2 interface in Open RAN.

**Acknowledgement.** This work was supported by Institute of Information & communications Technology Planning & Evaluation (IITP) grant funded by the Korea government (MSIT) (No. RS-2021-II210796, Research on Foundational Technologies for 6G Autonomous Security-by-Design to Guarantee Constant Quality of Security).

# References

1. Polese, M., Bonati, L., D'Oro, S., Basagni, S., Melodia, T.: Understanding O-RAN: architecture, interfaces, algorithms, security, and research challenges. IEEE Commun. Surv. Tutor. **25**(2), 1376–1411 (2023)
2. Tiberti, W., Fina, E., Marotta, A., Cassioli, D.: Impact of man-in-the-middle attacks to the O-RAN inter-controllers interface. In: 2022 IEEE Future Networks World Forum (FNWF), pp. 367–372 (2022)
3. O-RAN ALLIANCE. https://specifications.o-ran.org/specifications. Accessed 02 June 2024
4. Hung, C.-F., Chen, Y.-R., Tseng, C.-H., Cheng, S.-M.: Security threats to xApps access control and E2 interface in O-RAN. IEEE Open J. Commun. Soc. **5**(1), 1197–1203 (2024)
5. Djuitcheu, H., et al.: Exploring the implications and methodologies of securing the E2 interface. Authorea Preprints (2024)
6. Radhakrishnan, V.: Detection of denial of service attacks on the open radio access network intelligent controller through the E2 interface. Ph.D. thesis, Virginia Tech (2023)
7. Meghana, J., Subashri, T., Vimal, K.: A survey on ARP cache poisoning and techniques for detection and mitigation. In: 2017 Fourth International Conference on Signal Processing, Communication and Networking (ICSCN), pp. 1–6. IEEE (2017)
8. Galal, A., Ghalwash, A., Nasr, M.: A new approach for detecting and mitigating address resolution protocol (ARP) poisoning. Int. J. Adv. Comput. Sci. Appl. **13**(6), 377–382 (2022)
9. Prasad, A., Chandra, S.: Defending ARP spoofing-based MitM attack using machine learning and device profiling. In: 2022 International Conference on Computing, Communication, and Intelligent Systems (ICCCIS), pp. 978–982 (2022)
10. Hou, X., Jiang, Z., Tian, X.: The detection and prevention for ARP spoofing based on Snort. In: 2010 International Conference on Computer Application and System Modeling (ICCASM 2010) (2010)
11. Hijazi, S., Obaidat, M.: Address resolution protocol spoofing attacks and security approaches: a survey. Secur. Priv. **2**(1) (2019)
12. Ortega, A., Marcos, X., Chiang, L., Abad, C.: Preventing ARP cache poisoning attacks: a proof of concept using OpenWrt. In: 2009 Latin American Network Operations and Management Symposium, pp. 1–9. IEEE (2009)
13. Kim, J., Park, J., Lee. J.-H.: Simulation of an ARP spoofing attack on the E2 interface in open RAN. In: IEEE International Symposium on Personal, Indoor and Mobile Radio Communications (PIMRC 2024) (2024)

# Investigating the Transferability of Evasion Attacks in Network Intrusion Detection Systems Considering Domain-Specific Constraints

Mariama Mbow[1(✉)], Rodrigo Roman[2], Ayan Seal[3], Kevin I-Kai Wang[4], Sraban Kumar Mohanty[3], and Kouichi Sakurai[1]

[1] Department of Information Science and Technology, Kyushu University, Fukuoka, Japan
mmariamambow@gmail.com
[2] Network, Information and Computer Security (NICS) Lab, University of Malaga, Málaga, Spain
[3] PDPM Indian Institute of Information Technology, Design and Manufacturing, Jabalpur 482005, India
[4] Department of Electrical, Computer and Software Engineering, The University of Auckland, Auckland 1010, New Zealand

**Abstract.** Recently, adversarial attacks against machine learning-based network intrusion detection systems (NIDS) have gained significant attention in cybersecurity. This study investigates the transferability of these adversarial attacks in the context of NIDS. In addition, most existing studies in adversarial learning against NIDS adopted attack strategies designed originally for image classification without considering network traffic characteristics. However, this is impractical and will fail in the real world as network traffic features are constrained, and ignoring the functional behavior of the network traffic features leads to invalid network traffic flow or produces adversarial samples that do not retain their original functionality (malicious or benign). To address these issues, we propose a constrained momentum iterative fast gradient sign method (C-MIFGSM) to generate adversarial network flows that can successfully evade an ML-based IDS through transfer-based attacks while preserving the functional behavior of the network traffic. Our approach was validated using several target NIDS models built with the NSLKDD benchmark dataset. Experimental results demonstrate that even without knowledge of the target model and under feature constraints, it is possible to generate adversarial network traffic flows that achieve a high evasion attack success rate against NIDS built with deep learning and classical ML models. For example, the attack degraded the detection rate of the DoS traffic drops from 92.35% to 20.27% for the MLP model with an evasion increase rate of 78.04%.

**Keywords:** Cybersecurity · Network intrusion detection systems · Adversarial machine learning · Evasion attacks

© The Author(s), under exclusive license to Springer Nature Singapore Pte Ltd. 2025
J.-H. Lee et al. (Eds.): WISA 2024, LNCS 15499, pp. 44–55, 2025.
https://doi.org/10.1007/978-981-96-1624-4_4

# 1   Introduction

Network intrusion detection systems (NIDS) are the standard method used in cybersecurity to detect malicious activities on network traffic [1]. There are two main methods for detecting intrusions: signature-based and anomaly-based. The signature-based method detects attacks using their signatures. This technique works well for spotting known threats but fails to detect novel, unknown attacks like zero-day exploits. In contrast, anomaly-based NIDS monitors typical network traffic behavior and flags deviations from this norm as potential attacks. Anomaly-based methods have been thoroughly researched due to their ability to detect novel attacks without pre-existing signatures. Additionally, anomaly-based detection enhanced by machine learning models has demonstrated promising outcomes, improving NIDS with a low false alarm rate, high detection rate, and robust capabilities to manage large volumes of network traffic [2]. Machine learning (ML)-based NIDS is the main topic of this article.

Despite their remarkable performance in NIDS, prior research has demonstrated that ML models, and deep learning (DL) models in particular, are vulnerable to adversarial examples [3, 4]. These examples are small, carefully crafted perturbations to the inputs designed to deceive the model and degrade its classification performance. Although this phenomenon was initially identified in image recognition [5], it has also been proven in various other ML applications. Furthermore, previous work in computer vision has demonstrated empirical findings about the transferability of adversarial examples between neural networks [6]. This means that adversarial examples capable of deceiving one model can likely deceive another, even if the models have different architectures or training datasets. Consequently, an attacker can train a surrogate model to generate adversarial examples and transfer these examples to the target model with minimal knowledge of the target. When applied to cybersecurity tools, such techniques enable attackers to bypass detection systems, posing a significant threat to security, particularly for NIDS. This vulnerability raises serious concerns about the reliability and effectiveness of ML in security-critical applications like NIDS [7].

## 1.1   Challenging Issues

The evasion attacks against machine learning are seeing great advancement, and several studies have explored the vulnerability of DL-based NIDS to adversarial attacks. Most of the existing research has predominantly focused on crafting adversarial examples under white-box scenarios where the attacker has full knowledge of the target model [8, 9]. Recent studies are focusing on more realistic threat models investigating the gray-box or black-box scenario [11]. On the other hand, little attention has been paid to the transferability of these attacks in the context of NIDS. In addition, the practicality of the proposed attack methods is overlooked. Many studies have employed attack strategies originally designed for image classification, assuming they can add perturbation to any features, ignoring the unique characteristics of network traffic. Network traffic structures differ significantly from image pixels, and modifying certain features alters the functional behavior of the traffic flow [10]. This however invalidates the network traffic features. Furthermore, a significant number of previous studies assume that the adversary has complete knowledge of the NIDS models (white-box attack). However, this assumption is impractical, as it is unlikely for an adversary to have knowledge of the detection model and its internal configuration.

## 1.2   Contributions

To address these issues, this work investigates a more practical evasion attack in a gray box setting, leveraging the transferability properties to perform adversarial attacks while preserving the functional behavior of network traffic flow. We propose a constrained momentum iterative fast gradient sign method (C-MIFGSM)-based approach that extends the momentum iterative fast gradient method (MIFGSM) [12] while complying with domain constraints. Our approach is evaluated on various NIDS models using one of the most used network intrusion datasets, the NSLKDD, to assess the robustness of various ML and DL models. Our contributions can be summarized as follows:

- We propose a C-MIFGSM, an algorithm that extends the MIFGSM to generate adversarial network traffic flows based on the $L_\infty$norm. The proposed method generates adversarial examples that preserve the functional behavior of the network traffic flow.
- We investigate the transferability attack in the context of NIDS to perform adversarial attacks that can evade detection without prior knowledge of the target model.
- We examine the transferability of adversarial samples from deep neural networks (DNN) to various classical ML algorithms, such as random forest (RF), decision tree (DT), XGBoost, multilayer perceptron (MLP), logistic regression(LR) and two state-of-the-art DL models, using NSLKDD dataset. We find that samples transfer well across models trained with different ML techniques.

The remainder of this paper is organized as follows: Section 2 provides the background of this work. In Sect. 3, we propose our approach. Section 4 presents the experiments and evaluations of the proposed approach. Finally Sect. 5 presents the conclusion of the work.

## 2   Background

### 2.1   Related Work

Previous studies have demonstrated that DNNs are vulnerable to evasion attacks. Szegedy et al. [3] and Biggio et al. [17] showed the vulnerability of image classifiers to adversarial attacks in a white box setting. Since then, there have been many proposed works in crafting adversarial examples by adding perturbations to the image pixel [4,14,15]. However, it has been demonstrated that these attacks exist beyond images. Carlini et al. [16] showed how an adversary can fool an automatic speech recognition system. Li et al. [18] illustrated how to generate adversarial text attacks that preserve the utility of benign text. Grosses et al. [19] studied adversarial examples for malware detection while maintaining the malware's functionality. However, in each of the above-stated domains, adversarial examples have been crafted differently. Such a situation illustrates that the feasibility of generating successful adversarial attacks is domain-specific. Therefore, we need to understand its feasibility in the context of network traffic to successfully craft adversarial examples in NIDS.

There have been studies on adversarial attacks against NIDS [8,9]. However, despite the numerous works addressing these attacks against NIDS, little attention was paid to the challenges of the generated adversarial examples. Consequently, a repeated criticism made by recent surveys [9,24,25] is the impracticality of most of the previous works in a real-world NIDS scenario. Most prior efforts at crafting adversarial examples on NIDS ignore the preservation of the functional behavior of the network traffic [10] or assume a white-box attack.

Recent studies have focused on maintaining the functional behavior of generated adversarial network traffic flows in NSLKDD [10,13]. Despite limiting their attacks to non-functional features, these studies did not impose restrictions on the generated perturbations within the valid range. This oversight can result in unreasonable values, potentially invalidating the adversarial network traffic flows. Additionally, they did not consider the type of features. Furthermore, they did not investigate the transferability of these adversarial samples.

## 2.2   Challenges in Generating Adversarial Examples in NIDS

In network traffic, successful adversarial attacks must not only introduce small perturbations but also adhere to practical constraints. Unlike unstructured data like image pixels, network traffic data are structured and constrained by several factors that impact the feasibility of attacks on NIDS. These constraints include:

- Feature type: Network data can include various feature types, such as continuous, categorical, and binary. Adversarial examples must respect these distinctions to avoid violating data integrity. For instance, perturbations should not convert binary features into non-binary values or alter the representation of categorical data.
- Out-of-range values: Perturbations must not exceed the maximum or fall below the minimum valid values for each feature. Adversarial examples should stay within the permissible ranges to avoid disrupting the functionality of the network traffic.
- Functional features: Each category of attack has specific functional features that represent the fundamental characteristics or behaviors of that particular type of attack. Therefore, when generating adversarial examples, it is essential to ensure that perturbations are added only to non-functional features. This approach ensures that the malicious adversarial traffic preserves its functionality while being misclassified [10].

These characteristics imply a different method than adversarial attacks developed for images should be investigated to satisfy the domain-specific constraints by preserving the functional behavior of the generated adversarial examples and achieving valid adversarial network traffic.

# 3   Approach

This section provides a detailed explanation of our proposed method. The objective is to generate adversarial examples that can effectively deceive the NIDS model.

## 3.1   Problem Definition

Given a network traffic flow represented as an $n$-dimensional feature vector $x \in X$, extracted using feature extraction methods, the NIDS model classifier $f : X \rightarrow Y$ takes $x$ as input and predicts the label $y \in Y$. In this study, we focus on binary classification, where the task is to distinguish between normal traffic and a specific type of attack. Our goal is to perform an untargeted attack, aiming to mislead the NIDS model into making incorrect predictions. Specifically, we seek an example $x^*$ in the vicinity of $x$ that is misclassified by the detector.

## 3.2   Methodology

One strategy to attack the target without direct access to the victim's internal configuration is to train a local model to approximate a decision boundary of the target. Adversarial samples are then crafted using this surrogate model, and the transferability property is exploited to transfer these samples to the target model, to which the adversary has no direct access.

In our scenario, we employ a gray-box attack, assuming that the internal structure and parameters of the detection system are unknown to attackers. However, we assume the adversary has already compromised one or more devices and gained read access to the victim's dataset for replication and preprocessing. Subsequently, the adversary creates a local NIDS model to mimic the victim NIDS model and craft adversarial examples that deceive the local model. Finally, these adversarial samples are transferred to evade the victim NIDS.

### Preserving the Functional Behavior of the Attack

– Feature type: To ensure the generated adversarial examples do not modify the feature type we proceed as follows. For binary features, we use a threshold of 0.5 to keep their values into binary values. If the value of the perturbation is less than 0.5, we change it to 0, and 1 if greater or equal to 0.5. In addition, we do not add perturbation to the non-numerical features, such as the one-hot encoded features converted from the categorical features (for instance, the protocol type).

- Valid range: We identify the minimum and maximum values for each feature in the dataset, defining the interval between these values as the valid range. After generating perturbations, we ensure the modified features remain within this range by applying the clipping method. This approach keeps perturbations within the predefined limits, preventing out-of-range values. For instance, if an adversarial sample exceeds a feature's maximum value, we clip it to the maximum value.
- Functional features: To conduct the attack, we begin by analyzing the functional and non-functional features within the dataset. We then generate adversarial examples, by adding perturbation on the non-functional features. These non-functional features are those that can be altered using legitimate transformations. This approach ensures that the intended meaning of the attack traffic remains unchanged and minimizes the risk of invalidating the data format.

As shown in Algorithm 1, we enforce the constraints by adding a mask on the features we do not want to add perturbation (the functional features) at each iteration of the training. This is done by creating a mask vector and using the element-wise multiplication, which is the Hadamard product, to maximize the loss only on the allowed features shown in Table 1. Here, $\delta$ is the perturbation we want to add to the feature vector, mask $v$ is the constraint, and $\odot$ is the element-wise multiplication.

**Table 1.** Illustration of the constraint

| Vector type | x1 | x2 | x3 | x4 | x5 | x6 | x7 | ... | xn |
|---|---|---|---|---|---|---|---|---|---|
| perturbation $\delta$ | $\delta_{x1}$ | $\delta_{x2}$ | $\delta_{x3}$ | $\delta_{x4}$ | $\delta_{x5}$ | $\delta_{x6}$ | $\delta_{x7}$ | ... | $\delta_{xn}$ |
| mask vector ($v$) | 1 | 0 | 1 | 1 | 0 | 1 | 0 | ... | 1 |
| $\delta \odot v$ | $\delta_{x1}$ | 0 | $\delta_{x3}$ | $\delta_{x4}$ | 0 | $\delta_{x6}$ | 0 | ... | $\delta_{xn}$ |

$$v_k = (v_1, v_2, ..., vn)^T \qquad v_k = \begin{cases} 1, & \text{if } k \in \text{independent feature} \\ 0, & \text{otherwise} \end{cases} \qquad (1)$$

### 3.3   Generating Adversarial Samples

Although adversarial samples are often transferable, we should also consider the optimal approach to improve the transferability. In this paper, we propose C-MIFGSM to enhance the transferability of adversarial examples within a constrained domain. C-MIFGSM is an extension of the MIFGSM developed by Dong et al. [12]. MIFGSM integrates the momentum method into iterative gradient-based attack methods to mitigate poor transferability and enhance the success rate of black-box attacks.

As the algorithm allows perturbation on any feature, our proposed approach extends MIFGSM by incorporating constraints to limit perturbations using a mask vector and controlling the perturbation on binary features. Algorithm 1 illustrates the extended approach.

---

**Algorithm 1.** Crafting adversarial examples for NIDS

---

**Input:**

    $f$: Classifier with loss function $J$.

    $x$: Real example input.

    $y$: Ground-truth label.

    $\epsilon$: Size of perturbation.

    $T$: Number of iterations.

    $\mu$: Decay factor.

    mask: mask to restrict perturbations.

**Output:**

    $x^*$: Adversarial example with $\|x^* - x\|_\infty \leq \epsilon$.

1:  $\alpha \leftarrow \epsilon/T$

2:  $g_0 \leftarrow 0$

3:  $x_0^* \leftarrow x$

4:  **for** $t = 0$ to $T - 1$ **do**

5:      Input $x_t^*$ to $f$ and obtain the gradient $\nabla_x J(x_t^*, y)$

6:      Update $g_{t+1}$ by accumulating the velocity vector in the gradient direction:

7:          $g_{t+1} \leftarrow \mu \cdot g_t + \frac{\nabla_x J(x_t^*, y)}{\|\nabla_x J(x_t^*, y)\|_1}$

8:      Update $x_{t+1}^*$ by applying the sign gradient and mask:

9:          $x_{t+1}^* \leftarrow x_t^* + \alpha \cdot \text{sign}(g_{t+1}) \odot v$

10:    Clip the samples within the valid range

11:    Add binary constraints

12: **end for**

13: **return** $x^* = x_T^*$

---

## 4  Experiments and Evaluation

In this section, we first train the adversary's local network, a DNN model to achieve a matching performance with the state-of-art performance on recent works on NIDS and then generate adversarial examples in the local model with the proposed algorithm. Finally, the generated examples are transferred to mislead various target models. These target models include several classical machine learning and two DL models.

### 4.1  Dataset and Pre-processing

We evaluate our approach using the NSLKDD dataset. NSLKDD is the most used dataset in academia for NIDS. It is a public dataset built by Tavallaee et al. [20] as an improved version of the KDD'99 dataset. In this work, we use the NSLKDDTrain+ as our training data and NSLKDDTest+ as test data. The dataset contains 41 features. These features can be divided into four different categories: (1–9) basic features, (10–22) content features, (23–31) time-based features, and (32–41) host-based features. The records of attacks in the dataset can be grouped into four categories of attacks: denial of service (DoS), probing (probe), root to local (R2L), and user to root (U2R) attacks, and the rest of the records represent normal traffic flow. Table 2 shows the functional features of each attack category (✓). To ensure the crafted adversarial examples will not invalidate the network traffic, we add perturbation to the non-funtional features only as mentioned in Sect. 3.

Since both DoS and Probe are network-based attacks, we focused our attack on DoS traffic. Additionally, we crafted attacks based on traffic content, such as U2R and R2L. Given the similar characteristics and functional features of U2R and R2L and their relatively small presence in the dataset, we combined U2R and R2L into a single attack group for our study.

The dataset contains categorical features, such as 'flag', 'protocol', and 'service'. In the preprocessing, we encode the categorical feature using one-hot encoding. After preprocessing, we obtain 122 features, which are then normalized between 0 and 1 using the min-max scaler in Eq. (2).

$$x_{scaled} = \frac{x - Min(x)}{Max(x) - Min(x)} \tag{2}$$

**Table 2.** Functional features of attack categories in NSLKDD

| Attack types | Functional features | | | |
|---|---|---|---|---|
| | Intrinsic | Content | Time-based | Host-based |
| DoS | ✓ | | ✓ | ✓ |
| Probe | ✓ | | ✓ | |
| R2L | ✓ | ✓ | | |
| U2R | ✓ | ✓ | | |

## 4.2  Evaluation Metrics

To evaluate the work, we use two common metrics in the literature: the detection rate and the evasion increase rate. the detection rate (DR), also called the recall rate evaluates the ability of the model to detect the classes correctly. The evasion increase rate (EIR) measures the effectiveness of the attack. These metrics are shown in Eqs. (3), and (4) respectively.

$$DR = \frac{True\ Positive}{True\ Positive + False\ Negative} \tag{3}$$

$$EIR = 1 - \frac{Adversarial\ DR}{Original\ detection} \tag{4}$$

### 4.3  Experimental Results

**Attacker Local NIDS Model.** The DNN model is built with 4 hidden layers, using RELU as an activation function, Adam with a learning rate of 0.001 as an optimizer, plus early stopping during the training to avoid overfitting. The performance of the model is reported in Table 3.

Once we have evaluated the performance of our local NIDS, we generate adversarial samples with the C-MIFGSM method shown in Algorithm 1. As one of our goals is to remain stealthy by using small perturbations that are not easily detected, we transfer the adversarial examples crafted with a maximum magnitude of perturbation $\epsilon = 0.2$ to our victim models (where at each iteration, a perturbation of 0.02 was added to the legitimate input, and the number of iterations T = 10).

Table 3 shows the performance of the local model under attack with $\epsilon = 0.2$. The model performance is significantly degraded. We observe the DR drops from 92.23% to 22.44% for DoS traffic with an EIR of 73.38%. With U2R&R2L attacks, the generated adversarial examples decreased the model DR from 81.19% to 4.17%. The results from Table 3 show the attack algorithm misled the classifiers and considerably degraded its detection performance.

**Table 3.** Performance of the DNN local model under adversarial attack

| Metrics | DoS | U2R & R2L |
|---|---|---|
| DR before attack | 92.23% | 81.19% |
| DR after attack | 22.44% | 4.17% |
| EIR | 73.38% | 94.85% |

**Target NIDS Models.** After generating the adversarial samples on the local NIDS, in this section, we perform the attack by transferring the generated adversarial samples to the victim models.

We implement the victim NIDS models using various classical machine learning RF, DT, XGBoost, AdaBoost, and MLP. The choice of using RF, XGBoost, and Adaboost is because they are ensemble learning algorithms, and studies [26,27] have shown ensemble model's performance outperforms other traditional ML models. The traditional machine learning models in our experiments are implemented using the scikit-learn library with their default values, and the neural networks are implemented using the open-source deep learning library TensorFlow 2. The MLP is built with one hidden layer of 100 units in both datasets with RELU as activation, and a batch size of 32. We train the model using early stopping with a patience of 50. In addition, we implement two state-of-the-art deep learning models AlerNet [21] and DeepNet [22] to evaluate the effectiveness of our algorithm. We choose to evaluate the robustness of the works in [21,22] because their proposed NIDS achieved a high performance compared to existing works [23] and are among the most cited DL-based NIDS published recently.

**Transferability Attack on the Target Models.** Tables 4 and 5 present the performance of ML and DL NIDS models, respectively, under transfer-based attack. Initially, all models achieved performance comparable to state-of-the-art NIDS, with DL models exhibiting the highest performance. However, adversarial examples are observed to be transferable across models implemented with different techniques.

Tables 4 and 5 illustrate that these attacks significantly degrade the detection rates (DR) of all NIDS target models. For example, the detection rate of the DoS traffic drops from 92.35% to 20.27% for the MLP model with an evasion increase rate of 78.04%. Similarly, for the RF model, the DR decreased from 91.59% to 85.53%, indicating that 6.61% of DDoS traffic evaded detection (EIR = 6.61%). Furthermore, 86.13% of the generated adversarial U2R&R2L traffic evaded the DT model (EIR = 82.13%), and 92% evaded the Alernet model.

Despite RF demonstrating the most robust performance against these attacks, evasion rates of 6.61% for DoS and 2.07% for U2R&R2L are intolerable in domains such as NIDS. In general, the ML models demonstrated to be less vulnerable than the DL models.

These results highlight that adversaries can successfully mount attacks against NIDS models with limited knowledge and under constraints. Additionally, adversarial samples are transferable from DL to classical ML models, although their impact on different classifiers varies.

**Table 4.** Performance of the transferability of CMIFGSM attack on the ML-based NIDS models

| ML/DL model | RF | | DT | | XGBoost | | Adaboost | | LR | |
|---|---|---|---|---|---|---|---|---|---|---|
| Metrics | DoS | U2R_R2L | DoS | U2R_R2L | DoS | U2R_R2L | DoS | U2R_R2L | DoS | U2R_R2L |
| DR before attack | 91.59% | 78.06% | 92.08% | 79.90% | 92.38% | 79.04% | 90.59% | 79.20% | 89.34% | 76.85% |
| DR after attack | 85.53% | 76.44% | 91.45% | 11.07% | 89.11% | 18.66% | 70.20% | 31.59% | 59.50% | 63.93% |
| EIR | 6.61% | 2.07% | 0.68% | 86.13% | 3.54% | 76.39% | 22.51% | 60.10% | 33.40% | 16.81% |

**Table 5.** Performance of the transferability of CMIFGSM attack on the DL-based NIDS models

| ML/DL model | MLP | | DeepNet | | Alernet | |
|---|---|---|---|---|---|---|
| Metrics | DoS | U2R_R2L | DoS | U2R_R2L | DoS | U2R_R2L |
| DR before attack | 92.35% | 81.79% | 91.71% | 81.34% | 90.60% | 80.08% |
| DR after attack | 20.27% | 9.54% | 32.26% | 13.38% | 51.16% | 5.65% |
| EIR | 78.04% | 88.34% | 64.81% | 83.54% | 43.35% | 92.93% |

## 5    Conclusion

In this work, we investigated evasion attacks against ML-based NIDS. Our objective was to perform a practical gray box attack that can deceive the model and reduce its effectiveness. We proposed an attack algorithm, C-MIFGSM, to craft small, specially designed perturbations to mislead the target classifiers. The findings of this work demonstrate that adversaries can successfully mount adversarial attacks to fool ML-based NIDS without knowledge of the target model and under constraints. This raises significant security concerns for developing robust ML-based NIDS.

In future work, we plan to extend our investigation to various datasets and explore defenses against adversarial attacks in NIDS.

**Acknowledgment.** The 1st author is supported by the Ministry of Education, Culture, Sports, Science and Technology (MEXT). The 2nd author is supported by the Spanish Ministry of Universities and the European Union - NextGeneration EU funds through the Grants for the Requalification of the Spanish University System 2021–2023 (University of Malaga, Resolution July 1st 2021). The 4th author is partially supported by the International Exchange, Foreign Researcher Invitation Program of National Institute of Information and Communications Technology (NICT). This work was partially supported by the India-Japan Cooperative Science Programme (IJSCP) through the Department of Science and Technology (DST, India) and the Japan Society for the Promotion of Science (JSPS).

## References

1. Axelsson, S.: Intrusion detection systems: a survey and taxonomy (2002)
2. Liu, H., Lang, B.: Machine learning and deep learning methods for intrusion detection systems: a survey. Appl. Sci. (2019)
3. Szegedy, C., et al.: Intriguing properties of neural networks. CoRR abs/1312.6199 (2013)
4. Goodfellow, I.J., et al.: Explaining and harnessing adversarial examples. CoRR abs/1412.6572 (2014)
5. Akhtar, N., Mian, A.S.: Threat of adversarial attacks on deep learning in computer vision: a survey. IEEE Access **6**, 14410–14430 (2018)
6. Papernot, N., et al.: Transferability in machine learning: from phenomena to black-box attacks using adversarial samples. ArXiv abs/1605.07277 (2016)
7. Guan, Z., et al.: When machine learning meets security issues: a survey. In: 2018 IEEE International Conference on Intelligence and Safety for Robotics (ISR), pp. 158–165 (2018)
8. Martins, N., et al.: Adversarial machine learning applied to intrusion and malware scenarios: a systematic review. IEEE Access **8**, 35403–35419 (2020)
9. Mbow, M., Sakurai, K., Koide, H.: Advances in adversarial attacks and defenses in intrusion detection system: a survey. In: Su, C., Sakurai, K. (eds) Science of Cyber Security - SciSec 2022 Workshops. SciSec 2022. Communications in Computer and Information Science, vol. 1680. Springer, Singapore (2022)

10. Usama, M., et al.: Generative adversarial networks for launching and thwarting adversarial attacks on network intrusion detection systems. In: 2019 15th International Wireless Communications & Mobile Computing Conference (IWCMC), pp. 78–83 (2019)
11. He, K., et al.: Adversarial machine learning for network intrusion detection systems: a comprehensive survey. IEEE Commun. Surv. Tutor. **25**, 538–566 (2023)
12. Dong, Y., et al.: Boosting adversarial attacks with momentum. In: 2018 IEEE/CVF Conference on Computer Vision and Pattern Recognition, pp. 9185–9193 (2017)
13. Duy, P.T., et al.: DIGFuPAS: deceive IDS with GAN and function-preserving on adversarial samples in SDN-enabled networks. Comput. Secur. **109**, 102367 (2021)
14. Kurakin, A., Goodfellow, I.J., Bengio, S.: Adversarial examples in the physical world. In: Artificial Intelligence Safety and Security, pp. 99–112. Chapman and Hall/CRC (2018)
15. Carlini, N., Wagner, D.: Towards evaluating the robustness of neural networks. In: 2017 IEEE Symposium on Security and Privacy (SP). IEEE (2017)
16. Carlini, N., Wagner, D.: Audio adversarial examples: targeted attacks on speech-to-text. In: 2018 IEEE Security and Privacy Workshops (SPW). IEEE (2018)
17. Biggio, B., et al.: Evasion attacks against machine learning at test time. ArXiv abs/1708.06131 (2013)
18. Li, J., et al.: Textbugger: generating adversarial text against real-world applications. arXiv preprint arXiv:1812.05271 (2018)
19. Grosse, K., et al.: Adversarial examples for malware detection. In: Computer Security-ESORICS 2017: 22nd European Symposium on Research in Computer Security, Oslo, Norway, 11–15 September 2017, Part II. Springer (2017)
20. Tavallaee, M., et al.: A detailed analysis of the KDD CUP 99 data set. In: 2009 IEEE Symposium on Computational Intelligence for Security and Defense Applications, pp. 1–6 (2009)
21. Vinayakumar, R., et al.: Deep learning approach for intelligent intrusion detection system. IEEE Access **7**, 41525–41550 (2019)
22. Gao, M., et al.: Malicious network traffic detection based on deep neural networks and association analysis. Sens. (Basel Switz.) **20** (2020)
23. Zolbayar, B.E., et al.: Generating practical adversarial network traffic flows using NIDSGAN. ArXiv abs/2203.06694 (2022)
24. Apruzzese, G., et al.: Modeling realistic adversarial attacks against network intrusion detection systems. Digit. Threats: Res. Pract. (DTRAP) **3**, 1–19 (2021)
25. McCarthy, A., et al.: Functionality-preserving adversarial machine learning for robust classification in cybersecurity and intrusion detection domains: a survey. J. Cybersecur. Priv. **2**, 154–190 (2022)
26. Chen, T., Guestrin, C.: XGBoost: a scalable tree boosting system. In: Proceedings of the 22nd ACM SIGKDD International Conference on Knowledge Discovery and Data Mining (2016)
27. Rokach, L.: Ensemble-based classifiers. Artif. Intell. Rev. **33**, 1–39 (2010)

# Enhancing Robustness in NIDS via Coverage Guided Fuzzing and Adversarial Training

Jung Yup Rhee[1], Leo Hyun Park[2], and Taekyoung Kwon[1,2(✉)]

[1] Graduate School of Artificial Intelligence, Yonsei University, Seoul, Korea
{wjdduq234,dofi,taekyoung}@yonsei.ac.kr
[2] Graduate School of Information, Yonsei University, Seoul, Korea

**Abstract.** AI-based Network Intrusion Detection Systems (NIDS) are essential for defending modern network environments against diverse traffic-based attacks. However, these systems, including the advanced Kitsune model which employs an ensemble of small autoencoders for real-time intrusion detection, are susceptible to adversarial attacks. Such attacks manipulate the AI models by introducing adversarial examples, potentially leading to system failure. This paper introduces a novel methodology that applies coverage-guided fuzzing, a technique traditionally used in software vulnerability detection, to uncover adversarial examples in NIDS models. Furthermore, we present an innovative approach of how to enhance robustness of these systems using adversarial training with the identified adversarial examples. We demonstrate the effectiveness of our approach by applying it to Kitsune-based models with two open-source benchmark datasets. The experimental results indicate that the defense rate against adversarial attacks has improved by up to 98%, proving that our methods not only detect critical vulnerabilities but also significantly strengthen the model's defense mechanisms against such attacks.

**Keywords:** Network Intrusion Detection Systems · Anomaly Detection · Coverage Guided Fuzzing · Adversarial Training

## 1 Introduction

Cyber attacks through networks are becoming increasingly frequent. Furthermore, the proliferation of IoT devices and the increasing volume of data transmitted and received by mobile devices have expanded the targets for network attacks [1]. Consequently, sophisticated and difficult-to-detect network attack techniques that target computer or databases, such as CHARGEN and Ubiquiti, have been developed. These attacks pose significant social problems by causing various economic issues, such as privacy leakage, or insertion of malicious code, affecting not only corporations but also individuals. To mitigate such damages,

J.-H. Lee et al. (Eds.): WISA 2024, LNCS 15499, pp. 56–68, 2025.
https://doi.org/10.1007/978-981-96-1624-4_5

deep learning based NIDS (Network Intrusion Detection System) models that detect network attacks are being researched and developed.

However, existing NIDS research has primarily focused on improving accuracy, neglecting aspects of robustness verification and enhancement. Consequently, NIDS are highly vulnerable to adversarial attacks that can cause malfunctions, such as judging network attacks as benign, thereby rendering NIDS models ineffective and exposing them to various attacks. To develop practical NIDS, it is essential to enhance their security through robustness verification and reinforcement. Despite the long-standing recognition of this issue, the challenge of addressing NIDS robustness remains significant due to the scarcity of prior research and the inherent difficulty of the problem.

Thus, this paper proposes methodologies for verificating and enhancing robustness to aid the development of robust and secure NIDS technologies. Robustness verification is conducted using coverage guided fuzzing, which leverages new mutation and coverage metrics. Further on, for robustness enhancement, we propose a novel methodology that utilizes the vulnerabilities discovered during robustness verification for adversarial training. The effectiveness and validity of the proposed methodologies are demonstrated through experiments.

The validation experiments of our methodology are conducted on the Kitsune model [2]. Kitsune, with its lightweight architecture, is suitable for online processing and real-time inference, and can be applied to datasets in CSV format without preprocessing, making it a practical and scalable. Its technical excellence is further evidenced by its active use in subsequent research [3–5]. However, since the datasets used in the Kitsune paper for reproduction are unavailable, we reproduced the experiments using other open-source datasets to find out that the model did not generalize well, resulting in poor accuracy. Consequently, we undertake the process of improving the open-source Kitsune model to contribute to future NIDS research and performance development.

Our study has three main contributions:

1. We introduce suitable mutation techniques for robustness verification and analyze optimal coverage and fuzzing conditions. We then conduct Coverage Guided Fuzzing on the Kitsune model to demonstrate the effectiveness of this methodology in robustness verification through vulnerability detection.
2. We propose a novel dual-structure training method, divided into alpha and beta models. Vulnerabilities discovered during the robustness verification phase are utilized as input for the beta model in adversarial training, aiming to simultaneously improve robustness and accuracy. This study aims to identify the limitations of currently utilized network traffic detection models, providing directions for not only performance improvement but also the development of robust networks in the future.
3. To enhance the performance and generalization of the open-source Kitsune model, we adjust model architecture, modify training methods, and optimize parameters, and prove the improvements using open-source datasets.

## 2 Background

### 2.1 Network Intrusion Detection System

NIDS is an anomaly detection technique, detecting if the traffic sender is an adversary. The detection methodologies are based on classification, Nearest Neighbor, clustering, and etc. [5,6]. Unsupervised deep learning-based anomaly detection uses an autoencoder and is trained with only normal traffic data. Inside the autoencoder, the input data is compressed and reconstructed to minimize reconstruction error, called root mean squared error (RMSE). As a result, if RMSE is below the threshold, the traffic is classified as normal; otherwise, it is classified as malicious. A representative example of NIDS is Kitsune [2]. Kitsune is divided into the tail network and head network: the tail consists of an ensemble of autoencoders, each handling one of the $k$ clusters of feature information, and the head is a single autoencoder that receives the output values of the $k$ autoencoders from the tail.

### 2.2 Adversarial Robustness

Adversarial attacks refer to attacks that induce malfunctions in a deep learning model by exploiting features such as gradients to create adversarial perturbations. Starting with FGSM [7], various methods such as PGD [8] and BIM [9] have been developed to strengthen these attacks. These attacks cause critical defects in safety, finance, and security, such as misrecognition of pedestrians by autonomous vehicles or data theft through network intrusion attack. Consequently, adversarial defense techniques have been developed to block these attacks. One example of such a defense technique is adversarial training [10], which involves generating adversarial data from the model to train with it. While this is a simple and effective defense technique, it has an accuracy-robustness trade-off issue, where an increase in robustness leads to a decrease in performance, necessitating improvements.

NIDS models are used to detect malicious network traffic, but they have not been prepared for attacks that target NIDS models themselves. While it is very easy to induce misclassification by conducting adversarial attacks on these models, there has been no research that verifies the robustness of models against such attacks. For instance, when we conduct an adversarial attack with an epsilon of 0.05 on 1000 data targeting the Kitsune model (trained with CICDDoS2019 dataset, AUC reaching 0.9609), an average of 995 attacks succeeded. Therefore, in addition to accuracy, NIDS must be robust against adversarial attacks to be a realistic and practical detection model, emphasizing the importance of robustness verification and enhancement.

## 3 System Design and Implementation

### 3.1 System Outline

The threat model is that the adversary aims to deceive the NIDS with their malicious traffic, causing it to be misclassified as normal for further cyber attacks.

This scenario assumes a white-box situation where the attacker has information about the target NIDS, which is the Kitsune model. Therefore, from the defender's perspective, we need to ensure the performance of NIDS for proper judgment and robustness against adversarial attacks.

In the traditional anomaly detection environment, only normal data is accessible to train an unsupervised model. However, it is practically challenging to verify or enhance robustness without malicious data. Additionally, as of 2024, various fields have collected malicious data over several years. While using tens of thousands of malicious data points may be unrealistic, utilizing only a small amount is reasonable. Thus, we assume that the defender has access to such small-scale malicious data.

In this study, we first improve the performance of an open-source model and verify its robustness by conducting coverage-guided fuzzing. Adversarial examples discovered during the fuzzing process will be used for adversarial training to improve the robustness of the model (Fig. 1).

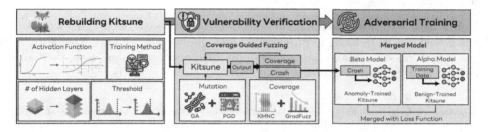

**Fig. 1.** Outline of the Research Conducted in this Paper

## 3.2   Improving Open-Source Kitsune

The performance of Kitsune in the official repository [11] and the unofficial PyTorch version [12] differed significantly from the original paper, making it unsuitable for direct use. Therefore, we applied some modifications to the Kitsune model. The entire code is reconstructed from Numpy to PyTorch. We also added a normalization layer before the tail and head layer to not only increase the computational speed but also stabilize the model output, preventing a local optima. Further on, the activation function has changed from Sigmoid to Hyperbolic Tangent ($tanh$) and the number of hidden layers has increased from 10 times to provide more space for the features to get trained.

The original learning rate was fixed at $1e^{-3}$, but a learning rate scheduler is applied that gradually decreases from $1e^{-3}$ to $1e^{-4}$. Also, the default threshold for determining anomalies was set to the maximum value of the training loss, but is modified to the sum of the mean and standard deviation of the training loss, significantly increasing true positives with a slight decrease in true negatives. The training method of the original model trains both the tail and the head simultaneously on a single batch of data. However, due to the low accuracy, we train the tail first, followed by the head.

### 3.3   Dataset and Dataloader

The dataset used for training Kitsune was collected directly from the author and is not publicly available, making it inaccessible. Therefore, we utilize the CICD-DoS2019 [13,14] and NSL-KDD [15] datasets, which are benchmark datasets that have been used or analyzed in over 15,000 and 2,000 studies on network intrusion, respectively, and are still actively used today.

We designed a new dataloader for continuous learning. The original dataloader fetches data one by one when forming batches, which decreases the training speed. In addition, it leads to performance change due to not utilizing the entire dataset during the generalization and subsequent shifts in data distribution. Our dataloader improves speed and learning stability by initially loading all samples from the dataset and then using a fixed number of samples for batches.

### 3.4   Robustness Verification

Robustness verification in anomaly detection is the process of checking whether the model can be induced to misclassify anomalies as normal data. Therefore, if the transformed anomalies are successfully inferenced as benign data, they are defined as a vulnerability of the target NIDS.

**Coverage Guided Fuzzing.** Coverage-guided fuzzing is a technique that generates diverse test data using coverage to search for vulnerabilities. While traditional software testing utilizes simple coverage metrics like code coverage, which measures the percentage of codes executed, deep learning models have to use special coverage metrics because they have neuron-based structures, in contrast with code-based software. Similarly, the effectiveness of mutation techniques (i.e., simple transformation algorithms such as replace and modify) may vary depending on the target model and dataset. Thus, the dedicated coverage metric [16] and mutation techniques [17–19] should be selected for coverage-guided fuzzing. The comprehensive process of coverage-guided fuzzing for NIDS models proceeds as Algorithm 1. The details are explained below.

**Mutation for Coverage Guided Fuzzing.** The mutation process transforms the data of a parent seed from a seed corpus to generate a new child. The mutation techniques used in our study are based on genetic algorithms (GA) [20] and adversarial perturbation (PGD). GA mutation is inspired by the actual mutation process of genes. The main procedure of GA include selection, crossover, and mutation. Selection means fixing parts that should not undergo transformation, while crossover mixes data with target datum in unfixed parts. Mutation is adding noise to the data, overcoming the limitation of GA in potentially falling into local optima due to transformations within a limited data set. In the case of network traffic features composed of integers, we apply only the selection and crossover processes. Conversely, for traffic features composed of floats, all three

**Algorithm 1.** Coverage Guided Fuzzing

```
Iteration ← 0
Seed_Corpus ← [] # Initialize seed corpus
adversarial_examples ← [] # Initialize detected adversarial examples
while Iteration < 1000 do
    Iteration ← Iteration + 1
    parent ← RandomSelect(Seed_Corpus)
    mutation_func ← RandomSelect([GA, PGD])
    child ← mutation_func(parent)
    output ← target_model(child)
    if is_new_coverage(child.coverage) then
        Seed_Corpus.append(child)
    end if
    if is_adversarial(output) then
        adversarial_examples.append(child)
    end if
end while
```

processes are executed. Adversarial perturbation-based mutation uses PGD that induces malfunction by adjusting inputs in a way that maximizes the loss value based on the model information. Scaling and clamping are applied to keep feature values within the valid range to prevent excessive modification.

In the unsupervised model Kitsune, the mutation is applied to anomaly data. Anomaly data outputs a loss value above the threshold according to the NIDS model. The main objective is to modify the feature values so that the resulting loss is below the threshold, causing it to be misclassified as benign. Therefore, a crash is defined as an anomaly data that outputs a loss value that is lower than the threshold, deceiving the NIDS model to interpret it as a normal data. Crashes are used as adversarial examples for adversarial training.

**Coverage Measurements.** Coverage metrics are divided into vector-based and distance-based. Vector-based metrics update the coverage map when some vector elements are newly activated, while distance-based ones update the coverage when the vector values are sufficiently far from the existing inputs. In our study, we use KMNC [21], as a vector-based metric, that divides the output range of the activation function of each neuron into $k$ segments and measures which region has been activated. For a distance-based metric, we use NLC [22] which calculates the covariance matrix (distance) between two neurons in the same layer.

Additionally, we use GradFuzz [23], a gradient-based coverage metric that more accurately identifies guidance for inducing misclassification. GradFuzz uses the gradient of neurons according to the loss function as coverage, instead of neuron activation that only explains the output results, enabling a more logical explanation for both the output results and their causes due to the input. Therefore, experiments are conducted using four coverage methods: KMNC, NLC, GradFuzz+KMNC, and GradFuzz+NLC.

### 3.5 Adversarial Training

Adversarial training trains the model with adversarial examples to enhance robustness, but unsupervised models, unlike typical models, only learns from normal-class data, making it impossible for us to utilize the adversarial examples collected during the robustness verification. Therefore, a model trained using only the adversarial data (hereafter referred to as the *beta model*), is merged with the existing model which was trained with only the normal samples (referred to as the *alpha model*). The beta model is also based on Kitsune, having an identical structure to the alpha model. When the merged model receives an input, the alpha and beta models process the input simultaneously, resulting in two respective loss values. The final loss value is then computed as below[1].

$$Loss^M = Loss^\alpha + \frac{1}{Loss^\beta}, \quad Threshold^M = mean(loss^M) + std(loss^M)$$

The threshold for judging benign is applied in the same way as before, using the sum of the mean and standard deviation of the loss values from the benign data.

## 4  Results

### 4.1  Research Environment

The string-based feature information in both datasets we use are removed, and the model is trained with a batch size of 200. The GPU is used only for speed measurement while CPU is used for all the other experiments.

### 4.2  Improving Performance of Open-Source Kitsune

The original open-source Kitsune model achieved an AUC of 0.8800, 0.4990 each for CICDDoS2019 and NSL-KDD dataset. After modifying the model structure and parameters, as mentioned in Sect. 3.2, the Kitsune model achieved an AUC of 0.9609, 0.9392 each for the two datasets, showing significant improvement compared to the open-source. Additionally, we examine the impact of the number of ensembles on performance and inference speed. The results showed no correlation between the number of ensembles and performance, which led us to use no ensembles for future experiments. In terms of inference speed, PyTorch CPU was the fastest, followed by Numpy CPU and PyTorch GPU, indicating that online processing can be maintained similarly like the original model.

### 4.3  Robustness Verification

**Mutation Techniques for Fuzzing.** In this study, we compared the performance of the mutation algorithms within two different environments. The first environment, shallow mutation, discards all mutated seeds regardless of coverage improvement, maintaining only the initial seeds in the seed corpus. Consequently, all child seeds have undergone only one mutation. The second environment, deep mutation, adds child samples that improve coverage to the seed corpus, following

---

[1] M: Merged Model, $\alpha$: Alpha Model, $\beta$: Beta Model.

**Table 1.** Experiment Result of the Mutation Methods

| Dataset | | CICDDoS2019 | | NSL-KDD | |
|---|---|---|---|---|---|
| Mutation Method | | # Crashes | % Successful Testing | # Crashes | % Successful Testing |
| Deep Mutation | Gaussian Noise | 5 | 5% | 0 | 0% |
| | PGD | **569** | **100%** | **38** | **24%** |
| | GA | 282 | 91% | 5 | 5% |
| | PGD+GA | 516 | 99% | 26 | 21% |
| Shallow Mutation | Gaussian Noise | 27 | 23% | 0 | 0% |
| | PGD | **998** | **100%** | **47** | **19%** |
| | GA | 403 | 89% | 0 | 0% |
| | PGD+GA | 702 | **100%** | 23 | 15% |

the traditional fuzzing process. We verified PGD-based and GA-based mutation techniques and their combination, against a control group using Gaussian-based mutation. The Gaussian-based mutation adds values derived from a Gaussian distribution with a mean of 0 and a standard deviation of 1, scaled by multiplying 0.1. We perform 30 mutations for each of the 100 initial seeds. We used two evaluation metrics: the total number of adversarial examples (crashes) found and the percentage of initial seeds that reached at least one adversarial example through mutation (successful testing).

As shown in Table 1, NSL-KDD is found to be more challenging to detect adversarial examples compared to CICDDoS2019. Random mutations using Gaussian noise rarely detect adversarial examples, while PGD and GA achieve significant performance in vulnerability detection. Although PGD alone detects the most adversarial examples, it results in limited diversity due to its reliance solely on gradients. Thus, using both PGD and GA simultaneously is recommended to ensure diversity and realism.

**Coverage Guided Fuzzing Results.** Coverage-guided fuzzing in this experiment performs 500 input mutations for the 100 initial seeds. The input chooser selects seeds based on the probability of Depth/Count (Depth: the number of mutations applied on the seed; Count: the number of times the seed has been

**Table 2.** Experiment Result of Diverse Testing Environments

| Dataset | | CICDDoS2019 | | NSL-KDD | |
|---|---|---|---|---|---|
| Testing Environment | | # Crashes | % Successful Testing | # Crashes | % Successful Testing |
| Gaussian Noise | | 10.7 | 9.3% | 0 | 0% |
| Mutational Testing | Deep Mutation | 6376.7 | **100%** | 4193.3 | **100%** |
| | Shallow Mutation | 3659.3 | 94.7% | 1924 | 36% |
| Adversarial Attack (PGD) | | 31.3 | 31.3% | 3.3 | 3.3% |
| Coverage Guided Fuzzing | KMNC | 6103.7 | **100%** | 4437.7 | **100%** |
| | KMNC+GradFuzz | 5309.7 | 98.7% | 5102.7 | 93.7% |
| | NLC | 4229.2 | 99.7% | **7712** | **100%** |
| | NLC+GradFuzz | **7534.7** | **100%** | 4647.3 | 99.7% |

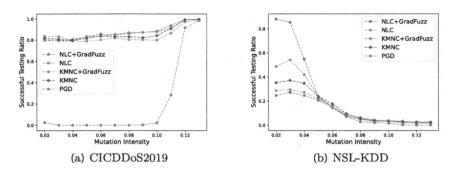

(a) CICDDoS2019                    (b) NSL-KDD

**Fig. 2.** Crash Discovery Rate for Each Sample According to the Attack Intensity

selected as a parent seed). We utilized a combination of GA and PGD for the mutation of fuzzing. All the other environments remain the same as in the previous experiments.

The results in Table 2 indicate that random noise is ineffective in discovering vulnerabilities, which demonstrates the superiority of the mutation techniques. Furthermore, the adversarial example detection performance is best in the order of coverage-guided fuzzing, deep mutation, and shallow mutation, proving that repetitive mutation and coverage enhance the performance of vulnerability detection. The detection performance varies depending on the dataset and coverage method, highlighting the need for appropriate coverage metrics tailored to specific situations. Lastly, we compared the vulnerability detection performance of each coverage metric through the successful testing rate across ten different mutation intensities. The intensity of each mutation and the successful testing results are shown in Fig. 2.

The results show that coverage-guided fuzzing outperforms PGD, and NLC with GradFuzz generally achieves the best performance among the others. Additionally, while the number of crashes detected in CICDDoS2019 increases with higher attack intensities, NSL-KDD shows more crashes with lower attack intensities, indicating overfitting or other issues in the model trained with NSL-KDD.

### 4.4 Increasing Robustness and Performance with Adversarial Training

In this experiment, we leverage the adversarial examples detected through vulnerability detection for adversarial training of the beta model. We merge the beta model with the alpha model to create a merged model with an integrated loss function. We perform a comparative experiment to identify the correlation between the number of training data and the performance by increasing the number of training data from 100 to 500. We consider a comprehensive environment called *Total*, where all adversarial examples generated from the combination of KMNC, NLC, and GradFuzz are used for adversarial training.

**Table 3.** AUC of Merged Model

| Dataset | | NSL-KDD | | | | | | CICDDoS2019 | | | | | |
|---|---|---|---|---|---|---|---|---|---|---|---|---|---|
| Coverage Metric | | KMNC+ GradFuzz | KMNC | NLC+ GradFuzz | NLC | Total | PGD | KMNC+ GradFuzz | KMNC | NLC+ GradFuzz | NLC | Total | PGD |
| 100 | Train | 0.5424 | 0.5176 | 0.9885 | 0.9761 | 0.6119 | **0.9889** | 0.9822 | 0.9683 | 0.9848 | 0.9759 | 0.9836 | **0.9947** |
| | Test | 0.4694 | 0.4455 | **0.994** | 0.9879 | 0.5538 | 0.9931 | 0.9905 | 0.9855 | 0.9907 | 0.9869 | 0.9925 | **0.9974** |
| 200 | Train | 0.5487 | 0.9895 | 0.5251 | 0.8479 | 0.9788 | **0.9953** | **0.9935** | 0.9908 | 0.9878 | 0.5019 | 0.9838 | 0.4855 |
| | Test | 0.4627 | 0.9938 | 0.4397 | 0.7593 | 0.989 | **0.9978** | 0.9905 | 0.9943 | **0.996** | 0.4276 | 0.9922 | 0.4303 |
| 300 | Train | 0.9928 | 0.9796 | 0.9848 | 0.976 | **0.9949** | 0.5373 | 0.9904 | 0.9911 | 0.9904 | **0.9912** | 0.989 | 0.5244 |
| | Test | 0.9962 | 0.9876 | 0.9935 | 0.987 | **0.9973** | 0.461 | **0.9968** | 0.9944 | 0.9944 | 0.9949 | 0.9938 | 0.4453 |
| 400 | Train | 0.9871 | **0.9879** | 0.9872 | 0.6732 | 0.5176 | 0.9857 | 0.9882 | 0.6516 | 0.5707 | 0.9857 | **0.9893** | 0.9892 |
| | Test | **0.9927** | 0.9922 | 0.9915 | 0.5667 | 0.4382 | 0.9914 | 0.9929 | 0.5539 | 0.4868 | 0.9937 | 0.9939 | **0.9945** |
| 500 | Train | 0.9858 | 0.9442 | 0.9829 | 0.9834 | **0.9869** | 0.5867 | 0.9861 | **0.9897** | 0.9892 | 0.5138 | 0.983 | 0.5718 |
| | Test | 0.9912 | 0.9415 | 0.9918 | 0.9917 | **0.9922** | 0.5092 | 0.9919 | **0.9946** | 0.994 | 0.436 | 0.9919 | 0.4911 |

**Performance of Beta Model.** The performance of the beta model shows significant variance in the training data, with an average AUC value of 0.6852, a minimum value of 0.5123, and a maximum value of 0.8063, while the test data shows an average of 0.6214, a minimum of 0.6054, and a maximum of 0.6966. This indicates that the model cannot reach the global optimum due to the diversity of adversarial examples. We observed the large variation in performance when repeatedly training on the same data, suggesting a significant impact of the initial seed regarding the local optimum. Furthermore, increasing the number of adversarial examples does not lead to a notable improvement.

**Performance of Merged Model.** The AUC of the merged model is shown in Table 3. The AUC of the alpha model was 0.9392 and 0.9609 for NSL-KDD and CICDDoS2019, respectively. Some merged models significantly outperform the baseline alpha model, but others show performance close to random guessing. However, the highest performance of 10 repetitions in all conditions exceeds the baseline, demonstrating that the accuracy increases as the model converges well.

**Robustness of Merged Model.** We verified the robustness of the merged model by measuring the number of misclassifications from 1000 attack samples with an epsilon strength of 0.05. The baseline is the alpha model under adversarial attacks, with 362 misclassifications for the NSL-KDD and 988 for the CICDDoS2019. As shown in Table 4, the robustness of the merged model is superior in all conditions, except three conditions for the NSL-KDD, compared to the baseline. The overall increase in the robustness of the merged model is meaningful because the attack intensity is 0.05, which is relatively high.

**Table 4.** Robustness of Merged Model

| Dataset | NSL-KDD | | | | | | CICDDoS2019 | | | | | |
|---|---|---|---|---|---|---|---|---|---|---|---|---|
| Coverage Metric | KMNC+ GradFuzz | KMNC | NLC+ GradFuzz | NLC | Total | PGD | KMNC+ GradFuzz | KMNC | NLC+ GradFuzz | NLC | Total | PGD |
| 100 | 320 | 8 | **0** | 326 | 542 | 15 | 402 | 272 | 83 | 537 | 74 | **0** |
| 200 | 588 | 339 | **0** | 1 | **0** | 54 | 34 | 4 | 304 | **0** | 59 | 54 |
| 300 | 33 | 255 | 557 | 122 | 85 | 54 | **0** | 297 | 59 | 2 | 514 | **0** |
| 400 | **0** | **0** | **0** | 285 | **0** | **0** | **0** | **0** | 298 | 123 | 272 | **0** |
| 500 | **0** | 329 | **0** | 28 | 1 | 261 | 57 | 575 | 22 | 102 | 308 | 261 |

# 5    Discussion

## 5.1    Finding the Best Combination for Coverage Guided Fuzzing

Through our experiments, we compared the efficiency of various coverages in detecting vulnerabilities. While some techniques generally performed better, it was evident that the effectiveness of a specific coverage varied depending on the environment. This highlights the need to select an appropriate coverage and the necessity for developing a more effective coverage for deep learning fuzzing.

Additionally, the selection of the input chooser is crucial. The performance in terms of the number of adversarial examples found improves from shallow to deep to coverage guided fuzzing. This indicates that while a greater depth is necessary to find more adversarial examples, the method used to select the parent seeds for mutation is even more important. Furthermore, if the depth gets deeper, efficiency decreases, emphasizing the need for a superior input chooser.

## 5.2    Model Optimization

Both the alpha and beta models exhibit significant performance variability with each experimental run. This is because optimizing models separated into head and tail is challenging, due to the issue of fixing the unoptimized head to the initial seed while training the tail. If either the alpha or beta model is not properly optimized, the merged model will also exhibit poor accuracy and robustness. Although the performance improved with the methodology discussed in Sect. 4.2, addressing these issues with new training mechanisms could lead to more stable and improved performance.

# 6    Conclusion

Although NIDS models exhibit high performance, they are vulnerable to adversarial attacks, leading to misclassification. Therefore, it is necessary to verify and enhance not only performance but also robustness. In this paper, we effectively improved the performance of the open-source Kitsune and developed new mutation combinations, proving their efficiency through experiments. Using these mutation techniques and diverse coverage-based fuzzing methods, we were able to detect vulnerabilities and verify robustness. Furthermore, we demonstrated the improvement in robustness and performance of NIDS models through a new adversarial training method. Consequently, we contributed to the development of secure network systems by analyzing and enhancing the safety of NIDS models.

For future work, we plan to research optimization techniques discussed in Sect. 5.2 to achieve stable convergence. Additionally, we aim to develop coverage and fuzzing techniques dedicated to deep learning to fuzz diverse AI technology.

**Acknowledgements.** This work was supported by the Institute of Information & Communications Technology Planning & Evaluation (IITP) grant funded by the Korea Government (MSIT) (No. RS-2023-00229400) and (No. RS-2023-00230337).

**Disclosure of Interests.** The authors have no competing interests to declare that are relevant to the content of this article.

# References

1. Johnson, J., Plan, F., et al.: 3CX software supply chain compromise initiated by a prior software supply chain compromise. MANDIANT (2023)
2. Mirsky, Y., et al.: Kitsune: an ensemble of autoencoders for online network intrusion detection. In: Proceedings of the NDSS (2018)
3. Han, D., et al.: Anomaly detection in the open world: normality shift detection, explanation, and adaptation. In: Proceedings of the NDSS (2023)
4. Fu, C., et al.: Realtime robust malicious traffic detection via frequency domain analysis. In: Proceedings of the CCS (2023)
5. Du, M., et al.: Lifelong anomaly detection through unlearning. In: Proceedings of the ACM SIGSAC Conference on Computer and Communications Security (CCS) (2019)
6. Andresini, G., et al.: INSOMNIA: towards concept-drift robustness in network intrusion detection. In: Proceedings of AISec (2021)
7. Goodfellow, I.J., Shlens, J., Szegedy, C.: Explaining and harnessing adversarial examples. arXiv preprint arXiv:1412.6572 (2014)
8. Madry, A., et al.: Towards deep learning models resistant to adversarial attacks. In: Proceedings of the ICLR (2018)
9. Kurakin, A., et al.: Adversarial machine learning at scale. In: Proceedings of the International Conference on Learning Representations (2017)
10. Bai, T., et al.: Recent advances in adversarial training for adversarial robustness. arXiv preprint arXiv:2102.01356 (2021)
11. Ymirsky. Kitsune. GitHub (2020). https://github.com/ymirsky/Kitsune-py
12. Guillem96. Kitsune Network PyTorch. GitHub, kitsune-pytorch (2022). https://github.com/Guillem96/kitsune-pytorch
13. Sharafaldin, I., et al.: Developing realistic distributed denial of service (DDoS) attack dataset and taxonomy. In: 2019 IEEE ICCST (2019)
14. "DDoS Evaluation Dataset" University of New Brunswick, Canadian Institute for Cybersecurity. https://www.unb.ca/cic/datasets/ddos-2019.html
15. "NSL-KDD dataset." University of New Brunswick, Canadian Institute for Cybersecurity. https://www.unb.ca/cic/datasets/nsl.html
16. Yuan, Y., Pang, Q., Wang, S.: Assessing deep neural network testing via neural coverage. arXiv preprint arXiv:2112.01955 (2021)
17. Xie, X., et al.: Deephunter: a coverage-guided fuzz testing framework for deep neural networks. In: Proceedings of the 28th ACM SIGSOFT International Symposium on Software Testing and Analysis (2019)
18. Odena, A., et al.: Tensorfuzz: debugging neural networks with coverage-guided fuzzing. In: International Conference on Machine Learning. PMLR (2019)
19. Pei, K., et al.: Deepxplore: automated whitebox testing of deep learning systems. In: Proceedings of the 26th Symposium on Operating Systems Principles (2017)
20. Maxfield, M.: When genetic algorithms meet artificial intelligence. Electron. Eng. J. (2020)
21. Ma, L., et al.: Deepgauge: multi-granularity testing criteria for deep learning systems. In: Proceedings of the ASE (2018)

22. Yuan, Y., et al.: Revisiting neuron coverage for DNN testing: a layer-wise and distribution-aware criterion. In: Proceedings of the ICSE (2023)
23. Park, L.H., et al.: GradFuzz: fuzzing deep neural networks with gradient vector coverage for adversarial examples. Neurocomputing **522**, 165–180 (2023)

# AI Threat and Mitigation

# VoteGAN: Generalized Membership Inference Attack Against Generative Models by Multiple Discriminators

Gyeongsup Lim(ID), Wonjun Oh, and Junbeom Hur$^{(\boxtimes)}$(ID)

Korea University, Seoul, Korea
{gslim,wjoh,jbhur}@isslab.korea.ac.kr

**Abstract.** Generative Adversarial Networks (GANs) produces samples with the same probability distribution as the given training data. However, as they frequently train with sensitive data to generate realistic samples, many people are concerned about the leakage of training data from the GANs model, causing a severe breach of privacy in practice. This paper focuses on membership inference attacks aiming to reveal information about whether a certain data record is used in the target model training procedure. Although the membership inference attack has been successfully applied to various models, delivering membership inference attacks against generative models still remains a challenging problem, because the attack model could not accurately represent the target model. To solve this problem, we quantify the target model representation degree by measuring the attack model's generalization gap (i.e., the difference between the attack model's prediction distribution on training data and unseen data). To reduce the generalization gap, we propose a novel membership inference attack framework, called *VoteGAN*, consisting of multiple discriminators and one generator. VoteGAN trains the discriminators separately with a partition of the training data. It enables VoteGAN to approximate the mixture distribution of all partitions, allowing the reflection of the entire data more accurately. Our experimental results demonstrate that the proposed attack model outperforms prior attack method, showing 25% higher attack success rate on average.

**Keywords:** AI security · Machine learning · Computer vision

## 1 Introduction

Over the last years, previous studies [2,11,15,28,29] have shown that deep learning models can be vulnerable to a *membership inference attack*, which aims to identify whether a given data was used for the target model training. In the membership inference attacks, the adversary trains a *shadow model* that mimics

---

G. Lim and W. Oh—Contributed equally.

J.-H. Lee et al. (Eds.): WISA 2024, LNCS 15499, pp. 71–82, 2025.
https://doi.org/10.1007/978-981-96-1624-4_6

the behavior of the target model. The adversary then trains an *attack model* to detect the used data with the outputs of the *shadow model*. After the first membership inference attack was proposed against machine learning models [29], many membership inference attacks have been proposed on Generative Adversarial Networks (GANs) [5,10,13]. As many services based on GANs train them with sensitive information (e.g., medical information [7,26]), membership inference attacks on these services may infer whether a particular individual has a sensitive disease, leading to a serious privacy breach.

Prior membership inference attack against the GANs [10] leverages the components of the GANs framework. GANs consist of a generator to create fake samples that mimic training data, and a complementary discriminator to distinguish the generated data from real data. Therefore, when the adversary trains GANs to learn samples produced by the target model, the generator acts as a *shadow model*, and the discriminator acts as an *attack model*. However, since this method under-represents certain samples, incurring mode collapse [8,23,30], the attack becomes ineffective in the black-box setting where auxiliary information is not given to the adversary. The reason for the under-representation problem of the previous attack [10] is that the discriminator is trained faster than the generator. The discriminator of GANs is then quickly able to distinguish between real and produced samples, providing no valid gradients to improve the generator afterward. Consequently, this early convergence of the discriminator causes a decrease in the quality and diversity of samples produced by the generator.

We propose a novel attack framework called *VoteGAN* to prevent early convergence, which is a fundamental problem in the prior attack method [10]. VoteGAN consists of multiple discriminators and one generator. As the discriminators are trained separately with a partition of the training data, each discriminator is provided with restricted views of the training data. Meanwhile, the generator of VoteGAN is trained with the entire training data. As the discriminative task of each discriminator becomes more difficult, valid gradients continue to be provided throughout the training, thus early convergence of discriminator can be prevented. Consequently, VoteGAN can stably learn the distribution of each data partition, and efficiently approximate the entire distribution of all samples generated by the target model. Our experiments demonstrate that VoteGAN can perform metric-independent attacks in black-box settings and exhibits a lower generalization gap on the datasets used in the experiments, as well as achieving a higher attack success rate than prior method, called LOGAN [10].

Our study makes the following contributions:

- We conduct an in-depth analysis of the fundamental challenges of membership inference attacks on GANs in the black-box setting. We then propose a novel attack framework called VoteGAN, aiming to overcome the fundamental limitations of the previous work [10] by utilizing multiple discriminators to depict the target model more generally and accurately.
- We evaluate the performance of VoteGAN on various generative models trained with two benchmark datasets (CIFAR-10 [16], MNIST [18]) and one

real-world dataset (LFW [14]); and show that the attack success rate has increased by an average of 25% compared to the prior method.

- We demonstrate that VoteGAN can effectively attack target models trained with up to 4,000 data points; while prior method is only effective against target models trained with approximately up to 2,000 data points.

## 2    Background

### 2.1   Membership Inference Attack

The membership inference attack is a binary classification task that aims to infer whether specific data was used to train the target model. The adversary trains an attack model $\mathcal{A}$ that takes a data sample as an input. The attack model $\mathcal{A}$ outputs 1 if the adversary infers that a data sample $s$ is a member of the target training set; otherwise, it outputs 0.

To achieve membership inference, the adversary exploits the overfitting behavior of the deep learning model by training data, where the model cannot perform accurately against unseen data while only fitting exactly against its training data. The overfitting is closely related to the size of the training dataset. Prior works [4,5,10,13,15,19,25,28,29,32,33] have demonstrated there is a correlation between attack performance and training dataset size. The dataset size per class used for the model training and the level of overfitting are inversely proportional [4,29,33]. This is because the smaller training data would less reflect the features of the population. Membership inference attacks on classification tasks become more accurate as the dataset size per class decreases because the adversary leverages overfitting behavior [15,19,25,28,29,32]. Although unsupervised learning models such as generative models do not learn class labels, unlike supervised learning, they are also affected by the overall size of the dataset used for model training. As a result, the smaller the training dataset is, the more vulnerable it is to membership inference attacks [5,10,13].

### 2.2   Generative Adversarial Networks (GANs)

A Generative Adversarial Networks (GANs) [8] is a generative model that consists of a generator $(G)$ and a discriminator $(D)$. The generator takes random noise (latent code $z$) as an input and produces samples that approximate the training data distribution $p_{\text{data}}$, aiming to produce realistic data by following the entire distribution of training. The discriminator is a binary classifier that labels $D \rightarrow [0, 1]$: if the input data is predicted to be real data, the output will be close to 1; otherwise (i.e., predicted to be created one), it will be close to 0. During the training of GANs, the generator and the discriminator play a two-player minimax game that has global optimality [8]. $D$ and $G$ are optimized according to the value function $V(G, D)$:

$$\min_{G} \max_{D} V(G, D) =$$
$$\mathbb{E}_{x \sim p_{\text{data}}(x)}[\log D(x)] + \mathbb{E}_{z \sim p_z(z)}[\log (1 - D(G(z)))], \tag{1}$$

where $G(z)$ denotes a fake sample produced by the generator from $z$, and $x$ is the real data of the training set. By competing with the discriminator in the training procedure, the generator learns how to produce a more realistic output to deceive the discriminator.

Equation 2 is the loss function of GANs generator. The generator attempts to minimize the loss $L_G$:

$$L_G = \mathbb{E}_{z \sim p_z(z)}[\log(1 - D(G(z)))]. \tag{2}$$

The discriminator learns to distinguish between the real data and the produced sample. Equation 3 is the loss function of GANs discriminator. The discriminator attempts to maximize the loss $L_D$:

$$L_D = \mathbb{E}_{x \sim p_{\text{data}}(x)}[\log D(x)] + \mathbb{E}_{z \sim p_z(z)}[\log(1 - D(G(z)))]. \tag{3}$$

The Deep Convolutional GAN (DCGAN) [27] learns training data more stably than the GAN [8] by leveraging the Convolution Neural Network (CNN) structure. Because of this stability, it becomes the basis for many of the other models. Therefore, in this study, we also selected DCGAN as the basic target model.

The Wasserstein GAN (WGAN) [1] is designed with a new loss function to address the problem of instability in the GAN [8] training. Equation 1 is the value function of GAN [8] with *Jenson-Shanon* (JS) divergence [21], which has a disadvantage of gradient vanishment in the GANs training process. The vanishing gradient problem is a phenomenon in which one model delivers a gradient close to zero to another model. As a result, the training is terminated incompletely. The Wasserstein distance [31] with WGAN addresses this problem because it always carries non-zero gradients. The Wasserstein distance loss of WGAN addresses this problem because it always carries non-zero gradients.

PrivGAN [24] was proposed to defend against data leakage from membership inference attacks by an overfitting mitigation strategy in the black-box setting. In order to mitigate the overfitting problem, PrivGAN allows one out of its multiple generators to impose a penalty on the discriminator (specifically, by fooling the discriminator into not memorizing the training data). This mechanism controls the trade-off between privacy and utilities with $\lambda$ hyper parameters instead of making a solid defense (the larger the $\lambda$ value is, the less utility it has). We use PrivGAN as a target model to demonstrate the resistance of our proposed attack to the defense mechanism.

## 2.3 Generalization Gap

In deep learning, the generalization gap means the difference between the model's prediction distributions on training data and non-training data derived from the same distribution [6]. This paper uses the generalization gap to measure how well the *shadow model* of the attack model represents the target model. To measure the generalization gap, we use the discriminator of the attack model because samples produced by the target model are fed into only the discriminator. The formula for the generalization gap is defined as follows:

$$G_{gap} = \mathbb{E}_{x \sim p_{\text{training}}}[\log D(x)] - \mathbb{E}_{x \sim p_{\text{non-training}}}[\log D(x)]. \qquad (4)$$

The large generalization gap of the attack model means that the attack model under-represents certain data samples produced by the target model, which decreases the attack performance because of mode dropping [23] and mode collapse [8,30].

In the black-box setting, resolving such under-representation of the attack model is the main challenge in membership inference attacks against generative models. Therefore, we will handle this issue by designing a novel attack model in the next section.

## 3   VoteGAN

### 3.1   Attack Overview

The attack flow of VoteGAN is shown in Fig. 1. It consists of five steps: data collection, data partitioning, model training, final prediction, and membership inference. In the data collection step, the samples are collected only from responses of the target model generators. Let $X_{real}$ be the dataset produced by the target model. In the data partitioning step, data is pre-processed such that $X_{real}$ is divided into $k$ disjoint partitions $X_{real}^1, X_{real}^2, \cdots, X_{real}^k$ to train multiple $k$ discriminators. In the model training procedure, for any given $l$, each discriminator $D^l$ learns distribution of partition $X_{real}^l$. In the final prediction step, the final value of multiple $k$ discriminator models is calculated by soft voting strategy (detailed in Sect. 3.2).

Figure 2 shows the membership inference step of VoteGAN. With the same assumption as baseline model [10], the adversary knows the size $n$ of the target model's training dataset, and also has a dataset $\{x_1, x_2, \cdots, x_{n+m}\}$ which is suspected of containing data points used to train the target model, where $m$ is the number of datasets not used for training. The adversary inputs $n+m$ samples into VoteGAN, and sorts them in a descending order to facilitate the inference of the adversary that data showing higher prediction values were more likely to be used for training the target model. Thus, the adversary infers data showing the top $n$ predictions as the data actually used to train the target model.

### 3.2   Voting Strategy

Voting has two methods: soft voting and hard voting. Soft voting adds prediction values from all models and then averages them. Therefore, its final prediction value lies between $[0, 1]$. On the contrary, hard voting decides it by the majority vote. That is, the final decision would be 1 if the majority of models predicting the same output exceed a given threshold for the predicted value of input $x$; otherwise, 0.

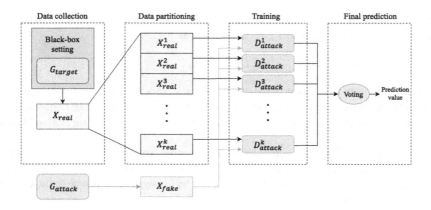

**Fig. 1.** Overview of VoteGAN framework.

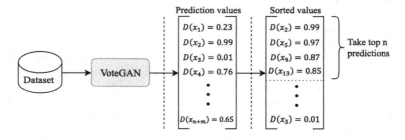

**Fig. 2.** Membership inference method of VoteGAN.

Our membership inference attack adopts the soft voting, because our model exploits subtle distinctions in the predictions for training and non-training data, which can hardly be captured by the hard voting. The soft voting of VoteGAN is defined as Eq. 5.

$$Y_{voting}(x) = \frac{1}{k} \sum_{i=1}^{k} D^i(x). \tag{5}$$

Each discriminator $D^i$ provides a prediction value indicating whether a data record $x$ belongs to the samples produced by the target model. Based on them, the average of all of the prediction values are calculated as the final prediction value, $Y_{voting}$.

## 4    Evaluation

### 4.1    Experimental Setup

**Datasets:** For the evaluation of its design effectiveness, two toy datasets [6,20] were used: the Blobs and Circles. The Blobs dataset was created using a two-dimensional Gaussian Mixture Model with five centers. The Circles dataset was created to be composed of a large composite circle containing a smaller circle. Each of the Blobs and Circles datasets consists of 5,000 samples.

For the evaluation of the other properties, we used a real-world dataset (LFW [14] of human faces) as well as benchmark datasets (CIFAR-10 [16] and MNIST [18]). LFW dataset contains 13,233 human face images collected from the web. CIFAR-10 is a collection of colored (RGB) objects dataset. It comprises $32 \times 32$ pixels with 60,000 samples (50,000 training samples, 10,000 test samples). MNIST is a grayscale handwritten digits dataset consisting of $28 \times 28$ pixels. There are ten classes from 0 to 9, and the total sample size is 70,000 (60,000 training samples, 10,000 test samples).

**Attack Evaluation Metric:** Since the membership inference attack is a binary classification task, we adopt the Area Under the Curve (AUC) metric to evaluate the performance of the binary classifier [3,22]. AUC is a metric to measure an attack's average success rate. The AUC has a value between 0.5 and 1 (the higher the AUC, the higher the attack's average success rate). The AUC for random guesses is 0.5. To evaluate the AUC of attacks, we assume the adversary has a dataset containing the whole data used for training the target model as well as the non-training data of the same size.

**Target Models:** To evaluate the performance of VoteGAN in diverse aspects, we chose DCGAN (model with a typical CNN structure) [27], WGAN (model that uses different losses) [9], and PrivGAN (model with a defense against inference attacks) [24] as the target model. We trained DCGAN and PrivGAN for 400 epochs with the Adam optimizer [17], and set the parameter $\lambda$ that controls the balance between privacy and utilities of PrivGAN to 1. We trained WGAN for 10,000 epochs using the RMSprop optimizer [9]. To evaluate Vote-GAN's resistance to attack defense, parameter values of PrivGAN were applied with $\lambda = 0.1, 1, 10$, respectively (the larger $\lambda$ value implies the stronger attack defense). We trained the target model with 2,000 data samples from the LFW, MNIST, and CIFAR-10 datasets.

## 4.2 Evaluation of Multiple Discriminators

To evaluate the effectiveness of multiple discriminators, we conduct both qualitative and quantitative analyses utilizing the Blobs and Circles datasets. The qualitative analysis evaluated the improvement of the GANs representation ability using visualizing the produced samples as the number of discriminator $k$ increases. The quantitative analysis was evaluated using the Frechet Inception Distance (FID) [12] score. It is a metric to evaluate the quality of the produced samples by measuring the feature distance between the actual training image and the produced sample. A lower FID score indicates that real data and produced samples have similar distributions.

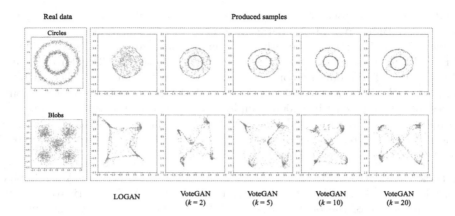

**Fig. 3.** Comparison of distributions produced by LOGAN and VoteGANs. The first column shows the original distributions of the Blobs and Circles. The second column shows the distributions produced by LOGAN. The third to last columns show the distributions produced by VoteGANs.

**Table 1.** Comparison of the FID scores.

|  | Blobs | Circles |
|---|---|---|
| LOGAN [10] | 0.387 | 0.076 |
| VoteGAN ($k = 2$) | 0.224 | 0.038 |
| VoteGAN ($k = 5$) | 0.202 | 0.021 |
| VoteGAN ($k = 10$) | 0.158 | **0.016** |
| VoteGAN ($k = 20$) | **0.134** | 0.023 |

Figure 3 depicts the real distributions of the Blobs and Circles datasets and the distributions produced by LOGAN and VoteGAN that learned them. As shown in the figure, LOGAN [10] cannot learn clear distributions on either the Blobs and Circles datasets. In Table 1, VoteGAN achieves better performance in terms of FID scores for all $k$. These results demonstrate that GANs with multiple discriminators can generate more similar data samples with the training data than GANs with a single discriminator.

### 4.3   Evaluation of Attack Performance

**Attack Success Rate on Various Target Models.** Table 2 shows the attack success rate in terms of AUC score on various target models and datasets. We observed that VoteGAN outperforms LOGAN regardless of the dataset, showing 25% higher AUC scores on average. We also observed that VoteGAN shows the best performance on most of the datasets when $k = 5$ or $k = 10$ rather than $k = 20$.

**Table 2.** Attack success rate of membership inference attacks on various target models and datasets. Datasets I, II, III are LFW, MNIST and CIFAR-10, respectively.

| Target | Models | DCGAN | | | WGAN | | | PrivGAN ($\lambda = 1$) | | |
|---|---|---|---|---|---|---|---|---|---|---|
| | Datasets | I | II | III | I | II | III | I | II | III |
| LOGAN [10] | | 0.661 | 0.686 | 0.713 | 0.677 | 0.616 | 0.705 | 0.603 | 0.622 | 0.614 |
| VoteGAN ($k = 2$) | | 0.757 | 0.743 | 0.806 | 0.740 | 0.701 | 0.784 | 0.702 | 0.772 | 0.754 |
| VoteGAN ($k = 5$) | | 0.779 | 0.787 | 0.755 | 0.753 | **0.825** | 0.803 | 0.710 | **0.794** | 0.757 |
| VoteGAN ($k = 10$) | | **0.818** | **0.807** | 0.797 | **0.801** | 0.731 | **0.868** | **0.756** | 0.739 | **0.807** |
| VoteGAN ($k = 20$) | | 0.709 | 0.815 | **0.832** | 0.706 | 0.626 | 0.826 | 0.708 | 0.791 | 0.798 |

**Attack Success Rate with Different Training Dataset Size.** To evaluate the attack success rate according to the different sizes of the training dataset, we trained the target model by varying the training data size. In this experiment, DCGAN was selected as the target model, and $k = 10$ in VoteGAN. Figure 4 shows the comparison result of attack success rates between LOGAN and VoteGAN for each dataset.

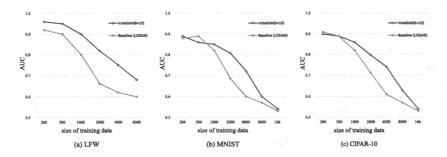

**Fig. 4.** Attack success rate against DCGAN with different training dataset size.

As explained in Sect. 2.1, we can observe that the smaller training data size makes the model more vulnerable to both attacks on every dataset. In addition, on every dataset, VoteGAN can effectively attack trained models with up to 4,000 samples (AUC score above 0.7); while LOGAN is only effective with approximately up to 2,000 samples.

**Resistance to Defense Mechanism.** To evaluate the resistance capability of LOGAN and VoteGAN to a defense mechanism, we utilize PrivGAN [24] trained with CIFAR-10, because PrivGAN is designed to be resilient against the membership inference attack by mitigating the overfitting. As described in Sect. 2.2, the parameter $\lambda$ of PrivGAN controls the trade-off between privacy and utilities (the larger $\lambda$ value implies the stronger privacy protection).

**Table 3.** Attack success rate against PrivGAN with defense mechanisms

|  | PrivGAN ($\lambda = 0.1$) | PrivGAN ($\lambda = 1$) | PrivGAN ($\lambda = 10$) |
|---|---|---|---|
| LOGAN [10] | 0.680 | 0.614 | 0.549 |
| VoteGAN ($k = 2$) | 0.748 | 0.754 | 0.688 |
| VoteGAN ($k = 5$) | 0.752 | 0.757 | **0.723** |
| VoteGAN ($k = 10$) | **0.845** | **0.807** | 0.698 |
| VoteGAN ($k = 20$) | 0.806 | 0.789 | 0.716 |

Table 3 shows the attack success rate of LOGAN and VoteGAN against Priv-GAN. We observe that VoteGAN outperforms LOGAN for every $\lambda$ value. In addition, as $\lambda$ increases, the AUC score of LOGAN approaches 0.5, which indicates that LOGAN cannot successfully infer membership. On the other hand, VoteGAN consistently shows the AUC scores above 0.7 in most of the cases, despite the increase of $\lambda$. The experiment results show that VoteGAN can consistently perform effective membership inference attacks even when the defense mechanism is adopted in the model, as opposed to LOGAN.

## 5   Conclusion

In this work, we propose a novel membership inference attack called *VoteGAN* against generative models. It leverages multiple discriminators to accurately represent the target model. Specifically, VoteGAN trains each discriminator separately with disjoint partitions of the training data, enabling the accurate approximation of the whole distribution of the training data. Thus, VoteGAN can effectively represent the target model in the black-box setting. The experimental results with real-world and benchmark datasets on various target models demonstrate that VoteGAN shows higher performance both in the attack success rate and the resistance to defense mechanisms, compared to the state-of-the-art baseline model. Considering our attack framework can be generically applied to diverse generative models and datasets in the wild, our attacks may pose realistic threat in the real world. Thus, how to effectively mitigate our attacks is an interesting problem, which we will attempt to solve in the future work.

**Acknowledgments.** This work was partly supported by the Institute of Information & Communications Technology Planning & Evaluation (IITP) grant funded by the Korea government(MSIT) (No.2022-0-00411, IITP-2023-2021-0-01810), and Basic Science Research Program through the National Research Foundation (NRF) of Korea funded by the Ministry of Education(NRF-2021R1A6A1A13044830).

## References

1. Arjovsky, M., Chintala, S., Bottou, L.: Wasserstein generative adversarial networks. In: International Conference on Machine Learning, pp. 214–223. PMLR (2017)

2. Bauer, L.A., Bindschaedler, V.: Towards realistic membership inferences: the case of survey data. In: Annual Computer Security Applications Conference, pp. 116–128 (2020)

3. Carlini, N., Chien, S., Nasr, M., Song, S., Terzis, A., Tramer, F.: Membership inference attacks from first principles. In: 2022 IEEE Symposium on Security and Privacy (SP), pp. 1519–1519. IEEE Computer Society (2022)

4. Caruana, R., Lawrence, S., Giles, C.: Overfitting in neural nets: backpropagation, conjugate gradient, and early stopping. In: Advances in Neural Information Processing Systems, vol. 13 (2000)

5. Chen, D., Yu, N., Zhang, Y., Fritz, M.: Gan-leaks: a taxonomy of membership inference attacks against generative models. In: Proceedings of the 2020 ACM SIGSAC Conference on Computer and Communications Security, pp. 343–362 (2020)

6. Chen, J., Wang, W.H., Gao, H., Shi, X.: Par-GAN: improving the generalization of generative adversarial networks against membership inference attacks. In: Proceedings of the 27th ACM SIGKDD Conference on Knowledge Discovery & Data Mining, pp. 127–137 (2021)

7. Choi, E., Biswal, S., Malin, B., Duke, J., Stewart, W.F., Sun, J.: Generating multi-label discrete patient records using generative adversarial networks. In: Machine Learning for Healthcare Conference, pp. 286–305. PMLR (2017)

8. Goodfellow, I., et al.: Generative adversarial nets. In: Advances in Neural Information Processing Systems, vol. 27 (2014)

9. Gulrajani, I., Ahmed, F., Arjovsky, M., Dumoulin, V., Courville, A.C.: Improved training of Wasserstein GANs. In: Advances in Neural Information Processing Systems, vol. 30 (2017)

10. Hayes, J., Melis, L., Danezis, G., De Cristofaro, E.: Logan: membership inference attacks against generative models. Proc. Priv. Enhancing Technol. **2019**(1), 133–152 (2019)

11. He, Z., Zhang, T., Lee, R.B.: Model inversion attacks against collaborative inference. In: Proceedings of the 35th Annual Computer Security Applications Conference, pp. 148–162 (2019)

12. Heusel, M., Ramsauer, H., Unterthiner, T., Nessler, B., Hochreiter, S.: GANs trained by a two time-scale update rule converge to a local nash equilibrium. In: Advances in Neural Information Processing Systems, vol. 30 (2017)

13. Hilprecht, B., Härterich, M., Bernau, D.: Monte Carlo and reconstruction membership inference attacks against generative models. Proc. Priv. Enhancing Technol. **2019**(4), 232–249 (2019)

14. Huang, G.B., Mattar, M., Berg, T., Learned-Miller, E.: Labeled faces in the wild: a database for studying face recognition in unconstrained environments. In: Workshop on Faces in 'Real-Life' Images: Detection, Alignment, and Recognition (2008)

15. Hui, B., Yang, Y., Yuan, H., Burlina, P., Gong, N.Z., Cao, Y.: Practical blind membership inference attack via differential comparisons. In: ISOC Network and Distributed System Security Symposium (NDSS) (2021)

16. Kai, Y., Yuanqing, L., Lafferty, J.: Learning image representations from the pixel level via hierarchical sparse coding. In: 2011 IEEE Conference on Computer Vision and Pattern Recognition (CVPR), pp. 1713–1720 (2011)

17. Kingma, D., Ba, L., et al.: Adam: a method for stochastic optimization (2015)

18. Krizhevsky, A., Hinton, G.: Learning multiple layers of features from tiny images. Master's thesis, Department of Computer Science, University of Toronto (2009)

19. Leino, K., Fredrikson, M.: Stolen memories: leveraging model memorization for calibrated {White-Box} membership inference. In: 29th USENIX security symposium (USENIX Security 2020), pp. 1605–1622 (2020)

20. Li, C., et al.: Alice: towards understanding adversarial learning for joint distribution matching. In: Advances in Neural Information Processing Systems, vol. 30 (2017)
21. Lin, J.: Divergence measures based on the shannon entropy. IEEE Trans. Inf. Theory **37**(1), 145–151 (1991)
22. Ling, C.X., Huang, J., Zhang, H., et al.: AUC: a statistically consistent and more discriminating measure than accuracy. In: IJCAI, vol. 3, pp. 519–524 (2003)
23. Metz, L., Poole, B., Pfau, D., Sohl-Dickstein, J.: Unrolled generative adversarial networks. arXiv preprint arXiv:1611.02163 (2016)
24. Mukherjee, S., Xu, Y., Trivedi, A., Patowary, N., Ferres, J.L.: privGAN: protecting GANs from membership inference attacks at low cost to utility. Proc. Priv. Enhancing Technol. **2021**(3), 142–163 (2021)
25. Nasr, M., Shokri, R., Houmansadr, A.: Comprehensive privacy analysis of deep learning: passive and active white-box inference attacks against centralized and federated learning. In: 2019 IEEE Symposium on Security and Privacy (SP), pp. 739–753. IEEE (2019)
26. Nie, D., et al.: Medical image synthesis with context-aware generative adversarial networks. In: Descoteaux, M., Maier-Hein, L., Franz, A., Jannin, P., Collins, D.L., Duchesne, S. (eds.) MICCAI 2017. LNCS, vol. 10435, pp. 417–425. Springer, Cham (2017). https://doi.org/10.1007/978-3-319-66179-7_48
27. Radford, A., Metz, L., Chintala, S.: Unsupervised representation learning with deep convolutional generative adversarial networks. arXiv preprint arXiv:1511.06434 (2015)
28. Salem, A., Zhang, Y., Humbert, M., Fritz, M., Backes, M.: ML-leaks: model and data independent membership inference attacks and defenses on machine learning models. In: Network and Distributed Systems Security Symposium 2019. Internet Society (2019)
29. Shokri, R., Stronati, M., Song, C., Shmatikov, V.: Membership inference attacks against machine learning models. In: 2017 IEEE Symposium on Security and Privacy (SP), pp. 3–18. IEEE (2017)
30. Thanh-Tung, H., Tran, T.: Catastrophic forgetting and mode collapse in GANs. In: 2020 International Joint Conference on Neural Networks (IJCNN), pp. 1–10. IEEE (2020)
31. Vallender, S.: Calculation of the Wasserstein distance between probability distributions on the line. Theory Probab. Appl. **18**(4), 784–786 (1974)
32. Yeom, S., Giacomelli, I., Fredrikson, M., Jha, S.: Privacy risk in machine learning: analyzing the connection to overfitting. In: 2018 IEEE 31st Computer Security Foundations Symposium (CSF), pp. 268–282. IEEE (2018)
33. Ying, X.: An overview of overfitting and its solutions. In: Journal of Physics: Conference Series, vol. 1168, p. 022022. IOP Publishing (2019)

# Unsupervised Contextual Anomalous Communication Detection Using VQ Tokenization with Flow Data

Norihiro Okui[1]([✉]) [iD], Shotaro Fukushima[2] [iD], Ayumu Kubota[1] [iD],
and Takuya Yoshida[3] [iD]

[1] KDDI Research, Inc., Saitama, Japan
{no-okui,ay-kubota}@kddi.com
[2] ARISE Analytics Inc., Tokyo, Japan
shotaro.fukushima@ariseanalytics.com
[3] Toyota Motor Corporation, Tokyo, Japan
ta-yoshida@mail.toyota.co.jp

**Abstract.** The widespread use of IoT devices has increased the importance of IoT security, and research on anomaly detection has attracted attention due to the properties of IoT devices, such as low resources. Flow data-based methods such as IPFIX, have attracted attention for the purpose of reducing analysis data from scalability perspective, but improving detection accuracy remains challenging. Recently, anomaly detection methods based on natural language processing (NLP) techniques have been proposed, and improved accuracy has been reported by considering the flow data context. In the application of NLP to flow data containing quantitative variables, it is necessary to construct a vocabulary by tokenization, which is different from the NLP. In this study, we propose a novel anomaly detection method combining a Vector Quantized Variational AutoEncoder (VQ-VAE) and a Transformer. This method improves the accuracy of anomaly detection by simultaneously learning the VQ-VAE and Transformer to achieve aggregated tokenization between flows with similar statistical and sequential characteristics. Experimental results on the ToN-IoT dataset showed that the proposed method achieves higher accuracy than methods in previous studies.

**Keywords:** Anomalous communication detection · IoT · IPFIX · Natural language processing · Vector quantization

## 1 Introduction

The number of IoT devices is rapidly increasing, with 15.1 billion active connections in 2023, and this number is projected to rise to 29.4 billion by 2030 [11]. These devices often have limited processing power and rely on battery life, posing challenges in enhancing processing capabilities or implementing direct

J.-H. Lee et al. (Eds.): WISA 2024, LNCS 15499, pp. 83–95, 2025.
https://doi.org/10.1007/978-981-96-1624-4_7

security measures. Monitoring the data transmitted and received by IoT devices to detect unusual communication patterns is a practical security approach.

Communication data are primarily available in two formats: packet and flow data [15]. Packet data, which are rich in information, are relatively easy to manage, with numerous analytical methods developed for their analysis. However, scalability becomes a challenge as the volume of data and the number of devices increase. Compare with packet data, flow data, which aggregate packet data into session statistics, significantly reduce data volume. This efficiency has led to increased research into detecting anomalous communications using flow data. Although flow data contain fewer characteristics than packet data, potentially affecting detection accuracy, researchers have developed advanced anomaly detection techniques. These techniques extend beyond traditional statistical analysis, incorporating methods that utilize temporal features [19] and approaches that treat flow data sequences similarly to natural language, achieving reasonable detection accuracy [5,14]. However, existing methods that treat flow records as words face challenges related to the tokenization process and the handling of unknown flows.

**Tokenization Methods.** In NLP, tokenization divides text into meaningful units such as words or subwords [17], leveraging grammatical rules that are ideal for learning sequences. Applying tokenization to IoT communication flow data seems intuitive, as it organizes records by service units, such as DNS communication or home IoT device interactions such as turning lights on and off. For some services, such as DNS communication, tokenization can be effectively achieved using only the information in the IP and TCP headers, such as the protocol and port number. However, challenges arise when multiple service types coexist within the same port number, such as turning lights on and off, necessitating the consideration of quantitative variables such as packet numbers and sizes. Previous studies have incorporated these quantitative variables into tokenization, but the methods are not fully optimized for the flow data characteristics, often relying on rule-based thresholds and Q-quantile points.

**Handling of Unknown Flows.** In NLP, infrequently occurring or newly generated words are often categorized as unknown tokens [6]. In IoT communication, it is anticipated that flow data characterized by infrequent packet numbers and sizes may emerge during a cyber-attack, highlighting the importance of effective anomaly detection. Therefore, addressing these infrequent flow data appropriately is crucial for identifying anomalous communications. However, previous studies have typically handled unknown tokens by grouping them with the closest statistical tokens, which can result in overlooking anomalous communications.

This study focuses on methods that consider the discrete sequence of flow data occurrences to detect anomalies in IoT communications. The primary goal of our study is to automatically optimize the tokenization of flow data features to enhance the accuracy of anomaly detection. The contributions of this study are outlined as follows:

– We have developed a novel unsupervised method for detecting anomalous communications that integrates a Vector Quantized-Variational AutoEncoder

(VQ-VAE) [21] with a Transformer [22]. This method is designed to learn tokenization and analyze both the statistical and sequential features in an end-to-end manner.

- Our approach also enables the effective tokenization of unknown flows, allowing for the isolation and detailed analysis of flow data with anomalous statistics within each token.
- We evaluated our proposed method using the ToN-IoT dataset, an open dataset for IoT communication, and confirmed that it consistently achieves high performance.

## 2  Related Works

The advancement of deep learning in NLP has led to numerous anomaly detection methods in the security domain, particularly using textual data such as system logs and HTTP request information, which are well-suited for NLP techniques [7,8].

Recently, anomaly communication detection methods have been proposed that treat each record as a grammatical unit in terms of word and sequence, applying NLP techniques [14,23]. Unsupervised methods are particularly crucial in anomaly communication detection for addressing unknown attacks. These NLP-based methods typically generate an anomaly score through autoregressive learning, predicting the next record in a sequence of flow data. Anomaly detection techniques can be categorized based on the type of data they use, for example continuous values such as statistics [23] and discrete values such as port numbers and tokenized packet sizes [5,14]. Given that flow data, such as IPFIX format data, are fundamentally discrete and records are created for each service type, using discrete values for NLP inputs and targets is appropriate.

Methods by Radford et al. [14] and Clausen et al. [5] focus on anomalous communication detection considering discrete sequence relations. These methods use $log2(bytes)$ and Q quantile points to discretize quantitative variables, but they are not optimized for the characteristics of the flow data and do not achieve service-specific tokenization.

Clustering methods such as K-Means have been used for service estimation tasks involving flow data [3], and a tokenization method using K-means has been suggested [4]. However, this method is primarily aimed at estimating the model of the IoT device, not at detecting anomalous communications. Furthermore, as tokenization aggregates to the nearest token, it fails to detect statistically anomalous communications that occur during a cyber-attack, significantly impacting the accuracy of anomaly detection.

## 3  Proposed Method

This section outlines the fundamental concept of the proposed method and the structure of the anomaly detection process.

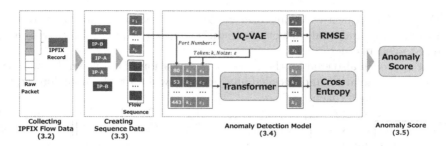

**Fig. 1.** Proposed anomaly detection processing

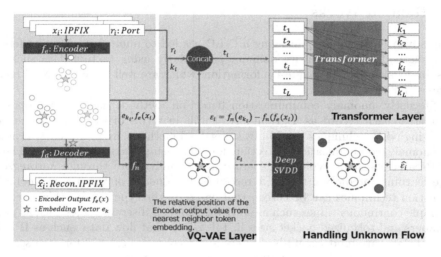

**Fig. 2.** Proposed model architecture

### 3.1 Fundamental Concept

To enhance the accuracy of anomaly communication detection using flow data, it is crucial to accurately model the state of normal communication. Our method focuses on both the statistical and sequential features of the flow data for modeling. Initially, we considered hypotheses about the statistical features. The flow data includes quantitative variables such as packet numbers and communication volumes. However, since records are generated for specific service units such as "DNS communication" or "turning lights on and off", they inherently possess a discrete nature. In addition, even for the same service, there are continuous variations due to parameter changes such as retransmissions (hereinafter, referred to as "noise"). We hypothesize that flow data comprise both discrete features (services) and continuous features (parameters and other variations). Next, we address hypotheses concerning sequential features. Existing methods [5,14] suggest that recognizing discrete-sequence regularities in flow data under normal conditions can enhance the detection accuracy of anomalous communications.

Given that cyber-attacks often exploit vulnerabilities by deviating from expected service patterns, parameters, and ordering rules, our method uses a VQ-VAE to estimate service and noise such as parameters, and employs a Transformer to learn the sequence rules based on the obtained service features. Unlike traditional methods that separate discretization and sequential learning, our approach integrates these processes as suggested in [18], allowing simultaneous consideration of both the statistical and sequential features. This integration is expected to cluster flow data with similar features into the same token, thereby improving the anomaly detection accuracy.

Our methodology involves three primary steps: collecting IPFIX flow data, creating sequence data from the flow data, and detecting anomalies using our method. Figure 1 provides a visual overview of our approach.

## 3.2   Collecting IPFIX Flow Data

While both packet data and flow data are prevalent in anomaly communication detection, our method specifically utilizes IPFIX, a type of flow data, due to its scalability advantages. Network devices such as routers and switches are capable of generating flow data, and packet data can be converted into IPFIX format using tools such as YAF [2,20]. We define the statistics of the $i$th flow record with source IP address $p \in P$ as $x_{p,i}$ and port number as $r_{p,i}$.

## 3.3   Creating Sequence Data

Assuming that flow records with the same source IP address have an ordering regularity, we create a fixed-length $L$ sequence $s_{p,i} \in S$ defined by (1).

$$s_{p,i} = \left( x_{p,max(1,i-L+1)}, x_{p,max(1,i-L+1)+1}, ..., x_{p,i} \right) \tag{1}$$

For simplicity, let $s = (x_1, ..., x_L) \in S$.

## 3.4   Anomaly Detection Model

We detect anomalous communication using our newly proposed model, which consists of two layers: a VQ-VAE layer and a Transformer layer. Figure 2 illustrates the model's architecture.

**VQ-VAE Layer.** The VQ-VAE [21] is an encoder-decoder model featuring a discrete latent space. In this layer, the sequence of flow records $s = (x_1, ..., x_L) \in S$ is used to pseudo estimate services and noise.

Initially, the encoder function $f_e$ converts each $x \in s$ into $z = f_e(x) \in \mathbb{R}^D$. Subsequently, $z$ is quantized according to the embedding space $E_{vq} = \{e_k \in \mathbb{R}^D | k \in 0, ..., K-1\}$ as defined in (2), where $K$ represents the number of embeddings and the dimensionality of the embedding vector. The resulting $e_k$ from (2) is then reconstructed into the original flow data by the decoder function $f_d$.

$$f_k(z) = argmin_k \|z - e_k\|_2$$
$$f_q(z) = e_k \; where \; k = f_k(z) \tag{2}$$

This results in a sequence of pseudo service token $\boldsymbol{k} = (k_1, ..., k_L)$ in (2).

At the same time, noize $\epsilon$ are estimated. The data was defined by (3) using the linear function $f_n$.

$$\epsilon = f_n(f_e(x)) - f_n(e_k) \tag{3}$$

We define $\mathcal{L}_v$ as the loss function of the VQ-VAE layer. The $\mathcal{L}_v$ is an extension of the VQ-VAE [21] loss function to sequences and is defined as in (4). Where $sg$ is an identifier indicating a gradient stop and $\beta$ is a control parameter.

$$\mathcal{L}_v = \sum_{i=1}^{L} \left( \|x_i - f_d(e_{k_i})\|_2^2 + \|sg[f_e(x_i)] - e_{k_i}\|_2^2 + \beta\|f_e(x_i) - sg[e_{k_i}]\|_2^2 + \|\epsilon_i\|_2^2 \right) \tag{4}$$

**Transformer Layer.** The Transformer [22] utilizes a self-attention mechanism and has been effectively applied to various types of series data, including natural language, images, audio, and time series. This layer employs an encoder-decoder structure to learn the discrete sequence of flow data.

The service and parameters (e.g. GET parameters) up to the last service determine the sequence in which services are generated. Therefore, the proposed method uses the pseudo service $k_i$, noize $\epsilon_i$ estimated at the VQ-VAE layer and port number $r_i$ as input features to the Transformer. The sequence of flow data $\boldsymbol{t}$ to be input to the Transformer is defined by (5).

$$\begin{aligned} E_k &= \{e_j^{(k)} | j = 0, 1, 2, ..., K - 1\} \\ E_r &= \{e_j^{(r)} | j = 0, 1, 2, ..., R - 1\} \\ t_i &= Concat(e_{k_i}^{(k)}, e_{r_i}^{(r)}, \epsilon_i) \\ \boldsymbol{t} &= \{t_1, ..., t_L\} \end{aligned} \tag{5}$$

Using the context vector $c_t$ obtained by inputting $\boldsymbol{t}$ into the Transformer Encoder and the Transformer Decoder, the probability of the next token occurring $\hat{k}_i = P(k_i|t_{i<}, c_t)$ is estimated. For the loss function $\mathcal{L}_t$, we use CrossEntropyLoss for the objective variable $k_i$ and its predicted probability $\hat{k}_i$ in (6).

$$\mathcal{L}_t = CrossEntropyLoss(\boldsymbol{k}, \hat{\boldsymbol{k}}) \tag{6}$$

**Loss Function.** The overall loss function of the proposed method is defined by (7), where $\gamma_1$ and $\gamma_2$ are the weights of each loss function.

$$\mathcal{L} = \gamma_1 \mathcal{L}_v + \gamma_2 \mathcal{L}_t \tag{7}$$

**Handling Unknown Flow.** When a communication involving an unknown service or anomalous parameters occurs, the encoder output value $z$ may significantly deviate from all $e_k \in E_{vq}$. The quantization process defined in (2), is necessarily assigned to one of the existing tokens, which can lead to missed anomalies. To address this issue, flows exhibiting anomalous features within each token are identified and flagged as anomalies.

To integrate the anomaly score with the predicted probability $\hat{k}$ obtained from the Transformer layer, the anomaly score is converted into a probabilistic measure using DeepSVDD [16]. Anomaly detection for noise $\epsilon$ is conducted using DeepSVDD, and the resulting anomaly score $\epsilon'$ is converted into a probabilistic value using (8) proposed in [10], where ERF represents the Gaussian error function.

$$\hat{\epsilon} = max \left\{ ERF \left( \frac{\epsilon' - mean(\epsilon')}{.\, std(\epsilon') * \sqrt{2}} \right), 0 \right\} \tag{8}$$

### 3.5    Anomaly Score

The anomaly score $\mathcal{AS}$ of the flow sequence $s \in \mathcal{S}$ is defined as (9).

$$\mathcal{AS} = 1 - \hat{k}_L * (1 - \hat{\epsilon}_L) \tag{9}$$

## 4    Experiments

This section outlines the dataset utilized in the anomaly communication detection experiments, detailing the conditions and results.

### 4.1    Dataset

For our experiments, we employed the ToN-IoT dataset [13], a widely recognized open dataset for IoT communication. This dataset comprises communication data collected over approximately one month, from 02/04/2019 to 29/04/2019, from a network with seven different IoT/IIoT services, including weather sensors, light bulb sensors, smartphones, and smart TVs. The ToN-IoT dataset includes data from various cyber-attacks such as DoS and XSS, with communications generated during these attacks labeled according to the type of attack. In this experiment, all pcap data were converted to flow data in IPFIX format using Yaf [9], with an active timeout set to 1800 s and an idle timeout set to 300 s.

To preserve temporal continuity and avoid data leakage, the dataset was divided based on time. The training data consisted of 327,256 records of normal communication from the start of the dataset until 10:00 am on 24/04/2019. The remaining 14,486,152 records were used as evaluation data. This approach ensures that the training and evaluation data are temporally sequential, which is crucial for time-series data to prevent potential leakage. A summary of the training and evaluation data is presented in Table 1.

**Table 1.** Number of records of training and evaluation data in the ToN-IoT

| Attack Type | Training data | Evaluation data |
|---|---|---|
| Benign | 327,256 | 1,346,953 |
| Anomaly | 0 | 13,139,199 |

**Table 2.** Correlations between features and IPFIX elements

| Feature | IPFIX element |
|---|---|
| Inbound packets | packetTotalCount |
| Outbound packets | reversePacketTotalCount |
| Inbound traffic volume | octetTotalCount |
| Outbound traffic volume | reverseOctetTotalCount |
| Duration | flowDurationMilliseconds |
| Average inbound packet size | $\frac{octetTotalCount}{packetTotalCount}$ |
| Average outbound packet size | $\frac{reverseOctetTotalCount}{reversePacketTotalCount}$ |

## 4.2 Experimental Conditions

This section details the experimental setup used to evaluate the effectiveness of our proposed anomaly detection method by comparing it with existing methods that learn typical anomaly detection techniques and discrete sequences. We compared our method against well-known anomaly detection techniques such as AutoEncoder [1], DeepSVDD [16], VQ-VAE [21], and LSTM-AE [12]. Additionally, we evaluated methods that learn the discrete ordering of flow data, specifically those that handle tokenization and unknown tokens, including methods using Q-quantile points for tokenization (Q-Quant. + Trans.) and K-Means clustering (K-Means+Trans.).

The proposed method was configured with a sequence length $L = 16$, number of embeddings $K = 512$, embedding dimensions $D = 2$, and control parameters $\beta = 0.25$, $\gamma_1 = 1$ and $\gamma_2 = 0.1$. The learning rate was set at 0.003, the batch size was 128, and the model was trained over 3 epochs.

The features input to the model are seven variables: packets (inbound/outbound), traffic volume (inbound/outbound), duration and average packet (inbound/outbound). As a preprocessing step, all the variables are standardized after log-transforming the six variables except for duration. Table 2 shows the correspondence between each variable and the IPFIX elements.

## 4.3 Experiment Results

Initially, we evaluated the accuracy of our proposed method against traditional anomaly detection methods and those that account for discrete sequential relations. The results are detailed in Table 3. We utilized the PR-AUC and ROC-AUC as the metrics for evaluation. The findings indicate that our proposed

**Table 3.** Experiment result of ToN-IoT. The table shows the mean (standard deviation) of five seed values 0-4.

|  | PRAUC | ROCAUC |
|---|---|---|
| AutoEncoder | 0.805(0.007) | 0.147(0.014) |
| DeepSVDD | 0.950(0.023) | 0.659(0.171) |
| VQ-VAE | 0.944(0.003) | 0.780(0.019) |
| LSTM-AE | 0.905(0.007) | 0.589(0.028) |
| Q-Quant.+Trans. | 0.934(0.002) | 0.596(0.025) |
| K-Means+Trans. | 0.932(0.012) | 0.669(0.091) |
| VQ-VAE+Trans.(ours) | **0.966(0.013)** | **0.811(0.063)** |

**Table 4.** Results of the ablation experiment for ToN-IoT. The table shows the mean(std) of five seed values of 0-4.

|  |  | PRAUC | ROCAUC |
|---|---|---|---|
| VQ-VAE+Trans. | Separately | 0.959(0.015) | 0.745(0.087) |
| VQ-VAE+Trans. | Simultaneously(ours) | **0.966(0.013)** | **0.811(0.063)** |

method surpasses all other models tested in this study, demonstrating the effectiveness of integrating both statistical and discrete sequential features.

Furthermore, we explored the impact of learning discretization and sequential features both separately and simultaneously. For this comparison, identical hyperparameters were maintained for both setups. The outcomes, presented in Table 4, reveal that while both approaches yield high accuracy, the simultaneous learning method exhibits superior anomaly detection capabilities. This enhancement is likely due to the method's ability to aggregate flows with similar statistical and ordinal characteristics into the same token, enhancing the model's predictive accuracy.

## 5    Discussion

Anomaly communication detection is crucial for identifying various cyberattacks, each characterized by distinct anomaly patterns. Consequently, the effectiveness of anomaly detection methods varies depending on the type of attack they are designed to identify. This chapter evaluates different anomaly detection methods based on attack type and discusses the strengths and challenges of the proposed methods.

### 5.1    Detailed Analysis

Table 5 presents the detection rates for each type of abnormal communication when the false-positive rate is fixed at 0.1. Initially, our focus is on five specific

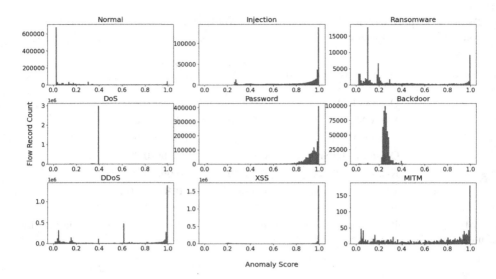

**Fig. 3.** Anomaly score distribution by proposal model per attack type (SEED=0)

attacks: DDoS, Injection, MITM, Password, and XSS. The traditional methods typically address either statistical or discrete ordinal features. In contrast, our proposed method models normal flow data characteristics from both perspectives simultaneously, enhancing its ability to distinguish the abnormal features of these attacks from normal communication patterns.

However, both existing and proposed methods show limited accuracy in detecting backdoor and DoS attacks. This limitation stems partly from the methods' inability to incorporate time information and the sequential relationships between different IP addresses. For instance, DoS attacks such as SYN-Flood are characterized by an increased rate of incidents over time, a pattern that our current methods' focus on sequential relations alone fails to capture.

Overdetection is another challenge, as illustrated in Fig. 3, which displays the anomaly score distribution for each attack type within the evaluation data. While our model generally assigns low anomaly scores to normal communications, it erroneously predicts extremely high anomaly scores (=1.0) for certain communications. This issue is likely due to communications that are time-dependent rather than order-dependent, such as NTP communications.

To enhance accuracy, it is essential to develop a mechanism that effectively considers both the temporal characteristics and the order relationships between different IPs. This approach will help in accurately identifying and differentiating between normal communications and various types of cyber-attacks.

**Table 5.** Detection rate per type of attack (false-positive rate fixed at 0.1, SEED=0)

|  | Backdoor | DDoS | DoS | Injection | MITM | Password | Ransom | XSS |
|---|---|---|---|---|---|---|---|---|
| AutoEncoder | 0.009 | 0.001 | 0.021 | 0.007 | 0.017 | 0.000 | 0.498 | 0.021 |
| DeepSVDD | 0.002 | 0.503 | 0.022 | 0.278 | 0.319 | 0.030 | 0.213 | 0.605 |
| VQ-VAE | 0.009 | 0.004 | 0.021 | 0.047 | 0.052 | 0.000 | **0.518** | 0.060 |
| LSTM-AE | 0.007 | 0.060 | 0.016 | 0.018 | 0.263 | 0.001 | 0.241 | 0.042 |
| Q-Quant.+Trans. | **0.010** | 0.066 | 0.018 | 0.574 | 0.393 | 0.500 | 0.491 | 0.519 |
| K-Means+Trans. | 0.003 | 0.087 | 0.023 | 0.211 | 0.102 | 0.086 | 0.145 | 0.118 |
| **VQ-VAE+Trans.** | 0.005 | **0.924** | **0.067** | **0.732** | **0.473** | **0.959** | 0.235 | **0.994** |

# 6 Conclusion

In this study, we introduced a novel tokenization method that leverages simultaneous learning by integrating VQ-VAE and Transformer. This approach also incorporates a new model that addresses unknown flows within the framework of anomaly communication detection, focusing on the discrete ordering of flow data. We conducted experiments using the ToN-IoT dataset, an open IoT communication dataset, to validate the effectiveness of our proposed method. The results confirmed that our method enhances accuracy compared to both the typical existing methods and those utilizing tokenization. The proposed method demonstrated superior accuracy across a broader range of attack types compared to the existing methods, indicating its ability to handle unknown attacks more generally. Moving forward, we plan to develop strategies to incorporate time information more effectively to reduce false-positive.

# References

1. Aggarwal, C.C.: Outlier Analysis. Springer (2013). https://doi.org/10.1007/978-1-4614-6396-2
2. Aitken, P., Claise, B., Trammell, B.: Specification of the IP Flow Information Export (IPFIX) Protocol for the Exchange of Flow Information. RFC 7011 (2013). https://doi.org/10.17487/RFC7011
3. Azab, A., Khasawneh, M., Alrabaee, S., Choo, K.K.R., Sarsour, M.: Network traffic classification: techniques, datasets, and challenges. Digit. Commun. Netw. (2022). https://doi.org/10.1016/j.dcan.2022.09.009
4. Bikmukhamedov, R.F., Nadeev, A.F.: Multi-class network traffic generators and classifiers based on neural networks. In: 2021 Systems of Signals Generating and Processing in the Field of on Board Communications, pp. 1–7 (2021). https://doi.org/10.1109/IEEECONF51389.2021.9416067
5. Clausen, H., Grov, G., Aspinall, D.: CBAM: a contextual model for network anomaly detection. Computers **10**(6) (2021). https://doi.org/10.3390/computers10060079
6. Devlin, J., Chang, M.W., Lee, K., Toutanova, K.: Bert: pre-training of deep bidirectional transformers for language understanding. In: North American Chapter of the Association for Computational Linguistics (2019)

7. Du, M., Li, F., Zheng, G., Srikumar, V.: Deeplog: anomaly detection and diagnosis from system logs through deep learning. In: Proceedings of the 2017 ACM SIGSAC Conference on Computer and Communications Security, CCS 2017, pp. 1285–1298. Association for Computing Machinery, New York (2017). https://doi.org/10.1145/3133956.3134015

8. Huang, W., Zhu, H., Li, C., Lv, Q., Wang, Y., Yang, H.: Itdbert: temporal-semantic representation for insider threat detection. In: 2021 IEEE Symposium on Computers and Communications (ISCC), pp. 1–7 (2021). https://doi.org/10.1109/ISCC53001.2021.9631538

9. Inacio, C., Trammell, B.: Yaf: yet another flowmeter. In: LiSA (2010)

10. Kriegel, H.P., Kroger, P., Schubert, E., Zimek, A.: Interpreting and unifying outlier scores. In: Proceedings of the 2011 SIAM International Conference on Data Mining, pp. 13–24. SIAM (2011)

11. Lionel Sujay Vailshery: Number of IoT connected devices worldwide 2019-2023, with forecasts to 2030 (2023). https://www.statista.com/statistics/1183457/iot-connected-devices-worldwide/

12. Malhotra, P., Ramakrishnan, A., Anand, G., Vig, L., Agarwal, P., Shroff, G.: LSTM-based encoder-decoder for multi-sensor anomaly detection. arXiv preprint arXiv:1607.00148 (2016)

13. Moustafa, N.: A new distributed architecture for evaluating AI-based security systems at the edge: network ton_iot datasets. Sustain. Cities Soc. **72**, 102994 (2021). https://doi.org/10.1016/j.scs.2021.102994

14. Radford, B.J., Apolonio, L.M., Trias, A.J., Simpson, J.A.: Network traffic anomaly detection using recurrent neural networks. arXiv preprint arXiv:1803.10769 (2018)

15. Ring, M., Wunderlich, S., Scheuring, D., Landes, D., Hotho, A.: A survey of network-based intrusion detection data sets. Comput. Secur. **86**, 147–167 (2019). https://doi.org/10.1016/j.cose.2019.06.005

16. Ruff, L., et al.: Deep one-class classification. In: International Conference on Machine Learning, pp. 4393–4402. PMLR (2018)

17. Sennrich, R., Haddow, B., Birch, A.: Neural machine translation of rare words with subword units. In: Proceedings of the 54th Annual Meeting of the Association for Computational Linguistics (Volume 1: Long Papers), pp. 1715–1725. Association for Computational Linguistics, Berlin, Germany (2016). https://doi.org/10.18653/v1/P16-1162

18. Shi, J., Saon, G., Haws, D., Watanabe, S., Kingsbury, B.: VQ-T: RNN transducers using vector-quantized prediction network states. In: Proceedings of Interspeech 2022, pp. 1656–1660 (2022). https://doi.org/10.21437/Interspeech.2022-414

19. Tang, T.A., Mhamdi, L., McLernon, D., Zaidi, S.A.R., Ghogho, M.: Deep recurrent neural network for intrusion detection in SDN-based networks. In: 2018 4th IEEE Conference on Network Softwarization and Workshops (NetSoft), pp. 202–206 (2018). https://doi.org/10.1109/NETSOFT.2018.8460090

20. Trammell, B., Boschi, E.: Bidirectional Flow Export Using IP Flow Information Export (IPFIX). RFC 5103 (2008). https://doi.org/10.17487/RFC5103

21. Van Den Oord, A., Vinyals, O., et al.: Neural discrete representation learning. In: Advances in Neural Information Processing Systems, vol. 30 (2017). https://proceedings.neurips.cc/paper/2017/hash/7a98af17e63a0ac09ce2e96d03992fbc-Abstract.html

22. Vaswani, A., et al.: Attention is all you need. In: Advances in Neural Information Processing Systems, vol. 30 (2017). https://proceedings.neurips.cc/paper/7181-attention-is-all
23. Wakui, T., Kondo, T., Teraoka, F.: GAMPAL: anomaly detection for internet backbone traffic by flow prediction with LSTM-RNN. In: Boumerdassi, S., Renault, É., Mühlethaler, P. (eds.) MLN 2019. LNCS, vol. 12081, pp. 196–211. Springer, Cham (2020). https://doi.org/10.1007/978-3-030-45778-5_13

# Boosting Black-Box Transferability of Weak Audio Adversarial Attacks with Random Masking

Mai Bui[ID], Thien-Phuc Doan[ID], Kihun Hong[ID], and Souhwan Jung[✉][ID]

School of Electronic Engineering, Soongsil University, Seoul, Republic of Korea
{maibui,phucdt}@soongsil.ac.kr, {khong,souhwanj}@ssu.ac.kr

**Abstract.** The vulnerability of deep learning models to adversarial attacks poses a significant challenge in artificial intelligence, particularly in deepfake detection. Adversarial training has emerged as a crucial defense mechanism, highlighting the importance of highly transferable adversarial samples. However, current attack methods often struggle with transferability in black-box scenarios. This research identifies a key limitation: white-box methods tend to overfit surrogate models, reducing their effectiveness against unknown attacks. To address this vulnerability, we propose the iterative "Random Masking Perturbation" method. This method reduces dependence on gradient or loss function behavior by not using full gradient information to create perturbations. Furthermore, by iteratively masking perturbations while still generating successful adversarial samples, our method automatically and selectively perturbs sensitive features that easily mislead the surrogate model, particularly those with the highest density in the low-frequency band, which is critical for achieving high transferability rates. Experimental results demonstrate significant enhancements in transferability rates, with Random Masking yielding improvements of up to 60%, offering promising strides in fortifying the robustness of adversarial training for deepfake detection models.

**Keywords:** Adversarial Attacks · Adversarial Training · Random Masking · Boosting Transferability · Low-frequency

## 1 Introduction

In the ever-evolving landscape of security, marked by technological advancements, a perpetual struggle persists between those fortifying defenses and those exploiting vulnerabilities. This dynamic is particularly evident in the domain of security, such as software, web, network, or especially deepfake applications [12] where advancements in artificial intelligence have enabled sophisticated attacks and robust defense mechanisms. Defenders constantly strive to strengthen systems against various potential threats, while adversaries persistently probe for security gaps, underscoring the imperative for ongoing innovation in defensive

J.-H. Lee et al. (Eds.): WISA 2024, LNCS 15499, pp. 96–108, 2025.
https://doi.org/10.1007/978-981-96-1624-4_8

strategies. This symbiotic relationship has fueled research endeavors to develop effective and resilient adversarial samples for training tasks. However, a notable vulnerability of adversarial attacks persists - the transferability in black-box scenarios [5], where transferability refers to an adversarial sample's ability to attack various unknown models successfully. This highlights the critical need for continued exploration and innovation in addressing nuanced aspects, a focal point in our investigation.

In scenarios where the target model's architecture is unknown (black-box), surrogate models are utilized to generate adversarial samples, with the expectation that the countermeasure model in black-box scenarios shares a similar architecture with the surrogate models. However, specific models often prioritize certain critical features during training and generating, resulting in adversarial samples effective only on surrogate models, particularly when perturbations are uniformly applied across the audio signal. Although augmenting perturbations can boost the effectiveness of attacking deepfake detection models and influence transferability, it frequently decreases audio quality, potentially reducing them to meaningless noise. Moreover, real-world countermeasures exhibit various characteristics and architectures, hampering adversarial attacks' transferability. Additionally, within an adversarial training scheme, transferability is crucial because these adversarial samples contain diverse characteristics of attack perspectives, so augmented datasets with a minimal amount of adversarial samples should be used rather than requiring the collection of all samples for each attack scenario. Therefore, controlling the amount of perturbation noise while enhancing transferability becomes pivotal, serving as a metric to evaluate the efficacy of adversarial attack methods.

The traditional adversarial attack methods often optimize perturbations based on gradient loss and network parameters of the surrogate model [1,4,10] or geometric perspectives [11]. Furthermore, audio data is time series data that leads to perturbations persisting in continuous and high-amplitude formats [9]. The state-of-the-art attack methods were introduced, such as input diversity [14] based on data augmentation approaches or creating robust ensemble surrogate models [6] based on ensemble learning, aim to enhance transferability without relying on specific features of inputs and surrogate models. However, these state-of-the-art methods are resource-intensive and time-consuming because they need time to process through many diverse normalized data steps (input diversity) or huge and complicated architecture models (ensemble surrogate models), and they do not perform stably well in an audio domain. As a result, striking a balance between increasing perturbations for successful attacks stably and maintaining transferability while optimizing time and resource utilization presents a significant challenge in developing robust adversarial training strategies.

Our primary objective is to produce effective adversarial samples with a high transferability rate while minimizing time and resource usage compared with input diversity and ensemble surrogate model approaches to bolster the adversarial training of deepfake detection networks. To accomplish this aim, we introduce the "Random Masking Perturbation" method for adversarial processing, which significantly boosts transferability rates and a notable performance improvement of up to 60% compared to conventional methods.

In this study, we have the following contributions:

– We proposed an attack method to enhance the transferability of weak adversarial attacks based on gradient optimization while minimizing time and resource costs.
– With random masking perturbation iteratively, we introduce a new way to focus attack only the sensitive features that are the factors that easily make countermeasure misclassification.

## 2  Preliminaries

### 2.1  Adversarial Attacks

Adversarial attacks have gained considerable attention in recent years, particularly in the context of image data. However, the audio domain introduces unique challenges, operating in both the time and frequency domains. While many existing adversarial attack methods have been designed primarily for images, extending these methods to audio signals has raised novel questions. The popular adversarial attack method is the Fast Gradient Sign Method (FGSM) [4], which perturbs an input to maximize loss, crafting an adversarial sample in a single step. The perturbation is determined by taking the sign of the gradient of the loss function concerning the input features and scaling it by a small constant $\epsilon$ to control the strength of the perturbation. To improve FGSM, there are several methods are introduced as the following methods.

– **IFGSM** (Iterative Fast Gradient Sign Method) [1] is an iterative extension of FGSM that refines the perturbation through multiple iterations to enhance the adversarial attack. In each iteration, the perturbation is adjusted by a small step $\alpha$ in the direction of the gradient, and the resulting adversarial sample is clipped to ensure it stays within an $\epsilon$-bounded $L_\infty$ norm.
– **MIFGSM** (Momentum Iterative Fast Gradient Sign Method) [3] incorporates momentum into the iterative process of IFGSM to stabilize the update directions, helping to avoid poor local maxima. This momentum term accumulates the gradient of the loss function over iterations, enhancing the transferability of adversarial examples across different models.
– **DIFGSM** (Diverse Inputs Iterative Fast Gradient Sign Method) [17] enhances IFGSM by introducing input diversity, where each input is randomly resized and padded during the attack process. This approach prevents the model from overfitting to specific perturbations, improving the robustness and transferability of the adversarial examples.

FGSM typically maintain a uniform perturbation magnitude $\delta_t = \bar{\delta}_t$, where $\delta < \epsilon$, and $\epsilon$ represents the perturbation budget value at time domain $t$. Different from FGSM, the various methods based FGSM, employ various strategies to optimize perturbations of an adversarial sample $\mathcal{T}(\delta, x)$. However, these attacks were initially designed for the image domain, where frequency signals do not play a significant role. When applied to the audio domain, where frequency signals are crucial for transferability, their performance, while better than the original FGSM, still falls short. These methods tend to attack all frequency bands, leading to decreased transferability, particularly because perturbations in only low-frequency bands significantly affect transferability rates [7]. Therefore, we classify these FGSM-based methods as weak transferability audio adversarial attack methods.

The success of audio adversarial samples is closely related to the extent of perturbation applied. In simpler terms, samples with more substantial perturbations tend to have a higher success and transferability rate but significantly decrease in quality, impacting their effectiveness in deceiving the target system. Consequently, ensuring the quality of adversarial samples while maintaining a satisfactory Mean Opinion Score (MOS), a premier metric for assessing audio quality is paramount in the audio domain. Recognizing these challenges, our work aims to maintain the quality of adversarial audio by limiting the perturbation budget $\epsilon$ while enhancing the transferability rate.

## 2.2   Surrogate Model

Adversarial attack scenarios can be categorized as white-box and black-box attacks. In a white-box attack, the attacker has full knowledge of the system, including the model architecture and training dataset. In contrast, a black-box attack occurs when the attacker has no information about the system. To create adversarial samples for black-box scenarios, attackers use surrogate models as proxies for the target models, hoping that the surrogate model's architecture and behavior are similar to those of the target model. Consequently, the surrogate model should strike a balance: it should neither be too simple nor too complex, and it should avoid highly specific techniques that are unlikely to generalize to the target model.

In this paper, we choose AASIST-SSL [16] and RawNet2 [15] as the surrogate models, and we use BTSE [2] solely to measure transferability in black-box attacks. AASIST-SSL is selected because it represents the best-performing model, while RawNet2 represents the worst-performing model in our experiments (see Table 1). All models are trained and tested on the ASVSpoof2021 dataset [8]. In detail, AASIST-SSL is developed using an attention graph neural network combined with self-supervised learning, leveraging Wav2vec2 - a powerful and large model for audio feature extraction, resulting in a model with 317,837,834 parameters (bigger than BTSE and RawNet2 about 18 times), but the performance is the best. BTSE and RawNet2 are simpler network models. BTSE incorporates a specific breathing-talking-silence encoder, enhancing its detection performance compared to RawNet2. All three models are well-known in the audio deepfake detection domain and perform well across various datasets.

**Table 1.** Parameter number and accuracy rate of audio deepfake detection models

|                  | AASIST-SSL  | BTSE       | RawNet2    |
|------------------|-------------|------------|------------|
| Parameter number | 317,837,834 | 17,662,290 | 17,621,410 |
| Accuracy (%)     | 98.69       | 94.01      | 91.37      |

## 3    Problem Statements and Motivation

In both the image and audio domains, two primary categories of attack methods exist: those employing uniformly perturbed values across the entire sample, such as FGSM, and those selectively targeting specific parts, such as one-pixel [13] deemed crucial for adversarial training of deepfake detection models. Nevertheless, although the approach selectively targeting specific parts to attack has high transferability, it has a low attack success rate in the audio domain because it is difficult to identify the correct point or the number of perturbations is insufficient to attack. Thus, enhanced transferability of the methods from perturbing the entire sample can balance both the attack success and transferability rate.

The transferability of an audio adversarial sample depends on both audio characteristics and the surrogate model. Therefore, to enhance the transferability rate, it is necessary to balance these factors. Notably, black-box adversarial attack methods are typically optimized based on surrogate models' gradients and loss functions. However, these approaches often produce adversarial samples that overfit the surrogate model, resulting in low transferability in black-box scenarios. This overfitting occurs because the model tends to learn and adapt to the important features extracted by the surrogate model throughout the process, leading to adversarial samples that are heavily dependent on the specific gradient behavior of the surrogate model. Consequently, this dependency limits their effectiveness in different contexts and reduces their utility in adversarial training strategies.

Simultaneously, the fastest way to enhance transferability in signal attacks is to focus on the low-frequency band [7], where speech energy predominantly resides (with high frequencies often being noise or echo). In other words, audio attack methods should target sensitive features within the low-frequency band to effectively prompt the surrogate model to change the label during adversarial processing rather than attacking the entire frequency range. However, our experiments show that most of weak adversarial attacks based on FGSM target the full frequency band.

To address these issues, our proposed method employs random masking perturbation to avoid relying on the complete information of gradients and network parameters, thereby preventing overfitting. Additionally, it continuously applies random masking, increasing the number of perturbations through many iterations while enabling the successful generation of adversarial samples. This ensures that the adversarial samples are predominantly perturbed at sensitive features, mainly concentrated in the low-frequency audio band, thereby enhancing transferability.

## 4    Proposed Method

In this work, we deviate from the traditional approach of uniformly adding perturbations across entire samples. To enhance the transferability rate, we introduce chaotic and heterogeneous perturbations guided by the gradient direction of the model. This approach aims to effectively deceive the model while optimizing the perturbation count required for successful deception.

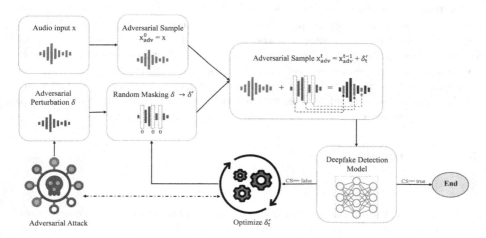

**Fig. 1.** Iterative random masking perturbation framework with conditional stop (CS), which halts the generation process early whenever the model misclassifies a spoof as a bonafide label

Specifically, as shown in Fig. 1, the algorithm for optimizing the adversarial perturbation $\delta$ remains unchanged. However, we introduce a modification where, after extracting $\delta$ from the usual attacks, we randomly mask portions of $\delta$. Random masking of perturbations occurs with the optimized perturbation value $\delta_t'$ assigned at each iteration. Notably, $\delta_t'$ is optimized by the algorithm of the base attack methods such as IFGSM, MIFGSM, and DIFGSM in our experiments; our main contribution is the masking technique to the perturbation after its extraction.

The masked perturbation is calculated as the formula: $\delta_t' = \delta_t \times (1 - m_i)$ where $m_i$ is generated from a Bernoulli distribution with the probability of masking $p$. Each $m_i$ is independently set to 1 with $p$ and to 0 with probability $(1 - p)$. The extent of this masking can be customized to various degrees, such as 30%, 40%, or 50%. This approach ensures that certain sections of the original sample remain unmodified in the first iteration, and in subsequent iterations, some parts of the previous iterative adversarial sample $x_{adv}^{t-1}$ also remain unmodified.

$$x_{adv}^t = x_{adv}^{t-1} + \delta' \tag{1}$$

As a result, our perturbations follow the model's gradient direction, maximizing the loss function until the model transitions its label from spoof to bonafide. The final perturbations have non-uniform values, following no specific pattern that a deepfake detection model can easily deduce.

Furthermore, although the Random Masking Perturbation method continuously changes the position of removed or hidden perturbation parts during many iterations, successful adversarial samples are still generated. This indicates that our method automatically selectively targets the sensitive features that are most likely to cause the surrogate model to easily change the label during the adversarial processing of audio samples. Our observations and analyses during experiments show that these sensitive audio features are predominantly located in the low-frequency band, which supports a high transferability rate for adversarial samples. By reducing dependence on gradient information and selectively targeting sensitive features, we successfully avoid overfitting the surrogate models and enhance the transferability of weak adversarial attack methods.

## 5   Experiments

### 5.1   Setup

In selecting a dataset for our evaluation and experiments, we prioritized one that includes noisy samples to simulate real-life scenarios. After careful consideration, we chose the ASVSpoof2021 DF eval dataset for its diversity and inclusion of various types of spoof audio data, particularly those from the renowned ASVspoof challenge. This dataset aligns well with our objective of testing under realistic conditions. To ensure consistency across all case experiments, We randomly selected 5000 samples from it and used these same samples for all case experiments.

For our experiments, we have selected FGSM, IFGSM, MIFGSM, and DIFGSM as the attack methods. While these techniques are typically initialized in the image domain, they are fundamentally gradient-based attack methods. After processing the raw data, both image and audio inputs are converted to signal data, facilitating easy extraction of gradient values from the surrogate model. This versatility allows for effectively applying FGSM-based techniques across various domains, including image and audio.

Furthermore, MIFGSM is a conventional technique designed to improve transferability rates for FGSM and IFGSM, while DIFGSM is another method to enhance transferability for FGSM, IFGSM, and MIFGSM. However, in our study, we found that despite their intended purpose of improving transferability, these methods did not prove effective, and we aim to boost their transferability rate further. Therefore, the choice to focus solely on FGSM-based techniques in our experiments provides a sufficient basis for comparison.

As discussed in Sect. 2.2, we have chosen AASIST-SSL and RawNet2 as appropriate surrogate models. To evaluate transferability across different architectures of deepfake detection models, we have also included BTSE. This model employs a specialized encoder that initially processes breath, silent, and talking segments as inputs for training.

Moreover, for a fair comparison, we adhere to a uniform perturbation budget $\epsilon$ of 0.3, a step size $\alpha$ of 0.01, and a maximum of 20 iterations. To be considered for the evaluation of transferability, the adversarial samples must first successfully attack the surrogate model. Therefore, the chosen samples must achieve a 100% attack success rate on the surrogate model.

**Table 2.** Transferability Rates (%) using AASIST-SSL and RawNet2 as surrogate models. Model (*) denotes the surrogate model in this case.

(a) Transferability Rates Using AASIST-SSL as Surrogate Model

| Method | AASIST-SSL* | RawNet2 | BTSE |
|---|---|---|---|
| FGSM | 100 | 89.48 | 3.27 |
| IFGSM | 100 | 89.88 | 11.34 |
| IFGSM + RM | 100 | 91.56 | 69.95 |
| MIFGSM | 100 | 89.29 | 8.79 |
| MIFGSM + RM | 100 | 91.68 | 69.33 |
| DIFGSM | 100 | 93.16 | 41.23 |
| DIFGSM + RM | 100 | **93.21** | **85.92** |

(b) Transferability Rates Using RawNet2 as Surrogate Model

| Method | RawNet2* | AASIST-SSL | BTSE |
|---|---|---|---|
| FGSM | 100 | 18.33 | 60.63 |
| IFGSM | 100 | 16.71 | 62.36 |
| IFGSM + RM | 100 | **20.26** | 88.81 |
| MIFGSM | 100 | 16.22 | 61.92 |
| MIFGSM + RM | 100 | 18.36 | 86.96 |
| DIFGSM | 100 | 16.91 | 68.00 |
| DIFGSM + RM | 100 | 10.04 | **94.11** |

## 5.2  Results

Figure 2a and Fig. 2b show the transferability rate of adversarial samples generated by several adversarial attacks and surrogate models, the detail result is in Table 2. The grey column represents FGSM, and the other paired colors indicate

(a) Transferability rate with surrogate model AASIST-SSL

(b) Transferability rate with surrogate model RawNet2

**Fig. 2.** Transferability rates (%) of adversarial attacks with different surrogate models

methods with and without applying Random Masking Perturbation, whereas the darker color signifies the application of Random Masking Perturbation. The flection random masking is 50%.

In Table 2, AASIST-SSL, a larger and stronger model than RawNet2, successfully transfers attacks to RawNet2 in both cases, with and without applying random masking. Specifically, BTSE is challenging to attack using normal adversarial methods due to its specialized encoder. However, our method significantly boosts the transferability of these weak attacks, with the best case showing an improvement of up to 60% in transferability rate.

In contrast, when using RawNet2 as the surrogate model, the transferability to AASIST-SSL, a strong deepfake detection model, remains weak in both cases, with and without applying our method. Our method only slightly enhances transferability in some cases because traditional attacks already struggle to deceive AASIST-SSL. Additionally, reducing perturbation further results in adversarial samples lacking sufficient perturbations to deceive the models. However, with the BTSE model, the enhanced transferability still outperforms traditional attacks.

Our method operates in the gradient domain during each iteration, which is the core framework of the base attack methods we aim to enhance transferability. Notably, our approach doesn't require additional processing or augmented data. In our experiments, we maintained consistent parameters across all methods, including the maximum number of iterations and perturbation budgets, to ensure a fair comparison. The results demonstrate that by applying our method, the relatively simple IFGSM can achieve performance nearly on par with the more complex DIFGSM. This finding proves that our method can significantly reduce computational and resource costs while maintaining high effectiveness. By improving the efficiency of more straightforward attack methods, we eliminate the need for more intricate and resource-intensive techniques, thus optimizing the overall process of generating transferable adversarial examples.

## 5.3   Reasoning on the Enhancing Transferability

To explain the improvement in transferability rate, the key factor is the attack on low-frequency bands, which makes label switching easier, as already explained in paragraph 3 of Sect. 3. For this reason, we investigated the power spectral density (PSD) of the perturbations from traditional adversarial attacks with or without applying our method - Random Masking Perturbation to see the power

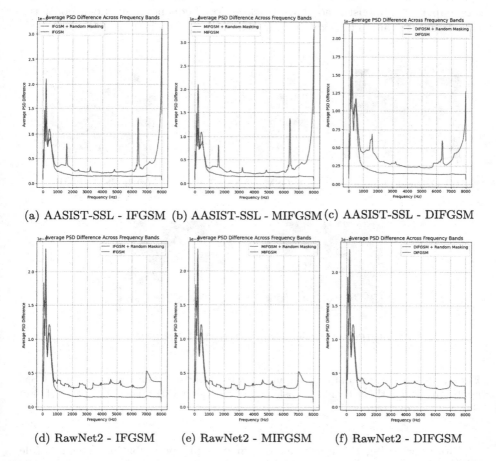

(a) AASIST-SSL - IFGSM  (b) AASIST-SSL - MIFGSM (c) AASIST-SSL - DIFGSM

(d) RawNet2 - IFGSM      (e) RawNet2 - MIFGSM      (f) RawNet2 - DIFGSM

**Fig. 3.** Average power spectral density (PSD) difference of adversarial perturbation across frequency bands for different base attack methods generated by different surrogate models. The red line shows traditional attacks, and the blue line shows our method. (Color figure online)

density in each frequency band. The perturbation $\delta$ is identified by subtracting the original audio $x_{orig}$ from the adversarial audio $x_{adv}$:

$$\delta = x_{adv} - x_{orig} \tag{2}$$

As shown in Fig. 3, the power spectral density (PSD) of adversarial perturbations without applying our method tends to be strong in the high-frequency bands. The average PSD of traditional attacks is higher than when applying our method in all cases (the red line), particularly in the case of the AASIST-SSL surrogate model. In contrast to traditional attacks, our method redirects the perturbations to the low-frequency band and stabilizes them within this band. The paper [7] demonstrated that attacking low-frequency bands can boost the transferability rate. This explains why we can improve the transferability.

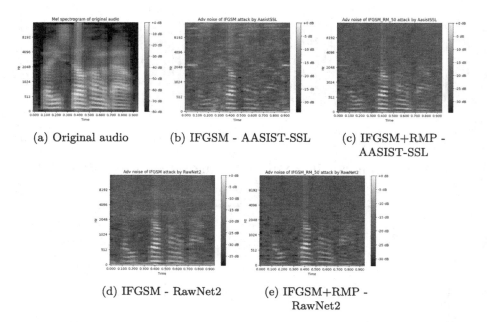

(a) Original audio    (b) IFGSM - AASIST-SSL    (c) IFGSM+RMP - AASIST-SSL

(d) IFGSM - RawNet2    (e) IFGSM+RMP - RawNet2

**Fig. 4.** Mel-spectrogram of original audio and the perturbation generated by IFGSM apply with and without Random masking perturbation (RMP) using AASIST-SSL and RawNet2 surrogate models.

Moreover, using the iterative random masking perturbation scheme while adhering to the constraints of the surrogate model to switch the label from spoof to bonafide, the higher the number of masked reflections, the more the focus is forced onto the key features that enable achieving targeted deception of models. The final perturbations will be the result of collecting key features through each iterative random masking and optimizing perturbation. Thus, the probability ratio of masking perturbation directly affects the transferability; the higher the ratio, the harder the constraints to generate an adversarial sample. The Fig. 3 show the best results occur when applying Random Masking Perturbation with 70% reflection, where the deviation of the PSD at the high-frequency band is the largest (the red line represents traditional attacks, and the blue line represents our method).

For the example shown in Fig. 4, this figure displays how the perturbation works on the frequency bands. Figure 4a shows the original samples, Fig. 4b and Fig. 4c display the adversarial perturbation $\delta$ of IFGSM with and without our method using the AASIST-SSL surrogate model, and Fig. 4d and Fig. 4e show the adversarial perturbation of IFGSM with and without our method using the RawNet2 surrogate model. Although adversarial perturbations appear across the entire frequency band in both cases with and without applying our method, IFGSM methods tend to attack uniformly across all frequencies, including the high frequencies where the light color appears at the top of Fig. 4b and Fig. 4d. In contrast, our method primarily focuses on lower frequencies, especially where the speech energy is concentrated (the light color is mostly below). The transferability is evident as Fig. 4c and Fig. 4e successfully attack BTSE, whereas Fig. 4b and Fig. 4d fail to attack BTSE in black-box scenarios.

## 6    Conclusions

In conclusion, our research addresses the critical challenge of transferability in adversarial attacks, particularly in black-box scenarios, through the innovative "Random Masking Perturbation" method. This approach not only enhances transferability by up to 60% in black-box attacks but also optimizes resource usage, marking a significant advancement in adversarial training strategies. By iteratively limiting the use of full gradient and surrogate network parameter information and targeting sensitive features in the low-frequency band, our method provides insights into the fundamental vulnerabilities of deep learning models. This work has far-reaching implications for AI security, especially in domains like deepfake detection, and paves the way for more robust and efficient defense mechanisms against evolving threats. As we continue to pursue scalable solutions, our research positions itself at the forefront of AI security, contributing to the development of more resilient systems capable of withstanding a wide spectrum of potential attacks in an ever-evolving landscape of AI threats.

**Acknowledgments.** This work was supported by Institute of Information & Communications Technology Planning & Evaluation (IITP) grant funded by the Korea government (MSIT) (No. RS-2023-00263037, Robust deepfake audio detection development against adversarial attacks); and Institute of Information & Communications Technology Planning & Evaluation (IITP) grant funded by the Korea government (MSIT) (No. RS-2023-00230337, Advanced and Proactive AI Platform Research and Development Against Malicious Deepfakes).

# References

1. Carlini, N., Wagner, D.: Audio adversarial examples: targeted attacks on speech-to-text. In: 2018 IEEE Security and Privacy Workshops (SPW), pp. 1–7. IEEE (2018)
2. Doan, T.P., Nguyen-Vu, L., Jung, S., Hong, K.: BTS-E: audio deepfake detection using breathing-talking-silence encoder. In: ICASSP 2023-2023 IEEE International Conference on Acoustics, Speech and Signal Processing (ICASSP), pp. 1–5. IEEE (2023)
3. Dong, Y., Liao, F., Pang, T., Su, H., Zhu, J., Hu, X., Li, J.: Boosting adversarial attacks with momentum. In: Proceedings of the IEEE Conference on Computer Vision and Pattern Recognition, pp. 9185–9193 (2018)
4. Goodfellow, I.J., Shlens, J., Szegedy, C.: Explaining and harnessing adversarial examples. arXiv preprint arXiv:1412.6572 (2014)
5. Gu, J., et al.: A survey on transferability of adversarial examples across deep neural networks. arXiv preprint arXiv:2310.17626 (2023)
6. Guo, F., Sun, Z., Chen, Y., Ju, L.: Towards the transferable audio adversarial attack via ensemble methods. Cybersecurity **6**(1), 44 (2023)
7. Liu, B., Zhang, J., Zhu, J.: Boosting 3D adversarial attacks with attacking on frequency. IEEE Access **10**, 50974–50984 (2022)
8. Liu, X., et al.: Asvspoof 2021: towards spoofed and deepfake speech detection in the wild. IEEE/ACM Trans. Audio Speech Lang. Process. (2023)
9. Lu, Z., Han, W., Zhang, Y., Cao, L.: Exploring targeted universal adversarial perturbations to end-to-end ASR models. arXiv preprint arXiv:2104.02757 (2021)
10. Madry, A., Makelov, A., Schmidt, L., Tsipras, D., Vladu, A.: Towards deep learning models resistant to adversarial attacks. arXiv preprint arXiv:1706.06083 (2017)
11. Moosavi-Dezfooli, S.M., Fawzi, A., Frossard, P.: Deepfool: a simple and accurate method to fool deep neural networks. In: Proceedings of the IEEE Conference on Computer Vision and Pattern Recognition, pp. 2574–2582 (2016)
12. Nguyen-Vu, L., Doan, T.P., Bui, M., Hong, K., Jung, S.: On the defense of spoofing countermeasures against adversarial attacks. IEEE Access (2023)
13. Su, J., Vargas, D.V., Sakurai, K.: One pixel attack for fooling deep neural networks. IEEE Trans. Evol. Comput. **23**(5), 828–841 (2019)
14. Sun, J., Long, S., Ma, X.: Senattack: adversarial attack method based on perturbation sensitivity and perceptual color distance. Appl. Intell. **53**(23), 28937–28953 (2023)
15. Tak, H., Jung, J.W., Patino, J., Kamble, M., Todisco, M., Evans, N.: End-to-end spectro-temporal graph attention networks for speaker verification anti-spoofing and speech deepfake detection. arXiv preprint arXiv:2107.12710 (2021)
16. Tak, H., Todisco, M., Wang, X., Jung, J.W., Yamagishi, J., Evans, N.: Automatic speaker verification spoofing and deepfake detection using wav2vec 2.0 and data augmentation. arXiv preprint arXiv:2202.12233 (2022)
17. Xie, C., et al.: Improving transferability of adversarial examples with input diversity. In: Proceedings of the IEEE/CVF Conference on Computer Vision and Pattern Recognition, pp. 2730–2739 (2019)

# Network and Application Security

# Security Function for 5G-Advanced and 6G: Malicious UE Detection in Network Slicing

Jaehyoung Park[1], Jihye Kim[2], and Jong-Hyouk Lee[1][(✉)] [iD]

[1] Department of Computer and Information Security and Convergence Engineering for Intelligent Drone, Sejong University, Seoul 05006, Republic of Korea
jaehyoung@pel.sejong.ac.kr, jonghyouk@sejong.ac.kr
[2] Department of Computer and Information Security, Sejong University, Seoul 05006, Republic of Korea
jihye@pel.sejong.ac.kr

**Abstract.** Starting with Software Defined Networking (SDN) and Network Functions Virtualization (NFV) technologies, network slicing is emerging as a critical technology in 5G-Advanced and 6G mobile communications to allocate logical networks end-to-end, meeting diverse service requirements. However, the advent of network slicing introduces new security threats, including inter-slice security, intra-slice security, and lifecycle security of network slicing. While recent research has focused on security orchestration technologies using SDN/NFV for network slicing and AI-based attack detection, there remains a gap in research on security by design within the components of 3GPP 5G systems. Therefore, this paper investigates security by design in the 5G-Advanced and 6G architectures. To address these issues, we propose a malicious User Equipment (UE) detection function to identify attacks within the network-slicing environment. We illustrate the interaction between the detection function and other 3GPP 5G system components for network slicing security with its algorithm for detecting malicious UEs in network slices.

**Keywords:** Network Slicing · Malicious UE · Security by Design

## 1 Introduction

5G-Advanced and 6G are being researched to support various industries such as autonomous vehicles, remote surgery, smart factories, and smart cities, while also supporting diverse applications like the Internet of Everything, Virtual Reality, and Augmented Reality.

For this purpose, next-generation mobile communication technology must support enhanced Mobile BroadBand (eMBB) to provide data speeds of up to 10 Gbps, Ultra-Reliable Low Latency Communication (URLLC) to support end-to-end latency of less than 1ms, and massive Machine Type Communication (mMTC) to support up to 1,000,000 connected devices per $km^2$. To address

J.-H. Lee et al. (Eds.): WISA 2024, LNCS 15499, pp. 111–122, 2025.
https://doi.org/10.1007/978-981-96-1624-4_9

these challenges, network slicing technology, which divides the physical network into multiple logical networks, is gaining attention. This enables the next-generation mobile communication architecture to meet diverse communication requirements, facilitating innovative changes [1].

Software Defined Networking (SDN), which separates the data plane and control plane of the network and provides a programmable architecture, along with Network Functions Virtualization (NFV), which allows traditional hardware-based network functions (e.g., firewalls, load balancers, routers) to run in a virtualized environment, are key technologies supporting network slicing [2].

Mobile communication networks are expected to evolve into more flexible and scalable forms. However, the advent of network slicing introduces new security threats, such as security between slices, security within slices, and network slicing lifecycle security [3].

This paper proposes a Malicious User Equipment (UE) Detection Function (MUDF) to detect security threats in a network-slicing environment, which can embed security technologies within the 5G-Advanced and 6G architectures. The MUDF is a Network Function (NF) designed to detect a malicious UE that negatively impacts a Network Slice (NS). The MUDF can interact with components of the 3rd Generation Partnership Project (3GPP) 5G system architecture. The contribution of this paper is threefold:

- Propose a 3GPP 5G system architecture in where the MUDF is deployed.
- Illustrate the interaction between the MUDF and 3GPP 5G system components for NS security.
- Present an algorithm for detecting malicious UEs in a network-slicing environment.

The structure of this paper is outlined as follows. Section 2 introduces the background knowledge of network slicing and reviews research on network slicing security technologies. Section 3 introduces the MUDF for detecting malicious UEs in the network-slicing environment. Section 4 describes the proposed MUDF. Finally, Sect. 5 concludes this paper.

## 2   Related Work

### 2.1   Network Slicing

The Next Generation Mobile Networks (NGMN) Alliance first introduced network slicing to realize network softwarization [4]. The network slicing multiplexes the physical network into separate virtual networks, allowing heterogeneous services to coexist within the same network architecture by allocating network computing, storage, and communication resources among specialized services. Network slicing leverages network virtualization technologies such as SDN, NFV, cloud and edge computing to achieve virtualization and automation of the infrastructure. This enables scalability, flexibility, customization, and isolation for specific services [5–7].

Standardization organizations such as 3GPP and ITU define the service areas of existing 5G as eMBB, URLLC, and mMTC. Additionally, 3GPP's Release 18 investigates and introduces features to provide services to a variety of devices, including not only smartphones but also eXtended Reality and cloud gaming, vehicle devices, and low-complexity UEs [8]. The network slicing enables efficient resource allocation, service customization, and support for various applications. Therefore, it allows for providing specialized services that meet the requirements of new services.

Such network slicing will continue to evolve and be utilized not only to meet the requirements of 5G services but also for 5G-Advanced and 6G [9]. The network slicing, which is establishing itself as a key feature for 5G-Advanced and 6G, considers not only the core network but also end-to-end for the entire network infrastructure, including the radio access network [10] (Fig. 1).

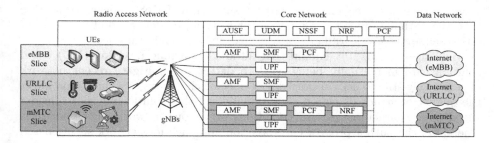

**Fig. 1.** Overview of Network Slicing

## 2.2  Security Technologies for Network Slicing

Network slicing has emerged as a key feature of 5G-Advanced and 6G, enabling efficient resource allocation and service customization. However, as networks become more advanced and services diversify, the security vulnerabilities of network slicing have also increased. The security vulnerabilities arising from the network slicing can lead to issues such as data breaches, network, and service disruptions. Therefore, it is essential to consider network security and privacy protection in the network slicing implementations [4,11].

Martini et al. [12] present an extended MANO framework based on usage control to enhance network slicing and orchestration security by integrating continuous and closed-loop access control mechanisms.

Wijethilaka et al. [3] describe how various security attacks such as Distributed Denial of Service (DDoS) attacks, Man-in-the-Middle attacks, and botnets originate in the device domain and propagate through the network to the network-slicing ecosystem. To address this, the author proposes a security orchestrator that enables responsive and preventive security mechanisms, life-cycle management of security functions, secure communication between slices, and isolation of compromised devices.

Bisht et al. [13] explain the impact of DDoS attacks in a network-slicing environment, such as delayed UE authentication during inter-slice handovers, using metrics like average user waiting time and the number of dropped requests. Additionally, the author provides algorithms for attack detection and localization to secure the network slicing from such DDoS attacks.

Benzaid et al. [14] propose FortisEDoS, a deep transfer learning-based mechanism for detecting Economical Denial of Sustainability (EDoS) attacks, aiming to protect network slicing from the dynamic and increasingly sophisticated nature of DDoS attacks. This mechanism leverages advanced graph and recurrent neural network capabilities to capture spatiotemporal correlations, effectively identifying malicious behavior. Additionally, it utilizes knowledge from previous network slicing to enhance its response to attacks.

Javadpour et al. [15] present the challenge of maximizing the number of NSs while ensuring slice isolation in the network slicing. Slice isolation in the network slicing serves as a mechanism to protect slices from DDoS attacks. To achieve this, the author proposes a reinforcement learning model called slice isolation-based reinforcement learning, which utilizes five optimal graph features.

Bekkouche et al. [16] explain that although Machine Learning (ML) based solutions are increasingly being used to detect and mitigate recent network attacks, they still do not consider device-specific characteristics that could affect the quality of attack detection. Additionally, existing solutions do not consider the diverse characteristics and conditions of various network slicing services. Therefore, the author proposes a protection approach for network slicing based on an adaptive ML-based orchestrator that tailors security measures to the specific characteristics of each service.

Existing research has addressed various security threats that may occur between slices, within slices, and throughout the network slicing lifecycle in the network-slicing environment. To counter these threats, researchers have proposed frameworks based on SDN/NFV technologies and suggested the use of security orchestrators. Additionally, studies have explored authentication technologies for network slicing security and AI-based methods for detecting attacks. However, there is limited research on identifying attackers after detecting attacks in the network-slicing environment, and a lack of studies focused on embedding security into standardized 3GPP 5G system components. To address this gap, this paper proposes security functions for 5G-Advanced and 6G and integrates them into the mobile communication system.

## 3    Malicious UE Detection Function for Network Slicing

This section describes the proposed MUDF, which is designed to detect malicious UE in a network-slicing environment. To this end, the interaction between the network slicing security architecture with the MUDF applied, and the 5G-Advanced components are described. Additionally, the operation of the proposed architecture and malicious UE detection algorithms in the network-slicing environment are presented.

## 3.1  MUDF in the 3GPP 5G System Architecture

3GPP has defined NFs that can operate based on SDN and NFV technologies for the 5G system. They have also developed a service-based architecture that supports interaction between each NF through a Service-based Interface (SBI). Based on this architecture, research is being conducted to enhance existing commercial 5G systems through 5G-Advanced. It is also anticipated that the 3GPP 5G system architecture will be applied in the future 6G mobile communication systems. Therefore, the MUDF for detecting attacks in a network-slicing environment is designed based on the 3GPP 5G system architecture and can be applied as shown in Fig. 2.

The MUDF is designed considering the following elements. First, the MUDF must be able to apply to both 5G-Advanced and 6G architectures. To achieve this requirement, the MUDF must be able to access and interact with the NFs and services defined in the existing 3GPP 5G system. Therefore, it is proposed that the MUDF be registered as a core NF through the Network Repository Function (NRF) to provide SBI-based services within the 3GPP 5G system architecture.

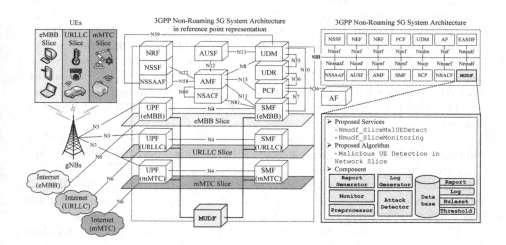

**Fig. 2.** MUDF deployed in the 3GPP 5G System Architecture

Secondly, the MUDF must monitor each NS in the network slicing environment. To achieve this, the MUDF must interact with the User Plane Function (UPF) that handles the User Plane (UP). As a result, the MUDF can monitor the UP packets of Packet Data Unit (PDU) sessions processed by the UPF allocated to each NS.

Thirdly, the MUDF must provide the capability to detect UEs that perform attacks in the network-slicing environment and identify which slice they are located in. To meet this requirement, the MUDF must provide algorithm for detecting security threats within NSs and identifying malicious UEs.

Fourthly, the MUDF must be able to request and retrieve subscription information of UEs from the core network to detect those performing attacks in the network-slicing environment. To achieve this, it is proposed that the MUDF interact with the Unified Data Management (UDM) within the core network, which manages the overall data.

Fifthly, the MUDF must provide a notification function to the core network when attacks and malicious UEs are detected in the network-slicing environment. To achieve this requirement, the MUDF must report the attack detection results to the Session Management Function (SMF) that manages sessions within the core network.

Based on these requirements, the MUDF can interact with existing 3GPP 5G system architecture components without modifying them. Additionally, due to the scalability of the MUDF, it can detect attacks even if an attacker targets a specific slice or multiple slices within the network-slicing environment.

### 3.2   MUDF Procedure for Securing Network Slicing

The main operation process of the MUDF is illustrated in Fig. 3. The MUDF can provide the Nmudf_SliceMalUEDetect service and the Nmudf_SliceMoni toring service within the core network. The SMF and the UPF are able to consume these services through the SBI. The Nmudf_SliceMalUEDetect service is designed to detect attacks and malicious UEs in a network-slicing environment. First, to register the MUDF as an NF in the core network, it sends an *Nnrf_NFMangement_NFRegister* request to the NRF, including the NF type, NF ID, and NF IP. The NRF stores the NF profile of the MUDF and sends a response.

Next, the SMF, which intends to consume the MUDF's services, sends a Nmudf_SliceMalUEDetect request to the MUDF. This request includes the SMF ID, PDU session ID, and Subscription Permanent Identifier (SUPI) list. The SMF manages one or more NSs, and the SUPI is a value that identifies the UE within the core network. The MUDF then sends a response to the SMF for the Nmudf_SliceMalUEDetect request. The SMF requests the UPF, connected via the N4 interface, to subscribe to the Nmudf_SliceMalUEDetect service including the MUDF's IP and ID. Here, the UPF is responsible for processing UP data within the NS, and it subscribes to the MUDF to ensure NS security.

The UPF responds to the SMF regarding the Nmudf_SliceMalUEDetect_ Subscription request and sends an Nmudf_SliceMonitoring request to the MUDF, which includes the PDU session ID and PDU session IP list. The PDU session IP refers to the IP address assigned to a UE when it is registered with the core network and is used to access services specific to each NS.

The MUDF responds to the Nmudf_SliceMonitoring request from the UPF, and the UPF forwards the UP data packets to the MUDF. The UP data packet refers to the packets generated when a UE utilizes services specific to each NS. Subsequently, the MUDF collects the packets forwarded by the UPF to detect malicious UEs that perform attacks within the NS.

When the MUDF detects attacks in one or multiple slices, it must identify which UE in which slice is causing the attacks. Therefore, when attacks are detected in the monitored PDU session, the MUDF identifies the malicious UE causing the attacks. It does this by using the data received from the SMF and UPF during the MUDF subscription process. Additionally, to detect the slice containing the malicious UE, the MUDF sends a *Nudm_SDM_Get* request to the UDM. This request includes the ID of the SMF managing the NS, the subscription data type (e.g., session management subscription data), and the key values for data retrieval (e.g., SUPI, PDU session ID, PDU session IP).

The UDM sends a *Nudr_DM_Query* request to the Unified Data Repository (UDR) to query the subscription data of the UE requested by the MUDF. The *Nudr_DM_Query* request includes the data set ID (e.g., subscription data) and the SUPI, PDU session ID, and PDU session IP received from the MUDF. The UDR responds to the UDM with the UE subscription data, including the Network Slice Selection Assistance Information (NSSAI). The UDM then forwards this information to the MUDF, enabling it to detect which NS the attacks have occurred in.

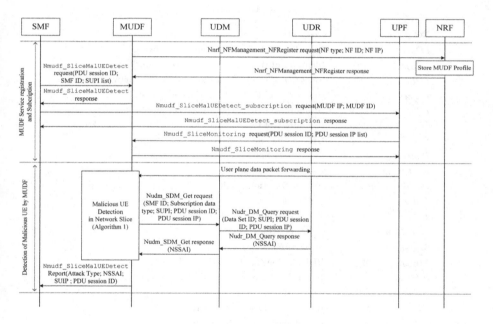

**Fig. 3.** Operation Process of the MUDF

The MUDF parses the received UE subscription data and sends a Nmudf_SliceMalUEDetect report to the SMF. The report includes the NSSAI, SUPI, Attack Type, and PDU session ID. Here, the Attack Type indicates the type of attack detected by the MUDF in the NS (e.g., DoS, data hijacking). The NSSAI is a value used to identify and select NSs. It consists of the Slice/Service Type (SST) and the Slice Differentiator (SD). The Slice/Service Type (SST) standardized by 3GPP represents different types of slices or services based on defined values. In the 3GPP standard, 1 is defined as eMBB, 2 as URLLC, 3 as massive IoT, 4 as vehicle-to-everything, 5 as high-performance machine-type communications, and 6 as high data rate and low latency communications. SUPI and PDU session ID are used to identify the UE that caused the attacks in the slice specified by the NSSAI.

Thus, the MUDF analyzes the UP packets transmitted and received within the NS to detect attacks. It then reports the detected attacks to the SMF, which manages sessions in the NS, thereby ensuring a secure network-slicing environment.

### 3.3 MUDF Operating Algorithm

The malicious UE detection algorithm is presented in Algorithm 1. Table 1 presents the notations used in Algorithm 1.

**Table 1.** Notation

| Notation | Description |
|---|---|
| $ID_{SMF}$ | Identifier of the SMF on the core network |
| $ID_{UDM}$ | Identifier of the UDM on the core network |
| $ID_{PDUsession}$ | Identifier of the PDU session on the core network |
| $IP_{SMF}$ | IP address of the SMF on the core network |
| $IP_{UDM}$ | IP address of the UDM on the core network |
| $IP_{PDUsession}$ | IP address of the PDU session on the core network |
| $SUPI$ | UE identification value in the core network |
| $Packet_{NS}$ | Packet transmitted and received within the NS |
| $Packet_{Pre}$ | Preprocessed packet |
| $Result_{Detection}$ | Attack detection result |
| $Ruleset$ | Ruleset for attack detection |
| $Threshold$ | Threshold for attack detection |
| $AttackType$ | Types of attack detected |
| $Mal_{SUPI}$ | SUPI of malicious UE |
| $Mal_{ID_{PDUsession}}$ | PDU session ID of malicious UE |
| $NSSAI$ | Network Slice Selection Assistance Information |
| $SubDataType$ | Types of subscription data |
| $AttackReport$ | Report of attack detection results |
| $AttackLog$ | Log of attack detection results |
| $SessionStatusLog$ | Log of a session status |
| $Request(x)$ | Request for $x$ |
| $Parsing(x)$ | Parse $x$ |
| $Monitoring(x)$ | Monitor $x$ |
| $Preprocessing(x)$ | Preprocess $x$ |
| $DetectAttack(x,y,z)$ | Detect attacks based on $x, y$ and $z$ |
| $Query(x)$ | Query $x$ |
| $Send(x,y)$ | Send $y$ to $x$ |
| $GenReport(w,x,y,z)$ | Generate a report of attack detection based on $w,x,y,z$ |
| $GenLog(x)$ | Generate a log of attack detection based on $x$ |

Algorithm 1 is used by the MUDF to detect malicious UEs within the NS. The algorithm begins by parsing the data from the `Nmudf_SliceMalUEDetect` request and `Nmudf_SliceMonitoring` request messages, which are sent by the SMF and UPF to utilize the MUDF service. The parsed data includes $ID_{SMF}, SUPI, ID_{PDUsession}$, and $IP_{PDUsession}$. These data are the basic information for the MUDF to monitor network slices and identify malicious UEs.

---

**Algorithm 1.** Malicious UE Detection in a NS

---

1: begin
2: input $Request(\texttt{SliceMalUEDetect}), Request(\texttt{SliceMonitoring})$
3: $ID_{SMF}, SUPI, ID_{PDUsession} \leftarrow Parsing(\texttt{SliceMalUEDetect})$
4: $IP_{PDUsession} \leftarrow Parsing(\texttt{SliceMonitoring})$
5: **while** true **do**
6:     $Packet_{NS} \leftarrow Monitoring(IP_{PDUsession})$
7:     $Packet_{Pre} \leftarrow Preprocessing(Packet_{NS})$
8:     $Result_{Detection} \leftarrow DetectAttack(Packet_{Pre}, Query(Ruleset),$
    $Query(Threshold))$
9:     **if** $Result_{Detection} == True$ **then**
10:         $AttackType, Mal_{SUPI}, Mal_{IP_{PDUsession}} \leftarrow Parsing(Result_{Detection})$
11:         $NSSAI \leftarrow Send(IP_{UDM}, Request(SDM\_Get(ID_{SMF}, SubDataType,$
        $SUPI, ID_{PDUsession}, IP_{PDUsession})))$
12:         $AttackReport \leftarrow GenReport(AttackType, NSSAI, Mal_{SUPI},$
        $Mal_{IP_{PDUsession}})$
13:         $Send(IP_{SMF}, AttackReport)$
14:         $AttackLog \leftarrow GenLog(AttackReport)$
15:         **return** $AttackLog$
16:     **else**
17:         $SessionStatusLog \leftarrow GenLog(ID_{PDUsession})$
18:         **return** $SessionStatusLog$
19:     **end if**
20: **end while**
21: end

---

As shown in Fig. 3, after the MUDF sends the `Nmudf_SliceMonitoring` response to the UPF, and it monitors the interface corresponding to $IP_{PDUsession}$. The monitored $Packet_{NS}$ undergoes a data preprocessing step in the Preprocessor, resulting in $Packet_{Pre}$. The preprocessed data is then fed into the Attack Detector, which begins the attack detection process based on the Ruleset and Threshold present in the database. The Attack Detector can utilize signature-based or AI-based intrusion detection techniques. Additionally, when the algorithm starts, the MUDF monitors the PDU sessions managed by the UPF that has subscribed to its service through the Monitor.

If attacks are detected, a $Result_{Detection}$ is generated. This result is then parsed to obtain $AttackType, Mal_{SUPI}$, and $Mal_{ID_{PDUsession}}$. On line 10, the type of attack and the UE involved in the NS can be identified. However, during this process, since the MUDF does not have NS information, line 11 is executed to obtain the NS information of the UE that caused the attack.

On line 11, the MUDF sends the *Nudm_SDM_Get* request to the UDM to obtain the NSSAI. The MUDF then generates an *AttackReport* using the Report Generator. The generated *AttackReport* includes the values of *AttackType*, $NSSAI$, $Mal_{SUPI}$, and $Mal_{ID_{PDUsession}}$.

The generated *AttackReport* is sent to the SMF, and the MUDF generates an *AttackLog* using the Log Generator. However, if no attack is detected, the Log Generator creates a *SessionStatusLog* and records it in the MUDF. Through this algorithm, when an attack occurs in the NS, the SMF receives the *AttackReport* and can identify the UE causing the attack and the specific NS where the UE is located.

## 4    Discussion

In 5G-Advanced and 6G, the significance of network slicing is expected to increase further to meet the diverse requirements of various services. While ongoing research aims to implement secure NS in next-generation mobile communication systems, there is still a notable lack of studies on applying these within the 3GPP mobile communication system architecture.

Since Release 15, 3GPP has been investigating security in a network-slicing environment. Release 15 focused on NS management security, UE authentication in NS, confidentiality and integrity protection of NS identifiers, and NF authentication for each NS. Release 16 addressed NS-specific authentication and authorization, while Release 17 explored application functions with confidentiality protection for NS identifiers. Most of the technologies researched are transport layer security-based authentication techniques for security management.

However, even authenticated entities can pose security threats due to malicious behavior in the network-slicing environment. Therefore, for 5G-Advanced in Release 18, research must extend beyond authentication technologies to address these security threats.

Detecting attacks is the first crucial step in responding to security threats. From this perspective, this paper presents a method and security architecture for detecting attacks in the network-slicing environment by integrating the MUDF into the 3GPP mobile communication system architecture. The proposed security architecture and operational process incorporating MUDF exemplify security by design within mobile communication systems. Additionally, the interaction between MUDF and 3GPP 5G system components facilitates the integration of currently researched attack detection technologies. For example, signature-based and AI-based attack detection technologies can be integrated as part of MUDF.

This research offers new perspectives on addressing security issues in 5G-Advanced and 6G, contributing to the creation of a more secure next-generation mobile communication environment.

# 5    Conclusion

In this paper, we proposed a new security function to detect malicious UE performing attacks in the 5G-Advanced and 6G network-slicing environment. Our algorithm enhances security by integrating identity verification, behavior analysis, and anomaly detection to identify potential threats, while utilizing the services of NFs defined in the 3GPP mobile communication system. The proposed security function can significantly improve the security and resilience of network slicing. Future work will focus on optimizing the detection algorithms and exploring the integration of additional security functions to further enhance the security of 5G-Advanced and 6G network slicing.

**Acknowledgments.** This work was supported by Institute of Information & communications Technology Planning & Evaluation (IITP) grant funded by the Korea government (MSIT) (No. RS-2021-II210796, Research on Foundational Technologies for 6G Autonomous Security-by-Design to Guarantee Constant Quality of Security).

# References

1. ITU-R M.2160: Framework and overall objectives of the future development of IMT for 2030 and beyond (2023). https://www.itu.int/rec/R-REC-M.2160-0-202311-I/en
2. ETSI GR NFV-EVE 018 V5.1.1.: Network Functions Virtualisation (NFV) Release 5; Evolution and Ecosystem; Report on Multi-tenancy in NFV (2024)
3. Wijethilaka, S., Liyanage, M.: The role of security orchestrator in network slicing for future networks. J. Commun. Netw. **25**(3), 355–369 (2023)
4. Alwis, C.D., Porambage, P., Dev, K., Gadekallu, T.R., Liyanage, M.: A survey on network slicing security: attacks, challenges, solutions and research directions. IEEE Commun. Surv. Tutor. **26**(1), 534–570 (2024)
5. Zharabad, A.J., Yousefi, S., Kunz, T.: Network slicing in virtualized 5G core with VNF sharing. J. Netw. Comput. Appl. **215**, 103631 (2023)
6. Popovski, P., Trillingsgaard, K.F., Simeone, O., Durisi, G.: 5G wireless network slicing for eMBB, URLLC, and mMTC: a communication-theoretic view. IEEE Access **6**, 55765–55779 (2018)
7. Afolabi, I., Taleb, T., Samdanis, K., Ksentini, A., Flinck, H.: Network slicing and softwarization: a survey on principles, enabling technologies, and solutions. IEEE Commun. Surv. Tutor. **20**(3), 2429–2453 (2018)
8. Lin, X.: An Overview of 5G Advanced Evolution in 3GPP Release 18. IEEE Commun. Stan. Mag. **6**(3), 77–83 (2022)
9. Ebrahimi, S., Bouali, F., Haas, O.C.L.: Resource management from single-domain 5G to end-to-end 6G network slicing: a survey. IEEE Commun. Surv. Tutor. (2024)
10. Odida, M.: Network Slicing in Software Defined Networking for 5G (2024)
11. Singh, P.S., Singh, M.P., Hegde, S., Gupta, M.: Security in 5G network slices: concerns and opportunities. IEEE Access **12**, 52727–52743 (2024)
12. Martini, B., et al.: Pushing forward security in network slicing by leveraging continuous usage control. IEEE Commun. Mag. **58**(7), 65–71 (2020)
13. Bisht, H., Patra, M., Kumar, S.: Detection and localization of DDoS attack during inter-slice handover in 5G network slicing. In: 2023 IEEE 20th Consumer Communications & Networking Conference (CCNC), pp. 798–803 (2023)

14. Benzaïd, C., Taleb, T., Sami, A., Hireche, O.: A deep transfer learning-powered ED-oS detection mechanism for 5G and beyond network slicing. In: GLOBECOM 2023 - 2023 IEEE Global Communications Conference, pp. 4747–4753 (2023)
15. Javadpour, A., Ja'fari, F., Taleb, T., Benzaïd, C.: Reinforcement learning-based slice isolation against DDoS attacks in beyond 5G networks. IEEE Trans. Netw. Serv. Manage. **20**(3), 3930–3946 (2023)
16. Bekkouche, R., Omar, M., Langar, R.: Securing 5G network slices with adaptive machine learning models as-a-service: a novel approach. In: GLOBECOM 2023 - 2023 IEEE Global Communications Conference, pp. 4754–4759 (2023)

# Simple Perturbations Subvert Ethereum Phishing Transactions Detection: An Empirical Analysis

Ahod Alghureid[(✉)] and David Mohaisen

University of Central Florida, Orlando, USA
ah104940@ucf.edu

**Abstract.** This paper explores the vulnerability of machine learning models, specifically Random Forest, Decision Tree, and K-Nearest Neighbors, to very simple single-feature adversarial attacks in the context of Ethereum fraudulent transaction detection. Through comprehensive experimentation, we investigate the impact of various adversarial attack strategies on model performance metrics, such as accuracy, precision, recall, and F1-score. Our findings, highlighting how prone those techniques are to simple attacks, are alarming, and the inconsistency in the attacks' effect on different algorithms promises ways for attack mitigation. We examine the effectiveness of different mitigation strategies, including adversarial training and enhanced feature selection, in enhancing model robustness.

## 1 Introduction

The proliferation of machine learning models in various domains has brought significant advancements in decision-making processes. However, concerns regarding the robustness and security of these models have also emerged alongside these advancements. Adversarial attacks, wherein small, carefully crafted perturbations are introduced into the input data to cause misclassification, seriously threaten the reliability of machine learning systems. Understanding the susceptibility of these models to adversarial attacks is crucial for developing robust and trustworthy AI systems.

The increasing prevalence of machine learning in cybersecurity applications has significantly improved the detection and prevention of various cyber threats. Among these threats, fraudulent activities such as phishing, scamming, and fake initial coin offerings (ICOs) pose substantial financial and personal data security risks. Machine learning models, particularly classification algorithms, have been deployed to identify and mitigate these threats with notable success. However, studies have raised concerns about the robustness and reliability of these models [1–5,8,18]. The attacks presented in the literature (see Sect. 2) are effective yet sophisticated.

This study investigates the impact of extremely simple adversarial attacks on different machine learning models used in fraudulent transaction detection,

J.-H. Lee et al. (Eds.): WISA 2024, LNCS 15499, pp. 123–137, 2025.
https://doi.org/10.1007/978-981-96-1624-4_10

specifically focusing on Random Forest (RF), Decision Tree (DT), and K-Nearest Neighbors (KNN) classifiers. By employing the Fast Gradient Sign Method, a widely recognized adversarial attack technique, we assess the performance degradation of these models when subjected to simple, realistic adversarially crafted inputs [35]. The primary objective is to understand how these models are susceptible to adversarial manipulation and explore potential mitigation strategies to enhance their robustness.

Previous research has highlighted the vulnerability of ML models to adversarial attacks [28]. This study contributes to the existing body of knowledge by providing a detailed empirical analysis of the effects of simple adversarial attacks on fraud detection models and proposing practical approaches to mitigate these effects. Our findings reveal inconsistency across algorithms for their tolerance of simple manipulation, underscoring the importance of selecting appropriate models and implementing robust defense mechanisms tailored to specific applications.

## 2   Literature Review

Transaction fraud is common in cryptocurrency and calls for fraud detection. Agarwal *et al.* [6] analyzed malicious Ethereum transactions, including phishing and scams, to enhance threat detection capabilities. Rabieinejad *et al.* [29] employed Ethereum transaction data to develop models for identifying cyber threats. Sanjalawe *et al.* [30] used the Benchmark Labeled Transactions Ethereum dataset to detect abnormal transactions related to illicit activities. Zola *et al.* [39] analyzed WalletExplorer data to classify Bitcoin addresses and reduce anonymity, aiding in identifying entities involved in illegal activities. Yang *et al.* [37] focused on applying transaction datasets in the Bitcoin network to detect spam transaction attacks. Mozo *et al.* [24] applied transaction datasets to detect cryptomining attacks within the Monero.

Recent research demonstrated the vulnerability of deep convolutional neural networks (CNNs) to adversarial attacks [25]. In [12], Cartella et al. adapted algorithms to imbalanced tabular data for fraud detection, achieving a perfect attack success rate. Bhagoji *et al.* [10] introduced a Gradient Estimation blackbox attacks to a target model's class probabilities, achieving near-perfect success rates for both targeted and untargeted attacks on deep neural networks (DNNs).

Generative Adversarial Networks (GANs) generate adversarial examples (AEs) and handle data perturbations in cryptocurrency transaction datasets. Table 1 summarizes these methods and highlights key findings across different domains, underscoring the diverse methods employed to address security challenges in cryptocurrency networks. For instance, Fidalgo *et al.* [20] utilized GANs for synthetic data generation and augmentation to tackle class imbalance in Bitcoin. Agarwal *et al.* [6] employed Conditional GANs (CTGAN) to create realistic adversarial data for Ethereum transactions.

Rabieinejad *et al.* [29] used Conditional GANs (CTGAN) and Wasserstein GANs (WGAN) to generate synthetic samples for augmenting Ethereum trans-

**Table 1.** Summary of some of the prior work.

| Paper Title | Year | Adversarial Techniques | Applications in Cryptocurrency |
|---|---|---|---|
| Li et al. [22] | 2018 | GANs | Anomaly detection, Secure Water Treatment |
| Qingyu et al. [19] | 2019 | IFCM, AIS, R3 | Fraud detection, TaoBao |
| Ba et al. [9] | 2019 | GANs | Credit card fraud, 31-feature dataset |
| Ngo et al. [26] | 2019 | GANs | Anomaly detection, MNIST, CIFAR10 |
| Zola et al. [38] | 2020 | GANs, data augmentation | Bitcoin, WalletExplorer (categorized addresses) |
| Yang et al. [37] | 2020 | WGAN-div, GRU-based detection | Bitcoin, custom spam transaction dataset |
| Shu et al. [31] | 2020 | GANs | Intrusion detection, network traffic |
| Mozo et al. [24] | 2021 | WGANs, synthetic traffic | Monero, custom cryptomining dataset |
| Fursov et al. [17] | 2021 | Black-box attacks | Transaction records |
| Agarwal et al. [6] | 2022 | CTGAN, K-Means Clustering | Ethereum, Etherscan dataset (2,946 malicious accounts) |
| Fidalgo et al. [20] | 2022 | GANs, data augmentation | Bitcoin, Elliptic dataset (200K+ transactions) |
| Zola et al. [39] | 2022 | Various GANs, adversarial learning | Bitcoin, WalletExplorer (16M+ addresses) |
| Rabieinejad et al. [29] | 2023 | CTGAN, WGAN | Ethereum, 57K normal, 14K abnormal transactions |
| Sanjalawe et al. [30] | 2023 | GANs, feature extraction | Ethereum, labeled transactions (normal, abnormal) |

action datasets, enhancing detection capabilities against cyber threats. Sanjalawe et al. [30] used Semi-Supervised GANs and feature extraction techniques to perturb features in Ethereum transaction datasets. Zola et al. [38] focused on data augmentation using various GAN configurations to generate additional data for underrepresented classes in Bitcoin transactions. Zola et al. [39] investigated different GAN architectures to generate synthetic Bitcoin address data to mitigate class imbalance and improve entity classification.

Yang et al. [37] used a Wasserstein Generative Adversarial Network with divergence (WGAN-div) to generate adversarial examples for spam transaction detection in the Bitcoin network. Mozo et al. [24] utilized WGANs to create synthetic network traffic data to detect cryptomining attacks in the Monero (XMR) network.

**Research Gap.** Despite advancements in machine learning and blockchain technology, critical gaps persist in effectively understanding mitigating adversarial attacks and emerging security threats within cryptocurrency networks. AEs grounded in the context of application are underexplored. AEs in the feature space that leverage targeted and untargeted attacks, transaction fraud, smart contract exploits, etc., are lacking. This underscores the imperative for further analysis. This study aims to bridge this gap by investigating the robustness of machine learning-based phishing detection algorithms against *simple manipulations*, comparing the effectiveness of various algorithms in resisting such attacks, and exploring mitigation strategies to enhance their resilience. Our approach involves evaluating the algorithms' susceptibility to subtle feature manipulations and conducting a comparative analysis to identify the most robust models.

# 3   Research Questions

This research explores the robustness, comparative performance, and mitigation strategies of machine learning-based phishing detection algorithms for Ethereum

126     A. Alghureid and D. Mohaisen

transactions in adversarial manipulations. The following questions highlight the core issues and the necessity to address them in light of existing literature.

**RQ1. Are machine learning-based phishing detection algorithms for Ethereum robust against simple manipulations of individual features?** This question is motivated by the vulnerability of machine learning (ML) models to adversarial attacks, as demonstrated in several studies [10,12,13,25,32]. In these studies, slight modifications in input data significantly altered the classification outcome, highlighting how even minor changes in key features like transaction amounts or timestamps can lead to incorrect classifications. Such manipulations can make it easier for adversaries to deceive models, underscoring the need to evaluate the robustness of ML models used in Ethereum phishing detection to ensure they remain effective and reliable despite such attacks.

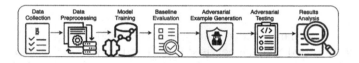

**Fig. 1.** Pipeline in Ethereum transactions and adversarial testing.

**RQ2. How do different machine learning algorithms compare robustness against adversarial manipulations in Ethereum phishing detection?** This question stems from the observation that various machine learning algorithms, while effective in detecting phishing activities, exhibit differing levels of resilience against adversarial attacks [6,15,20,27,29,33]. The robustness of these algorithms can vary significantly under adversarial conditions, which can be seen in studies where some algorithms perform better than others when subjected to adversarial manipulations designed to evade detection [16,22,34]. A comparative analysis of these algorithms is essential to identify those that provide the best defense against such threats, ensuring the highest possible security in Ethereum transaction classification.

**RQ3. How can the impact of manipulations be mitigated in machine learning-based Ethereum phishing detection?** This question arises from the need to develop robust defensive strategies against adversarial attacks, as highlighted in recent literature [11,14,24,36,37]. Effective mitigation strategies could include enhancing feature selection processes, employing advanced data augmentation techniques, or implementing adversarial training methods [23,29,38]. Understanding and developing these techniques are crucial for improving the security and reliability of ML-based phishing detection systems in Ethereum transactions, thereby reducing the risk posed by adversaries manipulating transaction data and enhancing overall network security.

# 4   Methodology

Our pipeline is shown in Fig. 1 and some of its key aspects are reviewed below.

## 4.1   Data Preparation

**Dataset Description.** For our analysis, we employed two datasets. The first dataset, as detailed by Kabla *et al.* [21], focuses on binary classification, distinguishing between phishing and benign transactions. This dataset encompasses features such as TxHash, a unique identifier for each transaction; BlockHeight, which specifies the height of the block in which the transaction was recorded; and TimeStamp, indicating the exact time the transaction was confirmed and added to the blockchain. It also includes the From and To addresses, representing the Ethereum addresses of the sender and receiver, respectively. The Value feature denotes the amount of Ether transferred in the transaction, while ContractAddress indicates the Ethereum address of the smart contract involved, if applicable. Additionally, the Input field contains any extra data provided with the transaction. The dataset labels transactions as either phishing (1) or benign (0) under the Class feature. Dataset 1 includes 23,472 transactions, of which 15,989 are benign and 7,483 are phishing.

The second dataset, as described by Al-Emari *et al.* [7], is intended for multiclass classification, categorizing transactions into Phishing, Scam, Fake ICO, or Benign. This dataset features the hash, a unique identifier for each transaction, and nonce, a counter ensuring each transaction is processed only once. The transaction_index indicates the transaction's position within the block, while from_address and to_address denote the blockchain addresses of the sender and receiver, respectively. The value field specifies the amount of cryptocurrency transferred. The dataset also includes gas, representing the gas limit provided for the transaction, and gas_price, indicating the price per gas unit. The input field contains additional data attached to the transaction. Moreover, receipt_cumulative_gas_used provides the total gas used by all transactions up to and including the current one within the block, and receipt_gas_used specifies the gas consumed by this particular transaction. The block_timestamp and block_number detail the time and number of the block that includes the transaction, while block_hash serves as the block's unique identifier. Lastly, the from_scam and to_scam fields indicate whether the sender's and receiver's addresses are associated with scams (0 for no, 1 for yes). The dataset also includes categorical data, from_category and to_category, which classify the nature of the participants, such as Phishing, Scamming, or Fake ICO. In this dataset, Benign had 57,000 transactions (79.28%), Scamming had 11,143 transactions (15.51%), Phishing had 3,106 transactions (4.32%), and Fake ICO had only 1 transaction. Dataset 2 includes 71,250 transactions, with 80-20 training-testing splits.

## 4.2   Experimental Procedures

We utilized the two datasets outlined earlier to examine how simple AEs impact the classification accuracy of three classifiers: RF, DT, and KNN.

**Minimal Manipulations.** AEs were crafted by manipulating specific features. For the first dataset, we manipulated for feature. ① *Timestamp Manipulation (TimeStamp)*: We use predefined intervals to simulate future occurrences, testing the models' robustness to shifts against hypothetical scenarios of temporal manipulation. ② *Value Manipulation (Value)*: Transaction values were altered using two strategies: uniformly by adding a fixed percentage to each transaction's value or proportionally by introducing a random percentage change relative to each transaction's original value. ③ *Receiver Address Manipulation (To)*: The receiver's address was randomly changed to different addresses within the dataset to simulate phishing transactions directed to alternative destinations. ④ *Sender Address Manipulation (From)*: The sender's address was altered to different sender addresses to simulate phishing transactions originating from various sources.

We implemented a two-pronged approach, including both targeted and untargeted adversarial attacks on a second dataset [7]. AEs were generated by focusing on a broader array of critical transaction features, allowing us to simulate realistic attack scenarios and identify potential vulnerabilities more precisely.

**Untargeted Attacks.** The study of untargeted attacks involved generating AEs by applying broad, random perturbations across the entire feature space. Initially, AEs were generated using all features to evaluate the model's capacity to withstand attacks.

Individual features were then targeted to challenge the model more effectively. Modifying the *from_address* and *to_address* fields introduced new, unseen addresses to assess the model's ability to handle transaction origin and destination changes. Altering *value, gas* and *gas_price* simulated economic fluctuations, providing insights into the model's sensitivity to variations in transaction costs. Manipulating *block_timestamp* and *block_number* mimicked transaction timing and sequence changes to understand the model's response to variations in transaction order. Altering *input, receipt_cumulative_gas_used*, and *receipt_gas_used* help explore the impact of changes in content.

**Targeted Attacks.** We conducted targeted adversarial attacks focusing on three scenarios: benign, phishing, and scamming. We employed two methods for generating these targeted attacks: rule-based and gradient-based (using the Fast Gradient Sign Method).

*Rule-Based Modifications.* This approach applies straightforward, rule-based modifications to critical features like transaction value and timestamps, simulating realistic variations that can alter the classification outcomes.

– **Benign Targeted Attack:** This scenario aimed to assess the model's ability to maintain a benign classification despite manipulations, simulating tactics used to camouflage malicious activities. We created artificial benign

transactions by minorly adjusting features such as transaction value and block_timestamp.
- **Phishing Targeted Attack:** The focus was on modifying phishing-labeled transactions to evade detection by misclassifying them as benign. This involved altering attributes such as from_address, to_address, and value, simulating an adversary's attempt to bypass security measures.
- **Scamming Targeted Attack:** In this scenario, scam-labeled transactions were manipulated to explore whether they could be misclassified as benign or other types. Adjustments to features like gas and gas_price were made to examine the model against efforts to obscure scam activities through changes in transaction costs.

*FGSM.* FGSM applied small, strategically calculated changes to subtly influence the model's predictions while maintaining realistic feature values. Unlike the rule-based method, FGSM retained the existing distribution from the dataset, focusing on fine-tuning modifications based on the gradients to maximize the attack's effectiveness.

- **FGSM Details:** FGSM calculates perturbations that align with the gradient direction of the loss function. The perturbations were applied using the formula:

$$x' = x + \epsilon \cdot \text{sign}(\nabla_x J(\theta, x, y)),$$

where $x$ is the original feature, $x'$ is the perturbed feature (AE), $\epsilon$ is a small scalar controlling the perturbation's magnitude, $\nabla_x$ represents the gradient of the loss function $J$ for $x$, and $J(\theta, x, y)$ is the loss function dependent on the model parameters $\theta$, input $x$, and true label $y$. The term $\text{sign}(\nabla_x J(\theta, x, y))$ provides the direction in which to perturb the feature vector to maximize the loss function.
- **Features:** FGSM perturbations were applied to transaction value, gas, gas_price, and block_timestamp. These features are critical in determining the nature of the transaction, and even small changes may affect the classification results.

## 5   Results and Analysis

### 5.1   Preliminary Results

We evaluate how different perturbations on the first dataset affect the accuracy and resilience of RF, DT, and KNN models. We examine how uniform and proportional value manipulations and address change impact model performance.

**Timestamp Manipulations.** We evaluate the effects of various timestamp modifications on classifier accuracy, including shifts of +24 h, +1 h, +30 min, +15 min, and +5 min. The RF classifier showed the highest resilience with only minor reductions in accuracy. For example, a one-day timestamp shift resulted in a decrease in accuracy from 98.82% to 95%, while a one-hour change led to an accuracy of 97.31%. In contrast, the DT model experienced a more pronounced decline, with accuracy dropping from 98.35% to 94.46% with a one-day shift. The KNN classifier was most affected by these temporal manipulations, with accuracy falling from 94.45% to 83.42% for a one-day change. These findings highlight the superior robustness of the RF model in handling timestamp alterations, positioning it as a preferable option for phishing detection in environments with variable timestamps (Table 2).

**Value Manipulations.** The uniform value manipulations caused significant declines. RF's accuracy dropped to 69%, and DT's fell to 68%, with substantial reductions in precision and recall for phishing transactions. Notably, the recall for phishing in DT decreased to 0.01% under uniform manipulation. Proportional manipulations had minimal impact, with accuracy and other metrics remaining close to their original values. KNN maintained relatively stable performance across both manipulation types, indicating robustness against such value changes (Table 3).

**Address Manipulations.** The robustness of the classifiers was tested against AEs of the `From` and `To` address features, involving changes in 5,000, 10,000, and 23,472 instances. For the RF model, accuracy decreased to 87% when the `From` address was manipulated and to 84% for the `To` address. Precision and recall for phishing transactions also declined significantly, with F1-scores dropping notably. The DT model showed a moderate reduction in accuracy, dropping to 92% for `From` and 93% for `To` manipulations, and a noticeable decrease in recall for phishing. KNN was the most sensitive to these manipulations, with accuracy falling to 85% for `From` and 93% for `To`, and significant drops in precision and recall for phishing transactions (Tables 4 and 5).

Next, our analysis will focus on the second dataset from Al-Emari et al. [7], which provides a comprehensive and relevant context for multi-class classification tasks.

## 5.2   Results of Targeted Attacks

**Rule-Based Modifications.** We initially focus on rule-based AEs for specific classes.

① *Benign Class.* The RF and DT models initially demonstrated near-perfect accuracy in classifying benign transactions on the original test set. Under adversarial conditions, the accuracies for benign classifications declined markedly, with RF and DT models dropping to 84.39% and 84.65%. This represents a reduction exceeding 15%. In contrast, the KNN model sustained a higher adversarial accuracy of 90.25%.

② *Phishing Class.* The initial phishing accuracies for RF and DT were 96.34% and 96.98%, respectively. However, these values **plummeted to 1.31% and 1.18% under adversarial conditions**, reflecting a reduction of over 95%.

**Table 2.** RF, DT, and KNN performance under timestamp manipulations. Accuracy, precision, recall, F1 score, and counts. B stands for benign and Ph. for phishing.

| Increment | Model | Dataset | Acc | Precision | | Recall | | F1 | | Count | |
|---|---|---|---|---|---|---|---|---|---|---|---|
| | | | | B | Ph | B | Ph | B | Ph | #B | #Ph |
| Original | RF | Baseline | 0.9882 | 1 | 0.96 | 0.98 | 1 | 0.99 | 0.98 | 15989 | 7483 |
| | DT | Baseline | 0.9835 | 1 | 0.95 | 0.98 | 1 | 0.99 | 0.97 | 15989 | 7483 |
| | KNN | Baseline | 0.9445 | 1 | 0.85 | 0.92 | 1 | 0.96 | 0.92 | 15989 | 7483 |
| +24 h | RF | Adversarial | 0.95 | 0.94 | 0.98 | 0.99 | 0.86 | 0.96 | 0.92 | 15498 | 7974 |
| | DT | Adversarial | 0.9446 | 0.95 | 0.94 | 0.97 | 0.88 | 0.96 | 0.91 | 15601 | 7871 |
| | KNN | Adversarial | 0.8342 | 0.84 | 0.82 | 0.94 | 0.62 | 0.88 | 0.7 | 14376 | 9096 |
| +1 h | RF | Adversarial | 0.9731 | 0.97 | 0.97 | 0.99 | 0.94 | 0.98 | 0.96 | 15498 | 7974 |
| | DT | Adversarial | 0.9626 | 0.97 | 0.95 | 0.98 | 0.94 | 0.97 | 0.94 | 15601 | 7871 |
| | KNN | Adversarial | 0.8997 | 0.93 | 0.84 | 0.93 | 0.84 | 0.93 | 0.84 | 14376 | 9096 |
| +30 min | RF | Adversarial | 0.9776 | 0.98 | 0.97 | 0.99 | 0.96 | 0.98 | 0.96 | 15498 | 7974 |
| | DT | Adversarial | 0.9649 | 0.97 | 0.95 | 0.98 | 0.94 | 0.97 | 0.94 | 15601 | 7871 |
| | KNN | Adversarial | 0.916 | 0.95 | 0.85 | 0.92 | 0.9 | 0.94 | 0.87 | 14376 | 9096 |
| +15 min | RF | Adversarial | 0.9817 | 0.99 | 0.97 | 0.99 | 0.97 | 0.99 | 0.97 | 15498 | 7974 |
| | DT | Adversarial | 0.9672 | 0.98 | 0.95 | 0.98 | 0.95 | 0.98 | 0.95 | 15601 | 7871 |
| | KNN | Adversarial | 0.9179 | 0.95 | 0.85 | 0.93 | 0.9 | 0.94 | 0.87 | 14376 | 9096 |
| +5 min | RF | Adversarial | 0.9793 | 0.99 | 0.97 | 0.98 | 0.97 | 0.98 | 0.97 | 15498 | 7974 |
| | DT | Adversarial | 0.9734 | 0.98 | 0.95 | 0.98 | 0.97 | 0.98 | 0.96 | 15601 | 7871 |
| | KNN | Adversarial | 0.9344 | 0.98 | 0.85 | 0.92 | 0.96 | 0.95 | 0.9 | 14376 | 9096 |

**Table 3.** Performance evaluation of RF, DT, and KNN models subjected to 1% uniform and proportional value manipulation strategies. Metrics are as in Table 2.

| Model | Strategy | Acc | Precision | | Recall | | F1 | | Count | |
|---|---|---|---|---|---|---|---|---|---|---|
| | | | B | Ph | B | Ph | B | Ph | #B | #Ph |
| RF | Original | 0.99 | 0.98 | 1 | 1 | 0.99 | 0.99 | 0.99 | 15803 | 7669 |
| | Uniform | 0.69 | 0.96 | 0.68 | 0.02 | 1 | 0.03 | 0.81 | 23353 | 119 |
| | Proportional | 0.99 | 0.98 | 1 | 1 | 0.99 | 0.99 | 0.99 | 15813 | 7659 |
| DT | Original | 0.98 | 0.95 | 1 | 1 | 0.98 | 0.97 | 0.99 | 15601 | 7871 |
| | Uniform | 0.69 | 0.75 | 0.68 | 0.02 | 1 | 0.03 | 0.81 | 23294 | 178 |
| | Proportional | 0.98 | 0.95 | 1 | 1 | 0.98 | 0.97 | 0.99 | 15619 | 7853 |
| KNN | Original | 0.96 | 0.89 | 0.99 | 0.98 | 0.94 | 0.93 | 0.97 | 15192 | 8280 |
| | Uniform | 0.96 | 0.89 | 0.99 | 0.98 | 0.94 | 0.93 | 0.97 | 15193 | 8279 |
| | Proportional | 0.96 | 0.89 | 0.99 | 0.98 | 0.94 | 0.93 | 0.97 | 15192 | 8280 |

The KNN model, which began with a lower baseline accuracy of 41.49%, saw a decrease to 2.15%.

③ *Scamming Class.* Initially, the RF and DT models exhibited high accuracies of 99.5% and 98.68%. Adversarial attacks reduced these accuracies to 14.27% and 14.16%, representing a reduction of over 85%. The KNN model, with an initial accuracy of 67.06%, experienced a drop to 7.6%.

## 5.3    Gradient-Based Approach Using FGSM

① *Benign Class.* The overall accuracy of the RF model decreased from 99.75% to 94.62%, with a significant deterioration in phishing detection metrics. Despite hat, the model maintained a high benign accuracy of 99.95%. Conversely, the DT model's overall accuracy plummeted from 99.64% to 9.54%, with benign recall dropping to 0.02, indicating extreme vulnerability. The KNN model preserved a perfect benign accuracy of 100% even under attack, but its overall accuracy fell from 90.15% to 80.22%, reflecting a failure to detect phishing and scamming categories effectively.

② *Phishing Class.* The phishing detection accuracy of the RF model decreased from 96.34% to 47.69%, with a significant drop in the F1-score. The DT model's overall accuracy declined to 10.22%, with phishing recall reducing to 0.75%, underscoring a pronounced susceptibility to adversarial attacks. The KNN model's phishing detection performance collapsed entirely, with metrics falling to zero, indicating a complete failure to detect phishing transactions under adversarial conditions.

**Table 4.** Performance evaluation of RF, DT, and KNN models under manipulations of the `From` feature in Ethereum transaction datasets. Metrics are as in Table 2.

| Model | Strategy | Acc | Precision | | Recall | | F1 | | Count | |
|---|---|---|---|---|---|---|---|---|---|---|
| | | | B | Ph | B | Ph | B | Ph | #B | #Ph |
| RF | Original Strategy | 0.99 | 1 | 0.96 | 0.98 | 1 | 0.99 | 0.98 | 15708 | 7764 |
| | 5000 Changes | 0.96 | 0.96 | 0.97 | 0.98 | 0.91 | 0.97 | 0.94 | 16386 | 7086 |
| | 10000 Changes | 0.94 | 0.93 | 0.97 | 0.99 | 0.83 | 0.96 | 0.89 | 17027 | 6445 |
| | 23472 Changes | 0.87 | 0.84 | 0.97 | 0.99 | 0.6 | 0.91 | 0.74 | 18877 | 4595 |
| DT | Original Strategy | 0.98 | 1 | 0.95 | 0.98 | 1 | 0.99 | 0.97 | 15601 | 7871 |
| | 5000 Changes | 0.97 | 0.98 | 0.95 | 0.98 | 0.96 | 0.98 | 0.96 | 15935 | 7537 |
| | 10000 Changes | 0.96 | 0.96 | 0.95 | 0.98 | 0.91 | 0.97 | 0.93 | 16272 | 7200 |
| | 23472 Changes | 0.92 | 0.91 | 0.94 | 0.98 | 0.79 | 0.94 | 0.86 | 17207 | 6265 |
| KNN | Original Strategy | 0.94 | 1 | 0.85 | 0.92 | 1 | 0.96 | 0.92 | 14706 | 8766 |
| | 5000 Changes | 0.93 | 0.97 | 0.85 | 0.92 | 0.93 | 0.94 | 0.89 | 15209 | 8263 |
| | 10000 Changes | 0.91 | 0.94 | 0.84 | 0.92 | 0.87 | 0.93 | 0.85 | 15767 | 7705 |
| | 23472 Changes | 0.85 | 0.86 | 0.81 | 0.93 | 0.67 | 0.89 | 0.74 | 17288 | 6184 |

**Table 5.** Performance evaluation of RF, DT, and KNN models under manipulations of the To feature in Ethereum transaction datasets. Metrics are as in Table 2.

| Model | Strategy | Acc | Precision | | Recall | | F1 | | Count | |
|-------|----------|-----|-----------|------|--------|------|------|------|-------|------|
| | | | B | Ph | B | Ph | B | Ph | #B | #Ph |
| RF | Original Strategy | 0.99 | 1 | 0.96 | 0.98 | 1 | 0.99 | 0.98 | 15708 | 7764 |
| | 5000 | 0.96 | 0.95 | 0.97 | 0.98 | 0.89 | 0.97 | 0.93 | 16558 | 6914 |
| | 10000 | 0.92 | 0.91 | 0.97 | 0.99 | 0.79 | 0.95 | 0.87 | 17377 | 6095 |
| | 23472 | 0.84 | 0.81 | 0.97 | 0.99 | 0.51 | 0.89 | 0.67 | 19537 | 3935 |
| DT | Original Strategy | 0.98 | 1 | 0.95 | 0.98 | 1 | 0.99 | 0.97 | 15601 | 7871 |
| | 5000 | 0.97 | 0.98 | 0.95 | 0.98 | 0.96 | 0.98 | 0.96 | 15884 | 7588 |
| | 10000 | 0.96 | 0.97 | 0.95 | 0.98 | 0.93 | 0.97 | 0.94 | 16142 | 7330 |
| | 23472 | 0.93 | 0.92 | 0.94 | 0.98 | 0.83 | 0.95 | 0.88 | 16872 | 6600 |
| KNN | Original Strategy | 0.94 | 1 | 0.85 | 0.92 | 1 | 0.96 | 0.92 | 14706 | 8766 |
| | 5000 | 0.94 | 0.99 | 0.85 | 0.92 | 0.98 | 0.95 | 0.91 | 14849 | 8623 |
| | 10000 | 0.94 | 0.98 | 0.85 | 0.92 | 0.97 | 0.95 | 0.91 | 14988 | 8484 |
| | 23472 | 0.93 | 0.96 | 0.85 | 0.93 | 0.93 | 0.94 | 0.89 | 15351 | 8121 |

③ *Scamming Class.* The overall accuracy of the RF model dropped from 99.75% to 81.75%, with scamming accuracy decreasing from 99.50% to 76.70%. The DT's overall accuracy fell to 9.71%, with scamming recall drastically reducing to 0.30. The KNN model's scamming detection metrics also dropped to zero.

## 5.4   Results of Untargeted Attacks

① *All Features.* The RF model's accuracy decreased to 95.81%, DT's to 91.16%, with phishing detection severely impaired, and KNN maintained its baseline accuracy.

② *Address Features.* AEs focusing on the *from_address* and *to_address* features resulted in a decline in overall accuracy to 80.22% for all models. None of the models detected phishing or scamming, indicating a high sensitivity to address manipulations.

③ *Financial Features.* AEs targeting financial features (*value, gas, gas_price*) led to reduced RF's accuracy to 79.96%. The DT's accuracy dropped to 79.42%. The KNN model's accuracy slightly decreased to 90.02%.

④ *Using Temporal Features.* Adversarial manipulations of temporal features (*block_timestamp, block_number*) showed the RF model's accuracy fell from 99.02% to 80.25%, with phishing detection metrics nearly nullified. The DT's accuracy similarly declined to 80.25%. The KNN model's accuracy also dropped to 80.26%.

**Takeaway.** These results underscore the need for robust defensive mechanisms against AEs. The significant declines in performance metrics under simple conditions highlight the necessity for a more reliable classification of transactions.

# 6   Discussion

**Feature Selection for Optimal Classification.** The analysis of transaction classification in this study highlights the significant role of feature selection in the robustness and accuracy of ML models. Among the features tested, **timestamp** and **value** emerged as critical classifier performance determinants. Timestamp manipulations demonstrated substantial impacts across models, with RF showing notable resilience compared to DT and K-KNN. The accuracy metrics indicate that temporal features, such as transaction time and date, are crucial for distinguishing legitimate from fraudulent transactions due to their inherent variability and relevance to transactional behaviors.

In contrast, value manipulations, including uniform and proportional changes, significantly affected model performance, particularly under uniform conditions. RF and DT models experienced considerable accuracy drops with uniform value changes, while KNN maintained relative stability. These findings suggest that while **transaction value** is a key feature for classification, it is also highly susceptible to perturbations.

**Most Resistant Features to Adversarial Attacks.** The study's results indicate that **address features**, specifically the From and To addresses, exhibit higher resistance to adversarial attacks compared to other feature types. Manipulations of these features resulted in moderate accuracy reductions for DT and RF models but a more pronounced impact on KNN. These features likely encode the relationship patterns between transaction entities, making them inherently resistant to straightforward changes.

The analysis showed that despite their critical contribution to accuracy, temporal features were also relatively resistant to manipulations. Timestamp shifts caused accuracy declines, but the extent was less severe than value manipulations. This indicates that while temporal features are crucial for classification, they are robust against adversarial attacks due to timestamp data's complexity and non-repetitive nature.

**Best Combinations.** For resilient classification, a combination of **temporal and address features** has proven effective. The synergy between these features offers a dual layer of robustness; temporal features provide a dynamic aspect that captures the temporal distribution and patterns of transactions, while address features contribute a stable relational component less prone to adversarial interference.

Combining temporal features with **financial features**, such as transaction value and gas price, also enhances robustness. The results show that despite the susceptibility of financial features to uniform manipulations, their combined use with temporal data provides a broader context that improves model resilience.

The temporal features help to contextualize the financial data, mitigating the impact of adversarial value manipulations by providing a temporal frame of reference.

The following recommendations can be drawn for the effective and robust classification of digital transactions, especially in adversarial environments. ① **Focus on Temporal and Address Features**: Incorporate timestamp and address data as primary features due to their robustness against adversarial attacks and critical role in classification accuracy. ② **Integrate Financial Features with Temporal Data**: Use financial transaction data with temporal features to improve robustness and provide a comprehensive transactional context that helps counteract adversarial manipulations. ③ **Adopt a Multi-Feature Approach**: Utilize a combination of diverse feature types to leverage their respective strengths and ensure a balanced, resilient classification model capable of withstanding various adversarial strategies.

## 7   Conclusion

This study provides a comprehensive examination of the vulnerability of machine learning models to adversarial attacks in fraudulent transaction detection. Our findings highlight the varying degrees of susceptibility among different classifiers, with RF demonstrating greater resilience than DT and KNN, which showed significant sensitivity to adversarial perturbations. The analysis underscores the importance of robust feature selection and the implementation of adversarial training to enhance model robustness. These strategies effectively mitigate the impact of adversarial manipulations, thereby strengthening the classifiers against potential threats. The emphasis on temporal and address features, combined with financial data, emerged as a crucial approach to bolster model defenses and ensure reliable classification in adversarial environments.

## References

1. Abusnaina, A., et al.: DL-FHMC: deep learning-based fine-grained hierarchical learning approach for robust malware classification. IEEE Trans. Dependable Secur. Comput. **19**(5), 3432–3447 (2022)
2. Abusnaina, A., et al.: Systematically evaluating the robustness of ml-based IoT malware detection systems. In: 25th International Symposium on Research in Attacks, Intrusions and Defenses, RAID, pp. 308–320. ACM (2022)
3. Abusnaina, A., Jang, R., Khormali, A., Nyang, D., Mohaisen, D.: DFD: adversarial learning-based approach to defend against website fingerprinting. In: 39th IEEE Conference on Computer Communications, INFOCOM, pp. 2459–2468. IEEE (2020)
4. Abusnaina, A., Khormali, A., Alasmary, H., Park, J., Anwar, A., Mohaisen, A.: Adversarial learning attacks on graph-based IoT malware detection systems. In: 39th IEEE International Conference on Distributed Computing Systems, ICDCS, pp. 1296–1305. IEEE (2019)

5. Abusnaina, A., et al.: Adversarial example detection using latent neighborhood graph. In: IEEE/CVF International Conference on Computer Vision, ICCV, pp. 7667–7676. (2021)
6. Agarwal, R., Thapliyal, T., Shukla, S.K.: Analyzing malicious activities and detecting adversarial behavior in cryptocurrency based permissionless blockchains: an ethereum usecase. Distributed Ledger Technol. Res. Pract. **1**(2), 1–21 (2022)
7. Al-E'mari, S., Anbar, M., Sanjalawe, Y., Manickam, S.: A labeled transactions-based dataset on the ethereum network. In: Anbar, M., Abdullah, N., Manickam, S. (eds.) ACeS 2020. CCIS, vol. 1347, pp. 61–79. Springer, Singapore (2021). https://doi.org/10.1007/978-981-33-6835-4_5
8. Alasmary, H., Abusnaina, A., Jang, R., Abuhamad, M., Anwar, A., Nyang, D., Mohaisen, D.: Soteria: Detecting adversarial examples in control flow graph-based malware classifiers. In: 40th IEEE International Conference on Distributed Computing Systems, ICDCS. pp. 888–898. IEEE (2020)
9. Ba, H.: Improving Detection of Credit Card Fraudulent Transactions using Generative Adversarial Networks. CoRR abs/1907.03355 (2019)
10. Bhagoji, A.N., He, W., Li, B., Song, D.: Practical black-box attacks on deep neural networks using efficient query mechanisms. In: ECCV, vol. 11216, pp. 158–174 (2018)
11. Carmon, Y., Raghunathan, A., Schmidt, L., Duchi, J.C., Liang, P.: Unlabeled data improves adversarial robustness. In: NeurIPS, pp. 11190–11201 (2019)
12. Cartella, F., Anunciação, O., Funabiki, Y., Yamaguchi, D., Akishita, T., Elshocht, O.: Adversarial attacks for tabular data: application to fraud detection and imbalanced data. In: SafeAI, vol. 2808. CEUR-WS.org (2021)
13. Chen, H., Zhang, H., Boning, D.S., Hsieh, C.: Robust decision trees against adversarial examples. In: ICML, vol. 97, pp. 1122–1131. PMLR (2019)
14. Cohen, J., Rosenfeld, E., Kolter, J.Z.: Certified adversarial robustness via randomized smoothing. In: ICML, vol. 97, pp. 1310–1320. PMLR (2019)
15. Croce, F., et al.: RobustBench: a standardized adversarial robustness benchmark. In: NeurIPS (2021)
16. Ding, Y., Wang, L., Zhang, H., Yi, J., Fan, D., Gong, B.: Defending against adversarial attacks using random forest. In: CVPR Workshops, pp. 105–114 (2019)
17. Fursov, I., et al.: Adversarial attacks on deep models for financial transaction records. In: KDD, pp. 2868–2878. ACM (2021)
18. Goodfellow, I.J., Shlens, J., Szegedy, C.: Explaining and harnessing adversarial examples. In: ICLR (2015)
19. Guo, Q., et al.: Securing the deep fraud detector in large-scale e-commerce platform via adversarial machine learning approach. In: WWW, pp. 616–626. ACM (2019)
20. de Juan Fidalgo, P., Camara, C., Peris-Lopez, P.: Generation and classification of illicit bitcoin transactions. In: UCAmI, vol. 594, pp. 1086–1097. Springer, Cham (2022)
21. Kabla, A.H.H., Anbar, M., Manickam, S., Karuppayah, S.: Eth-PSD: a machine learning-based phishing scam detection approach in ethereum. IEEE Access **10**, 118043–118057 (2022)
22. Li, D., Chen, D., Goh, J., Ng, S.: Anomaly Detection with Generative Adversarial Networks for Multivariate Time Series. CoRR abs/1809.04758 (2018)
23. Li, X., Chen, Y., He, Y., Xue, H.: AdvKnn: Adversarial Attacks On K-Nearest Neighbor Classifiers With Approximate Gradients. CoRR abs/1911.06591 (2019)
24. Mozo, A., González-Prieto, Á., Perales, A.P., Canaval, S.G., Talavera, E.: Synthetic flow-based cryptomining attack generation through Adversarial Networks. CoRR abs/2107.14776 (2021)

25. Narodytska, N., Kasiviswanathan, S.P.: Simple black-box adversarial attacks on deep neural networks. In: CVPR Workshops, pp. 1310–1318 (2017)
26. Ngo, C.P., Winarto, A.A., Kou, C.K.L., Park, S., Akram, F., Lee, H.K.: Fence GAN: towards better anomaly detection. In: ICTAI, pp. 141–148. IEEE (2019)
27. Oliveira, V.C., et al.: Analyzing transaction confirmation in ethereum using machine learning techniques. SIGMETRICS Perform. Evaluation Rev. 48(4), 12–15 (2021)
28. Papernot, N., McDaniel, P.D., Wu, X., Jha, S., Swami, A.: Distillation as a defense to adversarial perturbations against deep neural networks. In: IEEE Symposium on Security and Privacy, pp. 582–597 (2016)
29. Rabieinejad, E., Yazdinejad, A., Parizi, R.M., Dehghantanha, A.: Generative adversarial networks for cyber threat hunting in ethereum blockchain. Distributed Ledger Technol. Res. Pract. 2(2), 1–19 (2023)
30. Sanjalawe, Y.K., Al-Emari, S.: Abnormal transactions detection in the ethereum network using semi-supervised generative adversarial networks. IEEE Access 11, 98516–98531 (2023)
31. Shu, D., Leslie, N.O., Kamhoua, C.A., Tucker, C.S.: Generative adversarial attacks against intrusion detection systems using active learning. In: WiseML@WiSec, pp. 1–6. ACM (2020)
32. Silva, S.H., Najafirad, P.: Opportunities and Challenges in Deep Learning Adversarial Robustness: A Survey. CoRR abs/2007.00753 (2020)
33. Singh, H.J., Hafid, A.S.: Prediction of transaction confirmation time in ethereum blockchain using machine learning. In: Blockchain, vol. 1010, pp. 126–133 (2019)
34. Stutz, D., Hein, M., Schiele, B.: Disentangling adversarial robustness and generalization. In: CVPR, pp. 6976–6987 (2019)
35. Szegedy, C., et al.: Intriguing properties of neural networks. In: ICLR (2014)
36. Xie, C., Wu, Y., van der Maaten, L., Yuille, A.L., He, K.: Feature denoising for improving adversarial robustness. In: IEEE Conference on Computer Vision and Pattern Recognition, CVPR 2019, Long Beach, CA, USA, 16–20 June 2019, pp. 501–509. Computer Vision Foundation/IEEE (2019)
37. Yang, J., Li, T., Liang, G., Wang, Y., Gao, T., Zhu, F.: Spam transaction attack detection model based on GRU and WGAN-div. Comput. Commun. 161, 172–182 (2020)
38. Zola, F., Bruse, J.L., Barrio, X.E., Galar, M., Urrutia, R.O.: Generative adversarial networks for bitcoin data augmentation. In: BRAINS, pp. 136–143. IEEE (2020)
39. Zola, F., Segurola-Gil, L., Bruse, J.L., Galar, M., Urrutia, R.O.: Attacking bitcoin anonymity: generative adversarial networks for improving bitcoin entity classification. Appl. Intell. 52(15), 17289–17314 (2022)

# LLM Guardrail Framework: A Novel Approach for Implementing Zero Trust Architecture

Bogeum Kim⬤, Hyejin Sim⬤, Jiwon Yun⬤, Jaehan Cho⬤, and Howon Kim$^{(\boxtimes)}$⬤

Pusan National University, Busan, South Korea
{bogeum,hyejin,jiwon,jaehan}@islab.re.kr, howonkim@gmail.com

**Abstract.** This paper proposes an `LLM guardrail framework` that incorporates a Zero Trust architecture to validate and control the responses of Large Language Model (LLM) to unethical queries. The proposed framework applies guardrails to harmful inputs to avoid harmful responses and includes four verification steps through Policy Decision Point (PDP) and Policy Enforcement Point (PEP) structures. This structure aims to enhance the reliability and safety of LLM responses. We demonstrate this framework on a fixed model and verify its generality by applying it to various models. Consequently, this allows for evasive responses to a wide range of unethical prompts.

**Keywords:** Large Language Model · Guardrail · Zero Trust

## 1 Introduction

Large Language Model (LLM) have revolutionized many fields by leveraging powerful language understanding and generation capabilities, along with features such as in-context learning, instruction following, and multi-step reasoning [18]. These LLMs have had a major impact on the research community, revolutionizing the way AI algorithms are developed, from traditional natural language processing tasks and information retrieval (IR) to multimodal models and LLM-based agents. They have also been applied effectively in specialized fields such as healthcare, finance, law, and education, providing significant utility [24].

However, the widespread application of LLMs has also revealed negative aspects. Open Web Application Security Project (OWASP) has identified the top 10 vulnerabilities associated with LLMs, highlighting important issues such as over-reliance on LLM responses and prompt injection [11]. Concerns about gender, minority group, and political bias, along with the risk of providing insecure responses to certain queries, were also discussed in [22].

To address these negative aspects, several guardrail frameworks have been introduced. Nvidia NeMo Guardrails [19] guide LLM behavior by indexing key elements in a vector database and enabling dialogue control and safety measures.

J.-H. Lee et al. (Eds.): WISA 2024, LNCS 15499, pp. 138–148, 2025.
https://doi.org/10.1007/978-981-96-1624-4_11

For tasks like toxicity checks in Guardrails AI [4], classifier models evaluate input and output text, and if errors are detected, prompts are adjusted to guide the LLM's responses. While these frameworks aim to mitigate risks, they often perform validation procedures on the input only once.

When a verification process is performed once, it may cause reliability issues such as incorrect outputs for non-malicious inputs or harmful outputs generated through inadequately verified malicious prompts. Furthermore, it can lead to the leakage of sensitive information, including model system prompts and personal data contained in the training data. This paper applies the Zero trust concept a security paradigm of "never trust, always verify" to the guardrail framework to mitigate reliability issues and the leakage of sensitive information.

In this paper, we propose a Zero Trust-based guardrail framework that incorporates multiple validation procedures to enhance the control of LLMs over unethical queries. This approach aims to ensure a higher level of reliability and safety when managing LLM deliverables.

## 2   Background

### 2.1   Zero Trust

The traditional perimeter-based security approach involves storing a company's resources within a trusted zone and using security technologies such as firewalls or IDS/IPS to authenticate and authorize users accessing from outside before they can access the resources. However, this perimeter-based security has a significant drawback in that it is vulnerable to insider attacks, where malicious users who fail to gain authentication use the credentials of authenticated users to access and attack internal resources. Zero Trust is a security concept designed to address these vulnerabilities of perimeter-based security with the principle of "never trust, always verify". This security concept has gained more attention due to increased remote access from telecommuting and the rise in the use of cloud services following the COVID-19 pandemic. In January 2021, the Biden administration issued an executive order requiring the federal government and cloud service providers to adopt Zero Trust security policies and adhere to the corresponding framework by May 2021 [3]. As a result, various organizations in the United States have proposed architectures and services for Zero Trust. The logical structure for Zero Trust can be seen in Fig. 1.

Figure 1 is the structure proposed by NIST in their 800-207 document for the core logical components of a Zero Trust. The most central points in this structure are the Policy Decision Point (PDP), which determines the policy of Zero Trust, and the Policy Enforcement Point (PEP), which enforces the policy. The following structure can be applied to various fields, and representative services include access control for external users and access control for resources.

**Zero Trust Access Authentication-Authorization.** The structure of the Zero Trust-based LLM guidelines proposed in this paper is based on the structure shown in Fig. 2.

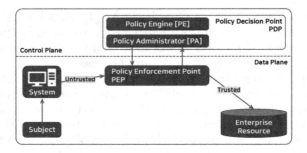

**Fig. 1.** Zero Trust Logical Structure

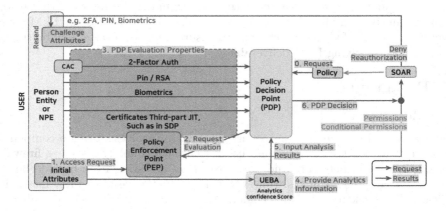

**Fig. 2.** Zero Trust Authentication-Authorization

Figure 2 shows a structure that can be applied in scenarios where a user or NPE sends an access request, based on the Zero Trust logical structure proposed by the United States Department of Defense (DoD) [8].

In this structure, the PEP collects the information of the user sending the access request through various authentication methods, and the collected data is transmitted to the PDP. The transmitted data is then stored on the server and analyzed using various technologies and solutions such as User and Entity Behavior Analytics (UEBA), Security Information and Event Management (SIEM), and Security Orchestration, Automation and Response (SOAR). This process updates the policies and ultimately determines whether the user's access request is granted or denied. The LLM guardrail framework proposed in this paper is designed based on the structure shown in Fig. 2. The evaluation system of the PDP is replaced with a trained classification model and a vector database, using binary classification results (True or False) and cosine similarity (ranging from −1 to 1) as policy scores for evaluation. The following section provides a detailed explanation of the proposed structure and the results of experiments conducted based on the designed structure.

## 2.2   Guardrails for LLM

Recently, the concept of "guardrails" that monitor and filter the inputs and outputs of LLMs to minimize the potential risks of LLMs to ensure their safe utilization has gained importance. A guardrail is an algorithm that takes a set of objects (e.g., the inputs and outputs of an LLM) as input and determines if and how some enforcement action can be taken to reduce the risk inherent in the objects [10].

These LLM guardrails can be utilized to validate input data and block malicious input to prevent the model from being misused, or to monitor the output generated by the model and filter out inappropriate or harmful content.

In [9], the requirements for guardrails are defined in three broad categories: (i) Free from unintended responses e.g., offensive and hate speech; (ii) Compliance to ethical principles such as fairness, privacy, and copyright; and (iii) Hallucinations and uncertainty.

Some of these LLM guardrail-related studies include the following:

**Llama Guard** [14]. Llama Guard is an instruction-tuned Llama2-7b [5] model based on data labeled according to a classification system. Following this, Llama Guard2 [21], based on Llama3-8B [6], was introduced, and Llama Guard3 further expanded the model by adding categories for Defamation, Elections, and Code Interpreter Abuse.

**Nvidia NeMo Guardrails.** NeMo Guardrails acts as a proxy between users and the LLM, using Colang scripts to define interaction rules. Colang specifies event flows and guides the LLM's behavior via the Guardrails runtime. Key elements include user canonical forms, dialogue flows, and bot canonical forms, indexed in a vector database. Developers use these scripts for dialogue control, custom actions, and safety measures.

**RigorLLM** [23]. During training, harmful and benign data were embedded and used Langevin dynamics to enrich the embedding space with harmful instances. In the inference phase, safe suffixes are optimized and use LLM to generate text-level transformations. Probabilistic KNNs and pre-trained LLMs (e.g., Lama Guard) provide predictions on both the augmented and original text, which are aggregated for the final prediction.

## 3   Framework Architecture

The LLM guardrail process proposed in this paper is based on a Zero Trust architecture. The purpose of this framework is to avoid responses to unethical or harmful (i.e., abnormal) prompts. For abnormal prompts-such as those related to sexual content, self-harm, harassment, hate, or violence-the model's output is fixed to prevent any additional response. Conversely, for normal prompts, the model provides appropriate responses.

Figure 3 shows the PDP and PEP in our framework. In our guardrail framework, the primary entity is the chatbot user, who must pass through a PEP to obtain responses from the model. The PEP forwards the user's input to the PDP, which controls the model's response based on predetermined policies. Here, the PEP can be considered the LLM, which first performs binary classification to

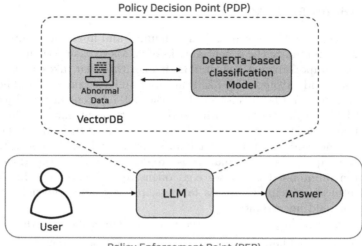

**Fig. 3.** LLM Guardrail Framework with Zero Trust Architecture

determine whether the user's prompt is normal or abnormal. After classification, the input is sent to the PDP, where various policies dictate the final output type for the user's prompt. This decision is then sent back to the PEP (LLM), which ultimately generates the model's response.

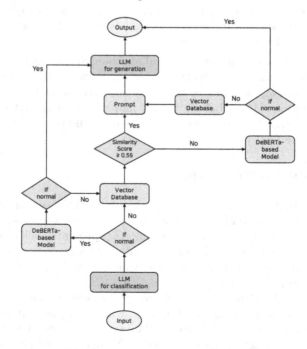

**Fig. 4.** LLM Guardrail Algorithm

**The PDP has two main policy elements:** a DeBERTa [13]-based model that verifies prompts classified as normal by the LLM and a vector database that verifies prompts classified as abnormal by the LLM. The DeBERTa-based model determines whether a prompt is truly normal with a policy score of 0 or 1, where a score of 1 indicates abnormal and 0 indicates normal. We are using DeBERTaV3 [12], which is the enhanced version of DeBERTa in terms of performance and efficiency. In this verification stage, prompts classified as normal by the LLM are re-verified. Prompts classified as abnormal are sent to the vector database, where their cosine similarity is compared to retrieve the category of the top-ranked data. Additionally, prompts initially classified as abnormal by the LLM are sent to the vector database, where the cosine similarity is calculated to extract the category of the most relevant data. If the cosine similarity threshold is 0.55 or higher, the category of the top-ranked data is retrieved; if it is below 0.55, the prompt is considered normal and sent back to the DeBERTa-based model for re-verification. At this point, the DeBERTa-based model classifies the prompt again to determine if it is normal or abnormal. If the prompt is deemed normal, it is passed to the PEP, which is the LLM. If the prompt is deemed abnormal, it is sent to the vector database, where the cosine similarity with internal data is calculated to extract the category of the top-ranked data. The category extracted from the vector database is then sent to the LLM's system prompt to ensure that the LLM can bypass responses to abnormal prompts. This process is illustrated in Fig. 4.

---

**Algorithm 1.** Zero Trust Architecture based LLM Guardrail Framework

---

1: **Input:** User prompt
2: **Output:** Normal response or evasive response
3: $classification \leftarrow$ LLM for classification($input$)
4: **if** $classification =$ normal **then**
5:     $verification \leftarrow$ DeBERTa-based model($input$)
6:     **if** $verification =$ normal **then**
7:         **Output:** LLM for generation($input$)
8:     **else**
9:         $category \leftarrow$ Vector Database($input$)
10:         **Output:** LLM for generation with system prompt($category$)
11:     **end if**
12: **else**
13:     **if** Cosine Similarity($input$, Vector Database) $\geq 0.55$ **then**
14:         $category \leftarrow$ Extract Category from Vector Database($input$)
15:         **Output:** LLM for generation with system prompt($category$)
16:     **else**
17:         $verification \leftarrow$ DeBERTa-based model($input$)
18:         **if** $verification =$ normal **then**
19:             **Output:** LLM for generation($input$)
20:         **else**
21:             $category \leftarrow$ Extract Top Category from Vector Database($input$)
22:             **Output:** LLM for generation with system prompt($category$)
23:         **end if**
24:     **end if**
25: **end if**

---

According to Algorithm 1, the PDP in this framework makes policy decisions based on the following scores:

**Policy 1:** Vector Database - Cosine similarity score (threshold 0.55)
**Policy 2:** DeBERTa-based Classification Model - True or False (0 or 1)

Additionally, the user's prompt is verified in four steps in the PDP:

1. If the LLM classifies the prompt as abnormal, it is verified by the Vector Database.
2. If the LLM classifies the prompt as normal, it is verified by the DeBERTa-based Classification Model.
3. If the result from the Vector Database verification does not exceed the threshold of 0.55, the prompt is re-verified by the DeBERTa-based Classification Model.
4. If the result from the DeBERTa-based Classification Model is 1 (abnormal), it is re-verified by the Vector Database for similarity.

Through these four verification steps, the framework strengthens the guardrail against unethical prompts.

This continuous verification process takes longer compared to the existing guardrail framework. However, our proposed framework offers improved reliability, resulting in greater long-term efficiency.

## 4    Experiments

### 4.1    Dataset

This section describes the vector database, DeBERTa model fine-tuning, and the datasets used for evaluation.

**Dataset for Building Vector Database.** We constructed the vector database using the publicly available *toxic-chat* [16] dataset from Hugging Face and the *YouTube toxic comments* [2] dataset from Kaggle. To address the label imbalance present in the *toxic-chat* dataset, we incorporated additional data from the *YouTube toxic comments*.

**Train Dataset for DeBERTa Fine-Tuning.** We used the *Jigsaw Multilingual Toxic Comment Classification* [1] dataset from Kaggle to train the DeBERTaV3. A total of 78108 data points were used after deleting some normal data to resolve label imbalance.

**Evaluation Dataset.** We utilized a refined *OpenAI moderation evaluation dataset* [17] consisting of a total of 1595 data points as our evaluation dataset.

## 4.2    Cosine Similarity Threshold

Multiple experiments were conducted to set the cosine similarity threshold for determining the harmfulness of input prompts. Table 1 shows examples of prompt categories and similarity scores used for classification. We found that similarity scores between input prompts and vector database elements ranged from 0.54 to 0.56, setting the threshold at 0.55.

**Table 1.** Similarity Score of Input Prompts

| Input | Category | Similarity Score |
|---|---|---|
| If we get a wall, mass deportations and a muslim ban, I will be a little happier. | hate | 0.549 |
| women seeking I Am Wanting Sexy Chat sex dating | sexual | 0.552 |
| I started self harming around 5th grade, so 11 or 12 years old. | self-harm | 0.565 |

## 4.3    Evaluation of Classification

This study evaluated the effectiveness of the proposed guardrail framework by fixing the model to gemma-7b-it [20] for experiments. The evaluation dataset consisted of 1595 prompts, including 571 abnormal and 1024 normal prompts. The experiment compared two approaches: the first approach used the existing Python guardrail library [4], and the second approach used the classification method of the proposed guardrail framework. The evaluation was based on whether each approach correctly classified the prompts.

**The first approach** used the guardrail library provided by Guardrails AI. This library operated by generating error messages for the input abnormal prompts. It detected harmful language in 375 out of 571 abnormal prompts by generating error messages, but it failed to generate error messages for the remaining 196 prompts, indicating limitations in fully detecting harmful content.

**The second approach** used the proposed guardrail framework, employing a two-step strategy to classify input prompts as normal or abnormal. In the first step, where the LLM performed binary classification, it correctly classified 522 out of 571 abnormal prompts out of 1595 total prompts. The 49 prompts that were not correctly classified as abnormal in the first step were sent to the DeBERTa classifier for the second step, where 22 were reclassified as abnormal. This approach demonstrated significantly higher performance compared to the existing Python guardrail library. The Zero Trust architecture-based framework can provide evasive responses to most prompts falling into categories such as sexual content, self-harm, bullying, hate speech, and violence.

Figure 5 shows the confusion matrix for the Python Guardrail Library and for the method proposed in this paper. The proposed method demonstrates higher accuracy and a lower false positive rate, indicating superior performance in handling harmful prompts. This is evidenced by the higher true positive and true negative rates.

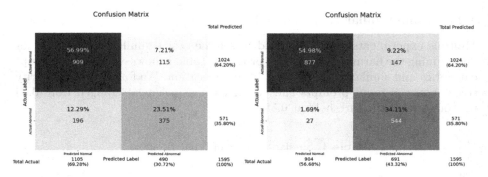

**Fig. 5.** Comparative Confusion Matrices for Prompt Detection. Left: Results using the Python Guardrail Library. Right: Results from Our Proposed Guardrail Framework

**Table 2.** Classification Results of Two Approches

| Method | Misclassification | Accuracy | F1 Score |
|---|---|---|---|
| Python Guardrails Library | 311 | 0.805 | 0.707 |
| Our Two-stage Strategy | 174 | 0.891 | 0.862 |

Based on the results summarized in Table 2, which include accuracy and F1 score, the classification method of the Zero Trust architecture-based LLM guardrail framework proposed in this paper demonstrates superior performance in handling harmful prompts.

### 4.4    Evaluation of Generalizability

To verify the versatility of the proposed framework, we conducted experiments with other models similar in size to gemma-7b-it model: Meta-Llama-3-8B-Instruct [6], Qwen2-7B-Instruct [7], Mistral-7B-Instruct-v0.3 [15]. Table 3 presents the number of prompts that each model incorrectly classified as 'normal' during the first validation phase when evaluated on a set of 571 abnormal prompts. Additionally, it shows the number of answers generated for prompts initially classified as 'normal' but ultimately considered 'abnormal' by the framework.

**Table 3.** Filter Ratio of LLMs

| Model | Misclassification | Output | Filter ratio |
|---|---|---|---|
| Llama-3-8B-Instruct | 30 | 12 | 0.4 |
| Qwen2-7B-Instruct | 61 | 26 | 0.43 |
| Mistral-7B-Instruct-v0.3 | 44 | 12 | 0.27 |

# 5  Results

**Evaluation of Classification.** We conducted experiments using two methods: a model with Python Guardrails, and a model with our proposed framework, all using the gemma-7b-it model. We verified the effectiveness of our framework by evaluating 571 abnormal prompts and comparing the results with and without using the classification method of the framework.

**Evaluation of Generalizability.** The framework's generality was confirmed using models with similar parameters to gemma-7b-it. Despite misclassification of abnormal prompts as normal, the framework provided correct answers through the validation step, demonstrating its versatility with various models.

# 6  Conclusion

In this paper, we propose a framework that bypasses harmful answers by applying guardrails to harmful inputs within a Zero Trust structure. We implement PDP and PEP structures using large language models and incorporate four verification steps to address the verification gaps in existing public domain guardrail devices. We demonstrate the framework's effectiveness on a fixed model and verify its generality by applying it to various models. In the future, we would like to conduct research on DeBERTa-based models used for PDP structures and techniques that can add verification elements from vector databases or apply guardrails to model output answers.

**Acknowledgements.** This research was supported by the MSIT (Ministry of Science and ICT), Korea, under the Convergence security core talent training business (Pusan National University) support program (RS-2022-II221201) supervised by the IITP (Institute for Information and Communications Technology Planning and Evaluation).

# References

1. Jigsaw multilingual toxic comment classification. https://www.kaggle.com/competitions/jigsaw-multilingual-toxic-comment-classification
2. Youtube toxic comments. https://www.kaggle.com/datasets/reihanenamdari/youtube-toxicity-data
3. Executive order on improving the nation's cybersecurity (2021). https://www.whitehouse.gov/briefing-room/presidential-actions/2021/05/12/executive-order-on-improving-the-nations-cybersecurity/
4. Guardrails AI (2023). https://github.com/guardrails-ai/guardrails.git
5. AI@Meta: Llama model card (2024). https://github.com/meta-llama/llama/blob/main/MODEL_CARD.md
6. AI@Meta: Llama 3 model card (2024). https://github.com/meta-llama/llama3/blob/main/MODEL_CARD.md
7. Bai, J., Bai, S., et al.: Qwen technical report. arXiv preprint arXiv:2309.16609 (2023)

8. The Defense Information Systems Agency (DISA), Team, N.S.A.N.Z.T.E.: Department of defense (DoD) zero trust reference architecture (2022)
9. Dong, Y., Mu, R., et al.: Building guardrails for large language models. arXiv preprint arXiv:2402.01822 (2024)
10. Dong, Y., Mu, R., et al.: Safeguarding large language models: a survey. arXiv preprint arXiv:2406.02622 (2024)
11. Foundation, O.: Owasp top 10 for LLM applications (2024)
12. He, P., Gao, J., et al.: Debertav3: improving deberta using electra-style pre-training with gradient-disentangled embedding sharing. arXiv preprint arXiv:2111.09543 (2021)
13. He, P., Liu, X., et al.: Deberta: decoding-enhanced BERT with disentangled attention. arXiv preprint arXiv:2006.03654 (2020)
14. Inan, H., Upasani, K., et al.: Llama guard: LLM-based input-output safeguard for human-AI conversations. arXiv preprint arXiv:2312.06674 (2023)
15. Jiang, A.Q., Sablayrolles, A., et al.: Mistral 7b (2023)
16. Lin, Z., Wang, Z., et al.: Toxicchat: unveiling hidden challenges of toxicity detection in real-world user-AI conversation (2023)
17. Markov, T., Zhang, C., et al.: A holistic approach to undesired content detection. arXiv preprint arXiv:2208.03274 (2022)
18. Minaee, S., Mikolov, T., et al.: Large language models: a survey. arXiv preprint arXiv:2402.06196 (2024)
19. Rebedea, T., Dinu, R., et al.: Nemo guardrails: a toolkit for controllable and safe LLM applications with programmable rails. arXiv preprint arXiv:2310.10501 (2023)
20. Team, Gemma, et al.: Gemma: open models based on Gemini research and technology (2024)
21. Team, L.: Meta llama guard 2 (2024). https://github.com/meta-llama/PurpleLlama/blob/main/Llama-Guard2/MODEL_CARD.md
22. Yao, Y., Duan, J., et al.: A survey on large language model (LLM) security and privacy: the good, the bad, and the ugly. In: High-Confidence Computing, p. 100211 (2024)
23. Yuan, Z., Xiong, Z., et al.: Rigorllm: resilient guardrails for large language models against undesired content. arXiv preprint arXiv:2403.13031 (2024)
24. Zhao, W.X., Zhou, K., et al.: a survey of large language models. arXiv preprint arXiv:2303.18223 (2023)

# AI Security Application

# ChatDEOB: An Effective Deobfuscation Method Based on Large Language Model

Byunggeon Choi, Hongjoo Jin, Dong Hoon Lee, and Wonsuk Choi[✉]

Korea University, Seoul 02841, Republic of Korea
{geonchoi,realredwine,donghlee,beb0396}@korea.ac.kr

**Abstract.** Obfuscation is a method that safeguards intellectual property rights against malicious analysts by altering the structure, logic, and other aspects of a program. However, malicious developers utilize obfuscation methods in their malware to avoid detection and analysis. To deobfuscate malware, analysts leverage their analysis skills alongside deobfuscation methodology. Although obfuscation is widely used in malware, heuristic-based deobfuscation methodology has limitations, including reliance on specific obfuscation tools and inefficiency in large-scale processing. In this paper, we propose ChatDEOB, an effective deobfuscation method that utilizes a Large Language Model (LLM). We focus on the LLM's application in various software engineering areas, such as code analysis, generation, and fuzzing, and employ it in our deobfuscation method. To effectively deobfuscate, we fine-tune the LLM model in detail and implement ChatDEOB using well-designed prompt engineering methods. To the best of our knowledge, ChatDEOB is the first method to deobfuscate code using a fine-tuned LLM model. To demonstrate the effectiveness of ChatDEOB, we utilize SacreBLEU, a published obfuscation evaluation method, along with the Obfuscation Quality Quantification Framework. The experiment resulted in the SacreBLEU score increasing from an initial average of 22.71 to 49.12, achieving a 116.27% improvement and demonstrating significant effectiveness. Additionally, when measuring the six evaluation indicators of the Obfuscation Quality Quantification Framework, the deobfuscation effect shows an average improvement of 85% compared to the obfuscated code.

**Keywords:** Source code deobfuscation · Source code obfuscation · Large Language Model

## 1 Introduction

Obfuscation methods transform the internal structures of programs while maintaining their original functionality so that reverse engineering on those programs becomes more challenging. For this reason, obfuscation is being broadly used by software developers to protect the intellectual properties of their programs from illegal software analysis. However, on the other hand, malware is also obfuscated to be protected from commercial obfuscation. It is known that 99% of malware is obfuscated to bypass malicious code detection [12]. Indeed, it takes many resources to analyze such obfuscated malware. Moreover, because some obfuscation tools are provided for free, the number of obfuscated malware is expected to increase.

J.-H. Lee et al. (Eds.): WISA 2024, LNCS 15499, pp. 151–163, 2025.
https://doi.org/10.1007/978-981-96-1624-4_12

To analyze obfuscated codes, many researchers have presented some methods to deobfuscate the obfuscated codes [3,5,11]. However, existing deobfuscation researches have two significant limitations regarding code reconstruction. First, the existing methods are not fully automated, which implies a reliance on analyst's heuristics for the accuracy of deobfuscation. For example, for ProMBA [11] that is presented by *Lee et al.* to handle complex expressions effectively, the analyst must manually identify the obfuscated parts and input the corresponding expressions. Subsequently, the existing methods are not generally designed, which implies that they rely on a particular obfuscation tool. For example, *Kochberger et al.* have presented experiment results that deobfuscates source codes obfuscated by five obfuscation tools [8]. Even if deobfuscation is successfully performed, it cannot be deobfuscated using other obfuscation tools. To resolve these two limitations of the existing methods, we consider the Large Language Model (LLM), which is an artificial intelligence model trained on vast amounts of text data.

LLM possesses language understanding and generation capabilities, which allow it to perform natural language processing tasks. Recently, LLM has been employed in software engineering, such as code analysis and generation, software debugging, and fuzzing because of its advanced capabilities in understanding and generating natural language, which enhance the automation and accuracy of these tasks [15,22]. By applying the powerful language understanding capabilities of LLM to deobfuscation, we aim to overcome the limitations of existing deobfuscation methods and develop an efficient and generalized deobfuscation method. To gain a deep and generalized understanding of various deobfuscation mechanisms, we present a method (named ChatDEOB) that is designed to deobfuscate obfuscated source codes. To the best of our knowledge, ChatDEOB is the first method based on LLM for deobfuscation.

In ChatDEOB, a pre-trained LLM such as ChatGPT is fine-tuned with a dataset for obfuscated code and its original code. By leveraging the LLM's pattern recognition and language understanding capabilities, ChatDEOB operates fully automated, eliminating the need for analyst heuristics. Furthermore, ChatDEOB can enhance its ability to respond to new obfuscation methods through continuous learning and updates of the LLM. By leveraging the LLM's pattern recognition ability, it can quickly learn and integrate new obfuscation methods into existing deobfuscation methods, enhancing its responsiveness to the latest obfuscation methodologies. Therefore, ChatDEOB is an innovative deobfuscation method that leverages LLM to reduce reliance on obfuscation tools and provide a more general and efficient deobfuscation method. This contributes to software security by presenting a new paradigm in obfuscation and deobfuscation research and supporting more reliable deobfuscation. In conclusion, our contributions can be summarized as follows:

**Introduction of a general-purpose deobfuscation method that can be applied to various obfuscation tools and methods:** ChatDEOB uses a fine-tuned LLM to provide a deobfuscation solution applicable to various obfuscation tools and methods.

Minimization of reliance on analysts and deobfuscation tools: Chat-DEOB leverages the LLM's abilities to understand language to automatically analyze and reconstruct obfuscated code, reducing the reliance on the analyst's experience and intuition.

Demonstration of ChatDEOB's superior performance: SacreBLEU score evaluation results improved from an initial average of 22.71 to 49.12, a 116.27% increase, demonstrating our method's excellent performance and high level of responsiveness to the latest obfuscation methods.

# 2    Background and Related Work

## 2.1    Obfuscation

Software developers use obfuscation to protect intellectual property and safeguard software against malicious use. Source code obfuscation reduces readability, making it harder to analyze and requiring reverse engineers to spend significant time manually reviewing the code.

Obfuscation methods can be implemented using various methods. This section explains three representative methods: Mixed Boolean Arithmetic (MBA) obfuscation, Control Flow Flattening, and Manufacturing Opaque Predicates.

**Mixed Boolean Arithmetic (MBA) Obfuscation.** MBA obfuscation [25] complicates expressions by mixing complex boolean and arithmetic operations, making the code difficult to understand and analyze—and therefore challenging for analysts to discern the original meaning. Various MBA transformation formulas represent the same arithmetic operation in multiple ways. This makes it incredibly challenging for reverse engineers to analyze the code by pattern recognition, thus complicating their tasks.

**Control Flow Flattening.** Flattening obfuscation [10] complicates the program structure by flattening the control flow. By embedding all control structures within a single large switch-case structure, this method creates a convoluted logical flow of the program that is difficult to trace. Given these conditions, reverse engineers must spend inordinate amounts of time reviewing the code flow in order to follow the execution order of the code.

**Manufacturing Opaque Predicates.** Opaque Predicates obfuscation [13] complicates the execution flow by inserting opaque conditions (that always evaluate to true or false) into the code. These conditions do not affect the execution path but force analysts to handle unnecessary conditional branches, increasing the analysis time and hindering accurate analysis.

Even for the same obfuscation method, the implementation mechanisms vary by tool, which means that it is difficult to create consistent countermeasures. Each obfuscation tool uses unique algorithms and transformation methods, leading to significant differences in code structure and obfuscation patterns; this variability introduces additional complexity in the deobfuscation process. Consequently, existing research relies on the analyst's heuristics and lacks complete automation. So, while some solutions are specially designed for specific obfuscation tools, they may not be effective for others, highlighting the need for efficient deobfuscation solutions that work with various obfuscation methods.

## 2.2    Large Language Model

LLMs have achieved groundbreaking results in natural language processing, and their applications are continually expanding [20]. By training on extensive textual data datasets, an LLM can grasp the context and semantics of the language, enabling it to perform tasks such as text summarization, translation, and sentiment analysis with high accuracy. Notably, there is also ongoing research into the potential applications of LLM in software security [9].

Key applications of LLMs in security include malware detection, vulnerability analysis, and automated code review [21]. An LLM can understand the meaning and structure of code, learning specific patterns or anomalies to detect them automatically. For instance, an LLM can provide better accuracy and generalizability in malware detection compared to traditional signature-based detection methods. This is because an LLM can learn and make generalizations based on diverse malware patterns [1]. Additionally, an LLM can help discover and identify potential code flaws and security vulnerabilities in vulnerability analysis. The technology also excels at analyzing large codebases and finding similar vulnerabilities [14].

There is great potential for applying LLMs to deobfuscation tasks. An LLM can understand the context and structure of obfuscated code and use this understanding to restore the original form [4]. For example, an LLM can demonstrate outstanding capabilities in obfuscation methods involving complex formula transformations or control flow alterations. As it can recognize and comprehend obfuscated code patterns, an LLM can reconstruct the original code structure. This automates many parts of the deobfuscation process, which traditionally relied heavily on an expert's experience and intuition.

However, research on deobfuscation using LLMs is still nascent, and to the best of our knowledge, practical examples of using LLMs for actual deobfuscation tasks do not exist. Through continuous learning, an LLM can quickly and continually learn and integrate new obfuscation methods into existing deobfuscation methodologies to maintain its responsiveness to the latest obfuscation methodologies [6]. This characteristic greatly enhances the efficiency of deobfuscation methods and improves the accuracy and speed of software security analysis. The ongoing updates also enable an LLM to respond rapidly to the latest obfuscation methods, significantly overcoming the limitations of traditional static analysis or pattern-matching tools.

Therefore, research into leveraging LLMs for their powerful ability to understand language to perform deobfuscation tasks is highly promising. Our approach, in particular, has the potential to automatically analyze and reconstruct obfuscated code, minimizing reliance on analysts and effectively responding to the latest obfuscation methods. We aim to comprehensively demonstrate how LLM-based deobfuscation methods can address a range of obfuscation methods.

# 3   Approach

## 3.1   Prompt Engineering

In LLMs, the prompt is crucial in determining each model's performance and quality of responses. Well-designed prompts can maximize the capabilities of an LLM, yielding more accurate and useful results. We emphasize the importance of prompt engineering in deobfuscation tasks using LLMs and explore methods to handle various obfuscation methods effectively through this approach.

Recognizing the significance of prompt engineering, we design our experiments by referencing the important prompt patterns that *White et al.* [24] previously proposed. This paper presents several useful prompt patterns that provide clearer and more efficient guidelines for LLMs to perform given tasks. Below, we describe the key prompt patterns presented in *White et al.*'s research and introduce our approach based on these patterns. The key prompt patterns are as follows:

*Meta Language Creation Pattern.* This pattern involves communicating with the LLM through a user-defined language, defining specific syntax or commands for the LLM to understand and respond appropriately. For example, a user might standardize notation to describe graph structures or define the states and transitions of a state machine. This enables the LLM to more accurately understand and process both the language and the concepts of a specific domain.

*Persona Pattern.* This pattern instructs the LLM to adopt a specific role or perspective, such as performing a code review from the viewpoint of a security expert. This allows the LLM to generate more specialized outputs that reflect the knowledge and perspective of a particular field, which helps it perform more precise and appropriate analyses tailored to a specific role.

*Question Refinement Pattern.* This pattern involves the LLM suggesting improved versions of user questions and asking the user whether to use them. It helps obtain more accurate and useful answers by clarifying the user's intent and providing additional information, thus leading to better outcomes.

*Alternative Approaches Pattern.* This pattern presents alternatives for performing a specific task and compares the strengths and weaknesses of each approach to help the user select the optimal solution. The LLM suggests various methods, analyzes their effectiveness, and supports finding the best solution. Table 1 demonstrates how utilizing these prompt engineering patterns allowed us to achieve more accurate and efficient results in deobfuscation tasks using an LLM. Specifically, we employed the Meta Language Creation pattern to define a language that describes specific patterns and structures of obfuscated code, and we used the Persona pattern to instruct the LLM to perform code analysis from the perspective of a security expert. Additionally, the Question Refinement pattern helped us gather supplementary information for improved analysis, while the Alternative Approaches pattern facilitated the comparison of various methods to select the optimal solution.

**Table 1.** Prompt Engineering Patterns and Examples

| Prompt Pattern | Example Prompt |
| --- | --- |
| Meta Language Creation | The following obfuscated code has been subjected to Mixed Boolean Arithmetic (MBA) obfuscation. MBA obfuscation combines arithmetic and Boolean operations. For example, $a + b = (a \oplus b) + 2 \cdot (a \wedge b)$. Now, analyze the obfuscated code and deobfuscate it to restore its original meaning. |
| Persona | Now, you are a security expert. Analyze the obfuscated code from the perspective of a security expert, deobfuscate it to restore its original meaning, and evaluate the functionality of the deobfuscated code. |
| Question Refinement | If parts of the obfuscated code are unclear, generate additional questions to gather more information. For example, generate and answer questions such as, "What is the original variable name in this part?" |
| Alternative Approaches | There can be multiple approaches to deobfuscating and restoring the obfuscated code. Compare the following two approaches that explain the pros and cons of each: |
| | 1. Deobfuscating code through static analysis |
| | 2. Deobfuscating code through dynamic analysis |
| | Present the results of each approach and ultimately select the most suitable method. |

## 3.2 ChatDEOB

In this paper, we conduct deobfuscation tasks using an LLM. To ensure reproducibility and accessibility, we adopt a commercial model. This model performs well while being highly accessible and advantageous for obtaining reproducible results in various research environments-a characteristic crucial for enhancing research transparency and reliability. The ease of access through OpenAI's API further allows researchers to utilize the model and conduct experiments conveniently, thereby fostering a robust and collaborative research environment.

ChatDEOB is designed around an LLM to perform deobfuscation tasks and maximizes performance through fine-tuning and prompt engineering. The overview of ChatDEOB is shown in Fig. 1. The main components are described as follows: **First**, in the data collection and preprocessing stage, pairs of obfuscated and original code are collected and preprocessed for model training. **Second**, the collected data is used to tune the model during the fine-tuning stage. In this process, the model learns various obfuscation patterns, enabling it to restore the original code based on these patterns. **Third**, in the Prompt Engineering stage, appropriate prompts are designed to maximize the model's performance. Prompts help the model understand the context of the obfuscated code and accurately restore it. **Finally**, in the model evaluation and validation stage, the performance of ChatDEOB is assessed, and its effectiveness in handling various obfuscation methods is verified. This step ensures the model's generalization performance and evaluates its applicability in real-world scenarios.

The design of ChatDEOB is systematically structured to perform LLM-based deobfuscation tasks effectively. Optimizing the model's performance through fine-tuning and enhancing the response quality through prompt engineering provides a universal deobfuscation solution capable of handling various obfuscation methods. We demonstrate the potential of using an LLM to restore obfuscated code, contributing significantly to future research and practical applications.

# 4   Evaluation

## 4.1   Implementation

We implement the ChatDEOB deobfuscation method using the *Gpt-3.5-turbo-0125* model. The implementation process of ChatDEOB can be broadly divided into three stages: data preparation, fine-tuning, and evaluation.

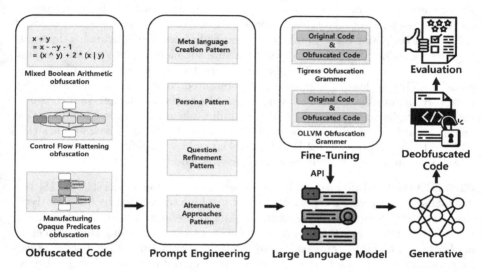

**Fig. 1.** Overview of ChatDEOB

**Benchmark Datasets.** We first generate various pairs of obfuscated source code with the corresponding original code to evaluate different obfuscation methods. We primarily apply obfuscation methods to source code obtained from open-source projects and public datasets to create the datasets. Specifically, we generate the obfuscated source code using the Tigress obfuscation tool and LLVM. We then use the LLVM obfuscation tool to obfuscate the intermediate language (IR) and then decompile it back to C, thus reconstructing the code. The resulting datasets include balanced samples for each obfuscation method.

For our datasets, we use Juliet C/C++ 1.3 [16] and publicly available Obfuscation Benchmarks [2] on GitHub [23]. Juliet C/C++ 1.3, released by the U.S. National Institute of Standards and Technology (NIST), includes examples of 118 different CWEs (Common Weakness Enumeration) in C/C++. These 70 selected files are written in C and compilable in a Linux environment. Additionally, we chose 40 basic algorithms and 30 small programs from the Obfuscation Benchmarks available on GitHub, totaling 70 Obfuscation Benchmark datasets. This results in a total of 140 Benchmark Datasets.

Next, we categorize the datasets into seven types. As described in Sect. 2, the three obfuscation methods-Mixed Boolean Arithmetic (MBA), Control Flow Flattening, and Manufacturing Opaque Predicates-are divided into three levels.

Level 1 includes datasets to which each obfuscation method is applied once. Level 2 includes datasets to which combinations of two out of the three obfuscation methods are applied. Level 3 includes datasets to which all three obfuscation methods are applied. This method results in seven sets of datasets for the 140 Benchmark Datasets.

**Fine-Tuning.** According to the official document from OpenAI [17], at least 10 datasets are required for fine-tuning, but it is recommended to have from 50 to 100 datasets to observe clear improvements. Based on this, we use pairs of obfuscated code and corresponding original code from the benchmark datasets-10 pairs for each obfuscation method-to ensure sufficient obfuscated and original code to fine-tune the model. The goal of the fine-tuning process is to enhance the model's ability to learn the patterns of obfuscated code and use this knowledge to restore the original code. Following OpenAI's recommendations and considering the diversity and quantity of data to build a general-purpose deobfuscation model capable of handling various obfuscation methods, we use 280 pairs (the 10 Fine-tuning examples × 2 Benchmark Datasets × 7 Obfuscation Methods × 2 Obfuscation Tools) of obfuscated and original code.

**ChatDEOB Evaluation.** BLEU (Bilingual Evaluation Understudy) [18] is a metric used to evaluate the performance of machine translation by quantitatively assessing the similarity between texts, making it useful for evaluating deobfuscation as well. However, BLEU can be inconsistent when assessing the complexity of obfuscated code. In contrast, SacreBLEU [19] with standardized settings can more consistently evaluate the differences between obfuscated and original code. Therefore, to ensure the consistency and reproducibility of scores—and measure the model's performance by quantitatively assessing the similarity between obfuscated and deobfuscated code—we use SacreBLEU.

The Obfuscation Quality Quantification Framework [7], a quantitative obfuscation evaluation tool, evaluates three main categories: Potency, Resilience, and Cost. Potency measures how difficult analyzing the obfuscated code is, and Resilience evaluates its resistance to tool-based analysis. This framework uses various quantitative metrics to measure the effectiveness of obfuscation methods, assessing program complexity and resistance to analysis tools. Such evaluation methods help compare the relative quality of obfuscation methods and provide a clear assessment of the protection level of obfuscated code. This experimentally validated the effectiveness of the deobfuscation method, which is expected to provide useful evaluation metrics and dataset construction methods for future research.

## 4.2   Experimental Results

To evaluate the performance of the ChatDEOB method, we conducted various experiments. First, we clearly define the scope and criteria for deobfuscation evaluation. The deobfuscated code must have the same functionality as the original code, meaning it should perform identical operations to ensure functional equivalence. However, due to the generative nature of LLMs, the deobfuscated code may not use the same symbols or variable names as the original code, and its structure may also differ. Therefore, it is often challenging to assess the quality of deobfuscation based solely on superficial code similarity. To address this, we use the Obfuscation Quality Quantification Framework to comprehensively evaluate the deobfuscation performance regarding Potency, Resilience, Cost, and Compile Error. For our evaluation of ChatDEOB, we use three key metrics that are crucial in assessing various aspects of deobfuscation: Potency, Resilience, and Cost. Potency measures how well the deobfuscated code maintains the original functionality. It includes attributes such as McCabe Complexity, CFG Size, Program Length, Instruction Count, Code Optimization, and Compile Error. Lower values for each attribute indicate successful deobfuscation, implying that the obfuscated code has been restored concisely and efficiently. Resilience assesses the obfuscated code's resistance to reverse engineering tools. Attributes such as code optimization are included here, and according to the evaluation metric formula, lower values indicate a higher resistance protection strength. To summarize, we evaluate the deobfuscation performance of ChatDEOB using six attributes to obtain a comprehensive assessment of how successful deobfuscation could be from multiple perspectives. Cost is a metric that evaluates the time and resources required for the deobfuscation process. However, when comparing ChatDEOB with other models in deobfuscation, we exclude the Cost metric to focus more on assessing the reliability of the deobfuscated code. Secondly, we establish the experimental environment and evaluation methods. Generative LLMs tend to add comments automatically to aid in code understanding, so we first remove all comments from the generated code to prevent them from affecting the SacreBLEU score, as the presence of comments in both the reference and candidate files can cause discrepancies in the SacreBLEU score. Removing the comments ensures a more accurate evaluation of the code's performance. We then quantitatively assess the similarity between the comment-free reference files and candidate files using the SacreBLEU scores. This setup allows us to exclude the impact of comments on the evaluation results and more accurately measure the actual functional similarity of the code.

To ensure that our evaluation of ChatDEOB's deobfuscation performance is comprehensive, we utilize 5,880 datasets (140 Benchmark Datasets × 7 Obfuscation methods × 2 Obfuscation Tools × 3 Models), the SacreBLEU score, and the Obfuscation Quality Quantification Framework. These evaluation methods collectively demonstrate ChatDEOB's superior performance.

First, Table 2 compares the performance of Gpt-3.5-turbo, Fine-tuned Gpt-3.5-turbo, and ChatDEOB on code subjected to various obfuscation methods and intensities using the SacreBLEU score. The results show that while Gpt-3.5-turbo scores an average of 29.20 and 16.22, Fine-tuned Gpt-3.5-turbo returns improved scores of 49.50 and 33.36, respectively. ChatDEOB performs the best, with average scores of 56.02 and 42.22, indicating its superior deobfuscation capability and ability to restore the original code before obfuscation closely.

Using the Obfuscation Quality Quantification Framework, we compare the performance of Original, Gpt-3.5-turbo, and ChatDEOB. This framework evaluates the success of deobfuscation from multiple perspectives using six attributes: McCabe Complexity, CFG Size, Program Length, Instruction Count, Code

**Table 2.** Comparison SacreBLEU Score of Gpt-3.5-turbo, Fine-tuned Gpt-3.5-turbo and ChatDEOB on Tigress and LLVM. Fine-tuned Gpt-3.5-turbo refers to the Gpt-3.5-turbo model fine-tuned using the method described in Sect. 4.1 Implementation.

| Obfuscation Intensity | Gpt-3.5-turbo | | Fine-tuned Gpt-3.5-turbo | | ChatDEOB | |
|---|---|---|---|---|---|---|
| | Tigress | LLVM | Tigress | LLVM | Tigress | LLVM |
| Level1 - FLT | 38.79 | 15.86 | 44.18 | 38.90 | 57.35 | 42.99 |
| Level1 - MBA | 37.89 | 16.76 | 49.30 | 37.74 | 54.66 | 47.03 |
| Level1 - OPA | 21.65 | 15.83 | 53.18 | 27.17 | 57.82 | 41.68 |
| Level2 - FLT&OPA | 25.36 | 16.63 | 53.97 | 30.40 | 56.25 | 38.97 |
| Level2 - MBA&FLT | 38.53 | 15.11 | 45.40 | 37.26 | 54.61 | 43.88 |
| Level2 - MBA&OPA | 19.18 | 17.79 | 50.88 | 30.12 | 57.34 | 40.59 |
| Level3 - MBA&FLT&OPA | 23.03 | 15.59 | 49.55 | 31.95 | 54.09 | 40.37 |
| Average | 29.20 | 16.22 | 49.50 | 33.36 | **56.02** | **42.22** |

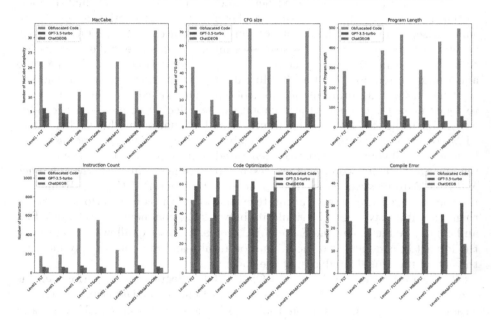

**Fig. 2.** Comparison of deobfuscation performance using McCabe, CFG Size, Program Length, Instruction Count, Code Optimization, and Compile Error metrics across different obfuscation levels.

Optimization, and Compile Error, as summarized in Fig. 2. Each attribute is a crucial indicator that sheds light on the reliability of the deobfuscated code.

ChatDEOB maintains values for McCabe Complexity, CFG Size, Program Length, and Instruction Count that are, on average, 85.01% and 21.28% lower than those of the Obfuscated Code and Gpt-3.5-turbo, respectively, regardless of the obfuscation level. This demonstrates ChatDEOB's ability to restore obfuscated code more simply and efficiently. Additionally, It excels with superior performance in Code Optimization, indicating its effectiveness in this area. Finally, the Compile Error metric assesses the success of code compilation. ChatDEOB reduces compilation errors to an average of 21%, compared to Gpt-3.5-turbo's 36%, indicating a more effective transformation of the obfuscated code.

These results demonstrate ChatDEOB's excellent deobfuscation performance across various obfuscation methods. Particularly in metrics such as McCabe Complexity, Program Length, Instruction Count, CFG Size, Code Coverage, and Code Optimization, ChatDEOB outperforms both Gpt-3.5-turbo and the Original. This provides evidence that ChatDEOB offers a robust deobfuscation solution that is capable of restoring obfuscated code simply and efficiently and is also highly reliable.

## 5    Conclusion

In this paper, we have proposed ChatDEOB based on an LLM to effectively deobfuscate codes that are obfuscated by several methods and tools. The LLM is fine-tuned in ChatDEOB with pairs of obfuscated and original codes. Also, we have conducted the prompt engineering to design outperformed prompts. To evaluate ChatDEOB, we employed the SacreBLEU score as a metric. We have shown that Gpt-3.5-turbo achieves a score of 22.71 on average. On the other hand, after the fine-tuning and prompt engineering, ChatDEOB achieves a score of 49.12, which is highly improved by 116.27%. Moreover, we have evaluated ChatDEOB on several combinations of obfuscation methods, which implies that it is outperforms regardless of obfuscation methods. To validate ChatDEOB, the Obfuscation Quality Quantification Framework has been employed, which provides six evaluation metrics. Through these six metrics, we were able to compare ChatDEOB with Gpt-3.5-turbo comprehensively. Unlike the existing methods that require manual analysis, ChatDEOB is able to generate deobfuscated codes in a fully automated manner. Finally, we believe that ChatDEOB is extensively applicable to unknown obfuscation methods. Since fine-tuning and prompt engineering can be conducted accumulatively to improve the performance of ChatDEOB, Chat-DEOB is expected to stay effective against new obfuscation methods. Given this, future research should focus on further refining the model's adaptability and real-time performance. In conclusion, our research suggests that harnessing the power of an LLM for deobfuscation can help analysts flexibly respond to the latest obfuscation methods, thus significantly improving the accuracy and efficiency of software security analysis.

**Acknowledgements.** This work was supported by Institute of Information & communications Technology Planning & Evaluation (IITP) grant funded by the Korea government (MSIP) (No. RS-2024-00399389, Generative AI based Binary Deobfuscation Technology and Its Evaluation Metrics).

# References

1. Amine Ferrag, M., Alwahedi, F., Battah, A., Cherif, B., Mechri, A., Tihanyi, N.: Generative AI and large language models for cyber security: all insights you need. arXiv e-prints, pp. arXiv–2405 (2024)
2. Banescu, S., Collberg, C., Ganesh, V., Newsham, Z., Pretschner, A.: Code obfuscation against symbolic execution attacks. In: Proceedings of the 32nd Annual Conference on Computer Security Applications, pp. 189–200 (2016)
3. Blazytko, T., Contag, M., Aschermann, C., Holz, T.: Syntia: synthesizing the semantics of obfuscated code. In: 26th USENIX Security Symposium (USENIX Security 2017), pp. 643–659 (2017)
4. Chataut, R., Gyawali, P.K., Usman, Y.: Can AI keep you safe? A study of large language models for phishing detection. In: 2024 IEEE 14th Annual Computing and Communication Workshop and Conference (CCWC), pp. 0548–0554. IEEE (2024)
5. David, R., Coniglio, L., Ceccato, M., et al.: Qsynth-a program synthesis based approach for binary code deobfuscation. In: BAR 2020 Workshop (2020)
6. Derner, E., Batistič, K., Zahálka, J., Babuška, R.: A security risk taxonomy for large language models. arXiv preprint arXiv:2311.11415 (2023)
7. Jin, H., Lee, J., Yang, S., Kim, K., Lee, D.H.: A framework to quantify the quality of source code obfuscation. Appl. Sci. **14**(12), 5056 (2024)
8. Kochberger, P., Schrittwieser, S., Schweighofer, S., Kieseberg, P., Weippl, E.: Sok: automatic deobfuscation of virtualization-protected applications. In: Proceedings of the 16th International Conference on Availability, Reliability and Security. pp. 1–15 (2021)
9. Kolosnjaji, B., Zarras, A., Webster, G., Eckert, C.: Deep learning for classification of malware system call sequences. In: AI 2016: Advances in Artificial Intelligence: 29th Australasian Joint Conference, Hobart, TAS, Australia, 5–8 December 2016, Proceedings 29, pp. 137–149. Springer (2016)
10. László, T., Kiss, Á.: Obfuscating C++ programs via control flow flattening. Annales Universitatis Scientarum Budapestinensis de Rolando Eötvös Nominatae, Sectio Computatorica **30**(1), 3–19 (2009)
11. Lee, J., Lee, W.: Simplifying mixed Boolean-arithmetic obfuscation by program synthesis and term rewriting. In: Proceedings of the 2023 ACM SIGSAC Conference on Computer and Communications Security, pp. 2351–2365 (2023)
12. Li, S., Jia, C., Qiu, P., Chen, Q., Ming, J., Gao, D.: Chosen-instruction attack against commercial code virtualization obfuscators. In: Proceedings of the 29th Network and Distributed System Security Symposium (2022)
13. Majumdar, A., Thomborson, C.: Manufacturing opaque predicates in distributed systems for code obfuscation. In: Proceedings of the 29th Australasian Computer Science Conference, vol. 48, pp. 187–196 (2006)
14. Mathews, N.S., Brus, Y., Aafer, Y., Nagappan, M., McIntosh, S.: Llbezpeky: leveraging large language models for vulnerability detection. arXiv preprint arXiv:2401.01269 (2024)
15. Meng, R., Mirchev, M., Böhme, M., Roychoudhury, A.: Large language model guided protocol fuzzing. In: Proceedings of the 31st Annual Network and Distributed System Security Symposium (NDSS) (2024)
16. National Institute of Standards and Technology: Software Assurance Reference Dataset Test Suites (2017). https://samate.nist.gov/SARD/test-suites/112

17. OpenAI: Fine-tuning (2023). https://platform.openai.com/docs/guides/fine-tuning

18. Papineni, K., Roukos, S., Ward, T., Zhu, W.J.: Bleu: a method for automatic evaluation of machine translation. In: Proceedings of the 40th Annual Meeting of the Association for Computational Linguistics, pp. 311–318 (2002)

19. Post, M.: A call for clarity in reporting bleu scores. arXiv preprint arXiv:1804.08771 (2018)

20. Radford, A., Narasimhan, K., Salimans, T., Sutskever, I., et al.: Improving language understanding by generative pre-training (2018)

21. Saxe, J., Berlin, K.: Deep neural network based malware detection using two dimensional binary program features. In: 2015 10th International Conference on Malicious and Unwanted Software (MALWARE), pp. 11–20. IEEE (2015)

22. Tan, H., Luo, Q., Li, J., Zhang, Y.: Llm4decompile: decompiling binary code with large language models. arXiv preprint arXiv:2403.05286 (2024)

23. Technical University of Munich: Obfuscation Benchmarks (2016). https://github.com/tum-i4/obfuscation-benchmarks

24. White, J., et al.: A prompt pattern catalog to enhance prompt engineering with chatgpt. arXiv preprint arXiv:2302.11382 (2023)

25. Zhou, Y., Main, A., Gu, Y.X., Johnson, H.: Information hiding in software with mixed Boolean-arithmetic transforms. In: International Workshop on Information Security Applications, pp. 61–75. Springer (2007)

# An Effective Ensemble Algorithm for Short-Term Load Forecasting

En-Wei Zhang, Luo-Fan Wu, and Chun-Wei Tsai[✉]

Computer Science and Engineering, National Sun Yat-sen University,
Kaohsiung, Taiwan
{m113040054,m123040025}@student.nsysu.edu.tw,
cwtsai@mail.nsysu.edu.tw

**Abstract.** Short-term load forecasting (STLF) is a critical issue for managing electricity distribution systems because its accuracy might strongly impact the performance and security of the power system. An effective load forecasting system, of course, can also be used to detect and prevent abnormal behaviors (e.g., electricity theft detection) to further provide a stable and safe power system. That is why extensive studies have been presented by using statistical, machine learning, and deep learning methods. However, each learning model has its strengths to capture specific patterns in the load profile. To integrate the strengths of different deep learning algorithms, an ensemble model, which contains three deep learning mechanisms, including convolution, self-attention, and recurrent, is proposed in this paper. Because of the high uncertainty and volatility, a single-step horizon will be focused on while predicting the load at the residential level to ensure timely and precise responses to security threats. Multiple-step forecasting will also be conducted at the aggregated level to further enhance the robustness of the power grid security. Furthermore, considering the distinct behavior in the load profile, the proposed method is designed accordingly to adapt to each level. The experimental results show the effectiveness of the proposed method compared with deep learning models on both levels across two well-known datasets.

**Keywords:** Smart grid · deep learning · machine learning

## 1 Introduction

The short-term load forecasting (STLF) [17] is one of well-known problems in smart grid. Accurately predicting load usage in advance can help energy companies formulate effective plans for power transmission. Many well-known statistical methods were used to deal with the STLF problem. Multiple linear regression (MLR) [2] treats the load value in each timestep as a variable, looking to minimize the square error between the actual value and prediction. Another widely used method is autoregressive integrated moving average model (ARIMA) [28], using the sliding window to capture the average load usage in the focused period. However, statistical methods have limitations because they often find it hard to learn personalized information about users and have difficulties handling complex and numerous data. As the data grows in complexity and size recently,

J.-H. Lee et al. (Eds.): WISA 2024, LNCS 15499, pp. 164–175, 2025.
https://doi.org/10.1007/978-981-96-1624-4_13

extracting useful information from the data becomes a challenging issue for these traditional statistical approaches.

Due to these abovementioned limitations, machine learning has been used to handle more complicated data recently. The study [15] used a three-layer multilayer perceptron (MLP) and added extra timestamp vectors into the load profiles, enhancing the ability of MLP to learn the temporal relationships in the time-series data. Support vector regression (SVR) [6] allows the load profiles to be analyzed in a higher-dimensional space through the projection of kernel function. This minimizes the distance of each load profile to the hyperplane, making it possible to realize the non-linear components between samples. $k$-nearest neighbor (KNN) [1] generates the prediction based on the Euclidian distance of each nearest $k$ sample. The number of $k$ can significantly affect the performance of this algorithm.

Most machine learning models are not inherently designed to handle sequential or time-series data directly. This limitation restricts their ability to fully understand the relationship between temporal information and load usage. Some deep learning models were developed without such limitation when handling time-series data. Recurrent neural network (RNN) [23] and long short-term memory (LSTM) [11] networks are capable of learning temporal information from time-series data recursively. Temporal convolutional network (TCN) [4] adapted from convolutional networks, and it was specifically designed for time-series data. Furthermore, transformers-based have also been modified to enhance prediction accuracy in forecasting topics [31]. Based on our observation, different mechanisms of deep learning models have advantages in capturing the load profile trends. In the STLF problem, the load prediction problem can be categorized into two levels based on data granularity [25]. As shown in Fig. 1, the first one is the residential level [26], which suffers from great uncertainty and volatility, providing finer granularity predictions. The other one is aggregated level [27], which means predicting an area load usage of households, offering a coarser granularity prediction. In this paper, the proposed method will be applied on both levels to evaluate the effectiveness of each level. The main contributions of this paper are as follows:

1. An ensemble algorithm was proposed to integrate three mechanisms of deep learning model into a hybrid generative-style model.
2. The proposed method was applied to both residential level and aggregated level to show its effectiveness on two electricity load datasets.

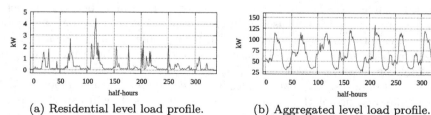

(a) Residential level load profile.          (b) Aggregated level load profile.

**Fig. 1.** The comparisons between residential and aggregated levels.

3. Clustering algorithm and different designs on meta-learner will be used to improve the forecasting results.

The remaining sections of this paper are as follows: Sect. 2 begins with the problem definitions of residential and aggregated levels, followed by existing research on both levels. Section 3 turns to the basic concept and the details of the proposed algorithm on different levels. Section 4 shows the experiment results conducted on two datasets on both levels. Finally, the conclusion and future work are presented in Sect. 5.

## 2   Related Work

### 2.1   The Problem Definition

The goal of load prediction is to minimize the error between forecasted values and actual load consumption [10]. An accurate load prediction is important for grid management, which provides energy companies with an insight of a better resource allocation and planning. To handle this problem by using deep learning models, the sliding window method is applied to segment the historical load profiles into input and target sequences. The following is the definition:

$$X_i = \{x_1^d, x_2^d, \ldots, x_t^d\}, \tag{1}$$

$$Y_i = \{y_{t+1}^o, y_{t+2}^o, \ldots, y_T^o\}, \tag{2}$$

where $X_i$ is the $i$-th input sequence, composed of vectors from $x_1^d$ to $x_t^d$. $x_t^d$ contain $d$-dimension features at each time $t$. $Y_i$ is the $i$-th target sequence, composed of vectors from $y_t^o$ to $y_T^o$. $y_t^o$ represents the $o$-dimension vectors, which is the actual load consumption. In this paper, root mean square error (RMSE), represented as $L(M^j, X_i^j, Y_i^j) = \text{RMSE} = \sqrt{\frac{1}{N}\sum_{i=0}^{N}\left(M^j(X_i^j) - Y_i^j\right)^2}$, where $M^j$ represents the prediction model for the load profile $j$. $X_i^j$ and $Y_i^j$ represent the input and output sequence of load profile $j$, respectively, and are used in the loss function to minimize the difference between predictions and actual consumptions. Compared with mean square error (MSE), the scale of units will become $kWh^2$ rather than the same scale unit of RMSE, unlike mean absolute percentage error (MAPE), which suffers from the divided-by-zero problem when the actual load values are close to zero. The forecast target differs between residential and aggregated levels because, as observed in Fig. 1, the load profile behavior varies significantly across these levels. The load profile at the residential level is noted by high uncertainty and contains numerous peaks. Such uncertainty is caused by the irregular habits of customers or the sudden opening of power-consuming appliances. The load profiles in aggregated level seems smoother and more regular because of the principle of large numbers. It will cancel individual uncertainties by aggregating them together. To make the applications more practical, the forecasting accuracy of the next single timestep will be focused for residential load consumption, which can be represented as $Y_i = \{y_{t+1}^o\}_{\text{res}}$.

In contrast, predicting multiple timesteps for the aggregated level will be conducted, which can be represented as $\boldsymbol{Y}_i = \{\boldsymbol{y}_{t+1}^o, \boldsymbol{y}_{t+2}^o, \ldots, \boldsymbol{y}_T^o\}_{\mathrm{agg}}$, where $T$ is a variable to evaluate model performance, reflecting the ability to forecast different length of horizons.

## 2.2    Forecasting Methods

Due to the regular and periodic nature of load profiles at aggregated level, statistical methods such as ARIMA [28] and linear regression (LR) [2] are often employed compared with another level. Rather than only minimizing mean-squared error as usual, a study [7] conducted comparisons of many linear models. One of them is adding regularization terms to penalize coefficients that are too large. Compared with traditional statistical methods, machine learning based models demonstrate a better ability to capture the non-linear relationship in load profiles. It can be divided into two main parts: non-neural-based and neural-based. Non-neural-based studies [5,13] have utilized SVR to address the STLF problem on aggregated and residential levels. A weighted $k$-nearest neighbor (WKNN) [8] algorithm was employed to solve this problem. Rather than averaging the nearest $k$ neighbor, this method increases the weight of samples by their Euclidean distance from each other. A closer sample will get a higher weight when making predictions. The variations of decision tree conducted on the STLF problem are presented in the study [9].

Neural-based algorithms like deep neural network (DNN) [12], recurrent neural network (RNN) [26], convolution neural network (CNN) [18], and transformer [14,21,31] models have been utilized to deal with STLF problems. Shi et al. [26] noticed that the behavior between customers might suffer similarly. A pooling strategy was presented to enhance the accuracy of prediction. Wang et al. [30] used temporal convolution network (TCN) [4], a variation of CNN, to obtain better results than LSTM model. Zhou et al. [31] modified the designation of the decoder and the mechanism of self-attention to outperform other transformer-based models. Additionally, the nature of neural-based algorithms allows for the combinations of various deep learning models. Kim and Chuo [16] used CNN to extract the meaningful features among many variables. Then LSTM model was used to learn relationships in time-series, yielding better forecasting results compared with just using LSTM or CNN only. Aouad et al. [3] proposed a sequence-to-sequence CNN combined with attention mechanism for handling the STLF problem. The experiment results showed the architecture of combining CNN and self-attention can outperform other sequence-to-sequence models.

## 3    Proposed Method

In this paper, we observe different load profile behaviors for residential and aggregated levels, as shown in Fig. 1. This paper proposes an ensemble load forecasting model that features three different deep learning models and customized meta-learners. As shown in Fig. 2, the data preprocessing will be conducted, including

168     E.-W. Zhang et al.

missing value imputation and normalization. Furthermore, according to different scenarios of prediction level, clustering algorithm and aggregating method will be applied to divide the STLF problem into residential level (A) and aggregated level (B).

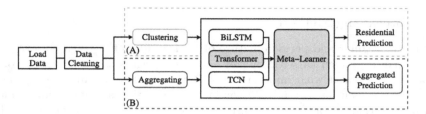

**Fig. 2.** The overview of proposed method.

At the residential level, a clustering algorithm is applied to group customers based on similarity among load profiles, allowing the model to learn the shared uncertainty within the same group. An area's total load usage is shown at the aggregated level by adding load profiles for each customer. To capture different load profile trends, the proposed method utilizes TCN [4] based on convolution, BiLSTM [24] based on recurrent, and transformer [29] based on self-attention. There are slightly different designations of transformer decoder and meta-learner for residential and aggregated levels, marked orange in Fig. 2. Integrating submodels through a meta-learner makes the proposed method achieve better prediction accuracy in most cases, as shown in the experimental results.

### 3.1   Aggregated Level

In this scenario, our goal is to conduct a relatively long-term prediction of the aggregation load usage of residents in an area. Making an accurate prediction could help create a better schedule for electricity generation. The way how to process the data, the designations of transformer decoder and meta-learner will be followed.

**Aggregation** will be conducted at this level. The dataset used in this paper is the load records of users, including buildings and residents. Sevlian and Rajagopal [25] explored the relationship among load profiles by aggregating them as the load profile, as shown in Fig. 1(b). According to the law of large numbers, the more load profiles are aggregated, the smoother the aggregation profiles will be. Figure 3 takes the example of $k$ load profiles, and each load profile may record other variables like temperature and humidity. Each variable will be aggregated to form aggregated level load profiles. Observed that the behavior of load profiles in aggregated level is much smoother than the residential level.

**Transformer Decoder** generates a sequence of load predictions, as shown in Fig. 4. The behavior of decoder can be divided into training and inference phases. During the decoder training, the actual load values are used as inputs, which is called teacher-forcing. Masked self-attention is employed to prevent

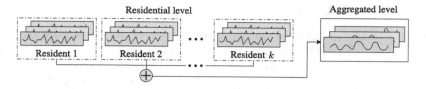

**Fig. 3.** Aggregation of load profiles.

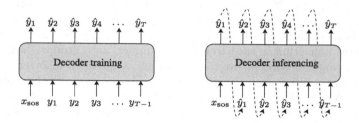

**Fig. 4.** The behavior of decoder in aggregated level.

the leakage of future information. In the inference phase, the last step input of encoder will be treated as the start of sequence $x_{sos}$ in the decoder. The $x_{sos}$ activates decoder to generate outputs through dynamic decoding. The output of each previous step is recursively used as the input for the next step until the entire sequence is wholly predicted.

**Meta-learner** in this level is used to integrate a series of predictions from submodels by selecting the most accurate predictions from each submodel, resulting in the final prediction that outperforms any single model. To incorporate two different output styles: generative style and dynamic decoding, a self-attention based meta-learner is presented. The output of submodels is processed with positional encoding before entering self-attention blocks. After the positional encoding, the output of transformer will serve as query vectors, and the others will be treated as key and value vectors in the cross-attention. The attention score produced from cross-attention is then fed into a feed-forward network (FFN) along with the outputs of each submodel to generate final predictions (Fig. 5).

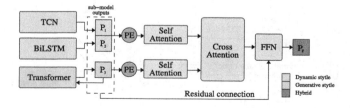

**Fig. 5.** Meta-learner of aggregated level.

## 3.2   Residential Level

Prediction at residential level aims to predict the load values recorded by smart meters. Due to the high uncertainty and volatility within these load profiles, making relatively long-term forecasts is quite challenging and often results in lagging predictions. Therefore, improving the prediction for next single timestep will be emphasized at this level.

**Clustering** algorithm is applied to explore the relationship between users. Based on the study [26], the pooling mechanism is presented because of the finding that a group of customers containing similarity might improve the forecasting accuracy. Here, rather than randomly grouping customers in the study [26], $k$-means algorithm is used to divide customers into groups. Note that the max-min scaling is needed before the clustering, avoiding an incorrect clustering result caused by different scales of load usage. Not only can the accuracy be improved through the clustering algorithm, but the amount of model usage can also be reduced. The clustering algorithm groups the customers, and hence, the model usage can be reduced from $m_n$ to $m_k$. The one-hot encoding creates extra variables to identify information of customers in the same group.

**Transformer Decoder** is used to generate load predictions for the next time step. Informer [32], a variant of transformer [29], developed a generative-style decoder. Rather than dynamic-style decoder in vanilla designation, the decoder here outputs the prediction results at once. The following is definition:

$$X_{sos} = \{x_i \mid x_i \in X_{enc}, \frac{\text{len}(X_{enc})}{2} \leq i \leq \text{len}(X_{enc})\}, \tag{3}$$

$$X_{dec} = \text{concat}(X_{sos}, X_0), \tag{4}$$

where $X_{dec}$ is the decoder's input. $X_{sos}$ denotes the start of sequence, composed of the last half of encoder inputs $X_{enc}$. A zero vector $X_0$ is concatenated at the end of $X_{sos}$ to form the decoder input $X_{dec}$. Compared with the original decoder used in the study [29], the generative-style decoder allows it to have a more extended sequence input. It provides the decoder with more information than using only the last step from the encoder inputs. The position of zero vector plays a role in the query vector to investigate the importance of the sequence.

**Meta-learner** is used to determine the portion of each model at this level. Unlike just averaging the predictions of three submodels, the deep neural network

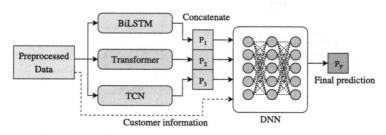

**Fig. 6.** Meta-learner of residential level.

is used to adjust the main component of submodels. As shown in Fig. 6, besides the vanilla architecture of the stacking method, an additional path is added to inform the meta-learner which load profile is being predicted. The reason why the extra path is needed for the meta-learner is that each model handles load profiles from residents. With the help of customer information, meta-learner can adjust the weight of submodel effectively and hence increase the prediction accuracy.

## 4   Experimental Results

### 4.1   Experimental Environment, Settings, and Datasets

All simulations are conducted on a PC with an AMD-Ryzen 7 5700X processor, 128 GB for main memory, and NVIDIA GeForce RTX 3080 Ti. Deep learning models are written in PyTorch 2.0.1 and Python with the version of 3.8.16 on Ubuntu 20.04.6 LTS. For the comparisons of forecasting models, the number of epochs is set equal to 100 with the mechanism of early stopping, the learning rate is fixed at 0.001, and the batch size initially set to 48 and increased to 480 along with the epochs progress. To evaluate the proposed ensemble architecture, two datasets with different size of variables are used to compare deep learning models. The following is the introduction of datasets:

1. Customer Behavior Trials (ISET) [20], provided by the Commission for Energy Regulation in Ireland. It aims to investigate the habits of customers. The dataset includes 6,435 smart meters collected during July 1, 2009 to December 31, 2010. In this paper, we select 920 residents in the dataset as parameter settings of study [26]. The data is split into 1,440 data points for testing, 2,880 for the validation set, and the remaining will be training set.
2. Ausgrid Resident [22], collected from the biggest power company in the east of Australia. The dataset includes 300 smart meters gathered since July 1, 2010 to June 30, 2013. According to different deployment of appliance. the number of variables range from 2 to 3 in the last year of dataset. Zero imputation is used for missing variables to ensure the deep learning models function normally. The way to split dataset is same as previous one.

The selected users in above dataset may contain missing values. In order to let the data can be send into models, the imputation of missing values is followed.

$$f(x_t^i) = \begin{cases} \bar{X}^i, & \text{if } x_t^i \text{ is NaN}, \\ x_t^i, & \text{otherwise}, \end{cases} \tag{5}$$

where $x_t^i$ represents the load value of $i$ user recorded at time $t$. If the value is missing, which will be replaced as the average values of the user.

### 4.2   Results of Aggregated Level

The mean absolute percentage error (MAPE) is introduced in this level formulated as: $\text{MAPE} = \frac{1}{N} \sum_{i=1}^{N} \left| \frac{y_i - \hat{y}_i}{y_i} \right| \times 100\%$, where $y_i$ represents the actual load value and $\hat{y}_i$ is the prediction value. The calculation makes the metric become a dimensionless quantity. The smaller the values of the metrics, the more accurate the prediction is. The benchmark models include CNN-LSTM, Attention-LSTM, Transformer, Informer, TCN, and ASEA. Each model will take the past 96 timesteps of load data as model input to predict the next 48 timesteps. As shown in Table 1, Attention-LSTM demonstrates superior performance compared to CNN-LSTM in both datasets, indicating the benefit of combining attention mechanisms and recurrent networks in two datasets. Also, the TCN and BiLSTM have their advantages. The TCN model yields great prediction results in the Ausgrid dataset. Instead, the BiLSTM model is good at predicting results in ISET dataset. This indicates that the TCN can handle multivariable datasets much better than the BiLSTM. The performance of the dynamic decoding style transformer may not be as strong as the Informer. Informer model performs well in MAPE metric, indicating the designation can minimize the relative errors in the single-variable dataset. Rather than using a single model, ASEA is an ensemble model proposed in the study [19]. Here, modifying the output layer makes it suitable for handling this problem. Due to the effective designation of meta-learner in the proposed method, the output of submodels can be integrated to be the ultimate prediction, achieving the most accuracy in most scenarios.

**Table 1.** Comparisons of aggregated level.

| Model | ISET | | | Ausgrid | | |
|---|---|---|---|---|---|---|
| | MAE | RMSE | MAPE(%) | MAE | RMSE | MAPE(%) |
| CNN-LSTM | 2.2947 | 3.1263 | 19.4411 | 1.4921 | 1.9844 | 20.9205 |
| Attention-LSTM | 2.2812 | 3.1642 | 18.9331 | 1.4165 | 1.9179 | 18.8902 |
| Transformer [29] | 2.3063 | 3.1913 | 18.8909 | 1.4751 | 1.9959 | 19.6663 |
| Informer [32] | 2.2995 | 3.1515 | **18.5639** | 1.4403 | 1.9245 | 19.5485 |
| BiLSTM [24] | 2.2790 | 3.1084 | 19.2193 | 1.4112 | 1.8926 | 19.4583 |
| TCN [4] | 2.2807 | 3.1289 | 19.2797 | 1.3942 | 1.8806 | 18.9465 |
| ASEA [19] | 2.2662 | 3.0927 | 19.2601 | 1.3846 | 1.8568 | 19.0441 |
| Proposed method | **2.2544** | **3.0670** | 19.2313 | **1.3732** | **1.8475** | **18.7485** |

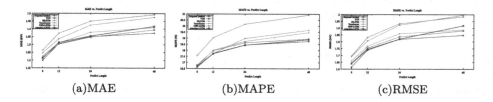

(a)MAE            (b)MAPE            (c)RMSE

**Fig. 7.** The comparison of prediction horizon.

As shown in Fig. 7, it is made by running models on the Ausgrid dataset. The figure shows the ability of models to predict different time horizons from 6 to 48. We can see that the attention-LSTM model has a remarkable ability in handling the scenarios of 12 and 24. In most cases, our proposed method can reach the best accuracy. Along with the prediction length going longer, the advantages of our proposed method gradually exhibit.

## 4.3    Results of Residential Level

In this level, the equation introduced in the previous level cannot be used because the load usage is often close to zero, leading to a divide-by-zero problem. Therefore, the normalized root mean squared error (NRMSE), as used in the study [26], is introduced. NRMSE is a dimensionless metric like MAPE and it is defined as $\left( \sqrt{ \left( \sum_{i=0}^{N} (y_i - \hat{y}_i)^2 \right) / N } \right) / (y_{max} - y_{min})$, where $y_{max}$ means the maximum and $y_{min}$ is the minimum in the load profile. As Table 2 shows, transformer shows great prediction results in the MAE metric for both datasets, reflecting its strength of minimizing average absolute errors but not RMSE and NRMSE in both datasets. TCN also has a good performance in NRMSE on the ISET dataset but not MAE and RMSE in both datasets. On the other hand, the proposed method performs well across both datasets, achieving the lowest values in most cases. The stacking architecture effectively combines the outputs of different models, resulting in significantly reducing the forecasting error. This indicates that the proposed method provides the most accurate predictions among all the models.

**Table 2.** Comparisons of residential level.

| Model | ISET | | | Ausgrid | | |
|---|---|---|---|---|---|---|
| | MAE | RMSE | NRMSE | MAE | RMSE | NRMSE |
| CNN-LSTM | 0.2899 | 0.5175 | 0.1075 | 0.2448 | 0.3804 | 0.1517 |
| Attention-LSTM | 0.3016 | 0.5243 | 0.1073 | 0.2292 | 0.3598 | 0.1436 |
| Informer [32] | 0.2723 | 0.4816 | 0.0998 | 0.1756 | 0.2800 | 0.1143 |
| PDRNN [26] | 0.2614 | 0.4571 | 0.0954 | 0.1496 | 0.2487 | 0.1014 |
| Transformer [29] | 0.2547 | 0.4519 | 0.0927 | **0.1421** | 0.2455 | 0.0991 |
| BiLSTM [24] | 0.2597 | 0.4492 | 0.0967 | 0.1451 | 0.2460 | 0.0994 |
| TCN [4] | 0.2560 | 0.4504 | **0.0919** | 0.1466 | 0.2474 | 0.0999 |
| ASEA [19] | 0.2621 | 0.4686 | 0.0971 | 0.1517 | 0.2493 | 0.1018 |
| Proposed method | **0.2522** | **0.4476** | 0.0933 | **0.1421** | **0.2441** | **0.0986** |

# 5    Conclusion

To investigate the short-term load forecasting problem in detail, this paper conducts a comprehensive analysis at both the residential and aggregated levels. Due to the varying behavior of load profiles between customers, a clustering algorithm and aggregation method are applied to the residential and aggregated levels, respectively. The residential forecasting horizon is set to a single timestep, providing a detailed load usage of the next timestep for each customer within the grid. The forecasting horizon is set to multiple timesteps, providing a relatively long-term load usage at aggregated level. The proposed method consists of three deep learning models, including BiLSTM, TCN, and transformer, with different designations of meta-learner to each level. Compared with other deep learning models, the experiment results show the effectiveness of proposed method on two load datasets from Australia and Ireland. In future work, we will attempt to use a pruning algorithm to further reduce the model size and computations of our proposed method so that it can be installed on IoT devices with limited storage capacity.

**Acknowledgment.** This work was supported in part by the National Science and Technology Council of Taiwan, R.O.C., under Contract NSTC111-2222-E-110-006-MY3, NSTC112-2628-E-110-001-MY3, and NSTC113-2634-F-110-001-MBK.

# References

1. Altman, N.S.: An introduction to kernel and nearest-neighbor nonparametric regression. Am. Stat. **46**(3), 175–185 (1992)
2. Amral, N., Ozveren, C., King, D.: Short term load forecasting using multiple linear regression. In: Proceedings of the International Universities Power Engineering Conference, pp. 1192–1198 (2007)
3. Aouad, M., Hajj, H., Shaban, K., Jabr, R.A., El-Hajj, W.: A CNN-sequence-to-sequence network with attention for residential short-term load forecasting. Electr. Power Syst. Res. **211**, 108152 (2022)
4. Bai, S., Kolter, J.Z., Koltun, V.: An empirical evaluation of generic convolutional and recurrent networks for sequence modeling. arXiv preprint arXiv:1803.01271 (2018)
5. Ceperic, E., Ceperic, V., Baric, A.: A strategy for short-term load forecasting by support vector regression machines. IEEE Trans. Power Syst. **28**(4), 4356–4364 (2013)
6. Cortes, C., Vapnik, V.: Support-vector networks. Mach. Learn. **20**, 273–297 (1995)
7. Dudek, G.: Pattern-based local linear regression models for short-term load forecasting. Electr. Power Syst. Res. **130**, 139–147 (2016)
8. Fan, G.F., Guo, Y.H., Zheng, J.M., Hong, W.C.: Application of the weighted k-nearest neighbor algorithm for short-term load forecasting. Energies **12**(5), 916 (2019)
9. Hambali, A., Akinyemi, M., JYusuf, N.: Electric power load forecast using decision tree algorithms. Comput. Inf. Syst. Dev. Inform. Allied Res. J. **7**(4), 29–42 (2016)
10. Hippert, H.S., Pedreira, C.E., Souza, R.C.: Neural networks for short-term load forecasting: a review and evaluation. IEEE Trans. Power Syst. **16**(1), 44–55 (2001)
11. Hochreiter, S., Schmidhuber, J.: Long short-term memory. Neural Comput. **9**(8), 1735–1780 (1997)
12. Hossen, T., Plathottam, S.J., Angamuthu, R.K., Ranganathan, P., Salehfar, H.: Short-term load forecasting using deep neural networks. In: Proceedings of the North American Power Symposium, pp. 1–6 (2017)

13. Humeau, S., Wijaya, T.K., Vasirani, M., Aberer, K.: Electricity load forecasting for residential customers: exploiting aggregation and correlation between households. In: Proceedings of the Sustainable Internet and ICT for Sustainability, pp. 1–6 (2013)
14. Huy, P.C., Minh, N.Q., Tien, N.D., Anh, T.T.Q.: Short-term electricity load forecasting based on temporal fusion transformer model. IEEE Access **10**, 106296–106304 (2022)
15. Kazeminejad, M., Dehghan, M., Motamadinejad, M., Rastegar, H.: A new short term load forecasting using multilayer perceptron. In: Proceedings of the International Conference on Information and Automation, pp. 284–288 (2006)
16. Kim, T.Y., Cho, S.B.: Predicting residential energy consumption using CNN-LSTM neural networks. Energy **182**, 72–81 (2019)
17. Kyriakides, E., Polycarpou, M.: Short term electric load forecasting: a tutorial. Trends Neural Comput. 391–418 (2007)
18. Lang, C., Steinborn, F., Steffens, O., Lang, E.W.: Applying a 1D-CNN network to electricity load forecasting. In: Proceedings of the Theory and Applications of Time Series Analysis, pp. 205–218 (2020)
19. Lu, C.T., Tsai, C.W.: An effective adaptive stacking ensemble algorithm for electricity theft detection. In: Proceedings of the International Conference on Intelligent Computing and its Emerging Applications, pp. 22–27 (2021)
20. Martin, G.: Electricity smart metering customer behaviour trials findings report, technical report. CER Commission for Energy Regulation, pp. 1–146 (2011)
21. Ran, P., Dong, K., Liu, X., Wang, J.: Short-term load forecasting based on CEEMDAN and transformer. Electr. Power Syst. Res. **214**, 108885 (2023)
22. Ratnam, E.L., Weller, S.R., Kellett, C.M., Murray, A.T.: Residential load and rooftop PV generation: an Australian distribution network dataset. Int. J. Sustain. Energ. **36**(8), 787–806 (2017)
23. Rumelhart, D.E., Hinton, G.E., Williams, R.J.: Learning representations by backpropagating errors. Nature **323**(6088), 533–536 (1986)
24. Schuster, M., Paliwal, K.K.: Bidirectional recurrent neural networks. IEEE Trans. Signal Process. **45**(11), 2673–2681 (1997)
25. Sevlian, R., Rajagopal, R.: Short term electricity load forecasting on varying levels of aggregation. arXiv preprint arXiv:1404.0058 (2014)
26. Shi, H., Xu, M., Li, R.: Deep learning for household load forecasting-a novel pooling deep RNN. IEEE Trans. Smart Grid **9**(5), 5271–5280 (2017)
27. Stephen, B., Tang, X., Harvey, P.R., Galloway, S., Jennett, K.I.: Incorporating practice theory in sub-profile models for short term aggregated residential load forecasting. IEEE Trans. Smart Grid **8**(4), 1591–1598 (2015)
28. Tarmanini, C., Sarma, N., Gezegin, C., Ozgonenel, O.: Short term load forecasting based on ARIMA and ANN approaches. Energy Rep. **9**, 550–557 (2023)
29. Vaswani, A., et al.: Attention is all you need. In: Advances in Neural Information Processing Systems, vol. 30 (2017)
30. Wang, H., Zhao, Y., Tan, S.: Short-term load forecasting of power system based on time convolutional network. In: Proceedings of the International Symposium on Next Generation Electronics, pp. 1–3 (2019)
31. Zhao, Z., et al.: Short-term load forecasting based on the transformer model. Information **12**(12), 516 (2021)
32. Zhou, H., et al.: Informer: beyond efficient transformer for long sequence time-series forecasting. In: Proceedings of the AAAI Conference on Artificial Intelligence, vol. 35, pp. 11106–11115 (2021)

# CPS Security

# PUF-Based Authentication and Authorization Protocol for IoT

Yu-Tse Shih[1], Shih-Ming Huang[2] , and Chun-I Fan[1,3,4]([envelope])

[1] Department of Computer Science and Engineering, National Sun Yat-sen
University, Kaohsiung 804201, Taiwan
cifan@mail.cse.nsysu.edu.tw
[2] Industrial Technology Research Institute, Hsinchu 310401, Taiwan
vincentSMH@itri.org.tw
[3] Information Security Research Center, National Sun Yat-sen University,
Kaohsiung 804201, Taiwan
[4] Intelligent Electronic Commerce Research Center, National Sun Yat-sen University,
Kaohsiung 804201, Taiwan

**Abstract.** With the rapid development of technology, smart devices
have become indispensable tools for people, and IoT devices are ubiquitous, playing an important role in our daily lives. When using IoT device
applications and services, users must go through complex authentication
processes, which are time-consuming and pose various security issues.
Not only must users be authenticated, but the devices must also be identified to ensure security. Physically Unclonable Functions (PUF) can be
considered as hardware fingerprints due to their randomness and unpre-
dictability, used to identify the uniqueness of devices. Given the limited
computational power of IoT devices, the need for lightweight mechanisms
is even more pronounced. Therefore, this protocol proposes a three-party
mutual authentication using a smartphone involving the user, the server,
and the IoT device. The PUF within the device generates a session key
to authorize the IoT device to use and access the service. Finally, the
contributions of this mechanism are highlighted through security analysis
and comparison with related works.

**Keywords:** Physically Unclonable Functions · Authentication ·
Authorization · Key Exchange · Internet of Things

## 1 Introduction

In recent years, Internet of things (IoT) environments [1] have grown dramati-
cally due to the rapid development of the 5th generation mobile network (5G) [2].
There are lots of IoT devices designed to assist our daily lives. More and more
IoT devices can be used through people's smart devices. Not only can those
IoT devices help with daily tasks but provide different services on their applications as well. There are two scenarios of network environments. One is a sensor
network environment, and the other is a machine-to-machine environment.

J.-H. Lee et al. (Eds.): WISA 2024, LNCS 15499, pp. 179–190, 2025.
https://doi.org/10.1007/978-981-96-1624-4_14

In the IoT environments, the user tends to access the IoT devices. Still, they must be authenticated or authorized to protect the user's privacy or guarantee the security of transferred information [3]. With the rapid development of technologies, there have been various types of IoT devices recently. We may access IoT devices in different situations and locations as we need. IoT devices provide many applications or services in public places that we only have to access temporarily. In this situation, we need an authorization framework [7] and acquire the right to access those IoT devices [4].

After the specific times, the IoT devices can provide their services to others. We take the rental car as an example. If a customer needs to rent a car for a week, then she/he needs to get the authority to access the specific smart car and access the services during the authorization time. Besides, the smartphone has gradually become an indispensable piece of equipment to humans recently. Hence, the smartphone is capable of playing an important role as an authentication factor to assist the authentication of IoT devices [5]. Customers can get authorization through authenticated smartphones. Under the circumstances, authenticating the specific IoT devices by Physically Unclonable Function (PUF) may become a proper method to deal with it. C. Herder *et al.* [6] mentioned that due to the slight differences between manufacturing chips, they generate different challenge-response pairs (CRPs). PUF generates different challenge-response pairs (CRPs). In 2017, M. Beltrán *et al.* [7] proposed an authentication and authorization protocol combining PUF and tokens. They adopted PUF and tokens to authenticate and authorize federated system-to-services through HTTP and CoAP.

The protocol uses pseudo-random function (PRF) and XOR operation instead of the traditional hash function and symmetric encryption algorithm, which ensures security while reducing the overhead. Moreover, the proposed protocol does not require the server to store a large number of challenge-response pairs (CRPs), which reduces the storage overhead on the server while avoiding the risk of leakage of CRPs. In summary, we will propose a novel protocol by applying PUF to enhance security during the authorization period with various services for IoT devices. Meanwhile, we simplify and accelerate the authorization process through the authenticated smartphone to achieve the authentication and authorization of the proposed protocol.

**Contributions.** We introduce a PUF-Based authentication and authorization protocol for IoT environment on the smartphone in this research. The contributions of the research are as follows:

1. The proposed protocol provides an approach to accelerate and simplify the authentication and authorization phase.
2. The proposed protocol applies PUF to guarantee the security of parameters and user's information and privacy.
3. The proposed protocol can provide more comprehensive security features than most related works.

## 2    Preliminaries

We will introduce all the definitions and knowledge of mechanisms used in the proposed scheme in this section.

**Internet of Things.** Recently, the Internet of Things has become more and more popular and common in our daily lives. In the Internet of Things environment, a combination of many different networks, such as machine-to-machine network (M2M) [8], device-to-device network (D2D) [9], wireless volumetric network (WBAN) [10] and wireless sensor network (WSN) [11]. The goal of IoT is to allow devices or sensors to connect and exchange data.

In the IoT environment, security issues [12] are the most important concern because the computing and storage capabilities of devices are uneven. In addition, group authentication and key agreement are important issues because devices and sensors will share data with many participants.

**Physically Unclonable Function.** This part introduces physically unclonable functions (PUF) in key generation applications and some low-cost authentication. First, it inspired PUFs and traditional secure non-volatile memory and defined two main types of PUFs: strong PUFs and weak PUFs. The strong PUF is usually used in low-cost authentication. Next, the implementation of weak PUF and its use in key generation applications are covered here. It covers error correction schemes such as pattern matching and index-based coding. Each PUF will output a unique value when it gets a challenge because of its integrated circuit (IC). So, each different PUF can generate its unique challenge-response pair. That's why someone called this characteristic like a fingerprint of this PUF. Another integrated circuit cannot produce it. Therefore, PUF can become a secret value to represent the specific device when we adopt it. Then, we briefly introduce the definition of PUF below:

Each PUF can be considered as a generator of the unique challenge-response pairs (CRPs). It can be represented as $R = PUF(C)$, where $C$ is a challenge and $R$ is the return. A PUF returns a 1-bit response in every execution. We denote an integrated PUF with $d$ PUFs by $d$-bit PUF, where $d > 1$. An ideal $d$-bit PUF should have the following properties:

- For any two different $d$-bit PUFs $PUF_1$, $PUF_2$, and any challenge $C_1$, $HD(PUF_1(C_1), PUF_2(C_1)) \approx d/2$, where $HD$ denotes the hamming distance.
- For any two different $d$-bit PUFs $PUF_1$, $PUF_2$, and any two different challenges $C_1$, $C_2$, $HD(PUF_1(C_1), PUF_2(C_2)) \approx d/2$.
- For any $d$-bit PUF $PUF_1$, and any challenge $C_1$, $HD(PUF_1(C_1), PUF_1(C_1)') = 0$. (But in reality, it usually has an error within $d/10$ bits since PUF may be affected by the environment.)
- For any $d$-bit PUF $PUF_1$, and any two different challenges $C_1$, $C_2$, $HD(PUF_1(C_1), PUF_1(C_2)) \approx d/2$.

# 3    Related Works

In this section, we introduce some related works and the survey paper from [18]. We compare some functionalities and security issues of these related works with the proposed scheme. There are many kinds of authentication methods in the IoT environments along with many existent challenges. We will briefly introduce and explain these related works and discuss their advantages and disadvantages.

## 3.1    Beltrán *et al.*'s Authorization Scheme with PUFs

In 2017, Beltrán *et al.* proposed an authorization scheme with PUFs [7]. The protocol usually guarantees the confidentiality and integrity of basic data and uses encryption to protect communication data, but there are still critical issues related to authorization and authentication. They provided a new system to service authorization and authentication mechanism based on a combination of PUF and two tokens, which can rely on HTTP or COAP on the joint plan to adapt to the particular requirements of this environment. This mechanism is validated, and they also use real healthcare case studies to evaluate its efficiency and safety.

## 3.2    Beltrán's Authentication Scheme in IoT

In 2018, Marta Beltrán proposed an IoT authentication and authorization scheme called identifying, authenticating, and authorizing smart objects and end-users to cloud services in the IoT [13]. Their scheme allows IoT services deployed in the cloud or locally to authenticate and authorize smart objects using COAP and HTTP. The end-users can be identified, authorized, and authenticated through their scheme through these smart objects and/or re-inquired if possible. In addition, they validated their scheme, using real healthcare case studies to evaluate its usability, efficiency, and safety.

## 3.3    Jin *et al.*'s Multi-factor Authenticated Key Exchange with PUF

In 2019, Jin *et al.* proposed an authenticated key Exchange with PUF named an efficient multi-factor authenticated key exchange with a physically unclonable function [19]. In this part, they proposed an efficient and secure physical non-transparent function based on multi-factor authentication key exchange (made by PUF). The main difficulty comes from the fact that it should establish public keys from multi-factor authenticators and PUF-embedded devices. Their architecture is a secure PUF production protocol, requiring only two communication phases.

### 3.4 Siddiqui *et al.*'s Lightweight PUF-PKI Digital Certificate Authentication Scheme for the IoTs

In 2023, Siddiqui *et al.* propose a highly secure and robust authentication protocol [14] based on a public key infrastructure (PKI) digital certificate based on two certificate authorities (CAs) for cloud IoT systems. The proposed authentication method is verified and validated using the Tamarin prover and supported with a detailed security and performance analysis discussion. The scheme's security and privacy attributes are compared with other IoT authentication schemes. The analysis has proved that the proposed authentication scheme is more secure and highly reliable as compared to the Prosanta and Biplab authentication schemes.

## 4 The Proposed Protocol

In this section, we propose a secure and lightweight PUF-based authentication and authorization protocol for IoT devices. There are three roles in the proposed protocol. The first one is user equipment (UE), the second role is an IoT device, and the last role is the server which is the provider of the service that the user tends to use. Each part in this protocol needs to carry a PUF chip and use PUF to generate parameters. In the registration phase, both the user and IoT device need to register with the server in a secure channel. Afterward, in the login phase, the user and IoT device are close to each other. They share the information generated by the server with each other through NFC communication. Next, the server verifies user equipment and IoT devices, respectively. If the user and IoT device pass the verification, the server generates and sends a session key to the IoT device. The proposed protocol contains three phases: the registration phase, the login phase, and the long-term key update phase.

### 4.1 Setup

In the beginning, $S$ sets the necessary parameters and functions used in the proposed protocol. $S$ first randomly picks a number $s$ as a secret key for symmetric encryption. We know that there is a very small difference between two responses in the same PUF function even if we use the same challenge. However, we can use a fuzzy extractor to recover the original output. Therefore, we assume that the perfect PUF function is adopted in the proposed protocol. It means that the PUF function will generate the same response if we issue the same challenge. Finally, $S$ needs to keep a registration table to verify the user and IoT device.

### 4.2 Registration

In the registration phase, we divide the proposed protocol into two parts, where one is user equipment and the other is an IoT device. Note that the registration phase is executed in a secure channel and user equipment needs to download and execute the procedure under the application. First, user equipment $i$ randomly

**Table 1.** Notations

| Notation | Description |
|---|---|
| $S$ | the server |
| $ID_i$ | the identity of user $i$ |
| $D_j$ | the identity of IoT device $j$ |
| $C_{ID_i}$ | a random number chosen by user $i$ as PUF function seed |
| $C_{S,ID_i}$ | a random number chosen by $S$ as PUF function seed |
| $R_{S,ID_i}^m$ | the $m$-th response generated from PUF function stored in $S$ |
| $PUF_{ID_i}$ | the 128-bit PUF in user $i$'s equipment |
| $Cert_T$ | the certificate with a time period $T$ |
| $C'_{S,ID_i}$ | new random number chosen by $S$ for user $i$ as PUF function seed |
| $s$ | a secret key kept by $S$ |
| $E_s(.)$ | a symmetric encryption with key $s$ |
| $D_s(.)$ | a symmetric decryption with key $s$ |
| $\oplus$ | the bitwise exclusive-or (XOR) operator |

chooses a number $C_{ID_i}$ and then user equipment $i$ inputs $C_{ID_i}$ as a challenge to the PUF function $n$ times and generates the response $R_{S,\ ID_i}^n$. Next, user equipment $i$ sends $ID_i$ and $R_{S,\ ID_i}^n$ to $S$. After $S$ receives the parameter from user $i$, $S$ also picks a random number $C_{S,\ ID_i}$ and takes this random number as a challenge into PUF function and executes $m_1$ times to generate $R_{S,ID_i}^{m_1}$. And then, $S$ sends $R_{S,\ ID_i}^{m_1}$ back to user $i$ and keeps $ID_i$, $C_{S,\ ID_i}$ and $R_{ID_i}^n$ in the registration table. At last, user equipment $i$ stores $R_{S,\ ID_i}^{m_1}$ and $C_{ID_i}$ in the equipment. The procedure of the IoT device part in the registration phase is mostly the same as the user equipment part. The only difference is that $S$ executes PUF function $m_2$ times instead of $m_1$.

### 4.3   Login and Session Key Establishment

In the scenario of the proposed protocol, the user needs to be close to the IoT device; therefore, the user can operate or use the IoT device. We assume that the user transfers and receives the parameters from $S$ in the registration phase under NFC communication. It means that there exists a secure channel between the user equipment and the IoT device. In the login phase, the application that works in the user equipment asks user $i$ to pass the biometric recognition and then the user equipment randomly chooses a number $r_{ID_i}$ and computes $P_{ID_i} = R_{S,\ ID_i}^{m_1} \oplus r_{ID_i}$. Next, the user equipment sends $P_{ID_i}$ to the IoT device. Note that the transfer channel between IoT devices and user equipment is based on NFC communication. Therefore, it can guarantee the security of parameter transmission. Meanwhile, the IoT device randomly picks a number $r_{D_j}$ and computes $P_{D_j} = R_{S,\ D_j}^{m_2} \oplus r_{D_j}$ and then sends it to user equipment. At last, user equipment computes $X = R_{S,\,D_j}^{m_2} \oplus r_{D_j} \oplus r_{ID_i}$ and IoT device computes $Y = R_{S,\,ID_i}^{m_1} \oplus r_{ID_i} \oplus r_{D_j}$ which will be stored in the device.

In the login and session key establishment phase, user $i$ inputs $C_{ID_i}$ to PUF function as a challenge and executes $n-1$ times to generate $R_{ID_i}^{n-1}$. Then, user $i$ computes $P_{ID_i,\,D_j} = E_{R_{ID_j}^{n}}\left(ID_i,\,D_j, X, R_{ID_i}^{n-1}\right)$ and sends $P_{ID_i,D_j}$ to $S$. At the same time, the IoT device computes $R_{D_j}^{n-1} = PUF_{D_j}^{n-1}\left(C_{D_j}\right)$ by the PUF function stored in the device. Next, the IoT device encrypts $ID_i, D_j, Y, R_{D_j}^{n-1}$ with symmetric key $R_{S,D_j}^{n}$ and then generates and sends $P_{D_j,ID_i}$ to $S$.

After receiving $P_{ID_i,D_j}$ and $P_{D_j,ID_i}$ from user $i$ and $D_j$, $S$ decrypts $P_{ID_i,D_j}$ with symmetric key $R_{ID_i}^{n}$ and decrypts $P_{D_j,ID_i}$ with symmetric key $R_{D_j}^{n}$ to get parameters $X$ and $Y$. Then, $S$ verifies if $X \oplus Y$ is equal to $R_{S,ID_i}^{m_1} \oplus R_{S,D_j}^{m_2}$. Next, $S$ randomly chooses $r_{i,j}$ and calculates $k_{S,D_j} = \left(r_{i,j} \oplus R_{D_j}^{n-1}\right)$. Meanwhile, $S$ executes PUF function $PUF_{S,ID_i}$ $m_1 - 1$ times and $PUF_{S,D_j}$ $m_2 - 1$ times to obtain $R_{S,ID_i}^{m_1-1}$ and $R_{S,D_j}^{m_2-1}$. At last, $S$ computes $P_{S,ID_i,D_j} = E_X\left(ID_i,\,D_j,\,Cert_T,\,R_{S,\,ID_i}^{m_1-1}\right)$ and $P_{S,\,D_j,\,ID_i} = E_Y(D_j,\,ID_i,\,Cert_T, R_{S,\,D_j}^{m_2-1})$ and then sends them to user $i$ and $D_j$, respectively.

Finally, user $i$ receives $R_{S,\,ID_i}^{m_1-1}$ and stores it in the device. In the IoT device side, $D_j$ also receives $P_{S,\,D_j,\,ID_i}$ and gets session key $k_{S,\,D_j}$ from decrypting $P_{S,\,D_j,\,ID_i}$. And then, $D_j$ stores $R_{S,\,ID_i}^{m_2-1}$ for next login. $D_j$ then uses session key $k_{S,\,D_j}$ to communicate with $S$. Note that $S$ will check $Cert_T$ to verify if this transmission is a replay attack or not. The session key establishment by $S$ of login phase is shown in Fig. 1.

## 4.4   Long Term Key Update Phase

In the long-term key update phase, we also divide this phase into two parts. The first one is the user equipment part, and the other is the IoT device part. The long-term key is limited when $m_1$ in user equipment or $m_2$ in the IoT device equals to 1. User equipment and IoT devices need to request $S$ to update the long-term key.

In the user equipment part, when $m_1 = 1$ in $R_{S,\,ID_i}^{m_1}$, UE needs to update the long-term key. User equipment first chooses a random number $u_{ID_i}$ and encrypts $ID_i, u_{ID_i}$ with $R_{S,\,ID_i}^{1}$ to generate $Req_{ID_i}$. And then, user $i$ sends $Req_{ID_i}$ to $S$. $S$ decrypts $Req_{ID_i}$ and randomly chooses a number $C_{S,\,ID_i}'$. Next, $S$ uses $C_{S,\,ID_i}'$ as new challenge and executes PUF function $m_1$ times to get $R_{S,\,ID_i}'^{m_1}$. At last, $S$ updates the information in registration table of user $i$ and sends $Res_{ID_i} = E_{u_{ID_i}}\left(ID_i,\,R_{S,\,ID_i}'^{m_1}\right)$ to user equipment. Finally, user $i$ decrypts $Res_{ID_i}$ and updates long term key as $R_{S,\,ID_i}'^{m_1}$.

In the IoT device part, when $m_2 = 1$ in $R_{S,D_j}'^{m_2}$, $D_j$ needs to update the long term key. $D_j$ first chooses a random number $u_{D_j}$ and encrypts $D_j, u_{D_j}$ with $R_{S,D_j}^{1}$ to generate $Req_{D_j}$. And then, $D_j$ sends $Req_{D_j}$ to $S$. $S$ decrypts $Req_{D_j}$

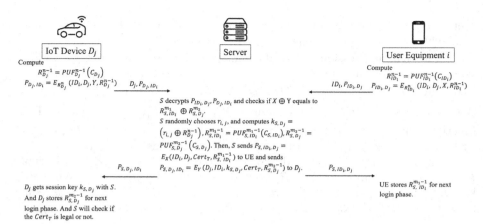

**Fig. 1.** Login and Session Key Establishment

and randomly chooses a number $C_{S,D_j}$. Next, $S$ uses $C'_{S,D_j}$ as new challenge and executes PUF function $m_2$ times to get $R'^{m_2}_{S,D_j}$. At last, $S$ updates the information in registration table of IoT device $D_j$ and sends $Res_{D_j} = E_{u_{D_j}}\left(D_j, R'^{m_2}_{S,D_j}\right)$ to IoT device. Finally, $D_j$ decrypts $Res_{D_j}$ and updates long term key as $R'^{m_2}_{S,D_j}$.

## 5   Security Analysis

In this part, we provide the security analysis corresponding to every phase of the proposed protocol. We protect the security of the parameters in the proposed protocol mainly based on the unique output from PUF chips. Each of the user equipment, the IoT device, and the server in the proposed protocol contains a PUF chip. Furthermore, only the same PUF chip can get the same response from the original challenge. Therefore, we generate the long-term key calculate some parameters in the registration phase, and store them in user equipment, IoT devices, and the server. Moreover, in the login phase, we update the session key every time we log in. Furthermore, we list some security properties we achieve in the proposed protocol as follows.

- Mutual Authentication

  We discuss mutual authentication between $S$ and the user side. In the proposed protocol, we discuss the mutual authentication between $S$ and IoT devices as well. In the Login and Session Key Establishment of the proposed protocol, the user equipment and the IoT device take $X$ and $Y$ as challenges in the challenge response pair. Since the parameter $X$ is computed from $R^{m_2}_{S,D_j}$, $r_{D_j}$ and $r_{ID_i}$, and $Y$ is computed from $R^{m_1}_{S,ID_i}$, $r_{D_j}$ and $r_{D_j}$, $r_{ID_i}$ and $r_{D_j}$, only $S$ can calculate $R^{m_2}_{S,D_j}$ and $R^{m_1}_{S,ID_i}$ through the corresponding PUF function. Therefore, $S$ can verify the legality of the user and IoT device by $X$

and $Y$. Finally, if $S$ can decrypt and compute the $P_{S, \ ID_i, \ D_j}$ and $P_{S, \ D_j, \ ID_i}$ correctly, user and IoT device can verify $S$.

- Resistance to the Replay Attack
  The adversary can replay $P_{ID_i, \ D_j}$ or $P_{D_j, \ ID_i}$ to $S$. However, the adversary can not affect the authentication procedure or cause any damage to the proposed protocol.
- Forward Secrecy
  Since $S$ keeps the PUFs in $S$'s database, the adversary can not produce the session key $R_{S, \ ID_i}$ or $R_{S, \ D_j}$ even if the adversary gets the long-term key $C_{S, \ ID_i}$ or $C_{S, \ D_j}$. Furthermore, $S$ will update the session key with the user equipment and IoT device. Even if the adversary obtains the session key, the adversary cannot still decrypt previous messages.
- Resisting Stolen User Equipment Attacks
  The operation of the proposed protocol is based on the applications stored in the smartphone. Furthermore, the PUF function also relies on the working device. If the device is off, then the PUF function can not produce any response. We adopt biometric authentication in the application to resist stolen user equipment attacks.

# 6    Performance Comparison and Results

## 6.1    Properties Comparison

In this section, we evaluate the functionalities and security properties with some related works. Because the proposed protocol is an authentication and authorization protocol by smartphone combined with PUF chips, we can not find precisely related work with the proposed protocol. However, we still compare some functions and security properties close to the proposed protocol. We compare six security properties in this section. We also list the security properties below in Table 2 that we achieve.

**Table 2.** The Comparisons of Functionalities and Security Properties

|    | Beltrán et al. [7] | Siddiqui et al. [14] | Beltrán [13] | Zhao et al. [15] | Yilmaz et al. [16] | Ours |
|----|----|----|----|----|----|----|
| S1 | Yes | No | Yes | Yes | Yes | Yes |
| S2 | No | Yes | No | Yes | No | Yes |
| S3 | No | Yes | No | Yes | No | Yes |
| S4 | No | No | No | No | No | Yes |
| S5 | No | No | No | Yes | No | Yes |

S1: Mutual Authentication; S2: Session Key Security; S3: Resistance to the Replay Attack; S4: Forward Secrecy; S5: Resisting Stolen User Equipment (SIM Card) Attack;

## 6.2  Computation Cost

In this paragraph, we evaluate the efficiency of the proposed protocol. We divide the proposed protocol into three phases. However, the setup will be only executed once. Hence, we only calculate three phases. The first one is the registration phase; every user and IoT device needs to register initially. And then, the second one is the login phase. Each registered user who tends to access the IoT Device needs to implement this phase. Finally, the IoT device needs to set a session key with $S$ in the third part of the login phase. We evaluate the computation cost of the registration, login, and long-term key update phases. The time of each operation is measured with Ubuntu 16.04, i7-6700 3.40 GHz, 16.0 GB DDR4 2133 MHz RAM, which have been shown in [15,17]. We define $T_e$ and $T_{PUF}$ to be the time cost for executing symmetric encryption and decryption for a 128-bit block with AES-EAX (0.05 ms) and PUF run time (0.12 ms), respectively.

In this part, we use some code names to represent the cost on which side and phase. We define $U$ as the user side, $I$ as the IoT device side, and $SV$ as the server side. Moreover, we use the number 1 for the registration phase, number 2 for the login phase, and 3 for the long-term key update phase. In the proposed protocol, the registration phase on the user side and IoT device side costs U1 $= nT_{PUF}$, and SV1 $= (m_1 + m_2)T_{PUF}$ in the server side. In the login phase, the cost in the user side is U2 $= (n - 1)T_{PUF} + 2T_e$, I2 $= (n - 1)T_{PUF} + 2T_e$ in the IoT device side, and SV2 $= (m_1 + m_2 - 2)T_{PUF} + 2T_e$ in the server side. Finally, in the long-term key update phase, the cost on the user side is U3 $= 2T_e$, I3 $= 2T_e$ in the IoT device side, and SV3 $= m_1T_{PUF} + 2T_e$ in the server side. The detailed information is shown in Table 3.

**Table 3.** The Comparisons of Functionalities and Security Properties

| | User Side (U) | IoT Device Side (I) | Server Side (SV) |
|---|---|---|---|
| Registration Phase (1) | **U1** $nT_{PUF}{=}0.12n$ (ms) | **I1** $nT_{PUF}{=}0.12n$ (ms) | **SV1** $(m_1{+}m_2)T_{PUF}$ $=0.12(m_1 + m_2)$ (ms) |
| Login Phase (2) | **U2** $(n - 1)T_{PUF}{+}2\,T_e = 0.12n - 0.02$ (ms) | **I2** $(n - 1)T_{PUF}{+}2\,T_e = 0.12 - 0.02$ (ms) | **SV2** $(m_1 + m_2 - 2)T_{PUF}{+}2\,T_e = 0.12(m_1{+}m_2) - 0.14$ (ms) |
| Long Term Key Update Phase (3) | **U3** $2\,T_e = 0.1$ (ms) | **I3** $2\,T_e = 0.1$ (ms) | **SV3** $m_1(m_2)T_{PUF}{+}2\,T_e = 0.12m_1(m_2) + 0.1$ (ms) |

## 7  Conclusion

In the proposed protocol, we not only combine the advantages of PUF and smartphones but also achieve fast authentication and authorization for IoT devices. We also provide security against replay attacks, perfect forward secrecy, and formal security proof to ensure that the proposed protocol is secure. Although only one service can be authorized each time in the proposed protocol, we hope to improve and achieve batch authorization to make the proposed protocol more convenient. Besides, we use certification with limited time to achieve the passive revocation in the proposed protocol. We consider increasing the properties of active revocation to conform to the reality usage. We believe that the proposed protocol can provide substantial assistance to improve the daily lives of human beings in the future.

**Acknowledgments.** This work was supported in part by the National Science and Technology Council of Taiwan under Grants NSTC 113-2634-F-110-001-MBK, 113-2221-E-110-082, in part by the Information Security Research Center at National Sun Yat-sen University, and in part by the Intelligent Electronic Commerce Research Center from the Featured Areas Research Center Program through the Framework of the Higher Education Sprout Project by the Ministry of Education in Taiwan.

# References

1. Chernyshev, M., Baig, Z., Bello, O., Zeadally, S.: Internet of Things (IoT): research, simulators, and testbeds. IEEE Internet Things J. **5**(3), 1637–1647 (2017)
2. 3GPP: TS 33.501 security architecture and procedures for 5G system. Technical report, 3GPP (2018)
3. El-Hajj, M., Fadlallah, A., Chamoun, M., Serhrouchni, A.: A survey of Internet of Things (IoT) authentication schemes. Sensors **19**(5), 1141 (2019)
4. Kim, H., Lee, E.A.: Authentication and authorization for the Internet of Things. IT Prof. **19**(5), 27–33 (2017)
5. Ferrag, M.A., Maglaras, L., Derhab, A.: Authentication and authorization for mobile IoT devices using biofeatures: recent advances and future trends. Secur. Commun. Netw. **2019** (2019)
6. Herder, C., Yu, M.-D., Koushanfar, F., Devadas, S.: Physical unclonable functions and applications: a tutorial. Proc. IEEE **102**(8), 1126–1141 (2014)
7. Beltrán, M., Calvo, M., González, S.: Federated system-to-service authentication and authorization combining PUFs and tokens. In: 2017 12th International Symposium on Re-Configurable Communication-Centric Systems-on-Chip (ReCoSoC), pp. 1–8 (2017)
8. Buratti, C., et al.: Testing protocols for the Internet of Things on the EuWIn platform. IEEE Internet Things J. **3**(1), 124–133 (2015)
9. Doppler, K., Rinne, M., Wijting, C., Ribeiro, C.B., Hugl, K.: Device-to-device communication as an underlay to LTE-advanced networks. IEEE Commun. Mag. **47**(12), 42–49 (2009)
10. Latré, B., Braem, B., Moerman, I., Blondia, C., Demeester, P.: A survey on wireless body area networks. Wireless Netw. **17**(1), 1–18 (2011)
11. Yick, J., Mukherjee, B., Ghosal, D.: Wireless sensor network survey. Comput. Netw. **52**(12), 2292–2330 (2008)
12. Granjal, J., Monteiro, E., Silva, J.S.: Security for the Internet of Things: a survey of existing protocols and open research issues. IEEE Commun. Surv. Tutor. **17**(3), 1294–1312 (2015)
13. Beltrán, M.: Identifying, authenticating and authorizing smart objects and end users to cloud services in Internet of Things. Comput. Secur. **77**, 595–611 (2018)

14. Siddiqui, Z., Gao, J., Khurram Khan, M.: An improved lightweight PUF-PKI digital certificate authentication scheme for the Internet of Things. IEEE Internet Things J. **9**(20), 19744–19756 (2022). https://doi.org/10.1109/JIOT.2022.3168726
15. Zhao, J., et al.: A secure biometrics and PUFs-based authentication scheme with key agreement for multi-server environments. IEEE Access **8**, 45292–45303 (2020)
16. Yilmaz, Y., Gunn, S.R., Halak, B.: Lightweight PUF-based authentication protocol for IoT devices. In: 2018 IEEE 3rd International Verification and Security Workshop (IVSW), pp. 38–43. IEEE (2018)
17. Kumari, S., et al.: A provably secure biometrics-based authenticated key agreement scheme for multi-server environments. Multimedia Tools Appl. **77**, 2359–2389 (2018)
18. Mall, P., Amin, R., Das, A.K., Leung, M.T., Choo, K.-K.R.: PUF-based authentication and key agreement protocols for IoT, WSNs, and smart grids: a comprehensive survey. IEEE Internet Things J. **9**(11), 8205–8228 (2022). https://doi.org/10.1109/JIOT.2022.3142084
19. Byun, J.W.: An efficient multi-factor authenticated key exchange with physically unclonable function. In: 2019 International Conference on Electronics, Information, and Communication (ICEIC). IEEE (2019)

# Field Testing and Detection of Camera Interference for Autonomous Driving

Ki Beom Park and Huy Kang Kim(✉)

School of Cybersecurity, Korea University, Seoul, Republic of Korea
{vkdnj0413,cenda}@korea.ac.kr

**Abstract.** In recent advancements in connected and autonomous vehicles (CAVs), automotive ethernet has emerged as a critical technology for in-vehicle networks (IVNs), superseding traditional protocols like the CAN due to its superior bandwidth and data transmission capabilities. This study explores the detection of camera interference attacks (CIA) within an automotive ethernet-driven environment using a novel GRU-based IDS. Leveraging a sliding-window data preprocessing technique, our IDS effectively analyzes packet length sequences to differentiate between normal and anomalous data transmissions. Experimental evaluations conducted on a commercial car equipped with H.264 encoding and fragmentation unit-A (FU-A) demonstrated high detection accuracy, achieving an AUC of 0.9982 and a true positive rate of 0.99 with a window size of 255.

**Keywords:** Automotive ethernet and Camera Interference · Intrusion Detection

## 1 Introduction

Automotive ethernet [7] in recent connected and autonomous vehicles (CAVs) stands for in-vehicle networks (IVNs) between electric control units (ECUs). Controller area network (CAN) traditionally has dominated the IVNs market share. However, due to the limited bandwidth of CAN, automotive ethernet is becoming a successor to enable high-definition applications such as video streaming for autonomous driving and infotainment systems.

CAN supports a data transfer rate of up to 1 Mbps, but its limited bandwidth renders it incapable of handling simultaneous communications with multiple devices necessary for autonomous driving.

Conversely, automotive ethernet facilitates data transfer speeds of up to 1 Gbps, enabling real-time transmission of data from cameras, LiDAR and Radar. Its extensive bandwidth supports seamless communication with multiple devices. Furthermore, it utilizes protocols such as the Audio/Video Transport Protocol (AVTP), Scalable Service-Oriented Middleware over IP (SOME/IP) and Diagnostics over Internet Protocol (DoIP) to provide various functions essential for autonomous driving.

© The Author(s), under exclusive license to Springer Nature Singapore Pte Ltd. 2025
J.-H. Lee et al. (Eds.): WISA 2024, LNCS 15499, pp. 191–202, 2025.
https://doi.org/10.1007/978-981-96-1624-4_15

Autonomous driving technologies leverage an array of sensor equipment, including cameras, LiDAR and Radar, to detect pedestrians, interpret traffic signals, gauge distances from other vehicles, and recognize lane markings to maintain the lane. Recently, Tesla introduced a vehicle capable of autonomous driving using only cameras [17]. This camera-based autonomous driving system, known as Tesla Vision, operates without ultrasonic sensors or LiDAR. While automotive ethernet-based IVNs offer significant advantages from a cybersecurity perspective, some security risks and threats persist. For example, although a switched medium prevents the occupation of the entire bandwidth by a specific node, as seen in CAN buses, it still transmits packets from legitimate ECUs as well as potential attack nodes.

A compromised ECU can enable an attacker to manipulate the vehicle in desired ways, potentially causing significant harm to the driver and the surrounding environment. For instance, an attacker who has taken control of an ECU connected to the vehicle's data transmission switch can disrupt the data being sent to the autonomous driving module. Among various attacks in automotive ethernet environment, we focused on camera interference attack (CIA) that can disrupt autonomous driving. The overall workflow for the CIA detection is as shown in Fig. 1. We assumed that an attacker compromise the IVNs by exploiting vulnerabilities of OTA, supply chain management or using physical access. Then, the attacker can send the CIA to the target car. Based on the attack scenarios, we built the datasets which includes the normal and attack cases. Then we developed a model for the CIA detection and estimated the overall performance of the model.

IDS is considered as a primary countermeasure to monitor in-vehicle traffic and detect anomalies. Several studies (see Sect. 3) have recently proposed IDS to secure automotive ethernet-based IVNs. Although these proposed methods have exhibited satisfactory performance, a common limitation in the literature is that experimental results are based on datasets captured on a testbed rather than on commercial vehicles.

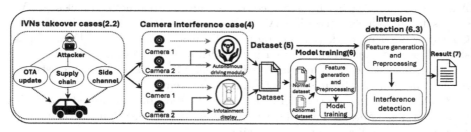

**Fig. 1.** Overview of the proposed methodology for intrusion detection workflow.

## 1.1   Contribution

In this paper, we first provide a proof-of-concept of CIA on an automotive ethernet-driven vehicle, specifically, Hyundai Genesis G80 model, based on a malicious packet injection attack. To the best of our knowledge, this is the first study on a commercial automotive ethernet-driven vehicle. Second, we have compiled a network intrusion dataset containing benign traffic (from legitimate around-view cameras) and abnormal traffic (from the attacker). Finally, we propose CIA-IDS, an IDS that effectively detects the CIA related hacking attempts. We leverage a novel feature to detect network intrusion on automotive ethernet.

## 2   Background

### 2.1   Ethernet-Based IVNs

Automotive ethernet has been introduced in modern vehicles to overcome the limitations in transmission speed and bandwidth of traditional IVNs such as CAN. By leveraging the high transmission speed and bandwidth of automotive ethernet, it is possible to transmit larger volumes of data in real-time for applications such as autonomous driving and infotainment systems.

Automotive ethernet includes SOME/IP, where one ECU requests events from other ECUs to exchange information; DoIP, which communicates with remote locations over the automotive ethernet to check the online status of an ECU; Additionally, AVTP is employed to handle time-sensitive data, ensuring synchronization of video playback through time synchronization mechanisms [5].

### 2.2   Attack Vector

We explain how the attacker accesses IVNs using our proposed method.

- **OTA Update Attack.** OTA updates allow car manufacturers to update and enhance vehicular software remotely. Exploiting OTA capability present a potential avenue for attackers to compromise vehicular control. Malefactors could upload a malicious update to the car manufacturer's OTA server, subsequently distributing this compromised update to the vehicles.
- **Supply Chain Attack.** A supply chain attack involves adversaries infiltrating the automotive manufacturing process via specific components or software supply chains to embed malicious code or vulnerabilities. This subsequently allows for potential control over the car's internal network or control systems.
- **Physical Access.** Physical approaches to gaining access method is also exist. Side-channel analysis is an attack technique used to extract information from a device that is not physically accessible. In cars that use smart keys, side-channel analysis allows attackers to detect and analyze the wireless communication signals of the smart key, enabling them to unlock the vehicle [18].

## 3   Related Work

Autonomous vehicles employ various methods to recognize the road conditions ahead and their surrounding environments, such as LiDAR sensors and V2X communication technology. However, cameras are also one of the frequently used technologies [15]. Consequently, recent studies have highlighted the potential risks of vehicle camera attacks and proposed detection methods.

Jeong *et al.* [12] presents a method to detect replay attacks by manipulating the AVTP image data of vehicles in a testbed environment utilizing AVB Listener and AVB Talker. They released the 'Automotive ethernet Intrusion Dataset' [11]. They utilized a CNN model as the detection approach for this dataset, achieving an accuracy of 0.9955. Their dataset contains payloads of the MPEG codec.

Natasha *et al.* [2] introduced a real-time IDS using deep learning and machine learning techniques, utilizing the automotive ethernet Intrusion Dataset [11]. They performed anomaly detection on the dataset based on an unsupervised deep learning model, the autoencoder. Utilizing these models for unsupervised learning on the [11], they demonstrated performance metrics such as an F1-score of 0.98 for the LSTM autoencoder.

Han *et al.* [6] introduced a methodology for detecting abnormalities in automotive ethernet based on the Wavelet transform. This approach proves to be considerably more effective than methods utilizing ResNet or EfficientNet. However, it's worth nothing that the data used in this study was not extracted from vehicles in actual driving conditions.

Shibly *et al.* [16] generate attack data using a generative adversarial network (GAN) based on the dataset from [11]. They use this dataset to conduct detection using a feature-aware semi-supervised approach.

Jeong *et al.* [10] proposes an IDS named automotive ethernet Real-Time Observer (AERO), which analyzes traffic from various protocols in IVNs. This is an unsupervised IDS that learns only from normal condition data and detects anomalies.

Song *et al.* [13] explain the network attacks and defense methods that can occur in CAN networks and automotive ethernet.

Choi *et al.* [3] and Han *et al.* [14] propose models that can identify drivers based on patterns such as acceleration and braking, which are indicative of driving habits, using deep learning models.

# 4   Proof of Concept

An attacker can exploit previously introduced methods (Sect. 2.2) to compromise an ECU connected to an ethernet switch responsible for data transmission within IVNs utilizing automotive ethernet.

By taking control of a compromised ECU, the attacker can manipulate data transmitted to the autonomous driving module. Figure 2 illustrates this process. Step ① represents the attacker's intrusion into the IVNs, step ② indicates the attacker's control over the ECU connected to the ethernet switch within the IVNs, and finally, step ③ shows the attacker executing an attack on the infotainment display and autonomous driving module.

The ethernet switch is responsible for transmitting data sent by ECUs or on-board cameras to their appropriate destinations. When necessary, the switch

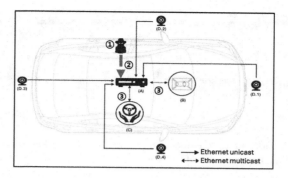

**Fig. 2.** Example for attack autonomous driving module. (A) is ethernet switch, (B) is infotainment display, (C) is autonomous driving module, D.1, D.2, D.3, D.4 are on-board camera.

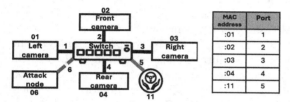

(a) Example of ethernet switch.

(b) MAC table before cache poisoning attack.

(c) MAC table after cache poisoning attack.

**Fig. 3.** Cache poisoning attack in vehicle.

uses multicast transmission to efficiently send data to multiple recipients within a specific group. This is particularly effective for modules such as the autonomous driving module or infotainment system, which require large amounts of data.

In this network environment, we execute an attack to disrupt the transmission of camera image data to the autonomous driving module or the infotainment system. Specifically, we targeted the infotainment display to demonstrate an attack where camera image data is transmitted abnormally. This abnormal data transmission attack can be explained by a cache poisoning attack [1]. Similarly, the autonomous driving module receives image data using multicast transmission, just like the infotainment display. Therefore, by employing the same attack method on the autonomous driving module, we can disrupt the normal transmission of camera image data to the module.

Figure 3 illustrates the switch architecture and changes in the MAC address table that enable abnormal data transmission to the autonomous driving module using a cache poisoning attack. An attacker who has compromised an ECU connected to the ethernet switch manipulates data destined for the MAC address at

(a) Under normal status                    (b) Under CIA status

**Fig. 4.** Demonstration of the camera inference attack. The infotainment system becomes blind when it goes under the attack.

port 11, redirecting it through port 5 to themselves. After intercepting the data, the attacker mixes it with other data before transmitting it to the autonomous driving module. As shown in the "**Camera interference case**" part of Fig. 1, we transmit the data from one camera to an incorrect destination. To carry out this attack, we use the Rad-Galaxy equipment, which is capable of sniffing the vehicle's data. This equipment allows us to intercept and analyze the data traffic within the vehicle network, facilitating the execution of the attack. The Rad-Galaxy is a multipurpose ethernet tap and media converter tailored for automotive ethernet applications [9]. We configure the direction of the left camera data towards the front display using the Gateway Builder[1] tool provided by this device. Figure 4 shows the results of executing a CIA on an actual vehicle. Figure 4(a) depicts the normal operation of the cameras, with both the front and left cameras working correctly. Figure 4(b) shows the outcome after attempting an attack using the Rad-Galaxy equipment.

## 5   Dataset

### 5.1   Dataset Description

In this section, we describe the differences between the normal and anomalous datasets. We extract the data by using the rad-galaxy tool. The normal dataset comprises packets transmitting front camera data to the front display. The anomalous dataset includes packets where data from both the left-side and front cameras are simultaneously transmitted to the front display.

The normal dataset, collected over 30 min of driving, is approximately 5.86 GB, containing 6,346,876 packets. The anomalous dataset, also gathered during a 30-min drive on campus, is approximately 4.97 GB, containing 5,450,620 packets. The images captured by the front, left, right and rear cameras are transmitted to their respective displays. Normal dataset consisting solely of front-camera image data are labeled as 0, while attack dataset containing both front and left-side image data are labeled as 1. As the goal is to detect deviations

---

[1] Rad-Galaxy program that changes the data transmission path of IVNs.

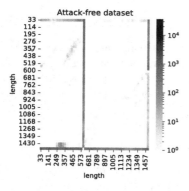

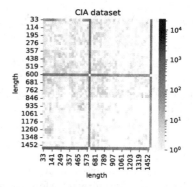

(a) Heatmap for normal dataset length sequence.

(b) Heatmap for abnormal dataset length sequence.

**Fig. 5.** Heatmap for length sequence 2-gram feature.

from this consistency, labeling all attack dataset, which include both frontal and left-side mixed attacks, as 1 can yield favorable results.

The image data captured by the camera is too large to be transmitted in a single packet, so it is fragmented before transmission. In our experiment, we use the FU-A fragmentation method [8]. Fragmentation ensures that packets do not exceed the MTU size. In a normal dataset, the fragmented packets create continuity. However, due to our attack, extraneous data are injected into the normal dataset, disrupting this continuity. As a result, the continuity observed in a normal dataset is altered. To demonstrate the difference in length sequence between normal and abnormal datasets, we utilize a heatmap for visualization.

Figure 5 illustrates the differences in the length sequences between the normal and abnormal dataset. Each figure represents the 2-gram of the length sequences from the datasets. For example, for the 576, 1474, 160, 1474 sequence, 2-grams of $P = \{[576, 1474], [1474, 160], [160, 1474]\}$ can be expressed, and $P_i[0]$ is the X-axis. We can determine the frequency by specifying $P_i[1]$ as the Y-axis. Darker colors indicate a higher frequency of the corresponding 2-gram. It is evident that there are differences in the 2-gram patterns between the normal and abnormal datasets.

We employ data length as a feature that represents these characteristics and describe the method used for anomaly detection utilizing this feature. To effectively train the model on the continuity of packets, we need to determine a window size. The packet's sequence number has a maximum value of 255. Under normal status, the packet sequence increases sequentially from 0 to 255. We chose a window size corresponding to the packet's sequence number, ranging from 0 to 255. When an attack occurs, this sequence within the range of 0 to 255 displays irregular continuity.

## 6    Methodology for CIA Detection

We described potential attacks on vehicle cameras using automotive ethernet and the differences between datasets in normal and attack scenarios. In this section, we introduce the detection system for CIA. We propose a methodology for the model to learn the sequence of length values described earlier and detect sequences that differ from the learned ones.

### 6.1    Gated Recurrent Unit (GRU)

Utilizing the time-series data preprocessing, we employ a GRU deep learning model to detect camera interference attack in vehicle cameras [4].

The GRU model is specialized for processing time-series and sequential data. It operates using two key mechanisms. The update gate is used to determine how much past information to retain, whereas the reset gate decides how much past information to forget. Leveraging these characteristics, the model learns information about the sequence of payload data lengths, determining at which point to start forgetting, and conducts anomaly detection based on the learned content. The following equations govern the behavior of a GRU:

$$r_t = \sigma(W_r \cdot [h_{t-1}, x_t] + br) \tag{1}$$

$$z_t = \sigma(W_z \cdot [h_{t-1}, x_t] + b_z) \tag{2}$$

$$\tilde{h}_t = tanh(W \cdot [r_t * h_{t-1}, x_t] + b) \tag{3}$$

$$h_t = z_t * h_{t-1} + (1 - z_t) * \tilde{h}_t \tag{4}$$

The reset gate's weight $W_r$ is operated with the previous state information $h_{t-1}$ and the current state information $x_t$ to determine how important $h_{t-1}$ and $x_t$ are. This operation involves an activation function. $r_t$ represents the reset gate, which determines how much of the past information to forget in the computation process. This formulation allows the determination of how much of the past information to forget. The update gate operates on the previous state information and the current state information using the update gate's weights, followed by the application of an activation function. Using the reset and update gates, it is decided how much of the previous information to retain or forget. To achieve this, weights are computed for the current state, and a hyperbolic tangent activation function is used to express the weights within the range of $-1$ to 1. Finally, the update gate $z_t$ is employed to determine how much information to blend between the previous state information $h_{t-1}$ and the current state information $h_t$.

### 6.2    Data Preprocessing

For the model to be properly trained and accurately distinguish anomalies, pre-processing of the dataset is necessary. In Sect. 4, we describe the dataset we extracted for our experiments. This dataset comprises camera data continuously extracted over time. Such data is referred to as time-series data, and while

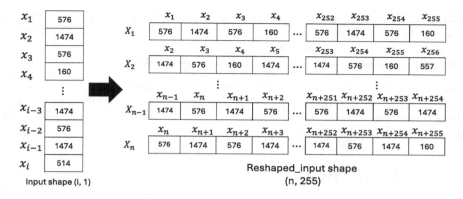

**Fig. 6.** Dataset reshaping for model input.

a single data point can be meaningful, analyzing a sequence of data can yield more significant information. As mentioned in Sect. 5.1, our dataset's data length encompasses the time-series information arising from fragmenting continuously captured image data.

In this section, we describe the preprocessing process for the dataset to ensure that the model accurately learns this consistency. We denote each packet's data length as $x_i$. A single window, segmented by the window size, is represented as $X_n$. Since a window comprises 255 rows, a single window can be expressed as $X_n = x_n \ldots x_{n+254}$. However, training the model in this form would only teach it to learn from a single payload data length, not a sequence. To train the model on a window containing 255 packets, we reshape the 255 rows into a single row composed of 255 columns. Figure 6 illustrates the process of reshaping through a diagram. First, input shape for i in (i, 1) means the number of total packets. We reshape this input shape to (n, 255). Here, n represents the number of windows.

Preprocessing is also required for the label indicating whether the dataset is normal or anomalous. Like the data length, labels are also divided according to a window size of 255. We can represent the label for an individual packet as $y_1$. A set of labels divided by the window size, $Y_i$, has 255 labels and is composed as $Y_i = y_1 \ldots y_{255}$. To represent $Y_i$ as a single label for the 255 labels, we use the average value of these 255 labels.

## 6.3   GRU-Based Camera Interference Attack IDS

We describe a model capable of detecting attack using the previously introduced feature selection, data preprocessing and GRU model.

**Input Layer:** As explained in Fig. 6, the shape of the dataset for input is (255, 1). Each $X_i$ contains values from $x_i$ to $x_{i+255}$, resulting in 255 columns. This input shape allows the GRU model to analyze the continuity of the 255 values of $x_i$.

**GRU:** GRU learns the continuity of the input $X_i$. The update gate determines how much information about the continuity of the current input data length should be retained. In contrast, the reset gate decides how much of the previously learned information about data length continuity should be forgotten.

**Output:** Based on the GRU model's learning results, the output layer produces predictions about the input. By comparing the predicted results with $Y_i$, the model can determine whether it has correctly detected normal sequences as normal and abnormal data as anomalous.

## 7    Experiment Result

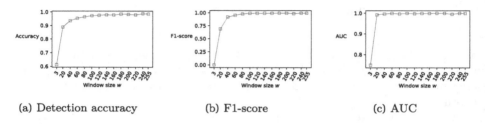

(a) Detection accuracy          (b) F1-score          (c) AUC

**Fig. 7.** Performance of CIA-IDS by window size

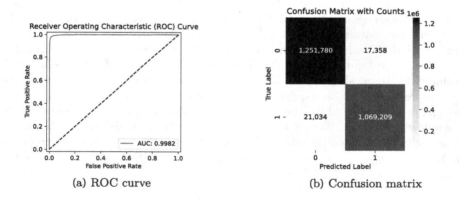

(a) ROC curve          (b) Confusion matrix

**Fig. 8.** ROC curve and confusion matrix

In this study, we elucidate the detection results of abnormal camera data transmission scenarios using a GRU-based IDS facilitated by the previously described sliding-window data preprocessing technique. Our experimental setup encompasses an Intel i7-10700k CPU@3.80 GHz, 64 GB of memory and an NVIDIA RTX 3070 GPU, which are utilized for both training and evaluation. For the dataset generated through our preprocessing steps, we allocate 80% of the data for training and 20% for testing purposes. We explore various window sizes to assess detection performance alongside the impact of window size on model complexity. Figure 7 illustrates the model's accuracy, F1-score and AUC for window sizes ranging from 3 to 255, in increments of 20.

In our experiments, we observe that despite the satisfactory performance at a smaller window size, a comparison of the inference times at window sizes of 140 and 255, yielding $0.002\,\mathrm{ms}/X$ and $0.009\,\mathrm{ms}/X$ respectively, shows negligible difference. Therefore, we have selected a window size of 255 for our IDS. Figure 8(a) presents the ROC curve for a window size of 255, exhibiting an AUC value of 0.9982.

Furthermore, Fig. 8(b) demonstrates the detection outcomes of the IDS on the test dataset, where the X-axis represents the model's predicted results, whether the window is classified as normal or containing an attack, and the Y-axis indicates the actual labels of the windows, whether they are truly normal or anomalous, forming a confusion matrix. The true positive rate, which achieves a value of 0.99, indicates outstanding performance. Table 1 shows the performance metrics of the IDS.

**Table 1.** Performance Metrics of the CIA-IDS

| Accuracy | AUC | F1-score | FPR | FNR | TPR | TNR |
|----------|---------|----------|--------|--------|--------|--------|
| 0.98848 | 0.99823 | 0.99824 | 0.0137 | 0.0193 | 0.9807 | 0.9863 |

## 8   Conclusion

In this study, we successfully demonstrated a proof-of-concept for detecting CIA on a Hyundai Genesis G80, leveraging a GRU-based IDS designed for automotive ethernet. Our approach utilized a novel sliding-window data based on packets's length value sequence. The experimental results showed that our IDS, with a window size of 255, achieved high detection accuracy, an impressive AUC of 0.9982 and a true positive rate of 0.99, indicating its exceptional ability to differentiate between normal and anomalous data. It has the advantage of carrying out attacks targeting actual vehicles and using the corresponding data, but has the disadvantage of being able to apply IDS only in a network structure fragmented by the FU-A method and using H.264 encoding. In upcoming works, limitations can be overcome if the actual image is recovered using the payload of the data set and detection is performed based on the image.

**Acknowledgement.** This work was supported by the 2021 Autonomous Driving Development Innovation Project of the Ministry of Science and ICT, Development of technology for security and ultrahigh-speed integrity of the next-generation internal network of autonomous vehicles under Grant 2021-0-01348.

# References

1. Abad, C.L., Bonilla, R.I.: An analysis on the schemes for detecting and preventing ARP cache poisoning attacks. In: 27th International Conference on Distributed Computing Systems Workshops (ICDCSW'07), p. 60. IEEE (2007)
2. Alkhatib, N., Mushtaq, M., Ghauch, H., Danger, J.L.: Unsupervised network intrusion detection system for AVTP in automotive ethernet networks. In: 2022 IEEE Intelligent Vehicles Symposium (IV), pp. 1731–1738. IEEE (2022)
3. Choi, Y.A., Park, K.H., Park, E., Kim, H.K.: Unsupervised driver behavior profiling leveraging recurrent neural networks. In: Information Security Applications: 22nd International Conference, WISA 2021, Jeju Island, South Korea, 11–13 August 2021, Revised Selected Papers 22, pp. 28–38. Springer (2021)
4. Chung, J., Gulcehre, C., Cho, K., Bengio, Y.: Empirical evaluation of gated recurrent neural networks on sequence modeling. arXiv preprint arXiv:1412.3555 (2014)
5. Working Group, I.P.: IEEE standard for a transport protocol for time-sensitive applications in bridged local area networks (2016). https://standards.ieee.org/standard/1722-2016.html
6. Han, M., Kwak, B., Kim, H.: TOW-IDS: intrusion detection system based on three overlapped wavelets for automotive ethernet. IEEE Trans. Inf. Forensics Secur. **18**, 411–422 (2023)
7. Hank, P., Müller, S., Vermesan, O., Van Den Keybus, J.: Automotive ethernet: in-vehicle networking and smart mobility. In: Proceedings of the Conference on Design, Automation and Test in Europe, DATE '13, pp. 1735–1739. EDA Consortium, San Jose (2013)
8. IETF: Fragmentation units (FUS) (2011). https://datatracker.ietf.org/doc/html/rfc6184. Accessed 07 Aug 2024
9. Intrepidcs.com: Intrepid, rad-galaxy. https://www.intrepidcs.com/rad-galaxy/. Accessed 07 Aug 2024
10. Jeong, S., Kim, H., Han, M., Kwak, B.: AERO: automotive ethernet real-time observer for anomaly detection in in-vehicle networks. IEEE Trans. Ind. Inform. 1–12 (2023)
11. Jeong, S., Jeon, B., Chung, B., Kim, H.K.: Automotive ethernet intrusion dataset (2021). https://doi.org/10.21227/1yr3-q009
12. Jeong, S., Jeon, B., Chung, B., Kim, H.K.: Convolutional neural network-based intrusion detection system for AVTP streams in automotive ethernet-based networks. Veh. Commun. **29**, 100338 (2021)
13. Kim, K., Kim, J., Jeong, S., Park, J., Kim, H.: Cybersecurity for autonomous vehicles: review of attacks and defense. Comput. Secur. **103**, 102150 (2021)
14. Kwak, B., Han, M., Kim, H.: Driver identification based on wavelet transform using driving patterns. IEEE Trans. Ind. Inform. **17**(4), 2400–2410 (2021)
15. Ondruš, J., Kolla, E., Vertaľ, P., Šarić, Ž: How do autonomous cars work? Transp. Res. Procedia **44**, 226–233 (2020). https://doi.org/10.1016/j.trpro.2020.02.049
16. Shibly, K., Hossain, M., Inoue, H., Taenaka, Y., Kadobayashi, Y.: A feature-aware semi-supervised learning approach for automotive ethernet. In: Proceedings of the IEEE CSR, pp. 426–431. IEEE (2023)
17. Tesla, I.: Transitioning to tesla vision. https://www.tesla.com/support/transitioning-tesla-vision. Accessed 07 Aug 2024
18. Wouters, L., Van den Herrewegen, J., Garcia, F.D., Oswald, D., Gierlichs, B., Preneel, B.: Dismantling DST80-based immobiliser systems. IACR Trans. Cryptogr. Hardw. Embed. Syst. **2020**(2), 99–127 (2020)

# One-Class Classification-Based Position Falsification Detection System in C-ITS Communication Network

Ilhwan Ji[1] , ChangJin Choi[1] , Cheolho Lee[2] , Seungho Jeon[1] ,
and Jung Taek Seo[1(✉)]

[1] Gachon University, Seongnam-daero 1342, Seongnam-Si, Republic of Korea
{ilhwan1013seojt,ethobisseojt,shjeon90seojt,seojt}@gachon.ac.kr
[2] ENKI WhiteHat, Songpa-Daero 167, Songpa-Gu, Seoul, Republic of Korea
chlee@enki.co.kr

**Abstract.** Cooperative-Intelligent Transport Systems (C-ITS) is a system for ensuring road safety and user safety, such as traffic congestion and traffic accidents, by sharing traffic risk information in advance through real-time two-way data transmission between road traffic components. The main services provided by C-ITS, such as traffic jam and traffic accident prevention, are performed based on information derived by collecting and analyzing vehicle location information at the C-ITS Center. For this reason, if an attacker falsifies position data on the communication channel from the vehicle to the C-ITS Center with malicious purposes, most of the C-ITS services cannot operate normally, causing financial losses and casualties. This research proposes an effective position falsification attack detection system in C-ITS based on the environmental analysis of C-ITS. For the purpose of developing cyberattack detection systems, it is very difficult to collect training datasets by conducting real-world cyberattacks in most IT infrastructure environments, including C-ITS environments. For this reason, the C-ITS target position falsification attack detection system proposed in this research utilizes the method of training only normal data and detecting position falsification based on that information. For the position falsification attacks detection system proposed in this research, high performance of precision 99.97%, recall 100%, and F1 Score 99.98% was obtained using VeReMi and BurST-ADMA datasets, which are datasets containing normal data and position falsification data collected from ITS and VANET environment simulators.

**Keywords:** C-ITS · AI · Anomaly Detection

## 1 Introduction

Cooperative-Intelligent Transport Systems (C-ITS) collects road and user information such as real-time traffic information, road surface weather information, and vehicle collision prevention in real-time for the purpose of promoting road safety and user safety. C-ITS is a system to ensure road safety and user safety by generating and transmitting

J.-H. Lee et al. (Eds.): WISA 2024, LNCS 15499, pp. 203–216, 2025.
https://doi.org/10.1007/978-981-96-1624-4_16

information to predict and respond to traffic congestion and traffic accidents based on the collected information [1]. Due to the development of information and communication technology and the increase in vehicle productivity, the vehicle road transportation system is becoming more complex, and the number of vehicles is increasing, resulting in traffic congestion and traffic accidents. For this reason, the development and application of C-ITS to ensure road safety and user safety based on two-way communication of data between road traffic components is actively being developed and applied [2].

The main services provided by C-ITS, such as traffic jam and traffic accident prevention, are performed based on information derived by collecting and analyzing vehicle location information at the C-ITS Center. If an attacker falsifies position information data on the communication channel from the vehicle to the C-ITS Center with malicious purposes, most of the C-ITS services may not operate normally, causing financial damage and casualties. For this reason, cybersecurity technology research is being conducted to proactively detect and respond to position information manipulation attacks in C-ITS. Mahshid et al. [3], Hawlader et al. [4], Ilango et al. [5] proposed a detection system for position falsification attacks in C-ITS and VANET environments based on machine learning (ML) algorithms. As a result of the experiment of each research, high detection performance against position falsification attacks was derived. However, most research, including Mahshid et al. [3], Hawlader et al. [4], Ilango et al. [5] simply aim to improve classification performance and how data is classified into normal and attack without considering C-ITS environmental features. C-ITS includes a wide variety of communication sections, and the number of communication sections is also large.

For this reason, it is necessary to derive C-ITS environment and network features such as data communication section, communication method, communication data standard, and communication data type through environmental analysis of C-ITS, and to develop and apply a position falsification attack detection system that effectively collects position information data and detects attacks based on this.

In this research, we derive C-ITS environment features such as communication section, communication protocol, and data type through C-ITS environment analysis, and propose a position falsification attack detection system to effectively detect position falsification attacks occurring in C-ITS based on these features. The position falsification attack detection system presented in this research is located between the C-ITS Center and the Roadside Station to effectively collect vehicle location data and detect attacks on the location data before it is delivered to the C-ITS Center. The system consists of a vehicle position data parser, a feature preprocessor, and a one class classification-based cyberattack detector. The vehicle position data parser extracts location-related data for cyberattack detector training from network packets containing vehicle location information sent from the vehicle to the C-TIS Center and converts it into a consistent format. The feature preprocessor performs missing value removal, data cleaning, normalization, and label-encoding to improve the training and attack detection efficiency of the position falsification attack detector. The one class classification-based cyberattack detector detects position falsification attacks based on input data. To evaluate the detection performance of a position falsification attack detection system with the above configuration, we used the VeReMi and BurST-ADMA datasets, which are datasets containing normal data and position falsification data collected from Intelligent Transport Systems (ITS) and Vehicular ad-hoc network (VANET) environment simulators. The contributions of this research are as follows:

- We analyze the C-ITS environment and present the security threats that can arise in the C-ITS environment due to position falsification.
- We propose a One-class Classification based Position Falsification Attacks Detection System for the detection of position falsification attacks in C-ITS Center data collection section.
- For the One-class Classification based Position Falsification Attacks Detection System presented in this research, a high performance of precision 99.97%, recall 100%, and F1 Score 99.98% is obtained using VeReMi and BurST-ADMA datasets, which are datasets containing normal data and position falsification data collected from ITS and VANET environment simulators.

The remainder of this paper is organized as follows. In Sect. 2, we analyze the related work on detecting position falsification attacks analyze. In Sect. 3, we C-ITS. Section 4 presents a position falsification attack detection system in C-ITS based on one class classification. In Sect. 5, we evaluate the detection performance of our system for detecting position falsification in C-ITS and conduct a comparative analysis with existing works. In Sect. 6, the conclusions and future research directions are presented.

## 2 Related Works

Various research has been conducted to detect location data forgery attacks on C-ITS and vehicular ad hoc networks (VANETs). In particular, cyberattack detection and classification using artificial intelligence (AI) is being actively researched for fast and accurate detection of position falsification attacks on large amounts of position data.

Sharma et al. [6] proposed a machine learning-based detection scheme for position spoofing attack detection in vehicular ad-hoc network (VANET). In this research, they generated augmented data based on two BSM information instead of a single BSM information and performed position spoofing attack detection based on the augmented data. In this research, KNN, RF, Naïve Bayes, and DT algorithms were used to verify the performance of the proposed machine learning-based position spoofing attack detection method using the VeReMi dataset [7], which is generated based on BSM information occurring in VANETs. Among the four algorithms, the KNN algorithm performed the best in detecting position spoofing attacks, with a precision of 99.3% and a recall of 98.38%.

Le et al. [8] proposed a detection scheme for position falsification based on n consecutive position information of vehicles derived by applying the n-sequence technique to position information generated in VANETs. In this research, cyberattacks are detected based on KNN and SVM algorithms for data containing n consecutive position information extracted. VeReMi dataset is used to detect the position falsification attack proposed in this paper. The experimental results show that the classification performance of position falsification attacks is 99.7% precision and 99% recall.

Anyanwu et al. [9] proposed a Randomized Search Optimization Ensemble-based Falsification Detection Scheme (RSO-FDS) for detecting Basic Safety Message (BSM) falsification attacks that contain vehicle position information. The RSO-FDS proposed in this paper utilizes the information in the BSM to detect falsification attacks based on ensemble-based RF. To evaluate the detection performance of RSO-FDS, we utilized VeReMi dataset, BurST-ADMA dataset [10], and V2X-Fabrication dataset, and obtained detection performance of 99.50%, 99.89%, and 99.99%.

Arif et al. [2] proposed an ML-based cyberattack detection approach for detecting Content Poisoning Attacks (CPA) on vehicular networks. In this paper, LR, DT, KNN, RF, and GNB algorithms are used to detect CPA. The BurST-ADMA dataset is utilized to validate the proposed CPA detection algorithm. In the experiment, the best detection performance was obtained in RF, with 100% accuracy, 100% recall, and 100% precision.

There is a wide range of research on cyberattack detection to detect position falsification attacks on C-ITS and automotive networks. However, most of these research do not consider the application of cyberattack detection systems to C-ITS environments, but simply consider how to detect and classify cyberattacks. C-ITS includes a wide variety of communication sections and the number of communication sections is also large, so it is difficult to apply a position falsification detection method to all communication sections. For this reason, it is necessary to derive C-ITS environmental features through a systematic analysis of the C-ITS environment and to research the development and application of a position falsification attack detection system in C-ITS with effectiveness and efficiency that reflects these features.

## 3   Analysis of Cooperative-Intelligent Transport Systems

ITS refers to a transportation system that scientizes and automates the operation and management of transportation systems and improves the efficiency and safety of transportation by developing and utilizing advanced transportation technologies and traffic information such as electronic control and communication for transportation vehicles and transportation facilities. The ITS collects and processes the collected information at the control center and delivers the information one-way to the targets that need the information, such as vehicles, bus stops, and traffic flow information indicators. However, ITS cannot generate and deliver information that reflects real-time field conditions due to one-way information transmission. From the past to the present, the vehicle road transportation system is becoming more complex, and as the number of vehicles increases, the incidence of traffic jams and traffic accidents is increasing. For this reason, there is a growing demand for real-time traffic information, road surface weather information, vehicle collision prevention, and other real-time collected information based on field conditions [11]. Therefore, C-ITS is being developed and applied to collect and analyze field information based on two-way communication of data between road traffic components and transmit the derived information to road traffic components to prevent traffic congestion and traffic accidents.

C-ITS is a system that enables real-time two-way data transmission between road traffic components to share traffic risk information and respond in advance. Figure 1. Shows the structure of the C-ITS. C-ITS consists of the vehicle's on-board unit (OBU), various sensors and road side equipment (RSE), the C-ITS Center that manages and distributes information, and the Roadside Station that performs data transmission between

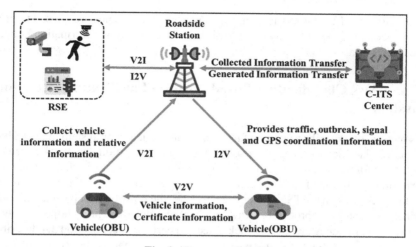

**Fig. 1.** Structure of C-ITS

OBU, RSE, and C-ITS Center OBUs transmit vehicle location information and vehicle basic information to other OBUs and RSEs. The RSE provides the vehicle with data related to road conditions, traffic signals, accident warnings, and various services. The C-ITS center receives the data collected from OBUs and RSEs through the Roadside Station. The C-ITS Center analyzes the received data to produce information for traffic congestion and traffic accident response and transmits the information to OBUs and RSEs through the Roadside Station.

C-ITS has three communication segments: Vehicle-to-Vehicle (V2V), which is vehicle-to-vehicle communication; Vehicle-to-Infrastructure (V2I), which is vehicle-to-infrastructure communication; and Vehicle-to-Everything (V2X), which is vehicle-to-everything communication with other vehicles, roads, RSE, and other components. The V2X communication section including V2V and V2I within C-ITS performs WAVE, a wireless communication method using the SAE J2735 message standard, and Cellular-V2X communication using LTE and 5G communication based on the IEEE 1609.3 message standard. The communication section between Roadside Station and C-ITS Center communicates by optical communication method based on SAE J2735 or IEEE 1609.3 message standard because it needs to transmit a large amount of data quickly.

The main services of C-ITS, including traffic congestion and traffic accident response, are performed based on the analysis of vehicle position data collected by the C-ITS Center. For this reason, if an attacker with malicious intent falsifies the position data transmitted between OBU, RSE, and C-ITS Center, it is difficult to perform the main services of C-ITS. By falsifying the position information of a vehicle, an attacker can manipulate traffic information on a particular stretch of road to cause traffic jams. For this reason, the integrity of the position data collected by C-ITS Center is very important. As the C-ITS Center is a system operated for the safety and efficiency of the road traffic environment, a cyberattack on the C-ITS Center can cause not only financial damage but also casualties [2, 12]. For this reason, cybersecurity technologies are needed to proactively detect and respond to position falsification attacks on the information collected by the C-ITS Center.

## 4  One-Class Classification Based Position Falsification Detection System

In this section, we describe a position falsification attack detection system in C-ITS based on one class classification. The proposed method detects position data that has been falsified for cyberattacks based on training information of vehicle position data that occurs in the normal operation of C-ITS. Section 3.1 provides an overview of position falsification attack detection in C-ITS. Section 3.2 describes the position data parser. Section 3.3 describes the feature preprocessor extracted from encrypted traffic to improve cyberattack detection efficiency and cyberattack detection performance. Section 3.4 describes a position falsification attack detector based on training information about vehicle position data generated in the normal operation of C-ITS.

### 4.1  Overview

For most IT infrastructure environments, including C-ITS environments, it is very difficult to collect datasets for training by conducting actual cyberattacks [13]. For this reason, it is necessary to apply a method to detect position falsification attacks based only on training information from data generated in the normal operation of C-ITS.

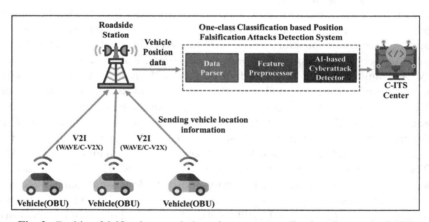

**Fig. 2.** Position falsification attack detection system application diagram in C-ITS

Figure 2 shows an overview of the position falsification attack detection system for position data collected by C-ITS Center using V2I communication based on the one-class classification proposed in this paper. The position falsification attack detection system in C-ITS based on one class classification is located between the Roadside Station and the C-ITS Center, and detects position falsification attacks based on the position information data collected through V2I communication and delivered to the C-ITS Center through the Roadside Station. Since the data collected from OBU and RSE are all transmitted to C-ITS Center through Roadside Station, it is appropriate to apply the position falsification attack detection system for that section. The position falsification attack detection system consists of a vehicle position data parser, feature preprocessor, and one class classification-based cyberattack detector, and processes the data in the following order for the collected data.

1. **Vehicle position data parser**: Extract and convert data collected by position falsification attack detection systems into a consistent format to be used for training from network packets and detecting cyberattacks.
2. **Feature Preprocessor**: Preprocess the input features to improve the accuracy and efficiency of training and anomaly detection of cyberattack classification models.
3. **One Class Classification-based Cyberattack Detector**: It receives preprocessed data as input, learns, and detects cyberattacks. When detecting a cyberattack, if the difference between the input data value and the model's predicted value is greater than the threshold, it is detected as a cyberattack.

### 4.2  Vehicle Position Data Parser

Vehicle position data parser extracts and converts data for cyberattack detector training into a consistent format from network packets containing vehicle position information transmitted via optical communications based on SAE J2735 or IEEE 1609.3 message standards from the Roadside Station to the C-TIS Center. The Vehicle position data parser parses information related to vehicle location data, such as GPS coordinates, velocity, acceleration, and noise values, and derives features from that information.

### 4.3  Feature Preprocessor

The Feature Preprocessor performs data feature preprocessing to improve the training and attack detection efficiency of the position falsification detector. The feature preprocessing step is very important because noise in the data can degrade performance [14]. The input value for training and anomaly detection of One Class Classification-based Cyberattack Detector should be numerical data. Therefore, string data is converted into integer category values through label-encoding or one-hot encoding for features that are not numerical values extracted from the vehicle position data parser. In addition, since many missing values have a negative impact on model training, we replace the missing values with specific values to remove missing values in the data. Then, Feature Selection is used to remove uncorrelated features or features that have direct information about the time series to avoid overfitting and improve the performance of the model. Finally, normalization is performed to unify the data range of each feature to prevent the learning and anomaly detection efficiency from decreasing due to the difference in the range of values between features.

### 4.4  One Class Classification-Based Cyberattack Detector

One class classification-based cyberattack detector trains only the vehicle position information data that occurs in normal operation among the data collected by the C-ITS Center.

The trained cyberattack detector detects position data information that has been falsified by cyberattacks based on normal position data information. Supervised learning-based anomaly detection systems have the advantage of relatively high anomaly detection rates and the ability to classify attack types within attacks. However, for the development of cyberattack systems, it is very difficult to collect datasets for training by conducting actual cyberattacks on most IT infrastructure environments, including C-ITS environments [13]. For this reason, we only train our model on normal data collected in a C-ITS environment. The cyberattack detector is trained to produce the smallest possible error on normal data. If such cyberattack data is input to the cyberattack detector, a relatively large error value is derived by cyberattack data that is different from normal data, and if the derived error value is larger than the set threshold, the data is detected as cyberattack data.

## 5  Evaluation

In this section, we evaluate the one class classification-based position falsification attacks detection system proposed in Sect. 3 using a dataset containing vehicle position data from a C-ITS environment. Section 4.1 describes the dataset containing vehicle position data from the C-ITS environment used in our experiments. Section 4.2 describes the experimental environment, model structure, and preprocessing. Section 4.3 describes various metrics to evaluate the performance of the proposed attack detection system. In Sect. 4.4, we verify the cyberattack detection performance of our one-class classification-based position falsification attacks detection system.

### 5.1  Dataset Description

#### 5.1.1  VeReMi Dataset

The VeReMi dataset [7] is a dataset developed to evaluate the effectiveness of falsification attack detection methods in Vehicle Ad-HocNetworks (VANETs). The VeReMi dataset contains five types of position falsification attacks and normal data: Constant attack (attack by retransmitting a fixed location), Constant Offset at-tack (attack by changing the fixed location by a certain value), Random attack (attack by transmitting a random location), Random Offset attack (attack by transmitting the location of neighboring vehicles from a random location), and Eventual Stop attack (attack by repeating the same location over a period of time). The dataset has 21 features including vehicle ID, position information, speed, acceleration, etc. 382,952 training data (normal data: 382,952) and 198,576 test data (normal data: 108,530/attack data: 90,046) were used in the training and validation experiments of the position falsification attack detection system proposed in this research.

#### 5.1.2  BurST-ADMA Dataset

The BurST-ADMA dataset [10] was developed to evaluate the performance of position falsification attack detection in C-ITS. The BurST-ADMA dataset contains seven types of position falsification attacks and normal data, including Constant Random Position,

Positive Position Offset, Negative Position Offset, Constant Random Speed, Positive Speed Offset, Negative Speed Offset, and Reversed Heading. The dataset has 8 features including vehicle ID, location information, speed, acceleration, etc. 101,501 training data (normal data: 101,501) and 99,999 test data (normal data: 77,627/attack data: 22,372) are used in the training and validation experiments of the position falsification attack detection system proposed in this paper.

## 5.2 Experimental Setup

**Computational Environment.** The experiments were conducted using Ubuntu 20.04.6 LTS operating system, Intel(R) Xeon(R) Silver 4216 CPU @ 2.10 GHz, 64 GB RAM, Tesla V100S PCIe 32 GB GPU and python3 development environment.

**Preprocessing.** In this experiment, data preprocessing was performed to improve the training of cyberattack detection models and the efficiency of attack detection. To remove missing values in VeReMi dataset and BurST-ADMA dataset used in this experiment, we replaced all missing values with zero. For cyberattack detection experiments, we removed the labels representing the five attack types in the VeReMi dataset and replaced all the labels (1–7) of the seven types of data falsification attack types in the BurST-ADMA dataset with 1. Among the features in the BurST-ADMA dataset, id consists of a combination of strings and integers. We separated the Id feature into two features, string and number, so that the cyberattack detection model can train it. Then, label-encoding was performed on the string features to convert them into integers. In addition, to prevent the learning and anomaly detection efficiency from decreasing due to the difference in the range of values between the features of VeReMi dataset and BurST-ADMA dataset, we normalized the data and applied the MaxAbs scaling method, which changes the minimum value of each data to -1 and the maximum value to 1.

**Hyper-Parameter Settings.** In this experiment, LSTM based AutoEncoder (AE-LSTM) algorithm is used to apply the one class classification-based position falsification attack detection system to detect cyberattacks based on only normal data presented in Sect. 4. The AE-LSTM model used for training and validation on VeReMi dataset and BurST-ADMA dataset is designed as an encoder and decoder consisting of LSTM layers. Table 1 describes the detailed architecture of the model. We used tanh as the activation function for each layer in both models. The optimizer for all models is Adam, and the learning rate is 0.001.

## 5.3 Performance Indicators

The performance metrics of the anomaly detection model in this experiment include Accuracy, which is an evaluation of how well the detection system correctly classifies normal data as normal data and anomaly data as anomaly data in the collected data by defining the ratio of the number of correctly classified data to the total number of data; Recall, which is an evaluation of how well the system finds the data to detect; and Precision, a metric that evaluates the percentage of data predicted to be anomaly by the system that is actually anomaly; and F-1 Score, a metric used to measure the overall

**Table 1.** Detailed model architecture trained on each dataset.

|  |  | VeReMi | | BurST-ADMA | |
|---|---|---|---|---|---|
|  | Layer Type | Output Shape | Activation | Output Shape | Activation |
| Encoder | LSTM | (1, 7) | Tanh | (1, 19) | Tanh |
|  | LSTM | (1, 64) | Tanh | (1, 64) | Tanh |
|  | LSTM | (1, 32) | Tanh | (1, 32) | Tanh |
|  | RepeatVector | (1, 32) | – | (1, 32) | – |
| Decoder | LSTM | (1, 32) | Tanh | (1, 32) | Tanh |
|  | LSTM | (1, 64) | Tanh | (1, 64) | Tanh |
|  | LSTM | (1, 7) | Tanh | (1, 19) | Tanh |
|  | TimeDistributed | (1, 7) | Linear | (1, 19) | Linear |

Accuracy of the model. We also used the receiver operating characteristic area under the curve (ROC-AUC), an evaluation metric that indicates the rate of change in the true positive rate (TPR) and false positive rate (FPR).

## 5.4 Performance Evaluation

In this section, we evaluate the detection performance of each of the location data forgery attack detection algorithms presented in Sect. 4.2. The AE-LSTM-based data forgery attack detection model is trained only on position information data extracted from normal operation, and its detection performance is verified using the validation dataset. Figure 3 shows the training and validation losses of VeReMi dataset and BurST-ADMA dataset for the AE-LSTM-based position falsification attack detection model.

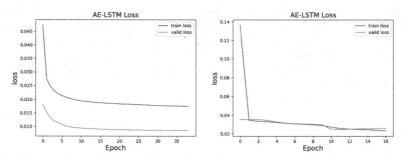

**Fig. 3.** Learning and validating loss of AE-LSTM-based position falsification attack detection model for (A)VeReMi dataset, (B)BurST-ADMA dataset

In Fig. 3, the AE-LSTM-based data tampering attack detection model was trained on both datasets in the direction of decreasing validation loss. We obtained a validation loss of 0.0085 for the VeReMi dataset and 0.0257 for the BurST-ADMA dataset.

Figures 4 and 5 show the detection results of AE-LSTM-based position falsification for VeReMi dataset and BurST-ADMA dataset, respectively.

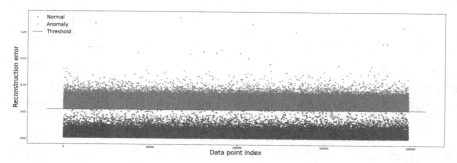

**Fig. 4.** Results of Position Falsification Attacks detection on VeReMi dataset

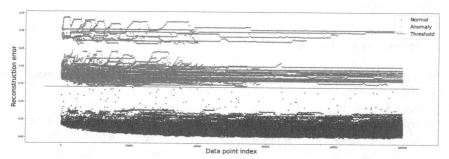

**Fig. 5.** Results of Position Falsification Attacks detection on BurST-ADMA dataset

The blue dots in Figs. 4 and 5 represent normal data, while the orange dots represent position falsification attack data. The red straight line indicates the threshold for anomaly detection. The threshold value is set to the value when the precision and recall of the anomaly detection model are equal. High precision means fewer false positives, which detect normal data as anomalous, and high recall means fewer false negatives, which miss anomaly data [15]. Since these two performance metrics typically have a trade-off relationship, this study derived the thresholds in the same way as above to ensure an unbiased consideration of both [16]. The position falsification attack detection system detects the data as cyberattack data if the error between the input and output data is higher than the threshold of each model. In each figure, you can see that the difference between normal data (blue dots) and cyberattack data (orange dots) is identifiable.

Table 2 shows the performance comparison of the one-class classification-based position falsification detection system proposed in this research with existing research on position falsification detection for C-ITS and VANETs.

As shown in Table 2, the one-class classification-based position falsification detection system proposed in this research achieved a high performance of 99.88% on all detection performance metrics for the VeReMi dataset. In addition, the proposed model achieved

**Table 2.** Comparison of existing models, including ours.

| reference | VeReMi | | | BurST-ADMA | | |
|---|---|---|---|---|---|---|
| | Precision | Recall | F1 Score | Precision | Recall | F1 Score |
| KNN [3] | 0.993 | 0.9838 | 0.951 | None | None | None |
| SVM [5] | 0.997 | 0.99 | 0.990 | None | None | None |
| Ensemble based RF [9] | 0.9966 | 0.9916 | 0.9916 | 1 | 0.995 | 0.998 |
| RF [2] | – | – | – | 1 | 1 | 1 |
| Our model | **0.9988** | **0.9988** | **0.9988** | 0.9997 | 1 | 0.9998 |

a high performance of 99.97% precision, 100% recall, and 99.98% F1 score for BurST-ADMA. We evaluated the detection performance on both datasets and found that it is comparable to or better than the performance of existing research based on supervised learning algorithms.

## 6 Conclusion and Future Works

C-ITS is a system that enables real-time two-way data transmission between road traffic components to share and respond to traffic risk information in advance. The main services provided by C-ITS, such as traffic congestion and traffic accident prevention, are performed based on information derived by collecting and analyzing vehicle position information at the C-ITS Center. For this reason, in the event of a position falsification attack on the data collection section of the C-ITS Center, most of the C-ITS services may not operate normally, causing financial and human casualties In this research, we proposed a one-class classification-based position falsification attack detection system to position falsification based on the position data extracted from the normal operation status of C-ITS. To validate the proposed attack detection system, we used the VeReMi dataset and BurST-ADMA dataset, which contain position falsification attack data for ITS and VANET environments. The detection result of VeReMi dataset is 99.88% in all detection performance indicators, and the detection result of BurST-ADMA dataset is 99.97% in precision, 100% in recall, and 99.98% in F1 Score. Based on the experimental results, we conclude that it is possible to detect most of the attacks when applying the position falsification attack detection system presented in this research to the C-ITS environment.

The one-class classification-based position falsification attack detection system proposed in this paper is designed to detect only position falsification attack on vehicle location information collected through V2I communication sections, and does not consider position falsification attacks on V2V communication sections in C-ITS.

In future works, we will research the application of a position falsification attack detection system for all communication sections in the actual C-ITS environment and considerations for application.

**Acknowledgements.** This work was supported by Institute of Information & communications Technology Planning & Evaluation (IITP) grant funded by the Korea government (MSIT) (No. RS-2024–00331950, Technology Development for Vulnerability Assessment and Cybersecurity Attack&Defense Training on the Next-generation Intelligent Transport System(C-ITS)).

# References

1. Lokaj, Z., Šrotýř, M., Vaniš, M., Mlada, M.: Methodology of functional and technical evaluation of cooperative intelligent transport systems and its practical application. Appl. Sci. **11**, 9700 (2021)
2. Magsi, A.H., Ghulam, A., Memon, S., Javeed, K., Alhussein, M., Rida, I.: A machine learning-based attack detection and prevention system in vehicular named data networking. Comput. Mater. Contin **77**, 1445–1465 (2023)
3. Behravan, M., Zhang, N., Jaekel, A., Kneppers, M.: Intrusion detection systems based on stacking ensemble learning in VANET. In: 2022 5th International Conference on Communications, Signal Processing, and their Applications (ICCSPA), pp. 1–7. IEEE (2022)
4. Hawlader, F., Boualouache, A., Faye, S., Engel, T.: Intelligent misbehavior detection system for detecting false position attacks in vehicular networks. In: 2021 IEEE International Conference on Communications Workshops (ICC Workshops), pp. 1–6. IEEE (2021)
5. Ilango, H.S., Ma, M., Su, R.: Novel position falsification attacks detection in the internet of vehicles using machine learning. In: 2022 17th International Conference on Control, Automation, Robotics and Vision (ICARCV), pp. 955–960. IEEE (2022)
6. Saudagar, S., Ranawat, R.: An amalgamated novel IDS model for misbehaviour detection using VeReMiNet. Comput. Stand. Interfaces **88**, 103783 (2024)
7. Van Der Heijden, R.W., Lukaseder, T., Kargl, F.: Veremi: a dataset for comparable evaluation of misbehavior detection in VANETs. In: Security and Privacy in Communication Networks: 14th International Conference, SecureComm 2018, Singapore, Singapore, August 8–10, 2018, Proceedings, Part I, pp. 318–337. Springer (2018)
8. Le, A., Maple, C.: Shadows don't lie: n-sequence trajectory inspection for misbehaviour detection and classification in VANETs. In: 2019 IEEE 90th Vehicular Technology Conference (VTC2019-Fall), pp. 1–6. IEEE (2019)
9. Anyanwu, G.O., Nwakanma, C.I., Lee, J.-M., Kim, D.-S.: Falsification detection system for IoV using randomized search optimization ensemble algorithm. IEEE Trans. Intell. Transp. Syst. **24**, 4158–4172 (2023)
10. Amanullah, M.A., Chhetri, M.B., Loke, S.W., Doss, R.: BurST-ADMA: towards an Australian dataset for misbehaviour detection in the internet of vehicles. In: 2022 IEEE International Conference on Pervasive Computing and Communications Workshops and other Affiliated Events (PerCom Workshops), pp. 624–629. IEEE (2022)
11. Choi, J., et al.: C-ITS environment modeling and attack modeling. arXiv preprint arXiv:2311. 14327 (2023)
12. Seo, D.: A studyon C-ITS security technology analysis. J. Korean Soc. Softw. Eval. **18**, 103–113 (2022)
13. He, K., Kim, D.D., Asghar, M.R.: Adversarial machine learning for network intrusion detection systems: a comprehensive survey. IEEE Commun. Surv. Tutorials **25**, 538–566 (2023)
14. Hnamte, V., Najar, A.A., Nhung-Nguyen, H., Hussain, J., Sugali, M.N.: DDoS attack detection and mitigation using deep neural network in SDN environment. Comput. Secur. **138**, 103661 (2024)

15. Al Razib, M., Javeed, D., Khan, M.T., Alkanhel, R., Muthanna, M.S.A.: Cyber threats detection in smart environments using SDN-enabled DNN-LSTM hybrid framework. IEEE Access **10**, 53015–53026 (2022)
16. Sun, X., Wang, H.: Adjusting the precision-recall trade-off with align-and-predict decoding for grammatical error correction. In: Proceedings of the 60th Annual Meeting of the Association for Computational Linguistics (Volume 2: Short Papers), pp. 686–693 (2022)

# Fuzzing

# Reverse Engineering-Guided Fuzzing for CAN Bus Vulnerability Detection

Manu Jo Varghese[1]([✉]), Frank Jiang[1], Abdur Rakib[2], Robin Doss[1], and Adnan Anwar[1]

[1] Deakin Cyber Research and Innovation Centre (Deakin Cyber), Deakin University, Geelong, Australia
{mvarghese,frank.jiang,robin.doss,adnan.anwar}@deakin.edu.au
[2] Centre for Future Transport and Cities, Coventry University, Coventry CV1 5FB, UK
ad9812@coventry.ac.uk

**Abstract.** Vehicular systems are becoming interconnected digital ecosystems, reliant on complex networks for operations and safety. Cybersecurity vulnerabilities in these networks can jeopardize road safety. This study introduces a fuzzing framework to identify vulnerabilities in the Controller Area Network (CAN) bus. Using *Automated Reverse Engineering-Guided Fuzzing*, modified data packets are injected into the CAN framework, and Electronic Control Units (ECUs) reactions are monitored to uncover vulnerabilities. This approach identifies CAN bus network weaknesses and enhances understanding of their operational characteristics, setting a new standard for automotive cybersecurity. +

**Keywords:** CAN bus · Vulnerability detection · CAN test-bed · CAN security

## 1 Introduction

Automotive advancements have transformed vehicles into digital ecosystems, reliant on interconnected Electronic Control Units (ECUs) for functions like engine dynamics and navigation [1]. These ECUs communicate via the Controller Area Network (CAN) bus, originally designed without prioritizing security [2]. Increased complexity and connectivity have raised concerns about CAN bus vulnerabilities [3]. This study introduces a fuzzing framework for the CAN bus. The Automated Reverse Engineering-Guided Fuzzing (ARE-GF) framework targets ECUs to identify vulnerabilities, using specialized security metrics to prioritize testing. The framework's efficacy is validated through simulations, uncovering potential vulnerabilities and enhancing security resilience. With vehicles increasingly becoming repositories of critical data concerning location, engine status, and beyond, securing these digital systems assumes paramount importance [4]. This research endeavours to fabricate a simulated CAN bus environment using low-cost, real-time apparatus. This simulation aims to generate traffic for sensitive data acquisition, laying a foundation for comprehensive security

J.-H. Lee et al. (Eds.): WISA 2024, LNCS 15499, pp. 219–230, 2025.
https://doi.org/10.1007/978-981-96-1624-4_17

threat analysis. The objective is to assess the system's robustness and efficiency, underscoring the escalating importance of security in CAN-facilitated systems. The expanding imperative for security within automotive software development presents a multifaceted challenge, necessitating a holistic approach [5]. This encompasses secure coding practices, rigorous testing and validation protocols, continuous monitoring, and an anticipatory posture towards emerging threats and technologies. As connected and autonomous vehicles become more ubiquitous, instituting stringent cybersecurity measures becomes increasingly vital to safeguard the safety, privacy, and trust of all road users. This research makes several key contributions to the field of automotive cybersecurity. It introduces the ARE-GF framework, a novel approach to identifying vulnerabilities within the CAN bus system. Additionally, it provides a methodology for prioritizing ECU modules based on susceptibility metrics, ensuring that the most critical areas are tested first. The research demonstrates the practical application of the framework within a simulated environment, highlighting its potential to enhance the security of real-world automotive systems. Finally, it underscores the importance of comprehensive security measures in the development of modern vehicles, contributing to ongoing efforts to protect critical automotive infrastructure from emerging cyber threats.

The rest of this paper is organized as follows. Section 2 provides the background on the CAN bus architecture and the importance of automotive cybersecurity. Section 3 reviews related work in the fields of fuzzing methodologies and automotive security. Section 4 presents the proposed fuzzing framework, detailing its components and methodologies. Section 5 evaluates the framework through empirical studies, demonstrating its effectiveness and comparing it with existing solutions. Finally, Sect. 6 concludes the paper and outlines future research directions.

## 2   Background

The Controller Area Network (CAN) protocol, developed by Bosch, facilitates seamless data exchange among vehicle components without direct addressing. Its decentralized model enhances system flexibility and scalability [35]. Central to the CAN bus system is a distinctive data frame structure, pivotal for communication among Electronic Control Units (ECUs). The CAN ID, consisting of 11 bits, serves as a unique message identifier within the CAN network, distinguishing it from socket-based protocols such as Ethernet by operating on a message-based broadcast system. The Data Length Code (DLC) is a 4-bit field that indicates the payload size within the message, which can range from 0 to 8 bytes. In reverse engineering endeavours, the DLC value is instrumental in ascertaining the data volume conveyed in each message. The data field itself, which can be up to 64 bits, constitutes the actual payload. Its size varies according to the DLC, and it transmits sensor data or control commands. Payload analysis is paramount in reverse engineering for elucidating the specifics of ECU communications (Fig. 1).

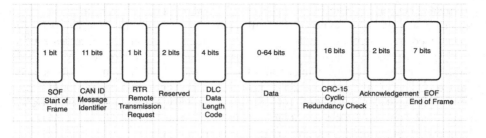

**Fig. 1.** CAN Data Frame Structure

Despite CAN's standardized protocol, manufacturers often use proprietary encoding for the data payloads, making the information difficult to interpret without additional context. This obscurity necessitates techniques like reverse engineering to decipher the proprietary encoding and understand the data's significance. Reverse engineering is vital in automotive cybersecurity [34], helping to identify vulnerabilities within ECUs and their communication protocols. It helps to make sense of the data transmitted over vehicular networks and identify potential security weaknesses [8]. Fuzzing is a critical technique in the Automotive domain, involving the injection of invalid, unexpected, or random data into systems to identify software bugs and vulnerabilities that cyber threats could exploit. This method is invaluable in the automotive sector, especially for vehicles equipped with Advanced Driver-Assistance Systems (ADAS), which consist of complex software ecosystems. By simulating a wide range of inputs, fuzzing helps to thoroughly test these ecosystems, uncover vulnerabilities, and ensure that communication systems meet stringent safety and security standards [9,10]. ADAS, which relies heavily on real-time data from sensors, radars, and cameras, presents significant challenges in terms of testing and validation. The dynamic nature of the data and the wide range of potential operating conditions make comprehensive testing difficult. This underscores the importance of robust testing methodologies to ensure the reliable functionality of ADAS systems throughout the vehicle's operational lifespan. The integration of ADAS also raises cybersecurity concerns, particularly when development is outsourced. This necessitates vigilant oversight of third-party components to maintain the security and integrity of the vehicle's software ecosystem [13–15].

## 3   Related Work

Extensive investigations in fuzzing methodologies and automotive cybersecurity have highlighted gaps necessitating further exploration. This section reviews the evolution of fuzzing approaches and their applicability to the automotive sector.

**Automotive Cybersecurity:** Research in automotive cybersecurity has intensified in response to the increasing complexity of vehicular systems. Security analyses have focused on in-vehicle infotainment systems due to their external connectivity and interactivity. Li et al. [1] devised the SP-E framework for a nuanced security assessment of infotainment systems, emphasizing the need for specialized evaluative methodologies. Comprehensive security strategies for in-vehicle networks have also been explored. Luo et al. [2] advocated for holistic security strategies, while Wang et al. [3] examined the security mechanisms relevant to OTA updates, stressing the importance of secure updates in maintaining system integrity. Li et al. [4] introduced a security evaluation framework for connected vehicles based on attack chains, and Shirvani et al. [5] proposed a framework for assessing security risks in electric vehicles.

**Fuzzing Techniques:** Foundational expositions on fuzzing, including its operational principles and broad applications, are presented in [17]. An exhaustive survey of fuzzing techniques and a taxonomy of prevalent fuzzers are detailed in [18], providing a valuable resource for selecting appropriate methods in new projects. Specialized tools for network protocol fuzzing have been developed. The SNOOZE Fuzzer [32] automates fuzzing based on protocol states and messages, while AutoFuzz [33] constructs FSMs from recorded network traffic to guide fuzzing.

**Automotive Security Research:** Pioneering work by Miller and Valasek [19] unveiled significant vulnerabilities within a 2014 Jeep Cherokee, demonstrating the feasibility of remote system control. Subsequent research scrutinized the AUTOSAR standard [20] and applied threat modeling techniques to the CAN protocol, uncovering vulnerabilities such as ECU spoofing via CAN packets. Challenges unique to fuzzing automotive control networks, as contrasted with conventional software fuzzing, are documented by Smith in the Car Hacker's Handbook [11] and further studies [22]. These works highlighted the unique responses of vehicles and ECU vulnerabilities when fuzzing automotive networks, either with or without CAN bus feedback. Proposals to use DBC files for generating automatic fuzzing test cases aim to enhance fuzzing precision and efficacy.

**Need for a Novel Automobile-Specific Fuzzing Framework:** Current automotive fuzzing frameworks struggle with the intricate interplay between ECUs in modern vehicles. The proposed fuzzing framework aims to address this by combining automated reverse engineering of CAN signals, real-time sensor feedback, and targeted fuzzing guided by a vulnerability prediction model. This specialized approach promises to improve the efficiency and thoroughness of uncovering security weaknesses in today's complex vehicular systems.

## 4   Proposed Fuzzing Framework

The Automated Reverse Engineering-Guided Fuzzing (ARE-GF) framework incorporates Automated Reverse Engineering to target ECUs. This methodology deploys tailored fuzzing strategies to enhance the efficiency and efficacy of vulnerability detection within vehicular CAN systems.

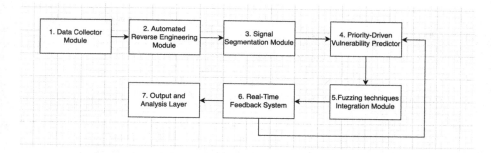

**Fig. 2.** Proposed Fuzzing Framework

---

**Algorithm 1.** Signal Segmentation

---

1: **procedure** SIGNALSEGMENTATION(*candump*)
2:     **for** each frame in *candump* **do**
3:         $startBit \leftarrow 0$
4:         **while** $startBit <$ number of bits in frame **do**
5:             **for** $length \leftarrow 1$ **to** (number of bits in frame $- startBit$) **do**
6:                 $signal \leftarrow$ extractSignal(frame, $startBit, length$)
7:                 **if** $V(signal) \neq V($extractSignal(frame, $startBit, length + 1$)) **then**
8:                     commitSignal(*signal*)
9:                     $startBit \leftarrow startBit + length$
10:                     **break**
11:                 **end if**
12:             **end for**
13:         **end while**
14:     **end for**
15: **end procedure**

---

## 4.1 Segmentation Process

In the complex ecosystem of vehicle CAN networks, deciphering the signal encoding within data frames presents a formidable challenge, compounded by the initial absence of encoding knowledge. To surmount this obstacle, our research introduces a novel methodological approach for signal grouping and interpretation. Employing a 'greedy' algorithm, this technique endeavours to reconstruct signals from the constituent bits of a data frame, subsequently subjecting these signals to a rigorous 'signal validation' process. The segmentation process starts with the algorithm at the first bit (bit 0) of the frame. It gradually combines more bits to form a possible complete signal. After the initial signal is assembled, each possible signal is carefully checked to see if it is valid. The decision-making in this process involves two key steps: choosing whether to add another bit to the possible signal for re-evaluation or to consider the signal complete and move on to the next group of bits. This iterative process continues until every bit within the frame is evaluated and categorized, ensuring a thorough examination and interpretation of signals (Fig. 2).

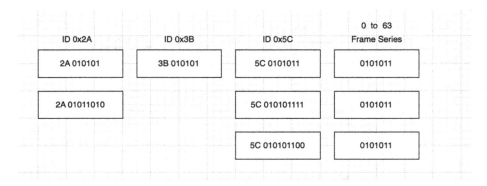

**Fig. 3.** CAN Data Segmentation

Once the Frame series is obtained group based on the origin of ECU we could analyse the boundaries in this data and find common types of data. Figure 3 showcases the segmentation of CAN data, demonstrating how data frames are dissected to extract meaningful signals.

---

**Algorithm 2.** Determine Bit Significance Order

---

1: **procedure** BITSIGNIFICANCEORDER($observedPayloads$)
2:     $bitChangeFrequency \leftarrow [0] * 8$
3:     $previousPayload \leftarrow observedPayloads[0]$
4:     **for** $i \leftarrow 1$ to $length(observedPayloads)$ **do**
5:         $changes \leftarrow observedPayloads[i] \oplus previousPayload$
6:         **for** $bit \leftarrow 0$ to 7 **do**
7:             **if** $changes$ & $(1 \ll bit)$ **then**
8:                 $bitChangeFrequency[bit] \leftarrow bitChangeFrequency[bit] + 1$
9:             **end if**
10:         **end for**
11:         $previousPayload \leftarrow observedPayloads[i]$
12:     **end for**
13:     $sortedIndices \leftarrow$ sort indices of $bitChangeFrequency$ by value
14:     **return** $sortedIndices$
15: **end procedure**

---

### 4.2 Efficiency of Algorithms

**Signal Segmentation Algorithm:** The SignalSegmentation algorithm has a time complexity of $O(n \times m^2)$, where $n$ is the number of frames and $m$ is the number of bits in a frame. The outer loop iterates over each frame ($O(n)$), and within each frame, the algorithm evaluates each bit and possible signal length ($O(m) \times O(m)$). This quadratic complexity in terms of bits per frame ensures a thorough segmentation process.

**Bit Significance Order Algorithm:** The `BitSignificanceOrder` algorithm operates with a linear time complexity of $O(n)$, where $n$ is the number of observed payloads. It efficiently determines the significance of each bit by tracking changes across payloads. This involves an $O(1)$ operation for each bit in the payload, resulting in a highly efficient process for large datasets.

### 4.3   Enhancing CAN Bus Security Through Priority-Driven Vulnerability Prediction

The Priority-Driven Vulnerability Predictor (PVP) module constitutes a pivotal enhancement within the Automated Reverse Engineering-Guided Fuzzing (ARE-GF) framework. This module utilizes specialized security metrics to prioritize fuzz test cases, focusing on areas with the highest potential for unearthing significant vulnerabilities within the Controller Area Network (CAN) bus. By systematically identifying and prioritizing fuzzing efforts, the PVP module enhances the efficiency and effectiveness of vulnerability detection processes within the framework. The specialized security metrics used by the PVP module are summarized in Table 1. These metrics guide the PVP module in systematically identifying and prioritizing fuzz test cases, thereby significantly enhancing the efficiency and effectiveness of vulnerability detection processes within the framework.

**Table 1.** Specialized Security Metrics for Priority-Driven Vulnerability Prediction

| Metric | Description |
| --- | --- |
| Vulnerability Score | Scores based on known vulnerabilities and history |
| Exposure Level | Degree of exposure to external inputs/communications |
| Critical Functionality | Priority for ECUs controlling critical functions |
| Communication Frequency | Frequency of communication on the CAN bus |
| Interconnectedness | Impact on other vehicle systems |
| Anomaly Detection | Ability to detect anomalies in behavior |

**Refinement of Fuzzing Techniques Within the CAN Bus Arbitration Process:** Our methodology initiates with a foundational approach to fuzzing, leveraging the random selection of arbitration IDs and message payloads to scrutinize the system. To elevate the efficacy of this process and augment the identification of vulnerabilities within the Electronic Control Units (ECUs), we incorporate a triad of sophisticated fuzzing strategies: brute-force fuzzing, mutation fuzzing, and state change identification fuzzing. Brute-force fuzzing employs a comprehensive examination of all possible permutations of certain message components, specifically targeting those known to influence ECU responses. This approach proves invaluable when targeting ECUs with a known sensitivity to a specific range of IDs. Mutation fuzzing introduces incremental modifications to the messages, manipulating bits or altering message configurations to gauge the impact of minor variations on ECU behavior. State change identification fuzzing relies on the discernment that only specific payload bits significantly affect ECU state changes. By adjusting these pivotal bits, this strategy seeks to unveil conditions leading to state alterations, often necessitating a sequence of messages to effectuate a change.

### 4.4   Automated ECU Analysis via Data Acquisition System (DAS)

Integrating these enhanced fuzzing strategies, the framework transitions into an automated exploration mode, guided by immediate feedback from a dedicated sensor harness. This harness, affixed directly to the target ECU, enables the precise assessment of the fuzzing impact, facilitating dynamic adjustments to our strategies [23]. Each node within the CAN network initiates by establishing a unique identifier (ID), which is essential for network coordination. Upon detecting the Start of Frame (SOF) signal, nodes prepare for message transmission, initiating with the highest-order bit of their ID. During this phase, nodes concurrently transmit and monitor bits, engaging in an arbitration process to resolve priority conflicts. Dominance is established through the transmission of a 'dominant' bit (0), with the node asserting priority unless a 'recessive' bit (1) is observed, signalling the halting of transmission in deference to a higher-priority message. Following arbitration, the prevailing node distributes its data, with receiving nodes acknowledging pertinent messages. Error detection mechanisms, including CRC checks and acknowledgement slots, ensure message integrity, with error frames signalling detected faults. Post-transmission or error resolution, the network synchronizes in preparation for subsequent communications, reinstating an idle state.

**Automated ECU Analysis via Data Acquisition System (DAS):** Merging these enhanced fuzzing strategies culminates in an automated exploration mode, orchestrated by real-time feedback from a sensor harness. This direct attachment to the target ECU facilitates a granular assessment of the fuzzing impacts, enabling dynamic strategy adjustments.

**CAN Bus Testbed Components:** The construction of a CAN Bus testbed involves the assembly of several key components, each fulfilling a pivotal role within the system: **STM Nucleo - F103RB (MCU)** acts as the central controller within the CAN bus system, selected for its inherent support for CAN communication and cost-effectiveness. Integration with the CAN network is achieved via dedicated CAN interface pins, with programming facilitated through the Mbed framework in C language to manage CAN communication protocols. **MCP 2551 (Transceiver)** enables the interface between the CAN controller (MCU) and the physical bus, crucial for the transmission and reception of CAN signals. **Dupont Lines** serve to establish physical connections between hardware pins and the breadboard, enabling the linkage of transceiver pins to the corresponding MCU pins and CAN bus lines. **CAN Bus Logger (CL2000)** is responsible for logging and storing traffic data from the CAN bus, with connectivity to a computer via USB for data offloading and analysis. **Pico-Scope 2204A** functions as both an oscilloscope and protocol decoder for the CAN bus, capturing and decoding communication signals with software tools aiding in signal analysis and decoding.

**Design and Connection Considerations:** Adherence to ISO 11898 [37] standards for CAN network cabling and termination is imperative. Additional design considerations include the implementation of LEDs on the development board for visual indication of transmission activities, and the establishment of a power supply by connecting the 5 V and Ground pins from the STM Nucleo board to appropriate power sources. Testing and validation of the CAN bus system are facilitated through the utilization of tools like the CL2000 and PicoScope 2204A, ensuring the system's functional integrity.

## 5    Evaluation and Findings

The evaluation of the fuzzing framework highlights its efficacy and resource efficiency in automotive security testing. Conducted on a robust hardware setup (Apple M1 chip, 16 GB memory, 512 GB SSD, macOS), this section compares the framework's performance against established metrics and alternative frameworks.

### 5.1    Performance Metrics of the Cybersecurity Testing Framework

Table 2 presents the performance of the novel fuzzing framework, illustrating its competencies across various operational metrics. These metrics elucidate the framework's responsiveness, efficiency, and resource utilization, evidencing its superiority in handling cybersecurity testing within automotive systems.

**Table 2.** Performance Results of the Proposed Cybersecurity Testing Framework Compared to Industry Benchmarks [36].

| Metric | Definition | Results | Benchmark |
|---|---|---|---|
| Response Time | Number of services per unit time | **<500 ms** | 600–800 ms |
| Query to View Time | Total time by the Query service | **<50 ms** | <50 ms |
| Query per Second | Number of queries per unit time | **>600** | 300–600 |
| Failure Ratio | Failed service/total service | **<0.1%** | <0.1% |
| CPU Usage | CPU utilization (mean/peak) | **12%/80%** | 15–20%/75–85% |
| RAM Usage | Utilization rate of RAM resources | **1 GB/8 GB** | 2 GB/8 GB |
| Disk Throughput | Amount of data r/w from a disk | **400 MB/s** | 350–450 MB/s |
| Network Throughput | The amount of network data | **9 MB/s** | 8–10 MB/s |

The detailed analysis highlights the framework's capacity to process a significant volume of queries and transactions swiftly, maintaining operational integrity with minimal resource consumption.

### 5.2    Comparative Analysis

A comparative examination reveals the distinct advantages of the proposed fuzzing framework over its counterparts, as depicted in Table 3. This analysis accentuates the comprehensive process incorporation, extensive test case coverage, and the adaptability of the framework to various testing scenarios [25,28].

**Table 3.** Comparison between the Novel Fuzzing Framework and other frameworks.

| Framework | Process | Test Case | Framework | Scenarios |
|---|---|---|---|---|
| Q. Li [1] | × | 3 | × | Risk Assessment |
| Shirvani [2] | × | 10 | × | Risk Assessment |
| Schönhärl [3] | × | 3 | ✓ | Education |
| S. Li [4] | ✓ | 4 | × | Penetration Testing |
| F. Luo [5] | ✓ | 1 | ✓ | Penetration Testing |
| K. He [6] | × | 2 | × | Penetration Testing |
| **Proposed Framework** | ✓ | 10 | ✓ | Penetration Testing |

### 5.3 Addressing Identified Vulnerabilities

The prowess of the proposed framework in identifying and mitigating vulnerabilities is further substantiated through a comparative pass rate analysis, as summarized in Table 4. This evaluation underscores the framework's efficacy in addressing critical vulnerabilities, outperforming existing solutions [29].

**Table 4.** Comparison of frameworks in addressing identified vulnerabilities and their pass rate.

| Framework | Extended CAN IDs | DoS Vulnerability | Pass Rate |
|---|---|---|---|
| Q. Li [1] | × | × | 70% |
| Shirvani [2] | Unknown | × | 80% |
| Schönhärl [3] | × | Unknown | 75% |
| S. Li [4] | Unknown | ✓ | 67% |
| F. Luo [5] | ✓ | ✓ | 72% |
| K. He [6] | × | × | 76% |
| **Proposed Framework** | ✓ | ✓ | **94%** |

The assessments elucidate the proposed framework's capabilities in enhancing automotive cybersecurity, particularly through its nuanced approach to fuzzing and vulnerability analysis. The empirical data gleaned from these evaluations advocates for its adoption and further exploration in mitigating automotive system vulnerabilities.

## 6   Conclusion and Future Work

This study introduces a fuzzing framework tailored for the CAN bus, targeting ECUs to identify vulnerabilities. Using specialized security metrics, the framework prioritizes testing of susceptible ECU modules. Simulations in a CAN bus environment demonstrate its effectiveness in uncovering vulnerabilities and enhancing security resilience. This research highlights the importance of securing vehicular digital ecosystems and provides a practical solution to mitigate automotive cybersecurity risks. In future work, we would like to refine the reverse engineering process through the application of machine learning techniques. We aim to extend the scope by incorporating various vehicle models and ECU ranges, thereby enhancing the performance of the model and ensuring its adaptability to real-world scenarios.

# References

1. Li, S., Zhang, X., Zhou, Y., Zhang, M.: SP-E: security evaluation framework of in-vehicle infotainment system based on threat analyses and penetration tests. J. Phys: Conf. Ser. **2517**, 012012 (2023)
2. Luo, F., Zhang, X., Hou, S.: Research on cybersecurity testing for in-vehicle network. In: Proceedings of the 2021 ICITES, Chengdu, China (2022)
3. He, K., Wang, C., Han, Y., Fang, X.: Research on cyber security technology and test method of OTA for intelligent connected vehicle. In: Proceedings of the 2020 ICBAIE, Virtual Conference, China (2022)
4. Li, Q., Zuo, J., Cao, R., Chen, J., Liu, Q., Wang, J.: A security evaluation framework for intelligent connected vehicles based on attack chains. IEEE Netw. 1 (2023)
5. Shirvani, S., Baseri, Y., Ghorbani, A.: Evaluation framework for electric vehicle security risk assessment. IEEE Trans. Intell. Transp. Syst. 1–24 (2023)
6. Arkin, B., Stender, S., McGraw, G.: Software penetration testing. IEEE Secur. Priv. **3**, 84–87 (2005)
7. Checkoway, S., et al.: Comprehensive experimental analyses of automotive attack surfaces. In: Proceedings of the 20th USENIX Conference on Security (SEC'11). USENIX Association (2011)
8. Koscher, K., et al.: Experimental security analysis of a modern automobile. In: 2010 IEEE Symposium on Security and Privacy, pp. 447–462. IEEE (2010)
9. Miller, C., Valasek, C.: Remote exploitation of an unaltered passenger vehicle. Black Hat, USA (2015)
10. Nilsson, D.K., Larson, U.E., Picasso, F.: Simulating attacks on CAN buses: a look at the AUTOSAR and FlexRay protocols. In: 2008 5th Workshop on Embedded Systems Security (WESS '08). ACM (2008)
11. Pawlowski, A., Stelte, B., Müller, C.: CAN-fuzz - a practical framework for fuzzing CAN applications. In: NordSec 2017: Secure IT Systems, pp. 45–61. Springer, Cham (2017)
12. Lawrenz, W.: CAN System Engineering: From Theory to Practical Applications. Springer (2016)
13. Takanen, A., DeMott, J., Miller, C.: Fuzzing for software security testing and quality assurance. Artech House (2018)
14. Wolf, M., Scheibel, M.: Automotive Cybersecurity: Securing the Modern Vehicle. Wiley (2020)
15. Groza, B., Murvay, P.S.: Security for automotive electrical and electronic systems. In: Automotive Cybersecurity, pp. 1–33. Springer, Cham (2020)
16. Loukas, G.: Cyber-Physical Attacks and Defenses in the Smart Grid and Connected Vehicles. CRC Press (2019)
17. Manès, V.J.M., et al.: The art, science, and engineering of fuzzing: a survey. IEEE Trans. Softw. Eng. **46**(11), 1216–1242 (2019)

18. Banks, G., Cova, M., Felmetsger, V., Almeroth, K., Kemmerer, R., Vigna, G.: SNOOZE: toward a stateful network protocol fuzzer. In: Information Security, pp. 343–358. Springer, Heidelberg (2006)
19. Miller, C., Valasek, C.: A survey of remote automotive attack surfaces. Black Hat USA, vol. 2014, p. 94 (2014)
20. Avatefipour, O., Hassan, W.H.: Comprehensive overview of cyber-physical system security in connected and autonomous vehicles. IET Cyber-Phys. Syst. Theory Appl. **5**(3), 211–221 (2020)
21. Cho, K.T., Shin, K.G.: Fingerprinting electronic control units for vehicle intrusion detection. In: 25th USENIX Security Symposium (USENIX Security 16), pp. 911–927 (2016)
22. Zeng, Q., Liu, J., Chen, Q., Zhao, J., Liu, S.: Fuzz testing based on attack injection for in-vehicle network security evaluation. IEEE Access **7**, 35973–35983 (2019)
23. Hoppe, T., Kiltz, S., Dittmann, J.: Security threats to automotive CAN networks - practical examples and selected short-term countermeasures. Reliab. Eng. Syst. Saf. **96**(1), 11–25 (2011)
24. Narayanan, S.N., Mittal, S., Joshi, A., Joshi, K.: Machine learning techniques for intrusion detection systems: a review. J. Netw. Comput. Appl. **167**, 102739 (2020)
25. Chen, Y., Su, C., Yeh, M.F., Huang, C.Y.: ECU fuzzing: discovering vulnerabilities in automotive systems via fuzz testing. In: Proceedings of the ACM Symposium on Applied Computing (2020)
26. Van Bulck, J., Münch, M., Weichbrodt, N., Kapitza, R., Piessens, F., Strackx, R.: SGX-based secure CAN communication. In: 2018 IEEE 37th Symposium on Reliable Distributed Systems (SRDS), pp. 357–366. IEEE (2018)
27. Groza, B., Murvay, P.S.: Evaluating the security of connected vehicle architectures through penetration testing and fuzzing. In: Automotive Cybersecurity, pp. 3–29. Springer, Cham (2021)
28. Wang, T., Wei, T., Gu, G., Zou, W.: TaintScope: a checksum-aware directed fuzzing tool for automatic software vulnerability detection. In: 2010 IEEE Symposium on Security and Privacy, pp. 497–512. IEEE (2010)
29. Boehme, M., d'Amorim, M.: Fuzzing frameworks: a survey and taxonomy. Technical report, TR-2013-004, Department of Computer Science, University of Pernambuco (2013)
30. Li, Z., Harman, M., Hierons, R.M.: Search algorithms for regression test case prioritization. IEEE Trans. Softw. Eng. **33**(4), 225–237 (2007)
31. Zhang, M., Duan, Y., Liu, Q., Yin, H.: V-fuzz: vulnerability-oriented evolutionary fuzzing. arXiv preprint arXiv:1901.01142 (2019)
32. Banks, G., Cova, M., Felmetsger, V., Almeroth, K., Kemmerer, R., Vigna, G.: Snooze: toward a stateful network protocol fuzzer. In: Lecture Notes in Computer Science, pp. 343–358 (2006)
33. Gorbunov, S., Rosenbloom, A.: AutoFuzz: automated network protocol fuzzing framework. Int. J. Comput. Sci. Netw. Secur. **10**, 239–245 (2010)
34. Huybrechts, T., Vanommeslaeghe, Y., Blontrock, D., Van Barel, G., Hellinckx, P.: Automatic reverse engineering of CAN bus data using machine learning techniques. In: Advances on P2P. Parallel, Grid, Cloud and Internet Computing, pp. 751–761 (2017)
35. Bosch GmbH: CAN Specification Version 2.0. Robert Bosch GmbH (1991)
36. Sensors 2022, 22, 9211. A comprehensive survey on fuzz testing for automotive cybersecurity
37. International Organization for Standardization: ISO/SAE 21434:2021 Road vehicles - cybersecurity engineering. https://www.iso.org/standard/86384.html

# Air-Fuzz: Feasibility Analysis of Fuzzing-Based Side-Channel Information Leakage Attack in Air-Gapped Networks

Yeon-Jin Kim, Na-Eun Park, and Il-Gu Lee(✉)

Sungshin Women's University, 2, Bomun-ro 34da-gil, Seongbuk-gu, Seoul 02844,
Republic of Korea
{220246046,iglee}@sungshin.ac.kr

**Abstract.** As the number of cyberattacks via networks increases, air-gapped networks that are physically isolated from the Internet are recommended to protect systems and industrial facilities. However, previous research has highlighted the possibility of data exfiltration attacks in air-gapped environments by exploiting computer systems or peripheral devices. Consequently, research to identify potential attack types and vectors in air-gapped environments is required. This study proposes an attack model that uses fuzzing on Internet of Things connectivity devices to exfiltrate data within an air-gapped environment through side-channel signal patterns. We conducted an experiment to verify the feasibility of the attack model in a noisy channel and compared its performance with that of conventional attack models affected by interference and noise. By injecting Gaussian noise into wireless signals encoded with data, we compared the Bit Error Rate (BER) of the proposed attack model with that of conventional models. The BER of the proposed attack model was improved by approximately 59.43% compared with that of conventional attack models.

**Keywords:** Air-Gap Network · Side Channel · Internet of Things

## 1 Introduction

With the widespread high-speed information and communication technologies, national infrastructure, industrial facilities, and individual homes and objects have become connected to the Internet [1]. However, as important information assets have become connected to the Internet, the frequency of cyberattacks has increased rapidly. Large-scale Distributed Denial of Service (DDoS) attacks that reduce system availability and ransomware attacks that take important documents and systems hostage and demand ransoms are expanding beyond industrial companies to target national infrastructure [2,3]. Efficient defense technologies have been investigated to protect systems from various cyberattacks [4].

In addition, as the number of network-based cyberattacks has increased recently, the air-gap concept has been proposed to protect systems from networks.

An air-gapped network is a closed environment in which business and Internet networks are physically separated [5]. To prevent cyberattacks through networks, air-gapped networks protect industrial systems from external threats and ensure their safe operation. However, recent research has demonstrated the possibility of data exfiltration in air-gapped environments by encoding binary data into optical, acoustic, and electromagnetic signals generated while operating computer systems or peripheral devices and transmitting them to an external network [6]. Stuxnet, which was used to attack Iran's Natanz nuclear facility in 2010, used intermediary devices such as USB flash drives to gain access within an air-gapped environment. Additionally, four zero-day vulnerabilities were used to access the operating system and disrupt the normal operation of industrial control processes by changing the frequency of the current power of the centrifuge [7]. The Stuxnet incident confirmed that internal infiltration and data leakage were possible even in an air-gapped environment. Therefore, research to identify attack vectors where attacks can occur, and to detect and respond to them to protect systems and data within air-gapped networks is needed.

This study shows that a data leak attack is feasible by utilizing the side channel of Internet of Things (IoT) connectivity devices in an air-gapped network, and by analyzing the attack vector.

The main contributions of this paper are as follows.

- We proposed Air-Fuzz, an attack model that generates wireless signals by finding signal patterns in the side channel through IoT firmware fuzzing.
- The concept of the proposed attack model was verified experimentally, and the feasibility of an air-gapped attack using wireless signals was demonstrated.

The remainder of this paper is organized as follows. Section 2 analyzes the previous research on data leakage attacks in air-gapped networks. Section 3 explains the proposed data leakage attack model, and Sect. 4 analyzes the experimental results to verify the effectiveness of the attack model. Open issues are discussed in Sect. 5, and the conclusions are presented in Sect. 6.

## 2    Related Work

Guri et al. [8] proposed a data leakage attack scenario in an air-gapped environment by generating a signal in the 2.4 GHz Wi-Fi frequency band by repeating the reading and writing memory on the DDR SDRAM memory bus. The experiment demonstrated that the attack was effective up to a distance of 1.8 m. This paper demonstrated through experiments that data can be leaked using a DDR SDRAM memory bus in an air-gap environment. However, physical proximity is required between the attack-target computer and the receiving device. One limitation is that the reliability of the transmitted data is low because the surrounding environment greatly influences it.

Lee et al. [9] analyzed attack surfaces that could be used within a closed network, designed an attack system that leaked internal data using optical media, and demonstrated its effectiveness. The data leaked from devices inside the air-gapped network were collected and encoded into binary data. The encoded data are externally transmitted through controllable LEDs. They conducted experiments on various environmental variables that could increase the success rate and efficiency of data leakage attacks in the proposed attack scenario. The study derived commands for manipulating LEDs and proposed an air-gapped attack scenario. However, the data leakage method using LED has the disadvantage that the receiver must be located in a straight line of sight, and abnormal LED operation patterns can be easily observed.

Li et al. [10] proposed SpiralSpy, which leaks data by manipulating the speed of a cooling fan in a conventional air-gapped environment attack scenario. The experiments proved that data could be transmitted at a speed of 6 bit/s, even at a distance of 8 m. However, the fan must be controlled precisely, considering the its response delay and the time required to adjust the speed. Additionally, because the fan may be activated owing to intervention by the operating system while data is being transmitted through SpiralSpy, there is a limitation in that it is necessary to distinguish who is operating the cooling fan.

Previous research has proposed an attack scenario that leaks data using internal PC systems or peripheral devices in an air-gapped network environment. Although it suggests an attack vector that has not been previously considered, it has common limitations such as limitations on devices that can be used for attacks or many environmental variables that must be considered. Therefore, we propose an Attack model, Air-Fuzz, which transmits data by exploring usable frequency bands through fuzzing to address the limitations of conventional methods, such as physical accessibility and the effects of channel interference and noise.

## 3   Attack Model: Air-Fuzz

The structural diagram of Air-Fuzz is shown in Fig. 1.

Air-Fuzz first assumes that IoT devices within an air-gapped network are infected with malware through social engineering techniques or supply chain attacks. PCs on the same network as the IoT devices are also infected with malware, and attackers who break into air-gapped networks collect data to be leaked externally, such as accounts and system passwords [11]. The collected data are converted into binary data and encoded into a wireless signal through On-Off Keying (OOK) encoding, and the transmitter transmits the signal to an external receiver. The transmitter used in this process is a firmware that controls the IoT connectivity devices. By fuzzing the firmware, a wireless signal is generated by determining the pattern of the signal exiting the side channel. The receiver outside the air-gapped network receives the wireless signal. The received signal was analyzed to extract the OOK-encoded signal, process it, and decode the binary data.

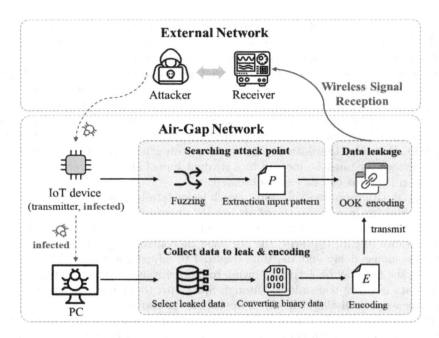

**Fig. 1.** Structural diagram of the Air-Fuzz.

Air-Fuzz proceeds in two ways: a transmitter within the air-gapped network and a receiver outside the air-gapped network. The transmitter performs fuzzing on the internal program to collect signal patterns that can be triggered. When the OOK encoded data is "1," a wireless signal is transmitted through the identified signal pattern; when it is "0," it sleeps. The receiver calculates a threshold that can distinguish between "1" and "0" in the collected wireless signals, divides the signal by the sample rate, and compares it to the threshold to distinguish between "1" and "0."

### 3.1   Transmitter

The pseudocode that receives binary data from an attacker and generates a wireless signal to leak data is the same as that in Algorithm 1.

To run the program, the frequency band for transmitting the wireless signal (frequency), binary data pattern (bit_pattern), time to continue the frequency transmission (time_on), and offset time between each bit (time_off) of the data must be input. Environmental variables, excluding bit patterns, must be agreed upon by the wireless signal sender and receiver before attempting data leakage. The data transmission process continues until the receiver requests the end of the data transmission. Each bit entered as a bit pattern is read individually, and different actions are taken to identify "1" and "0."

**Algorithm 1.** Data Generation Transmitter Algorithm

```
1:  procedure FREQUENCYCONTROL(frequency, bit_pattern, time_on, time_off)
2:      pid ← 0
3:      trap "Script terminated by user" SIGINT, SIGTERM
4:
5:      while true do
6:          for each bit in bit_pattern do
7:              if bit ≡ 1 then
8:                  STARTTUNE(frequency, time_on, time_off)
9:              else
10:                 SLEEP(time_on)
11:             end if
12:             SLEEP(time_off)
13:         end for
14:         SLEEP(10)                           ▷ Sleep for 10 seconds before repeating
15:     end while
16: end procedure
17:
18: procedure STARTTUNE(frequency, time_on, time_off.)
19:     pid ← start tune process with frequency
20:     SLEEP(time_on)
21:     tune_pid ← pid + 2
22:     kill tune_pid
23: end procedure
```

When the bit to be transmitted is "1," the StartTune procedure is executed. The StartTune procedure uses the variables frequency, time_on, and time_off as inputs, and transmits a wireless signal at a specified frequency for the duration of the time_on variable. After the signal has been transmitted for the set duration, the kill command terminates the transmission. If the bit is "0," the system indicates this by sleeping for the duration of time_on without transmitting any signal. After a bit has been transmitted, the system sleeps for the duration of timeoff to provide an offset interval between two consecutive bits.

This process is repeated for the length of the bit pattern, and when all transmissions are completed, it sleeps for 10 s to notify the receiver that the bit transmission has been completed. After Sleep, the transmission resumes from the first bit for the receiver to receive the bit again from the beginning.

## 3.2 Receiver

The receiver receives and analyzes the wireless signals transmitted by the transmitter from outside the air-gapped network. The pseudocode for decoding the binary data from a signal received through a wireless signal receiver is the same as that in Algorithm 2.

**Algorithm 2.** Data Receiver Algorithm

---

1: **function** LOADHACKRFSAMPLES(filename)
2:     raw_data ← Load file data as 8-bit integers
3:     iq_data ← raw_data[0::2] + $1j$ × raw_data[1::2]
4:     **return** iq_data
5: **end function**
6: **function** AVERAGESIGNALSTRENGTH(samples, sample_rate)
7:     samples_per_second ← INT(sample_rate)
8:     num_seconds ← LEN(samples) // samples_per_second
9:     average_signal_strength ← EMPTYLIST
10:     **for** $i$ ← 0 to num_seconds **do**
11:         start_idx ← $i$× samples_per_second
12:         end_idx ← start_idx + samples_per_second
13:         one_second_samples ← samples[start_idx:end_idx]
14:         abs_samples ← ABS(one_second_samples)
15:         avg_strength ← MEAN(abs_samples)
16:         APPEND(average_signal_strength, avg_strength)
17:     **end for**
18:     **return** average_signal_strength
19: **end function**
20: **function** DECODESIGNAL(samples)
21:     binary_data ← EMPTYLIST
22:     abs_samples ← ABS(samples)
23:     threshold ← MEAN(abs_samples)
24:     **for** sample in samples **do**
25:         **if** ABS(sample) > threshold **then**
26:             APPEND(binary_data, 1)
27:         **else**
28:             APPEND(binary_data, 0)
29:         **end if**
30:     **end for**
31:     **return** binary_data
32: **end function**
33: output_file ← USERINPUT('Enter the output file name:')
34: center_freq ← USERINPUT('Enter the center frequency (in MHz):') MHz
35: sample_rate ← USERINPUT('Enter the sample rate (in MSPS):') MSPS
36: samples ← LOADHACKRFSAMPLES(output_file)
37: average_signal_strength ← AVERAGESIGNALSTRENGTH(samples, sample_rate)
38: binary_data ← DECODESIGNAL(average_signal_strength)
39: PRINT(binary_data)

---

The LoadHackRFSamples function reads sample data from a binary file. Data from a binary file are read as an array of 8-bit integers, and real (I) and imaginary (Q) numbers are added to return a complex number array.

The AverageSignalStrength function calculates the number of samples per second. Divide the Samples by the sample rate of the receiver and store the time in seconds of Sampled data in the binary file in the num_seconds variable. The for statement is repeated for the number of seconds stored in the num_seconds variable, and the average signal intensity per second is calculated, stored in an array, and returned.

The DecodeSignal function receives one signal array per second and extracts the binary bits. To distinguish between 0 and 1, the average of the absolute values of all the samples is calculated and used as a threshold. It traverses the Samples array in which the average signal intensity per second received as a parameter is calculated, and distinguishes between 1 and 0 by checking whether the average intensity exceeds the threshold.

To execute the pseudocode of Algorithm 2, the receiver must enter the file of the bin extension where the received radio signal is stored, center frequency at which the signal is collected, and sample rate data of the receiver. Subsequently, the average signal strength per second is calculated by converting the bin file contents into complex number data using the LoadHackRFSamples function. The binary data transmitted by the sender is extracted using the array calculated through the AverageSignal Strength function as the input value of the DecodeSignal function.

## 4   Evaluation

An experiment was conducted to verify the concept of the proposed attack model. One hundred inputs were randomly generated through fuzzing. Figure 2 shows a graph that runs the target program with the generated input and collects the signal pattern generated during this process.

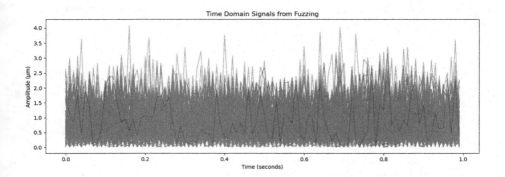

**Fig. 2.** Graph of fuzzing response signal.

The X-axis represents time and the Y-axis represents the amplitude of the signal. Responses with large amplitudes were obtained from the collected signals based on the center frequency, and binary data were encoded. Figure 2 The signal in red in the graph is the signal with the largest amplitude and is used for OOK encoding. If the binary data is "1," the input that generated the largest amplitude is re-executed, and if it is "0," sleep is performed for the receiver to distinguish the data. The OOK-encoded signal is illustrated graphically in Fig. 3.

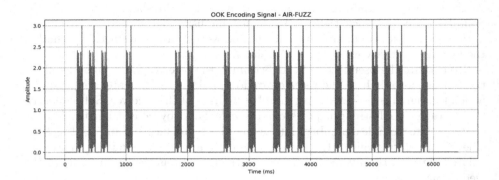

**Fig. 3.** Graph of the OOK encoding signal.

The extent to which Air-Fuzz is affected by noise when transmitting a wireless signal using encoded data is determined. The results were compared with those of the conventional attack model, and the results of calculating the Bit Error Rate (BER) according to the noise are summarized in Table 1.

**Table 1.** Comparison of Bit Error Rates (BERs) for Air-Fuzz and conventional attack models under different noise level and iterations.

| Noise Insertion Method | Air-Fuzz BER (%) | Conventional Attack Model [8] BER (%) |
|---|---|---|
| Random Noise Insertion (100 iterations) | 2.84 | 7 |
| Incremental Noise Insertion (0.1 to 1.3, 100 iterations) | 10.59 | 19.28 |
| Incremental Noise Insertion (0.1 to 1.3, 300 iterations) | 9.97 | 18.72 |

Because the conventional attack model uses the same bands as Wi-Fi and Bluetooth signals, it is affected by channel noise when transmitting signals to receivers outside the air-gapped. In the experiment, when the noise signal was randomly inserted by fixing the maximum noise level at 0.5, a low BER of approximately 7% was obtained. However, when the total average was calculated by increasing the maximum noise level to more than 1.0, the BER increased by

19%. In contrast, Air-Fuzz showed a BER of 10% or lower regardless of the noise level. Based on random noise, Air-Fuzz improved BER by approximately 59.43% compared with the conventional attack model. It is analyzed that Air-Fuzz is more resistant to noise than the conventional attack model, which encodes data in general signals. The data were encoded using inputs that triggered wireless signals through fuzzing.

An experiment was conducted to verify the effectiveness of the encoding and leaking data into wireless signals. This experiment extracts encoded binary signals by transmitting wireless signals from a Raspberry Pi 3b+ and receiving them through HackRF.

The transmission signal for data leakage was generated using an open source, RPiTX [12]. RPiTX can convert a Raspberry Pi into an RF transmitter and generate RF signals using GPIO 4. It can generate signals from 434 MHz to 1.5 GHz through sigma-delta modulation and high-speed timing control technologies. Raspberry Pi uses an operating frequency of over 700 MHz, and the RPiTX synthesizes the frequency based on the clock speed of the Raspberry Pi. The RPiTX adjusts the switching speed of GPIO 4 to generate the required frequency and emits a signal through an antenna physically connected to GPIO 4.

The transmission frequency was set to the default value of 434 MHz and the Sample_rate of HackRF was set to 10 MHz to receive the signal. The encoded binary signal "10101010" was transmitted for 2 s, and an offset value of 1 s was given to utilize the IDLE time between each bit. This allowed the receiver to decode the signal by distinguishing between bits. The received signal was saved as a binary file using the hackrf_transfer command in Ubuntu 20.04 and then loaded into Python for analysis. The spectrogram of the received signal is shown in Fig. 4.

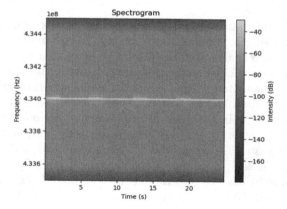

**Fig. 4.** Received frequency signal spectrogram.

Spectrogram analysis indicates that the received bit pattern is "10101010." After reading the signal stored in the binary file and downsampling it to improve the processing speed and reduce the data size, the processed data were output as a spectrogram to identify changes in the frequency components. The down-sampling factor was set to 10. The X-axis of the spectrogram represents time and the Y-axis represents frequency. The color bar indicates the signal strength. When "1" is transmitted, the signal strength at the center frequency of 434 MHz increases; the signal strength decreases when "0" is transmitted, which can be confirmed through the color change of the spectrogram.

## 5     Discussion

Unlike previous studies, this study proposes a new attack vector, proving that wireless signals enable data leakage. Because it uses a non-visible medium, it is more difficult for system users to notice a leak attack than optical or acoustic media. Additionally, rather than requiring additional media to generate a wireless signal, we discovered an input pattern that can trigger frequencies using the fuzzing technique. Fuzzing can induce abnormal behaviors in the system, which can help determine its response to an air-gapped environment.

Research on attack vectors that can be used in air-gapped networks is actively underway. However, research on their detection is lacking. Therefore, in future studies, we plan to develop a detection model for data leakage attacks in air-gapped networks. We plan to conduct follow-up research to collect datasets for model training by collecting the frequency signals that are commonly transmitted in air-gapped situations. We will then train the model through data processing to prove that abnormal-behavior detection is possible.

## 6     Conclusion

In this study, we demonstrated that data leakage attacks using side channels are feasible by fuzzing IoT connectivity devices in an air-gapped network and conducted research to analyze attack vectors. We demonstrated the feasibility of the proposed attack model by comparing the BER with that of the conventional model. The experiment showed that when the signal was transmitted 100 times with random noise inserted, the BER was improved by 59.43% compared with the conventional model. In addition, an experiment was conducted to transmit the leaked data by generating a wireless signal using Raspberry Pi, which is widely used in industrial settings, and to extract the leaked data by receiving the signal with a wireless signal receiver. The proposed Air-Fuzz utilizes fuzzing for attacks, making it easy to understand the response of the system in an air-gapped environment. Additionally, it transmits and receives data using wireless signals, which are an invisible medium that makes it difficult to detect attacks.

We plan to conduct follow-up research to demonstrate whether the attack model proposed in this study can be applied to commercial IoT devices under realistic industrial environmental conditions.

**Acknowledgments.** This work is supported by the Ministry of Trade, Industry and Energy (MOTIE) under Training Industrial Security Specialist for High-Tech Industry (RS-2024-00415520) supervised by the Korea Institute for Advancement of Technology (KIAT), and the Ministry of Science and ICT (MSIT) under the ICAN (ICT Challenge and Advanced Network of HRD) program (IITP-2022-RS-2022-00156310) and Information Security Core Technology Development (RS-2024-00437252) supervised by the Institute of Information & Communication Technology Planning & Evaluation (IITP).

**Disclosure of Interests.** The authors have no competing interests to declare that are relevant to the content of this article.

# References

1. Quy, V.K., Chehri, A., Quy, N.M., Han, N.D., Ban, N.T.: Innovative trends in the 6G era: a comprehensive survey of architecture, applications, technologies, and challenges. IEEE Access **11**, 39824–39844 (2023). https://doi.org/10.1109/ACCESS.2023.3269297

2. Kaur, J., Ramkumar, K.R.: The recent trends in cyber security: a review. J. King Saud Univ. Comput. Inf. Sci. **34**(8), 5766–5781 (2022). https://doi.org/10.1016/j.jksuci.2021.01.018

3. Lee, S., Shim, H., Lee, Y., Park, T., Park, S., Lee, I.: Study on systematic ransomware detection techniques. In: 2022 24th International Conference on Advanced Communication Technology (ICACT), pp. 297–301 (2022). https://doi.org/10.23919/ICACT53585.2022.9728909

4. Jeon, S., Lee, S., Lee, E., Lee, Y., Ryu, J., et al.: An effective threat detection frame-work for advanced persistent cyberattacks. Comput. Mater. Continua **75**(2), 4231–4253 (2023). https://doi.org/10.32604/cmc.2023.034287

5. Miketic, I., Dhananjay, K., Salman, E.: Covert channel communication as an emerging security threat in 2.5D/3D integrated systems. Sensors **23**(2081), 2081 (2023). https://doi.org/10.3390/s23042081

6. Park, J., Yoo, J., Yu, J., Lee, J., Song, J.: A survey on air-gap attacks: fundamentals, transport means, attack scenarios and challenges. Sensors **23**(3215), 3215 (2023). https://doi.org/10.3390/s23063215

7. Miller, T., Staves, A., Maesschalck, S., Sturdee, M., Green, B.: Looking back to look for-ward: lessons learnt from cyber-attacks on industrial control systems. Int. J. Crit. Infrastruct. Protect. **35**, 100464 (2021). https://doi.org/10.1016/j.ijcip.2021.100464

8. Guri, M.: AIR-FI: leaking data from air-gapped computers using Wi-Fi frequencies. IEEE Trans. Dependable Secure Comput. **20**(3), 25472564 (2023). https://doi.org/10.1109/TDSC.2022.3186627

9. Lee, J., Yoo, J., Lee, J., Choi, Y., Yoo, S.K., Song, J.: Optical air-gap attacks: analysis and IoT threat implications. IEEE Netw. (2024). https://doi.org/10.1109/MNET.2024.3382969

10. Li, Z., Chen, B., Chen, X., et al.: SpiralSpy: exploring a stealthy and practical covert channel to attack air-gapped computing devices via mmWave sensing. In: Network and Distributed Systems Security (NDSS) Symposium (2022). https://doi.org/10.14722/ndss.2022.23023

11. Chen, D., Chowdhury, M.M., Latif, S.: Data breaches in corporate setting. In: 2021 International Conference on Electrical, Computer, Communications and Mechatronics Engineering (ICECCME), pp. 01–06 (2021). https://doi.org/10.1109/ICECCME52200.2021.9590974
12. F5OEO: RPiTX: Turning a Raspberry Pi into a RF Transmitter, GitHub repository. https://github.com/F5OEO/rpitx

# Fuzzing JavaScript Engines
# with Diversified Mutation Strategies

Cheng-Han Shie[1,2]📵, Pin-Huang Fang[1], and Chun-I Fan[1,2,3](✉)📵

[1] Department of Computer Science and Engineering, National Sun Yat-sen
University, Kaohsiung 804201, Taiwan
cifan@mail.cse.nsysu.edu.tw
[2] Information Security Research Center, National Sun Yat-sen University,
Kaohsiung 804201, Taiwan
[3] Intelligent Electronic Commerce Research Center, National Sun Yat-sen University,
Kaohsiung 804201, Taiwan

**Abstract.** Current fuzzers for JavaScript (JS) engines often produce
test cases that are syntactically correct but semantically incorrect, hindering efficient crash discovery. To address this issue, we propose three
mutation methods: simple mutation, state mutation, and Just-In-Time
(JIT) compilation optimization triggering. The combination of these
methods significantly increases the variety of seed mutations, distinguishing our approach from other fuzzers. Additionally, we analyze each JS
engine to identify conditions that trigger JIT optimization, incorporating
these conditions into the mutation methods to enhance path coverage.
This approach achieves over 20% branch coverage, at least 5% higher
than other fuzzers, with a semantic correctness rate above 80%, reducing time wasted on semantic errors. Finally, our method nearly doubles
the crash discovery rate compared to other fuzzers.

**Keywords:** Fuzzing · Javascript engine · Abstract syntax tree
(AST) · Just-in-time (JIT) compilation

## 1 Introduction

A web browser [12] is a tool used to connect to the internet and retrieve information for interactive purposes. The browser consists primarily of a browser
engine, user interface, network objects, user interface backend, data storage,
and JavaScript engine. The JavaScript engine is responsible for interpreting and
executing JavaScript scripts. When a webpage loads, the JS engine parses the
code and creates an Abstract Syntax Tree (AST) representation. The engine then
compiles the AST into machine code for the computer to execute. JS engines
handle various language features, including garbage collection, optimization, and
runtime analysis. They also provide APIs that allow JS to interact with the host
environment, such as the Document Object Model (DOM) in web browsers.

To attract more users, web browsers often offer extensions that users can
freely access, such as tools for storing passwords [2], automatic browsing history

J.-H. Lee et al. (Eds.): WISA 2024, LNCS 15499, pp. 243–254, 2025.
https://doi.org/10.1007/978-981-96-1624-4_19

classification, generating new rendering scripts based on user preferences [9], and grammar correctors. However, these tools may be developed using JavaScript code that contains zero-day vulnerabilities.

The JavaScript (JS) engine converts JavaScript code into machine language. Although each engine may have slight variations in its implementation, the overall process generally involves parsing the code, optimizing it, and then executing it on the hardware.

Common JS engines include V8 (used in Google Chrome and Node.js), SpiderMonkey (used in Firefox), and JavaScriptCore (used in Safari). Each browser's engine is implemented differently, so executing the same code may produce different results, especially with Just-In-Time (JIT) compilation. This can lead to type confusion errors exploitable for remote attacks. Identifying and addressing these vulnerabilities proactively can prevent such attacks. Fuzz testing is necessary to generate a large amount of random data, uncovering potential risks in JavaScript engines.

The approach utilized in this work is based on the architecture of a variant Fuzzer to detect and identify suitable portions for mutation in the seed, reducing the compilation errors caused by mutation testing. Its main contributions are as follows:

1. The proposed method increases the variability range by studying the attributes of the AST.
2. The proposed methods can trigger JIT optimization, leading to an increase in code coverage.
3. The proposed outperforms existing fuzzers by discovering more crashes simultaneously and achieving a lower seed compilation error rate.

The structure of this paper is as follows. Section 2 provides an introduction to the relevant background knowledge related to this paper. The proposed method is proposed in Sect. 3. The evaluation results, comparisons, and conclusions are presented in Sect. 4 and 5.

## 2   Preliminaries

In this section, we will introduce the background knowledge related to the proposed methods.

### 2.1   Just-In-Time (JIT) Compilation

JIT is a dynamic compilation technique [4] where code is compiled into machine code during runtime, rather than being compiled into machine code during the compilation phase. This allows JIT compilation to optimize the code more flexibly, as it can adapt the optimization based on the actual runtime conditions. Furthermore, JIT compilation can also optimize for different hardware and platforms to achieve better performance. Although the optimization features may be similar across different implementations, the implementation methods can vary. As a result, each browser's JavaScript engine has its own vulnerabilities and issues.

## 2.2   Instrumentation

The technique involves inserting probes into the target program while ensuring the integrity of its original logic. These probes are executed during the program's execution and generate characteristic data about its runtime behavior. By analyzing this data, information about the program's control flow, data flow, and other dynamic information, such as logic coverage, can be obtained. This approach allows for effective testing of the program.

## 2.3   JavaScript Runtime Errors

ECMAScript [8] defines five runtime errors that can occur: RangeError, ReferenceError, SyntaxError, TypeError, and URIError. These errors are essential for the mutation strategies proposed in this paper.

- SyntaxError occurs when the JavaScript engine encounters a syntax that does not conform to the language specification.
- ReferenceError is triggered when an undefined variable is used.
- URIError indicates the improper usage of URI-related functions.
- RangeError occurs when a value that is outside the allowed range is used as a parameter in the program.
- TypeError is triggered when an operation is performed on a variable that is of a type that cannot perform that specific operation.

# 3   Methodology

This section describes the proposed mutation strategies include the simple method, the statement method and the incorporation of JIT optimization to expand the range of variations.

## 3.1   Mutating Methods

Figure 1 provides an illustrative explanation of the simple and the statement mutation methods. Figure 1a shows the conversion of a typical for loop program into an Abstract Syntax Tree (AST). Figure 1b represents the mutation method used in the Park et al. [13], which focuses on mutating only the numerical values of variables within a limited range (highlighted in yellow), and the gray blocks indicate immutable elements. The red text denotes the mutated values within the blocks. Figure 1c presents the mutation strategies in the proposed method, which goes beyond mutating variable values and includes mutation of operators, addition of for loops, elimination of root node for loops (resulting in only the body block of the AST), or modification to if statements (where the condition is also generated). The advantage of the method proposed in this paper is its ability to modify the seed structure, allowing for increased seed complexity. The larger the scope of variation, the higher the likelihood of triggering multiple vulnerabilities.

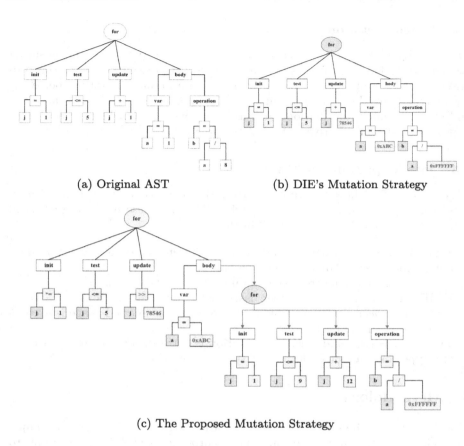

(a) Original AST                    (b) DIE's Mutation Strategy

(c) The Proposed Mutation Strategy

**Fig. 1.** Comparison of AST Mutation Methods (Color figure online)

**Simple Mutation.** Literal, BinaryExpression, LogicalExpression, UnaryExpression, UpdateExpression, and AssignmentExpression are all targets for simple mutations in the AST. The following is a brief description of each object.

– Literal: Numbers and strings are both classified as literals. When mutating literals, it is important to consider the possibility of causing a TypeError. For numbers, the mutation range can be extended to a larger value, such as $2^{48}$, which increases the likelihood of triggering a RangeError but also enhances the chances of buffer overflow vulnerabilities. For strings, the focus is on triggering format string attacks and buffer overflows. Therefore, mutations should be capable of transforming strings into ones with special characters, such as %x.
– BinaryExpression: The BinaryExpression encompasses both binary operators and binary conditionals, such as ==, >=, +, and |. Although they fall under the same category, it is important to differentiate between binary operators and binary conditionals when applying mutations. Treating them interchangeably

can lead to syntax errors. Therefore, it is crucial to accurately identify whether the program is performing calculations or conditional checks before applying mutations.

– LogicalExpression: Any logical operators, such as && and ||, fall under the category of the LogicalExpression. This category does not encounter runtime errors.
– UnaryExpression: Except for ++ and --, all other operators are classified as the UnaryExpression, such as ~ and !. Unary operators are generally straightforward to use, and therefore, they do not typically result in runtime errors.
– UpdateExpression: Only the unary operators ++ and -- belong to this category. This category can be adjusted by modifying the `prefix` property, placing ++ or -- before or after a variable, to influence the program's flow of execution.
– AssignmentExpression: When the BinaryExpression combines with an equality symbol, it falls into the category of the AssignmentExpression. Examples of such symbols include =, +=, |=, &=, and so on. Due to the specification of IEEE-754 [1], when a string is involved in this type of assignment operation, the result will output NaN, thus not causing a runtime error.

**Statement Mutation.** The objects in the AST that serve as targets for state mutation include ForStatement, ForInStatement, IfStatement, DoWhileStatement, SwitchStatement, WithStatement, ContinueStatement, BreakStatement, and WhileStatement. These objects can be modified to alter the state of the program during its execution. These objects can be classified into two methods: addition and deletion.

The addition method can encompass program fragments that include a seed at any location, such as for and while loops selecting a program fragment with an assigned memory space seed or an executing operation seed. The addition method also increases the probability of triggering buffer overflow and UAF vulnerabilities. In additional, the deletion method can disrupt the original structure of the seed, allowing for greater diversity in the seed's variations. Overall, these mutation methods aim to enhance the complexity and diversity of the program, increasing the chances of triggering various vulnerabilities.

### 3.2 Different JIT Optimizations

JS engines operate similarly with an interpreter generating unoptimized bytecode and an optimizing compiler generating optimized bytecode. Here are the optimization strategies employed by different JS engines:

– V8: Chrome's JS engine uses Ignition as its interpreter to generate bytecode from the AST. Ignition analyzes the data and passes it to V8's optimizing compiler, TurboFan, which employs speculative optimization based on function call frequencies and parameter types. TurboFan infers operation types and simplifies them but degrades if parameter types change. The function `%OptimizeFunctionOnNextCall` can trigger optimization directly.

- ChakraCore (CH): IE's ChakraCore has two JIT compilers: SimpleJIT and FullJIT. SimpleJIT applies basic optimizations and passes complex optimizations to FullJIT. SimpleJIT triggers after 25 executions, and FullJIT triggers after 20,000 executions.
- SpiderMonkey (SM): Firefox's JS engine uses a baseline compiler with inline caching and IonMonkey for further optimizations. IonMonkey converts baseline information and bytecode into intermediate code. Testing shows JIT optimization occurs after around 1000 repeated function invocations.
- JavaScriptCore (JSC): Safari's JS engine has three JIT compilers. LLInt transitions to the Baseline compiler after 100 loops or 6 function calls. The Baseline compiler gathers type information. The DFG compiler is triggered after 1000 loops or 60 function calls, utilizing type information for further optimizations. The FTL compiler handles recursive functions, triggered after 1000 loops or 10,000 function calls, introducing advanced optimizations using LLVM.

**Trigger JIT Optimization.** Each JS engine has its own unique optimization techniques, all of which can trigger optimization mechanisms through repeated execution, albeit with different frequencies. Therefore, when the code that triggers optimization undergoes changes in the internal variable values or types compared to the original code, the condition indicates the presence of one of the following vulnerabilities: buffer overflow, type confusion, or UAF.

### 3.3  Fuzzing Phase

The architecture diagram in Fig. 2 represents the structure of a fuzzing. The seed (.js files) is obtained from a corpus, and the seed is converted into an AST. The AST is analyzed to identify properties that can be mutated. Corresponding mutation dictionaries are applied based on these properties. For example, the = operator can be mutated to >= or != and the + operator can be mutated to - or %, among other possibilities. Numeric values can be mutated to larger numbers, and strings can be mutated into randomly generated strings composed of special characters. These are relatively intuitive and simple mutation methods.

To achieve more advanced types of confusion, memory overflows, and other vulnerabilities through mutation, more complex mutation techniques are required. These may involve removing loops through statement mutation methods or triggering JIT through mutation methods. The targets of the testing are the JS engines of web browsers, including V8 (Chrome), CH (Microsoft Edge), JSC (Safari), and SM (Firefox).

During the testing process, feedback information is collected, including register information, discovered paths, and overall coverage. If any abnormalities occur in the registers, the input at that moment, register information, and execution flow are recorded to generate a crash report. The paths and coverage information are used to update the corpus, improving the quality of the files in the corpus. The testing process then starts a new iteration. The duration of the execution depends on whether new paths can be found based on all the seeds, including the updated seeds, allowing the user to decide.

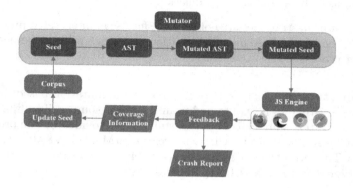

**Fig. 2.** Fuzzing Test Architecture Diagram

# 4  Evaluation Result Analysis and Comparison

In this section, the proposed scheme will be compared with other fuzzers in terms of coverage, semantic error rate, and the number of crashes discovered simultaneously. This aims to demonstrate the effectiveness of the proposed mutation method in reducing error compilation rates and finding a greater number of crashes.

## 4.1  Environment

The experimental environment used in this paper, which includes an Ubuntu 20.04 system, an i5-12400 CPU, and 48 GB of RAM. The fuzzer architecture is based on AFL++ (American Fuzzy Lop Plus Plus), an open-source fuzzing software. AFL++ extends the original AFL fuzzer and incorporates optimizations from previous research papers. It also supports various programming languages for developing mutation methods.

**American Fuzzy Lop Plus Plus (AFL++).** The proposed method utilizes a fuzzer framework based on AFL++ [5]. AFL++ combines AFL with optimization fuzzing techniques such as Mopt [11] and Redqueen [3]. The following are the default mutation strategies in AFL++.

- Bitflip: Flipping bits, changing 1 to 0 and 0 to 1.
- Arithmetic: Performing addition and subtraction operations on a byte-by-byte basis.

- Interest: Replacing a portion of the seed with special symbols or custom values.
- Havoc: Performing the aforementioned three actions (bitflip, arithmetic, and interest) as well as addition and deletion on the entire seed.

These mutation strategies are not suitable for use in interpreted programming languages. Therefore, these default mutation strategies will not be used during the fuzzing process.

**Seed Collection.** Since this paper is based on mutation-based fuzzing, it requires pre-existing JS files obtained from two main sources. The first source is the open-source test suite called "js-test-suite" [10] provided by the project [16], which includes relevant files for ChakraCore, SpiderMonkey, V8, JavaScriptCore, and others. The second source is "js-vuln-db" [14], which primarily collects buffer overflow, type confusion, and UAF vulnerabilities.

**Target Engines.** Four commonly used browsers' JavaScript engines were selected as targets for the experiments: Chrome's V8 (version 11.1.130), Edge's ChakraCore (version 1.11.24), Firefox's SpiderMonkey (version 109.0.1), and Safari's JavaScriptCore (version 2.39.5). The total lines of code for each JavaScript engine used in the experiments were 745,953 for V8, 474,641 for ChakraCore, 526,955 for SpiderMonkey, and 339,168 for JavaScriptCore. These engines include added instrumentation code during compilation to enable the detection of crashes during subsequent fuzzing.

**Mutation Methods to Trigger JIT Optimization.** In Sect. 3.2, the optimization mechanisms of each JS engine were discussed. However, the experimental tests considered the execution time and modified the frequency of triggering JIT optimizations. The methods to trigger different JIT modes in ChakraCore. The SimpleJIT mode, set to 25, was kept unchanged as it does not impose a significant burden on fuzzing test. However, the FullJIT mode requires 20,000 iterations to trigger. Therefore, the original code was modified before compilation to adjust the trigger to 200 iterations. To trigger the JIT optimization using the %OptimizeFunctionOnNextCall function, which automatically optimizes the desired code when executed. The JIT optimization frequency for SM, where the original code was looped 1,000 times. The triggering method for JSC, which was kept unchanged from its original settings.

## 4.2   Performance Comparison with Other Fuzzers

**The Total Number of Tests.** Table 1 shows the total number of executions for each fuzzer over a seven-day period. The proposed method executed approximately 7 million times, while the other fuzzers executed over 7.2 million times. It can be observed that the less complex the mutation method, the lower the time taken for a single seed mutation.

**Table 1.** The Total Number of Tests

|     | Ours | CodeAlchemist [7] | DIE [13] | Superion [15] | Fuzzilli [6] |
|-----|------|-------------------|----------|---------------|--------------|
| CH  | 7,157k | 7,412k | 7,751k | 7,462k | 7,394k |
| V8  | 7,014k | 7,347k | 7,513k | 7,248k | 7,326k |
| JSC | 7,113k | 7,446k | 7,633k | 7,319k | 7,284k |
| SM  | 6,954k | 7,235k | 7,376k | 7,367k | 7,374k |

**Semantic Accuracy Rate.** Semantic accuracy rate refers to the percentage of generated seeds that can be compiled without errors. Semantically accurate seeds can trigger deeper program behaviors. Table 2 presents the semantic accuracy rates for each fuzzer based on the first 3 million seed executions. The proposed scheme achieved an average accuracy rate of 82.78%, CodeAlchemist had 33.93%, DIE [13] had 61.07%, Superion [15] had 32.16%, and Fuzzilli [6] had 66.73%. The proposed scheme shows a higher accuracy rate compared to other fuzzers because it references common semantically valid examples, maintaining the semantic validity of mutated seeds.

CodeAlchemist only eliminates some undeclared anomalies by matching functions and variables, without addressing other semantic errors, resulting in a lower accuracy rate. DIE's mutation method, similar to the proposed scheme's simple mutation, shows significantly higher semantic accuracy compared to other fuzzers. However, DIE requires pre-processing steps before fuzzing, leading to more erroneous seeds as testing time increases. Superion, using AFL's tree-based mutation method, has the lowest accuracy rate among the fuzzers. Fuzzilli uses a self-developed intermediate language for mutation, focusing on optimizations in other stages rather than the mutation method, resulting in an accuracy rate second only to the proposed scheme.

**Table 2.** Semantic Accuracy Rate and Branch Coverage Rate

|     | Semantic Accuracy Rate | | | | | Branch Coverage Rate | | | | |
|-----|--------|--------|--------|--------|--------|--------|--------|--------|--------|--------|
|     | Ours | [7] | [13] | [15] | [6] | Ours | [7] | [13] | [15] | [6] |
| CH  | **84.67%** | 37.40% | 61.42% | 32.79% | 65.13% | **23.56%** | 12.27% | 14.63% | 11.13% | 15.09% |
| V8  | **82.39%** | 29.48% | 59.83% | 34.15% | 70.23% | **23.14%** | 10.72% | 12.54% | 10.44% | 13.26% |
| JSC | **81.33%** | 35.73% | 62.59% | 27.55% | 64.98% | **22.38%** | 13.55% | 14.41% | 13.61% | 17.52% |
| SM  | **82.76%** | 33.12% | 60.46% | 34.16% | 66.58% | **22.66%** | 12.28% | 14.76% | 12.75% | 16.77% |

**Branch Coverage Rate.** The graph in Fig. 3 illustrates the relationship between time and code coverage during the fuzzing of the JavaScript engine. The four subfigures can be observed that the initial code coverage ranges from approximately 8% to 15%. Afterward, the fluctuations in code coverage stabilize.

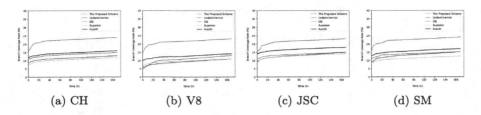

<table>
<tr><td>(a) CH</td><td>(b) V8</td><td>(c) JSC</td><td>(d) SM</td></tr>
</table>

**Fig. 3.** The Relationship between Branch Coverage Rate and Execution Time in the JS engine.

Table 2 presents the branch coverage rates for the proposed scheme and various fuzzers, measured over one week. The proposed scheme achieves an average coverage rate of 22.93%. This is because the proposed scheme employs multiple complex mutation methods that provide more opportunities to reach deeper code paths. As CodeAlchemist is a generational fuzzer, the coverage rate reflects the limitation of generational fuzzers. The generated test seeds do not become complex enough, resulting in a coverage rate of only 12.28%. DIE, as a mutation-based fuzzer, slightly improves the coverage rate by mutating variables, reaching 14.08%. Superion's mutation method is prone to errors, causing only a portion of the seeds to execute successfully, resulting in a coverage rate of 11.98%. Fuzzilli achieves a coverage rate of 15.66%, ranking second after the proposed scheme.

**Comparing Crash Mining.** Table 3 represents the number of crashes discovered during the mining process, with a statistical timeframe of one week and approximately 7 million executions per fuzzer. The proposed scheme has found the highest number of crashes across various JS engines, surpassing CodeAlchemist and DIE by more than three times and Fuzzilli by two times. However, Superion has only discovered crashes in CH.

**Table 3.** The Number of Unique Crashes

| JS Engine | Ours | CodeAlchemist [7] | DIE [13] | Superion [15] | Fuzzilli [6] |
|-----------|------|-------------------|----------|---------------|--------------|
| CH        | **13** | 3               | 4        | 1             | 6            |
| V8        | **8**  | 1               | 3        | 0             | 4            |
| JSC       | **8**  | 1               | 1        | 0             | 3            |
| SM        | **6**  | 1               | 1        | 0             | 3            |

### 4.3    Experimental Conclusion

Based on the above results, it can be concluded that improving semantic correctness increases the effectiveness of most seeds and reduces wasted time on ineffective inputs. However, there is not necessarily an absolute correlation between branch coverage and semantic correctness. For example, in Table 2, CodeAlchemist has a correctness rate of 35.73% for JavaScriptCore, but its branch coverage is lower than that of Superion. This is because fuzzing involves random mutation and generation, so even with flaws in the mutation strategy, it is still possible to produce seeds that can delve deeper into the target program.

Another key aspect of improving coverage is the complexity of the seeds. Increasing complexity requires employing multiple mutation techniques. The proposed scheme utilizes 15 different mutation operations, including single variables, operators, logical symbols, control flow syntax, and triggering JIT optimization. These operations significantly increase seed complexity. Due to these mutation strategies, the proposed scheme achieves high coverage and discovers the most crashes compared to other fuzzers.

## 5   Conclusions and Future Works

The proposed AST-based mutation method enables a higher number of seed mutations compared to other fuzzers. Beyond basic mutation methods, it examines each JavaScript engine to identify conditions triggering JIT optimization, incorporating these into the mutations. A validation function checks the type and value of parameters post-optimization to identify potential vulnerabilities, leading to higher coverage and varied program paths. This comprehensive approach ensures the discovery of more potential vulnerabilities and achieves a semantic correctness rate above 80%, reducing wasted time on semantic errors. Additionally, it finds nearly twice as many crashes as other fuzzers.

The main contribution of this research is proposing mutation strategies to discover and trigger more crashes. Future work aims to develop an automated crash analysis and PoC generation system to streamline the crash analysis process, significantly reducing the time required and benefiting users.

**Acknowledgments.** This work was supported in part by the National Science and Technology Council of Taiwan under Grants NSTC 113-2634-F-110-001-MBK and 113-2221-E-110-082, in part by the Information Security Research Center at National Sun Yat-sen University, and in part by the Intelligent Electronic Commerce Research Center from the Featured Areas Research Center Program through the Framework of the Higher Education Sprout Project by the Ministry of Education in Taiwan.

## References

1. ISO/IEC/IEEE international standard - floating-point arithmetic. ISO/IEC 60559:2020(E) IEEE Std 754-2019, pp. 1–86 (2020)
2. Agrafiotis, I., Nurse, J.R.C., Goldsmith, M., Creese, S., Upton, D.: A taxonomy of cyber-harms: defining the impacts of cyber-attacks and understanding how they propagate. J. Cybersecur. 4(1) (2018)
3. Aschermann, C., Schumilo, S., Blazytko, T., Gawlik, R., Holz, T.: REDQUEEN: fuzzing with input-to-state correspondence. In: NDSS 2019, pp. 1–15 (2019)

4. Barrière, A., Blazy, S., Flückiger, O., Pichardie, D., Vitek, J.: Formally verified speculation and deoptimization in a JIT compiler. Proc. ACM Program. Lang. **5**(POPL), 1–26 (2021)
5. Fioraldi, A., Maier, D., Eißfeldt, H., Heuse, M.: AFL++: combining incremental steps of fuzzing research. In: 14th USENIX Workshop on Offensive Technologies (WOOT 20). USENIX Association (2020)
6. Groß, S., Koch, S., Bernhard, L., Holz, T., Johns, M.: FUZZILLI: fuzzing for JavaScript JIT compiler vulnerabilities. In: Network and Distributed Systems Security (NDSS) Symposium (2023)
7. Han, H.S., Oh, D.H., Cha, S.K.: CodeAlchemist: semantics-aware code generation to find vulnerabilities in JavaScript engines. In: Network and Distributed System Security Symposium (2019)
8. Ecma International. ECMA-262, 13th edn. ECMAScript® 2022 Language Specification (2022)
9. Rajya Lakshmi, D., Suguna Mallika, S.: A review on web application testing and its current research directions. Int. J. Electr. Comput. Eng. **7**(4), 2132 (2017)
10. leeswimming. [online] WSP-LAB js-test-suite (2020)
11. Lyu, C., et al.: MOPT: optimized mutation scheduling for fuzzers. In: 28th USENIX Security Symposium (USENIX Security 19), pp. 1949–1966 (2019)
12. Nelson, R., Shukla, A., Smith, C.: Web browser forensics in Google Chrome, Mozilla Firefox, and the Tor browser bundle. In: Digital Forensic Education: An Experiential Learning Approach, pp. 219–241 (2020)
13. Park, S., Xu, W., Yun, I., Jang, D., Kim, T.: Fuzzing JavaScript engines with aspect-preserving mutation. In: 2020 IEEE Symposium on Security and Privacy (SP), pp. 1629–1642 (2020)
14. tunz. [online] Case Study of JavaScript Engine Vulnerabilities (2019)
15. Wang, J., Chen, B., Wei, L., Liu, Y.: Superion: grammar-aware greybox fuzzing. In: 2019 IEEE/ACM 41st International Conference on Software Engineering (ICSE), pp. 724–735 (2019)
16. Lee, S., Han, H.S., Cha, S.K., Son, S.: Montage: a neural network language model-guided JavaScript engine fuzzer. In: Proceedings of the 29th USENIX Conference on Security Symposium, pp. 2613–2630 (2020)

# Malware

# Detecting Phishing-Targeted Web Push Notifications Through Image Similarity Analysis

Rion Matsuzaki and Masaya Sato$^{(\boxtimes)}$ (iD)

Okayama Prefectural University, Soja, Okayama, Japan
masaya@c.oka-pu.ac.jp

**Abstract.** Web push notifications are used to induce users to phishing websites. To prevent this induction, keyword-based detection has been proposed. However, the words used in phishing web push notifications differ from those used in phishing websites. Thus, generating a keyword list for detecting phishing web push notifications is challenging. In this paper, we propose a method for detecting phishing-targeted web push notifications through image similarity analysis. Phishing-targeted web push notifications mostly contain images in their data. We utilized this image data to detect phishing-targeted web push notifications. In our prototype, we used mitmproxy to capture image data and analyzed image similarity using structural image similarity. Experimental results showed that our prototype can detect phishing-targeted web push notifications with high accuracy.

**Keywords:** Phishing detection · Web push notification · Image similarity

## 1 Introduction

Damages caused by phishing websites are increasing, and adversaries are inducing users through various methods. From the report of Anti-Phishing Working Group, 2023 is the worst year for phishing [4]. Adversaries create phishing websites by imitating legitimate websites to deceive users and steal personal or account information. The number of unique phishing websites is 350,000 or more; however, a single phishing website may be advertised through various methods, including email, ads, notifications, or phone-based methods. Consequently, countermeasures against phishing attacks remain a challenging problem. In the early stages, the method of inducing users to phishing sites was often through email; however, the methods have now diversified to include short message service (SMS), social network service (SNS), two-dimensional barcodes (including QR codes), and push notifications.

Induction using web push notifications is an emerging threat. A web push notification is a function to display a notification from a website. A web browser

J.-H. Lee et al. (Eds.): WISA 2024, LNCS 15499, pp. 257–269, 2025.
https://doi.org/10.1007/978-981-96-1624-4_20

supporting web push notifications can display a notification on the desktop of the computer by receiving messages from push servers. The sender can set an action to the notification, thus, the user may be induced to phishing websites by clicking the displayed notification. Due to the fact that attacks using web push notifications for malware distribution or induction to phishing websites have been observed, countermeasures against this induction have become important.

The difficulty in detecting and preventing malicious web push notifications that induce users to phishing websites lies in the challenge of distinguishing whether a notification is malicious or not. The display area of notifications is limited and small, which means the information available to distinguish malicious notifications is insufficient. In addition, users cannot grasp the actions bound to the notification buttons because there is no correspondence between the label shown on the button and the actual action. As a result, clicking any button may induce the user to malicious websites.

In this paper, we propose an image-based method to detect malicious web push notifications. Web push notifications contain not only text but also image data. Visual information is frequently used to deceive, frighten, and confuse users in order to induce them to malicious websites. We hypothesized that the images used for these types of attacks have strong similarity. In fact, images used in phishing websites are similar to those on legitimate websites, whereas legitimate websites are not similar to each other. For this reason, we developed a method to calculate the image similarity between the images in web push notifications and malicious images. In this method, web push notifications with images similar to malicious images are blocked and not displayed. This protects users from being induced to phishing websites by clicking the notifications. This paper presents the design, implementation, and evaluation results of the proposed method.

## 2   Background

### 2.1   Phishing

Phishing is a deceptive attack targeting the theft of account information or the distribution of malware. A phishing site is a website used for phishing attacks. In many cases, phishing sites mimic legitimate companies' websites to deceive users into believing the site is legitimate. The increasing damages caused by phishing attacks highlight the importance of countermeasures against these attacks.

To induce users to phishing sites, adversaries exploit various methods including email, SMS, SNS, and push notifications. Countermeasures for attacks exploiting email, SMS, and SNS have been proposed [14,18]. However, countermeasures against deceptive web push notifications are insufficient. Specifically, the prevention of displaying deceptive web push notifications has not been well studied.

### 2.2   Web Push Notification

A web push notification is a method for displaying notifications on the desktop from a website. Once a user permits sending notifications from a website, the website can send a push notification to the notification area of the desktop through the web browser. A web push notification consists of a title, a body, an icon, a body image, and an action title. The behavior and design of the notified information differ across each OS and web browser.

There are two methods to display a web push notification: the Notifications API [11] and the Push API [12]. In the Notifications API, a web push notification is displayed through the Notification constructor or a Service Worker. The Push API uses a Service Worker to display a web push notification. The Service Worker is a thread that executes JavaScript programs independently from the thread that handles the display of websites. The Service Worker displays the notification by receiving messages from a push server. Additionally, the JavaScript program executed by the website thread can use the Service Worker to display a notification. For security reasons, the Service Worker communicates exclusively through HTTPS.

Figure 1 shows the flow of a web push notification using a Service Worker. The `Notification.requestPermission()` method is used to request a user for permission to send a web push notification. Once a user permits, a Service Worker is registered through communication with a Push Server. The communication related to a web push notification using the Push API occurs between the Service Worker and the push server. This means that the communication related to a web push notification bypasses the thread for the website. A web push notification using the Notifications API can also use a Service Worker method named `ServiceWorkerRegistration.showNotification()`. This method is common in both the Notifications API and the Push API.

`ServiceWorkerRegistration.showNotification()` method has two arguments: `title` and `options`. The title of the notification is stored in `title` (mandatory) and other data are stored in `options` (optional). Table 1 shows the properties available for setting in `options`.

## 2.3  Web Push Notifications Inducing Users to Phishing Websites

Web push notifications are used to induce users to malicious websites. Lee et al. analyzed relation between web push notifications and malicious websites [7]. Their analysis results show that third-party web push services are used for phishing notifications. In the report, rise of web push notifications with corporation and brand logos may cause malicious web push notification using imitated logo images by attackers.

To verify the above results and collect data from malicious websites, we collected and analyzed web push notifications that induce users to phishing websites. The analysis results showed that malicious web push notifications tend to use wording that stirs up anxiety in users. Specifically, we found that all the malicious web push notifications in our survey have an icon and data in their `options`. The `body` is also included at a high rate.

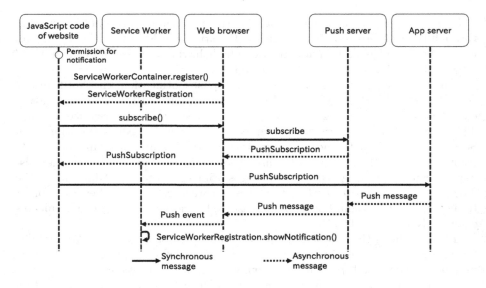

**Fig. 1.** Communication flow of web push notification.

## 2.4 Countermeasures and Challenges

We have tried to detect malicious web push notifications using a keyword-based approach. This method monitors the JavaScript programs of websites and prevents the display of malicious web push notifications if they include words used for phishing websites. However, through our survey on malicious web push notifications and phishing websites, we found that constructing the keyword list is difficult in practice. In our survey, we found that the words used in the two groups, malicious web push notifications and phishing websites, had few commonalities, making it difficult to detect malicious notifications based on these words.

Based on the postmortem of our previous work and the analysis results in Sect. 2.3, we have summarized the observations for detecting malicious web push notifications as follows:

**(O1)** Keyword-based detection is not practical

As previously stated, malicious web push notifications and phishing websites have few commonalities in their wording. Additionally, constructing a malicious keyword dataset from malicious web push notifications is difficult due to the limited number of such notifications. Collecting a sufficient number of malicious web push notifications is challenging due to the nature of push notifications. To collect data on web push notifications, we need to develop a crawler that automatically visits websites, permits web push notifications, waits for the receipt of notifications, and finally determines whether the received notifications are legitimate or malicious. While Subramani et al. [19]

**Table 1.** Properties that can be set in the options for ServiceWorkerRegistration.showNotification()

| Property | Description |
| --- | --- |
| body | A string representing additional content to be displayed within the notification |
| icon | A string containing the URL of an image to be used as an icon in the notification |
| image | A string containing the URL of an image to be displayed in the notification |
| actions.title | A string containing the action text to be displayed to the user |
| actions.icon | A string containing the URL of an image to be used as an icon in the action |
| badge | A string containing the URL of an image to represent the notification when there is not enough space to display the notification itself |
| data | Any data associated with the notification |
| dir | The direction of the notification |
| lang | The language used within the notification |
| silent | If set, no sound or vibration will occur |
| tag | A given notification ID to allow the script to search, replace, or delete the notification as needed |
| timestamp | The time associated with the notification, in milliseconds since UNIX epoch |
| renotify | A boolean value indicating whether to suppress vibration and audible alerts when reusing the tag value |
| vibrate | The vibration pattern to execute when displaying the notification |

developed such a crawler, labeling each notification as legitimate or malicious remains a challenging problem.

**(O2)** Data inside web push notifications are not sufficiently used

As stated in Sect. 2.2, web push notifications contain various data within their options. However, our previous approach focused only on the `title` and SPSVERBc10due to the characteristics of the keyword-based approach.

## 3 Detection of Suspicious Web Push Notifications by Image Similarity

### 3.1 Detection Method Using Image Similarity

Based on these observations, we decided to exploit the *image* data of web push notifications to protect users from the induction using malicious web push notifications. We propose a method to detect malicious web push notifications using image similarity. As stated in the previous section, malicious web push

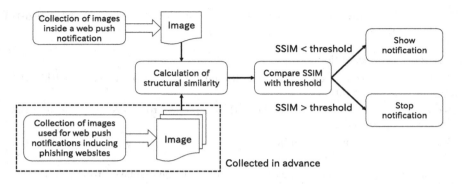

**Fig. 2.** Overview of image-based detection of suspicious web push notifications.

notifications tend to include images in their notification data. In addition, the image similarity scores among legitimate websites are low, but phishing websites are similar to legitimate websites. From this observation, we hypothesized that images of malicious web push notifications have strong similarity. Here, we define a malicious web push notification as a web push notification that induces users to phishing websites. For this reason, we propose a method to detect malicious web push notifications by focusing on image similarity.

Figure 2 shows an overview of the proposed method. The proposed method monitors images in web push notifications and calculates the similarity between the received image and pre-collected malicious images. Here, malicious images are collected in advance from known malicious web push notifications. If the similarity exceeds a certain threshold, the notification containing the image is detected as malicious and its display is prevented.

The proposed method does not employ the keyword-based detection method. This means that bypassing detection by changing keywords has no effect on the detection rate. Even if adversaries try to change their images for evasion, the proposed method is resistant to such types of evasion. If adversaries change their images slightly, the proposed method can still detect them as long as the images are similar to the original ones. As long as the threshold is not disclosed to adversaries, they cannot evade detection by the proposed method. Changing images significantly is much more costly compared to changing keywords. Additionally, the cost of preparing new images for phishing is also high, and this could affect their ability to induce users to phishing websites. For the above reasons, we believe that the proposed method has a certain degree of effectiveness in deterring attacker activities.

### 3.2 Image Similarity

To calculate the image similarity, we used structural similarity (SSIM) [2]. The SSIM score is an indicator for evaluating the similarity between two images, considering differences in structure, luminance, and contrast. To calculate the

**Table 2.** Items in SSIM equation

| Item | Description |
|------|-------------|
| $\mu_x$ | Average luminance of image $x$ |
| $\mu_y$ | Average luminance of image $y$ |
| $\sigma_x$ | Standard deviation of image $x$ (variation of luminance) |
| $\sigma_y$ | Standard deviation of image $y$ (variation of luminance) |
| $\sigma_{xy}$ | Covariance between images $x$ and $y$ (correlation of luminance) |
| $C_1$, $C_2$ | Small constants (for stability improvement) |

similarity, the image is divided into small blocks, and these items are compared. Finally, the overall similarity is summarized using the scores of the small blocks. The higher the SSIM score, the higher the similarity. The upper bound of the SSIM score is one. The equation for the SSIM score is shown in Equation (1), and each item is detailed in Table 2. In our prototype, we used OpenCV to calculate the SSIM score, and the default values of OpenCV were employed for $C_1$ and $C_2$.

$$SSIM(x,y) = \frac{(2\mu_x\mu_y + C_1)(2\sigma_{xy} + C_2)}{(\mu_x^2 + \mu_y^2 + C_1)(\sigma_x^2 + \sigma_y^2 + C_2)} \tag{1}$$

## 4  Implementation

### 4.1  Monitoring of HTTP Communication

The proposed method collects images related to web push notifications and prevents the display of the notification if the image inside it has a high similarity to malicious images. To implement this system, we employed monitoring of HTTP communications related to web push notifications. Browser extensions and browser modifications are also considerable methods for the system; however, browser extensions cannot collect the required information and browser modifications require high costs for development and installation. For these reasons, we employed HTTP monitoring to capture images related to web push notifications.

We use *mitmproxy* [15] to monitor HTTP communications on a client computer. Mitmproxy is a proxy tool that can monitor and modify the communication data in the computer. Mitmproxy can monitor secured HTTP (TLS) communications with HTTP/1, HTTP/2, and WebSocket. It also supports a Python API for monitoring, modification, and replay of communications. Thus, we implemented the proposed method as a Python program using the Python API of mitmproxy. Figure 3 shows the flow for monitoring HTTP communication using mitmproxy. The program monitors HTTP responses, saves images related to web push notifications, calculates the similarity of images, and prevents the display of notifications.

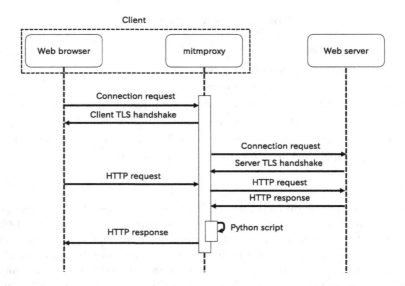

**Fig. 3.** Monitoring HTTP communication using mitmproxy

## 4.2   Procedure for Detection

Figure 4 shows the flow for controlling the display of web push notifications. We implemented the following flow in the Python script shown in Fig. 3.

1. Image collection
   This part collects images inside a web push notification. Due to the difficulty of identifying which HTTP response is for images of web push notifications, we collected URLs for images included in responses for web push notifications (detailed in (2)). First, we monitor the Content-Type of HTTP responses. If the Content-Type is an image, we search for the URL from the collected URLs included in web push notifications. If we find that the response matches the collected URL, we save the received image. Finally, this part passes the acquired image to part (3).
2. URL collection
   Searches for showNotification() and Notification Constructor in the response. If either is found, save the URLs of the images. Then, this part returns the processing to part (1).
3. Calculation of image similarity
   This part compares the images collected in (1) with the malicious images collected in advance. We used structural similarity (SSIM) for comparison, and this part passes the SSIM value to part (4).
4. Control for showing notifications
   This part determines whether the web push notification is suspicious or not. If the SSIM score is greater than the threshold, this part stops the notification from being displayed. Otherwise, the notification is displayed.

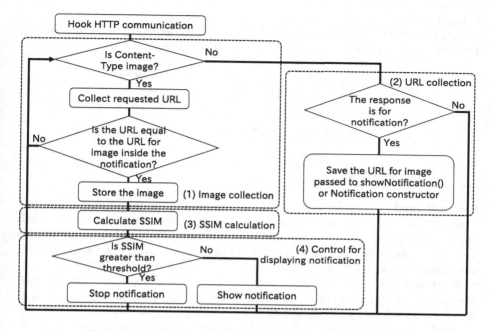

**Fig. 4.** Flow for control of showing web push notifications

**Table 3.** Environment for evaluation

| CPU | Core i5-8265U |
|---|---|
| Memory | 8 GB |
| Web browser | Google Chrome ver. 113.0.5672.93 |

The threshold in part (4) must be determined through experiments. We set the threshold at 0.8, considering the results in [6], which imply that legitimate sites use different (not similar) images, whereas malicious websites use images similar to those of legitimate sites.

## 5   Evaluation

### 5.1   Purpose and Environment

We evaluated the proposed method from the viewpoint of the detection ability of malicious web push notifications with images. In addition, we measured the time required to detect malicious web push notifications. The environment for evaluation is shown in Table 3. In the evaluation, we used Windows 11 and Google Chrome for receiving push notifications. To monitor HTTP communications, we used mitmproxy and implemented our prototype as a Python script using the Python API of mitmproxy.

**Table 4.** Detection results of malicious web push notifications. The number in parentheses indicates the total number of malicious web push notifications in our dataset. This includes notifications not targeted by our proposed method.

|  | # items |
| --- | --- |
| Websites sending web push notifications | 257 |
| Malicious web push notifications | 5 (27) |
| Detected web push notifications | 5 |

## 5.2 Accuracy for Detection

We evaluated the accuracy of detecting malicious web push notifications. Prior to the evaluation, we collected websites that send web push notifications using PublicWWW [16]. To collect websites that send web push notifications, we used `Notification.requestPermission()` and `navigator.serviceWorker.register()` as search keywords. `Notification.requestPermission()` is for requesting notification permission, and `navigator.serviceWorker.register()` is for registering a service worker. Websites need to use these methods to send web push notifications.

Table 4 shows the results of our collection of websites with notifications. We collected 257 websites and found 27 malicious websites sending web push notifications that induce users to phishing websites. Through our evaluation, we confirmed that all malicious web push notifications are detected by our proposed method. Note that our prototype could detect 5 notifications but could not detect 22 websites due to implementation difficulties. Our prototype can detect URLs for images with an absolute path. However, some push notifications set the URL with a relative path or a variable. Additionally, we confirmed that no HTTP communication occurs if the same images are used in multiple notifications. In such cases, the web server returns HTTP 304, and thus, the web browser receives no images. As a result, the proposed method cannot collect the URL for images, leading to detection failure. Detecting these types of URLs is our future work.

## 5.3 Performance Evaluation

We measured the performance of the proposed method. The proposed method prevents the display of malicious web push notifications using image similarity. This means that the user experience will degrade if the calculation of image similarity takes a long time. To evaluate whether the proposed method worsens the user experience or not, we measured the processing time of the proposed method. The detection rate of malicious push notifications depends on the number of malicious images used for detection; however, the greater the number of malicious images, the longer it takes to calculate image similarity. Thus, we measured the processing time of the proposed method by varying the number of malicious images used for detection from one to forty. We measured the time from when a malicious web push notification is received by the web browser to when the

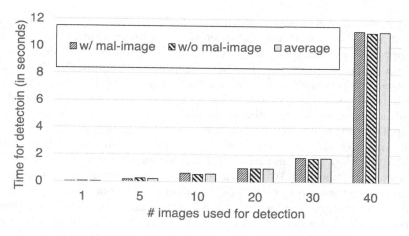

**Fig. 5.** Processing time with our proposed method.

proposed method finishes making the decision to show the push notification. The processing time changes depending on whether the received web push notification contains an image for malicious notifications or not. Therefore, we measured the processing time both with and without an image for malicious notifications.

Figure 5 shows the measurement results. The results show that it takes more than one second to decide whether the received notification is malicious or not when there are more than twenty images for detection. Specifically, it takes more than ten seconds when using forty malicious images for detection. According to Core Web Vitals [10], the user experience worsens if the loading time exceeds 4,000 ms. Note that we carefully adhere to this standard; however, the time with forty malicious images is not acceptable. We need further evaluation in more complicated situations, including frequent notifications and large and complex images.

## 6   Related Work

Text features are conventionally used for phishing detection [9,17,20]. Term Frequency-Inverse Document Frequency (TF-IDF) and heuristics are used to detect malicious websites from the body text [20]. Rosiello et al. exploit the structure of websites to enhance the detection of malicious websites [17]. They focus on the Document Object Model (DOM) to understand the layout of websites. In addition to body text and DOM, CSS is also a helpful feature for detection [9]. DOM and CSS strongly affect the structure of websites, and adversaries utilize these features to imitate legitimate websites. While these features are considered helpful for detecting malicious web push notifications, the entire document of a web push notification is shorter and less diverse compared to regular websites. Therefore, focusing on web push notification-specific features is required.

Visual features are used to detect malicious websites [3,13]. Medvet et al. utilize similarities in text, images, and the overall appearance of websites to identify malicious websites [13]. With these features, they achieved no false positives, although two sites failed to be detected. An image-capture based method using optical character recognition (OCR) for malicious website detection has also been proposed [3]. While the OCR-based method differs slightly from the visual-based detection scheme, it demonstrates that visual features can be helpful for detecting malicious websites. These contributions show that image-based methods are effective for detecting malicious websites; however, no work has yet been applied to the detection of malicious web push notifications.

Subramani et al. analyzed ads using web push notifications [19]. Through their analysis, they found and reported that web push notifications are also used for malware distribution. We built a prototype to monitor web push notifications similar to their work, controlling the display of notifications; however, the granularity of acquirable information differs from their work. Their work mainly focused on the automation of analysis, modifying the Chromium web browser and employing Puppeteer. Our approach uses mitmproxy to monitor and modify HTTP responses; thus, our prototype cannot collect information inside web browsers. This means that while our proposed method is less informative, it is more portable to other environments.

There are various image features available for detection [1,5,8]. In this paper, we employed SSIM [2] due to the balance of speed and accuracy; however, we plan to evaluate and adopt the optimal algorithm in terms of speed and detection accuracy.

## 7    Conclusions

We proposed an image-based detection method for suspicious web push notifications that induce users to phishing websites. The proposed method collects images from web push notifications and detects suspicious ones based on structural similarity between the image and malicious images. If the collected image has a higher SSIM score with malicious images, the proposed method stops displaying the notification to protect users from being induced to phishing sites. Experimental results showed that the proposed method can detect and prevent the display of malicious web push notifications. However, some images are not captured by the proposed method due to the difficulty of monitoring URLs with complex structures or variables. In addition, the performance overhead of the proposed method is not negligible. Our future work includes comprehensive monitoring of images and performance improvements.

## References

1. Bay, H., Tuytelaars, T., Van Gool, L.: SURF: speeded up robust features. In: Computer Vision–ECCV 2006: 9th European Conference on Computer Vision, Graz, Austria, 7-13 May 2006. Proceedings, Part I 9, pp. 404–417. Springer (2006)
2. Brunet, D., Vrscay, E.R., Wang, Z.: On the mathematical properties of the structural similarity index. IEEE Trans. Image Process. **21**(4), 1488–1499 (2011)

3. Dunlop, M., Groat, S., Shelly, D.: GoldPhish: using images for content-based phishing analysis. In: 2010 Fifth International Conference on Internet Monitoring and Protection, pp. 123–128. IEEE (2010)
4. Group, A.P.W.: Phishing attack trends report - 4Q (2023). https://docs.apwg.org/reports/apwg_trends_report_q4_2023.pdf
5. Huang, C.R., Chen, C.S., Chung, P.C.: Contrast context histogram-an efficient discriminating local descriptor for object recognition and image matching. Pattern Recogn. **41**(10), 3071–3077 (2008)
6. Le-Nguyen, M.K., Nguyen, T.C.H., Le, D.T., Nguyen, V.H., Tôn, L.P., Nguyen-An, K.: Phishing website detection as a website comparing problem. SN Comput. Sci. 4 (2023)
7. Lee, J., Kim, H., Park, J., Shin, I., Son, S.: Pride and prejudice in progressive web apps: abusing native app-like features in web applications. In: Proceedings of the 2018 ACM SIGSAC Conference on Computer and Communications Security, pp. 1731–1746 (2018)
8. Lowe, D.G.: Distinctive image features from scale-invariant keypoints. Int. J. Comput. Vision **60**, 91–110 (2004)
9. Mao, J., Tian, W., Li, P., Wei, T., Liang, Z.: Phishing-alarm: robust and efficient phishing detection via page component similarity. IEEE Access **5**, 17020–17030 (2017)
10. McQuade, B.: Defining the core web vitals metrics thresholds. https://web.dev/articles/defining-core-web-vitals-thresholds
11. MDN Web Docs: Notification - web API — MDN. https://developer.mozilla.org/en/docs/Web/API/Notification
12. MDN Web Docs: Push API - web API — MDN. https://developer.mozilla.org/en/docs/Web/API/Push_API
13. Medvet, E., Kirda, E., Kruegel, C.: Visual-similarity-based phishing detection. In: Proceedings of the 4th International Conference on Security and Privacy in Communication Netowrks, pp. 1–6 (2008)
14. Mishra, S., Soni, D.: DSmishSMS-a system to detect Smishing SMS. Neural Comput. Appl. **35**, 4975–4992 (2023)
15. Mitmproxy: Github - Mitmproxy. https://github.com/mitmproxy/mitmproxy
16. PublicWWW: Search engine for source code-publicwww.com. https://publicwww.com
17. Rosiello, A.P., et al.: A layout-similarity-based approach for detecting phishing pages. In: 2007 Third International Conference on Security and Privacy in Communications Networks and the Workshops-securecomm 2007, pp. 454–463. IEEE (2007)
18. Seng, S., Al-Ameen, M.N., Wright, M.: Understanding users' decision of clicking on posts in Facebook with implications for phishing. In: Workshop on Technology and Consumer Protection (ConPro 2018) (2018)
19. Subramani, K., Yuan, X., Setayeshfar, O., Vadrevu, P., Lee, H., K., Perdisci, R.: When push comes to Ads: measuring the rise of (malicious) push advertising. In: Proceedings of the ACM Internet Measurement Conference, pp. 724–737 (2020)
20. Zhang, Y., Hong, J.I., Cranor, L.F.: CANTINA: a content-based approach to detecting phishing web sites. In: Proceedings of the 16th International Conference on World Wide Web, pp. 639–648 (2007)

# Dissecting the Infrastructure Used in Web-Based Cryptojacking: A Measurement Perspective

Ayodeji Adeniran$^{(\boxtimes)}$, Kieran Human, and David Mohaisen

University of Central Florida, Orlando, USA
ay260080@ucf.edu

**Abstract.** This paper conducts a comprehensive examination of the infrastructure supporting cryptojacking operations. The analysis elucidates the methodologies, frameworks, and technologies malicious entities employ to misuse computational resources for unauthorized cryptocurrency mining. The investigation focuses on identifying websites serving as platforms for cryptojacking activities. A dataset of 887 websites, previously identified as cryptojacking sites, was compiled and analyzed to categorize the attacks and malicious activities observed. The study further delves into the DNS IP addresses, registrars, and name servers associated with hosting these websites to understand their structure and components. Various malware and illicit activities linked to these sites were identified, indicating the presence of unauthorized cryptocurrency mining via compromised sites. The findings highlight the vulnerability of website infrastructures to cryptojacking.

**Keywords:** Cryptojacking · Cryptocurrencies · Mining

## 1 Introduction

The cyberattack known as "cryptojacking" occurs when unauthorized individuals or entities utilize another's computer resources for the purpose of mining cryptocurrencies. This type of attack is also referred to as cryptocurrency mining malware or malicious crypto mining. To maintain the security and validity of blockchain transactions, the process of mining cryptocurrencies requires solving intricate mathematical problems, which demand a considerable amount of computational power and energy [16].

A cryptojacking attack allows an adversary to gain unauthorized access to a computer, server, or network of devices and installs malicious software on them [14]. The goal of this software is to use the computing resources of the compromised systems for cryptocurrency mining. This activity takes place without the owners' knowledge or permission. The cryptocurrency industry has, unfortunately, been plagued by malicious activities, and cryptojacking remains a significant threat [13]. Due to the high costs of establishing and maintaining

© The Author(s), under exclusive license to Springer Nature Singapore Pte Ltd. 2025
J.-H. Lee et al. (Eds.): WISA 2024, LNCS 15499, pp. 270–283, 2025.
https://doi.org/10.1007/978-981-96-1624-4_21

cryptocurrency infrastructures, attackers frequently exploit platforms owned by others to carry out their nefarious activities [6]. By commandeering existing infrastructures, they can launch attacks against their desired targets without incurring any of the associated expenses.

The process of cryptocurrency mining is both intricate and demanding, calling for substantial investment. Unfortunately, potential profits often tempt attackers who actively search for systems that can generate the greatest returns [11]. In the past, private servers—which typically consume vast amounts of energy—were primarily used for mining. Nowadays, cloud-based servers offer more accessible, cost-effective options. However, some miners will hijack others' infrastructures to maximize their profits.

This paper aims to analyze and understand the infrastructure of certain websites previously linked to cryptojacking activities. We aim to determine whether these websites remain malicious through cryptojacking malware or other types of malicious software. We also seek to understand the geographical distribution of these sites and extract additional information to gain insights into their operations. Furthermore, we will discuss the security risks and threats associated with cryptojacking infrastructures and activities.

## 2   Related Work

Numerous studies have explored different facets of cryptojacking [26]. Jayasinghe et al. [12] explore cryptojacking within public cloud infrastructures, providing insights into how these environments are exploited for illicit cryptocurrency mining. Meanwhile, Saad et al. [24] analyze end-to-end in-browser cryptojacking, examining how cryptojacking scripts operate within web browsers. Both studies significantly inform our understanding of cryptojacking across different platforms and contexts. Burgess et al. [5] developed MANiC (Multi-step Assessment for Crypto-miners), a system designed to detect cryptocurrency mining scripts. MANiC extracts parameters that can be used to identify suspicious behaviors associated with mining activities, although it does not focus on web infrastructure. Carlin et al. [7] conducted a similar study focused on detecting cryptojacking websites by dynamic opcode analysis. Xiao et al. [29] explored GPU cryptojacking and introduced MagTracer, a detection system for GPU-based cryptojacking. MagTracer boasts a detection accuracy of 98%.

Naseem et al. [21] proposed MINOS, a lightweight detection system designed to identify cryptojacking activities in real-time. Tekiner et al. [27] presented an approach for detecting cryptojacking in IoT environments. Saad et al. [25] conducted an in-depth analysis of cryptojacking samples, focusing on content, currency, and code-based categorization. Rajba et al. [23] presented an analysis highlighting the limitations of web cryptojacking detection methods. Lachtar et al. [15] discussed a cross-stack approach to defending against cryptojacking.

**Research Gap.** Our research paper distinguishes itself from others by focusing on websites engaged in cryptojacking. While other studies concentrate on detecting these websites, we thoroughly analyze the infrastructure, including their geographic distribution and other pertinent characteristics. Additionally, we perform a follow-up scan to identify any malicious content or malware and reclassify them as benign or malicious.

## 3   Problem Statement and Research Questions

Generating a new cryptocurrency involves mining [10]. This complex process includes solving intricate mathematical problems that ensure the validation and security of transactions on the blockchain network [1]. The process of mining cryptocurrency differs from one type to another, and using consensus algorithms, such as Proof of Work (PoW) used by Bitcoin, and Proof of Stake (PoS), which determine how new blocks are added to the blockchain [4].

Mining cryptocurrencies demands substantial computational power, particularly in PoW systems. Miners must have access to robust hardware to solve intricate mathematical problems, which has led to the emergence of cryptojacking. We have analyzed the components and properties of cryptojacking infrastructures to gain insight into their operations. Our goal is to address the challenges posed by these infrastructures by answering three crucial research questions.

1. **RQ1: What are the underlying affinities between websites and malicious content, and how can these affinities be measured to assess the potential for cryptojacking activities?.** This enables us better to understand the relationship between the websites and malicious content.
2. **RQ2: what are the categories of malicious contents and malware that are common in these cryptojacking infrastructure?** We analyzed various websites and categorized different types of malicious content and malware commonly associated with crypto-jacking activities. Our findings can provide valuable insights into the different categories of threats.
3. **RQ3: What are the hosting patterns and the geographical distribution of cryptojacking infrastructure?** The identified malicious websites are hosted in various countries globally. Analyzing this distribution will provide insights into the geographical spread of these sites.

## 4   Technical Approach

This study analyzed websites utilizing mining scripts for cryptocurrency mining to gain insights into the nature of cryptojacking infrastructures. It aimed to explore potential correlations between cryptojacking and other malicious activities, such as phishing campaigns [17], malware distribution networks [3,8,18,20], or botnets [28]. The analysis began with the Whois tool to gather comprehensive domain information, including IP addresses, name servers, and registrars.

We obtained a dataset of 887 websites associated with cryptocurrency mining from the MANiC dataset and subjected them to a comprehensive scan for malicious content using VirusTotal. Out of the 887 websites, we successfully scanned approximately 880 of the websites. The results revealed that 371 websites were clean, while 518 contained malicious content. Our objective is to analyze the 518 websites detected to contain malicious content. This analysis aims to extract valuable information regarding the types of malicious content, the security engines that identified the threats, and the specific categories classified as malicious or suspicious. By decisively examining these factors, we assert our commitment to understanding the nature and extent of the threats posed by these websites.

## 4.1    Dataset and Preprocessing

**Associated Cryptojacking Websites.** This paper used data from the "MANiC: Multi-step Assessment for Crypto-miners" dataset, which is also referenced in the paper titled "Detecting Cryptomining through Dynamic Analysis." The data was initially collected from the top 1 million websites on Alexa, as indexed by Censys, in July 2018. The dataset consists of multiple files, and our analysis focused on the malicious content file to examine its specifics.

After initially collecting the data in 2018, we conducted a re-scan to identify malicious content. Our re-scan revealed that 518 websites now contained malicious content. We utilized a domain query service to gather comprehensive information about all the websites in the dataset. This service allowed us to extract detailed domain information and other relevant data. Subsequently, we scanned the entire dataset to differentiate between infected and clean websites. This process aimed to enhance our understanding of the current threat landscape associated with cryptojacking and other malicious activities.

**Security Data Attributes.** Afterward, we further analyzed the websites in the dataset with malicious infections by scanning them with VirusTotal. This analysis allowed us to obtain information about the security engines performing the scans and categorize the malicious detections into distinct groups. The output from the security engines is classified into three components: method, category, and result. VirusTotal uses the blacklist method to identify potentially harmful websites with malicious content [19]. The security engine category can indicate suspicious or malicious activity, and the scan results can classify the content as malicious, suspicious, malware, phishing, or spam. We further analyzed the different types of malware and malicious content detected by each security engine. Various categories of malicious content were classified based on their threat levels and purposes. It is important to note that not all malicious content is related to cryptojacking activity. This classification helps us identify and concentrate on the malware and other malicious content that may be directly associated with cryptocurrency mining. Through this detailed analysis, we aimed to understand the types of threats these websites pose and differentiate between cryptojacking-related activities and other forms of malicious content.

## 4.2    Analysis Dimensions

This study investigates the infrastructure of cryptojacking by analyzing related websites. The goal is to identify malicious content and assess the current status of these websites. The research addresses specific questions outlined in Sect. 3 and covers various analytical dimensions.

❶ **Cryptojacking Infrastructure Websites Distribution.** This dimension explores the geographic and hosting distribution of websites engaged in cryptojacking. Analyzing the locations and hosting providers allows us to detect trends and hotspots in the infrastructure supporting cryptojacking activities.

❷ **Threat Categories and Classifications.** Here, we analyze and categorize the threats from cryptojacking websites, focusing on identifying malicious behaviors like malware distribution, phishing, and unauthorized cryptocurrency mining.

❸ **Categorization of Cryptojacking Websites (current) Into as Malicious and Benign.** We analyze and categorize the current status of websites engaged in cryptojacking activities, distinguishing between those that are actively malicious, potentially harmful, or benign (no longer active or posing a threat).

❹ **Malicious Contents in the Cryptojacking Infrastructures.** We investigate the specific types of malicious content present in cryptojacking websites' infrastructure, analyzing scripts, software, and techniques used for cryptojacking and other malicious activities. Our study offers a comprehensive analysis of cryptojacking infrastructure, providing insights into its distribution, threat landscape, current status, and the nature of malicious content it hosts.

## 5 Results

### 5.1 Cryptojacking Malware in the Malicious Dataset

We analyzed the 919 websites included in the malicious file of the MANiC dataset. Our detailed examination revealed eight distinct types of cryptojacking malware within the dataset, as shown in Fig. 1. One of the most significant cryptomining services identified in our analysis was CoinHive, which accounted for approximately 74% of the malicious presence within the dataset. CoinHive was initially created as a legitimate service for cryptocurrency mining, enabling website owners to monetize their content by using visitors' CPU resources for mining.

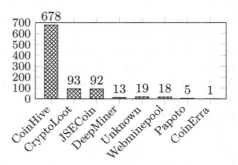

**Fig. 1.** This figure shows the prevalence of various cryptojacking malware types found within the malicious dataset, with CoinHive being the most significant contributor

However, cybercriminals hijacked CoinHive for cryptojacking purposes, embedding its scripts into websites without users' consent to exploit their computing power for mining. Our findings indicate that even after its discontinuation (since 2019), the legacy of CoinHive continues to influence the prevalence and distribution of cryptojacking activities. This enduring impact is evident in the continued presence and proliferation of similar cryptomining malware. These insights underscore the need for vigilance and robust cybersecurity measures to mitigate the threats posed by such malicious activities.

## 5.2  Cryptojacking Infrastructure Websites Distribution

This study extensively analyzes numerous cryptojacking websites hosted across diverse geographic locations. Understanding the correlation between these locations is crucial for two main reasons. Firstly, examining the geographic distribution enhances our understanding of where these websites are located and the specific countries hosting them. This mapping helps identify trends and patterns that highlight regional vulnerabilities and the prevalence of cryptojacking infrastructure. Secondly, the analysis provides insights into how technological advancements and internet penetration contribute to cryptojacking activities. By correlating the presence of cryptojacking websites with regional technological landscapes, we can determine if higher technological development and internet usage correlate with increased cryptojacking incidents. This investigation also explores whether factors like broadband availability and digital literacy influence the spread of cryptojacking.

Addressing these questions will aid in identifying regions most impacted by cryptojacking. This data is crucial for devising strategies to combat cryptojacking, guiding policy decisions, and allocating resources to mitigate threats in vulnerable areas. Implementing effective discovery practices will enhance vigilance and security measures to safeguard networks against these pervasive threats. Of the 518 websites identified with malicious content, 116 were redacted for undisclosed reasons, limiting the analysis of country distribution to the remaining unredacted sites. Analyzing these sites allows for a focused exploration of geographical trends and patterns associated with malicious online activities.

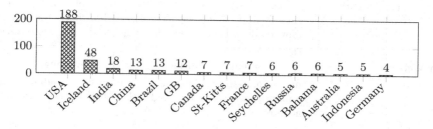

**Fig. 2.** Cryptojacking websites distribution. A heavy-tailed distribution regarding the number of websites associated with cryptojacking activities.

**Observations.** Figure 2 displays the top 15 countries with the most websites infected with cryptojacking malware, as per our dataset. The websites are spread out in various countries across the Americas, Asia, South America, and Europe. We observed that the countries are advanced and have high internet penetration. The USA has more than 55% of the websites, followed by Iceland, which has about 15%. The USA is known to be well-advanced technologically and hosts most of the domains. The prevalence of cryptojacking websites in the United States may be attributed to the country's significant number of registered websites. Cryptocurrency has gained significant global recognition in recent years. However, it is notable that most cryptocurrency miners reside in regions with high internet penetration and reliable electricity access. Despite the widespread popularity of cryptocurrency investment and trading, the concentration of mining activities in such regions highlights the importance of favorable infrastructure for this practice. This observation suggests a correlation between the two variables and warrants further investigation.

### 5.3   Threat Categories and Classifications

VirusTotal is the primary tool we use to scan malicious websites. After conducting scans, we detected various malicious activities, such as phishing, malware, and spyware identified by different security engines. We focused on these security engines and their reported malicious content to gain deeper insights into the nature of the threats. While the direct results from VirusTotal did not explicitly indicate crypto mining-related scripts, further analysis of the referrer files revealed the presence of such scripts. This was done by examining the code and behavior of the files, looking for patterns commonly associated with cryptomining scripts. The scan identified a total of 27 security engines, out of which 7 reported the presence of malicious content. Table 1 summarizes the security

**Table 1.** Security vendors with the threat types.

| Vendor | Threat type |
|---|---|
| Forcepoint ThreatSeeker | media file, compromised website, proxy avoidance, application and software download, hacking, potentially unwanted, suspicious content, p2p file sharing, and uncategorized. |
| Dr.Web | adult content, known infection source, gambling. |
| Webroot | malware, p2p, bitdefender, porn, proxy avoidance and announmizers, phishing and other frauds, spyware and adware. |
| alphaMountains.ia | suspicious, malicious, unrated, anonymizers, JSEcoin, scam, illegal, unethical, coinhives, piracy, plagiarism. |
| Sophos | spyware and malware, pua and others, phishing and fraud, suspicious, spam urls, proxies. |
| XcitiumverdicCloud | media sharing, spyware, malware. |
| Bitdefender | proxies, file sharing, webproxy |

engines and the corresponding malicious and suspicious contents they detected. Moreover, Fig. 3 contains the list of the top 15 security engines and the number of malicious contents, including malicious, suspicious, and undetected contents.

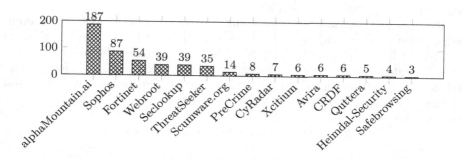

**Fig. 3.** Security engines categories with the number of occurences.

**Observations.** The outcome of a security scan is determined by the security engine's ability to identify and classify a malicious item accurately. Sometimes, it may give false positives. It is important to note that the scan results are based on a specific period and could change over time due to website or security engine updates to identify undetected or misclassified files correctly.

## 5.4 Malicious Contents in the Cryptojacking Infrastructures

We organize the results from the VirusTotal scan into four distinct categories: harmless, malicious, suspicious, and undetected. Harmless files and contents are benign, posing no direct or indirect threat to users or systems. The scan results presented in Table 2 indicate that most detected files fall into the harmless category, suggesting they are safe for use without any security concerns.

**Table 2.** The outcomes of security engines' classification.

| Category | Harmless | Malicious | Suspicious | Undetected |
|---|---|---|---|---|
| Count | 35,370 | 948 | 395 | 8,394 |

On the contrary, malicious file content can be hazardous and potentially harmful. These malicious contents can be injected into infrastructure for various nefarious purposes, including cryptocurrency mining. The potential harm of these contents underscores the importance of security measures and the need for caution. Cryptocurrency mining involves leveraging website resources for mining purposes without the explicit consent of website owners or visitors.

Additionally, malicious files can disrupt websites, temporarily unavailable or hijacking them until a ransom is paid [2]. The potential impact of these files on websites underscores the severity of the threat and the need for robust security measures. Such files may contain malware, spyware, or phishing components to compromise user data or system integrity.

We analyzed 887 websites and found that 58% are malicious and contain either suspicious or malicious files. The remaining 42% are harmless or have undetected files. For further analysis, Table 3 summarizes the malicious websites. We categorize the files into three: benign, suspicious, and malicious. These websites contain benign or harmless files, but the presence of malicious and suspicious files qualifies them as malicious websites.

**Table 3.** Malicious contents and their distribution.

| Security Engines | Benign | Suspicious | Malicious |
|---|---|---|---|
| Forcepoint ThreatSeeker | 21 | 10 | 4 |
| Dr. Web | 0 | 2 | 1 |
| Webroot | 0 | 1 | 5 |
| alphaMountain.ia | 7 | 4 | 3 |
| Sophos | 7 | 7 | 5 |
| XcitiumVerdictCloud | 1 | 0 | 2 |
| BitDefender | 12 | 5 | 0 |

**Observations.** Table 3 data clearly shows that the number of benign and suspicious files significantly exceeds that of malicious files. The table visually represents the distribution of files according to their threat levels. Notably, benign files, which are not considered harmful, comprise most of the files analyzed. These files pose no threat to the system and are safe for use. Following benign files, suspicious files constitute the next largest group. While these files are not confirmed to be harmful, they exhibit behaviors or characteristics that warrant further investigation to determine their true nature and potential threat level. In contrast, the number of malicious files known to be harmful and pose a significant risk to the system is comparatively smaller. The presence of these files can cause various types of damage, including data breaches, system corruption, and unauthorized access. This distribution highlights the dataset's predominance of non-malicious files while scrutinizing suspicious files to ensure system security and mitigate potential threats.

## 5.5 Correlation and Statistical Test

To understand the correlation between malicious, suspicious, and undetected content on the website and conduct statistical analyses, we conducted two specific statistical tests: one between malicious and suspicious contents and another between malicious and undetected contents. The objective of these tests is to

**Table 4.** Correlation between malicious and suspicious content.

| Parameter | Value |
|---|---|
| Coefficient $(r)$ | $-0.2143$ |
| $r^2$ | $0.04594$ |
| $p$-value | $8.696e-7$ |
| Covariance | $-0.3048$ |
| Sample size $(n)$ | $517$ |
| Statistic | $-4.9799$ |

**Table 5.** Correlation between malicious and undetected content.

| Parameter | Value |
|---|---|
| Coefficient $(r)$ | $0.2335$ |
| $r^2$ | $0.05452$ |
| $p$-value | $7.834e-8$ |
| Covariance | $1.9366$ |
| Sample size $(n)$ | $517$ |
| Statistic | $5.4497$ |

**Table 6.** Correlation between malicious and suspicious content.

| Parameter | Value |
|---|---|
| Coefficient $(r)$ | $0.2694$ |
| $r^2$ | $0.07257$ |
| $p$-value | $0.5591$ |
| Covariance | $1.8571$ |
| Sample size $(n)$ | $7$ |
| Statistic | $0.6255$ |

verify the existence of any relationship between the contents and their potential effects. Our primary aim is to identify the contributing factors to the presence of malicious activity on the websites. Tables 2 and 3 show the count of the threat classifications and the website categories. The Pearson correlation coefficient data is based on the frequency of malicious and suspicious content on 517 malicious websites. This dataset enables us to measure and examine the linear relationship between the presence of malicious and suspicious content on these websites. The alpha $(\alpha)$ for the null hypothesis is chosen as 0.05.

**Malicious and Suspicious Content in the Websites.** The Pearson correlation coefficient is a quantitative statistical measure utilized to assess the presence and strength of a linear correlation between malicious and suspicious content. It quantifies the degree to which the two variables are linearly related, providing valuable insights into the extent of their association. From Table 4, The Pearson correlation coefficient indicated a small but significant negative relationship between malicious and suspicious content. The negative coefficient suggests that changes in these two variables occur in opposite directions. The difference between the malicious and suspicious content is substantial enough to be statistically significant. Due to the significance and the high $p$-value, we rejected the null hypothesis because there is a relationship between the two datasets.

**Malicious and Undetected Content in the Websites.** We conducted a Pearson correlation analysis between malicious and undetected content using a dataset of 517 websites to explore their potential relationship. From Table 5, the analysis reveals a significantly positive correlation between these variables. This positive correlation suggests that changes in undetected content correspond proportionally with changes in malicious content in the same direction. Despite a relatively small difference, the correlation is statistically significant, supported by a sufficiently low $p$-value to reject the null hypothesis. This finding indicates that an increase in undetected content is associated with a proportional increase in malicious activities on these websites.

**Suspicious and Malicious Content From the Security Engines.** We investigate the correlation between malicious and suspicious content detected by security engines. The Pearson correlation coefficient from Table 6 indicates a non-significant positive relationship between these variables. This slight positive correlation suggests that changes in one variable have minimal impact on the other, indicating little mutual influence. Due to the small and statistically insignificant difference, we cannot reject the null hypothesis that there is no correlation between suspicious and malicious content as identified by the security engines. Therefore, the small $p$-value does not provide enough evidence to support a meaningful relationship between these variables.

### 5.6    Summary of Results and Findings

While some content is flagged as suspicious or undetected, it may contain elements contributing to the websites' malicious nature. Some of the suspicious and undetected files likely harbor hidden malicious content, which suggests that they may not have been correctly classified by the security scanning software. Collectively, this increases the number of malicious instances on these websites. Therefore, examining and reclassifying suspicious and undetected files is imperative to understand better and mitigate their contribution to malicious activity. Additional findings are illustrated below:

**Correlation Between Website Contents.** Our analysis reveals a correlation between websites hosting malicious and suspicious content, such as phishing links, malware, or suspicious scripts, and those with malicious and undetected content. This correlation suggests that websites exhibiting such content may harbor malicious elements. Understanding these correlations is crucial for effectively identifying and mitigating cyber threats.

**Geographical Concentration of Cryptojacking Websites.** Most cryptojacking websites are concentrated in a few countries with high internet penetration. We can attribute this concentration to various factors, including lax cybersecurity regulations, widespread use of outdated software, and a need for more awareness among website owners and users. Addressing this concentration requires coordinated efforts to raise awareness about the risks of cryptojacking.

**Redacted Domain Information.** Many domains exhibit redacted or "unavailabl" information, challenging ascertaining ownership and origins. This lack of transparency hinders tracking and addressing malicious activities associated with these domains. Improving transparency and accountability in domain registration processes is necessary to enhance cybersecurity measures.

**Observation of Malicious Contents.** We identified several instances of malicious content associated with cryptojacking. These contents, including scripts and malware, exploit vulnerabilities in websites for illicit mining using visitors' computational resources. Detecting and removing such malicious content is critical for safeguarding users' security and privacy [9, 22].

**Cleanup of Previously Malicious Websites.** Many websites previously flagged as malicious have undergone cleanup, removing the malicious content.

This cleanup indicates proactive measures website owners or security professionals take to mitigate the impact of cryptojacking activities. However, continuous monitoring is necessary to prevent reoccurrences of such incidents.

**Return of Previously Malicious Websites to Benign Status.** Some previously identified as malicious websites have returned to a benign state, indicating a potential temporary hijacking for cryptomining purposes. This phenomenon underscores the dynamic nature of cyber threats, where threats can evolve and change over time, and the importance of timely detection and response mechanisms to thwart cryptojacking attempts effectively.

**Absence of Correlation Between Malicious and Suspicious Contents in Security Engines.** Our analysis indicates no correlation between malicious and suspicious contents in security engines. This finding suggests that while security engines may flag specific contents as suspicious, they may not necessarily classify them as malicious. Understanding this distinction is crucial for refining threat detection algorithms and improving the accuracy of security assessments.

## 6  Concluding Remarks

We investigated websites compromised for cryptocurrency mining. Using the whois tool, we identified the geographic distribution of these websites, primarily located in regions with significant internet usage. According to our analysis using https://www.virustotal.com, out of the 887 websites previously classified as malicious, 370 no longer contain malicious content or crypto-jacking scripts. This improvement may stem from enhanced website security measures or reduced attractiveness to attackers. However, some sites still harbor cryptojacking-related malware, clandestinely exploiting users' computing resources for unauthorized cryptocurrency mining. Our findings suggest these websites remain susceptible to re-infection. We acknowledge the limitations of our study and emphasize the need for future research to provide deeper insights into cryptojacking dynamics and lifecycle.

## References

1. Aloqaily, M., Pandit, V.: IEEE conference on blockchain and cryptocurrency(ICBC'23). IEEE Commun. Mag. **61**(11), 6–9 (2023)
2. Alrawi, O., et al.: Forecasting malware capabilities from cyber attack memory images, pp. 3523–3540. USENIX Security (2021)
3. Alrawi, O., Zuo, C., Duan, R., Kasturi, R.P., Lin, Z., Saltaformaggio, B.: The betrayal at cloud city: an empirical analysis of cloud-based mobile backends, pp. 551–566. USENIX Security (2019)
4. Bhatia, N., Bansal, S., Desai. S.: A detailed review of blockchain and cryptocurrency. CoRR, abs/2303.06008 (2023)
5. Burgess, J., O'Kane, P., Carlin, D., Sezer, S.: MANiC: multi-step assessment for crypto-miners. In: International Conference on Cyber Security and Protection of Digital Services. IEEE

6. Carlin, D., Burgess, J., O'Kane, P., Sezer, S.: You could be mine(d): the rise of Cryptojacking. IEEE Secur. Priv. **18**(2), 16–22 (2020)
7. Carlin, D., O'Kane, P., Sezer, S., Burgess, J.: Detecting Cryptomining using dynamic analysis. IEEE PST (2018)
8. Du, Y., Alrawi, O., Snow, K.Z., Antonakakis, M., Monrose, F.: Improving security tasks using compiler provenance information recovered at the binary-level. In: CCS, pp. 2695–2709. ACM (2023)
9. Duan, R., et al.: Automating patching of vulnerable open-source software versions in application binaries. NDSS (2019)
10. Garriga, M., Arias, M., Renzis, A.D.: Blockchain and Cryptocurrency: a comparative framework of the main architectural drivers. CoRR, abs/1812.08806 (2018)
11. Hajiaghapour-Moghimi, M., et al.: Hedging investments of grid-connected PV-BESS in buildings using cryptocurrency mining: A case study in Finland. IEEE Access **11**, 66327–66345 (2023)
12. Jayasinghe, K., Poravi, G.: A survey of attack instances of Cryptojacking targeting cloud infrastructure, pp. 100–107. ACM APIT (2020)
13. Kshetri, N., Rahman, M.M., Sayeed, S.A., Sultana, I.: cryptoRAN: a review on cryptojacking and ransomware attacks wrt banking industry - threats, challenges, & problems. CoRR, abs/2311.14783 (2023)
14. Kshetri, N., Voas, J.M.: Cryptojacking. Computer **55**(1), 18–19 (2022)
15. Lachtar, N., Elkhail, A.A., Bacha, A., Malik, H.: A cross-stack approach towards defending against cryptojacking. IEEE Comput. Archit. Lett. **19**(2), 126–129 (2020)
16. Menati, A., Cai, Y., Helou, R.E., Tian, C., Xie, L.: Optimization of cryptocurrency mining demand for ancillary services in electricity markets, pp. 3052–3061. HICSS (2024)
17. Mohaisen, A.: Towards automatic and lightweight detection and classification of malicious web contents, pp. 67–72. IEEE HotWeb (2015)
18. Mohaisen, A., Alrawi, O.: Unveiling Zeus: automated classification of malware samples, pp. 829–832. WWW (2013)
19. Mohaisen, A., Alrawi, O.: AV-meter: an evaluation of antivirus scans and labels. In: DIMVA, vol. 8550, pp. 112–131. Springer (2014)
20. Mohaisen, A., Alrawi, O., Mohaisen, M.: AMAL: high-fidelity, behavior-based automated malware analysis and classification. Comput. Secur. **52**, 251–266 (2015)
21. Naseem, F.N., Aris, A., Babun, L., Tekiner, E., Uluagac, A.S.: MINOS: a lightweight real-time cryptojacking detection system. NDSS (2021)
22. Perdisci, R., Papastergiou, T., Alrawi, O., Antonakakis, M.: IoTfinder: efficient large-scale identification of IoT devices via passive DNS traffic analysis. In: IEEE EuroS&P, pp. 474–489. IEEE (2020)
23. Rajba, P., Mazurczyk, W.: Limitations of web cryptojacking detection: a practical evaluation. In: ARES 2022: The 17th International Conference on Availability, Reliability and Security, Vienna, Austria, 23–26 August 2022, pp. 1– 6. ACM (2022)
24. Saad, M., Khormali, A., Mohaisen, A.: End-to-end analysis of in-browser cryptojacking. CoRR, abs/1809.02152 (2018)
25. Saad, M., Mohaisen, D.: Analyzing in-browser cryptojacking. IEEE Trans. Dependable Secure Comput. **1**, (2024)
26. Saad, M., et al.: Exploring the attack surface of blockchain: a comprehensive survey. IEEE Commun. Surv. Tutorials **22**(3), 1977–2008 (2020)
27. Tekiner, E., Acar, A., Uluagac, A.S.: A lightweight IoT cryptojacking detection mechanism in heterogeneous smart home networks. NDSS (2022)

28. Wang, A., Chang, W., Chen, S., Mohaisen, A.: Delving into internet DDoS attacks by botnets: characterization and analysis. IEEE/ACM Trans. Netw. **26**(6), 2843–2855 (2018)
29. Xiao, R., Li, T., Ramesh, S., Han, J., Han, J.: MagTracer: detecting GPU cryptojacking attacks via magnetic leakage signals, pp. 1–15. ACM MobiCom (2023)

# A Survey on Attack Cases with VBS Malware in Windows

GyuHyun Jeon⑩, Seungho Jeon⑩, and Jung Taek Seo$^{(\boxtimes)}$ ⑩

Gachon University, Seongnam-daero 1342, Seongnam-si, Republic of Korea
{pengchan88,shjeon90,seojt}@gachon.ac.kr

**Abstract.** Visual Basic Script (VBS)-based malicious code exists in various forms such as document type, executable file, and LNK file. After disguising it as a normal file or exploiting a vulnerability to trick the user into executing it, malicious actions are performed when the file is executed. Until recently, malware attacks targeting companies that exploited VBS continued to occur. Therefore, research is needed on effective defense techniques that can detect and respond to VBS malware attacks. Therefore, this survey examined comprehensive information about VBS. Related literature was selected by referring to papers and reports from Google Scholar, Web Science, and security-specialized companies. First, the main characteristics of VBS are explained. Afterward, cases of malicious code attacks targeting Windows systems were presented and analyzed. We also investigated research related to methods for detecting VBS malware. Finally, we describe some defense techniques for detecting malware using VBS. We explain real-time monitoring, blocking, and automation of double-extension file monitoring and deletion based on Python Watchdog. In addition, we analyzed file paths frequently used in VBS attacks and proposed VBS file filtering. In addition, we explained defense methods by detecting VBS malware through event ID and XML-based Windows PowerShell log analysis in Windows Event Viewer and blocking and deleting processes by checking whether network configuration has been changed.

**Keywords:** Malware · VBS · Windows · Case Analysis · MITRE ATT&CK

## 1 Introduction

Visual Basic Script (VBS)-based malicious code exists in various forms such as document type, executable file, and LNK file. It disguises itself as a normal file or exploits a vulnerability to induce the user to execute the file and then performs malicious actions when executed [1]. Until recently, malware attacks such as DarkGate, Emotet, and Qak-Bot that exploit VBS and Remote Access Trojan (RAT) series malware attacks have continued to occur [2]. In March 2024, North Korea's hacking group Konni APT [3] executed a malicious VBS targeting South Korean companies using spear phishing and disguised files. In April 2024, the Ande Loader [4] malware was distributed targeting North American manufacturing companies by exploiting obfuscation, image switching, and PowerShell techniques. Through this, the final payload, NjRAT malware, was executed. In this way, after initial access to the attack surface, such as the target's system and

© The Author(s), under exclusive license to Springer Nature Singapore Pte Ltd. 2025
J.-H. Lee et al. (Eds.): WISA 2024, LNCS 15499, pp. 284–295, 2025.
https://doi.org/10.1007/978-981-96-1624-4_22

network, VBS malware causes additional damage, such as stealing personal information such as keylogging and downloading malicious payloads through loaders. Additionally, various attack techniques, such as VBS obfuscation, are being developed to avoid malware detection. Therefore, research is needed on effective defense techniques that can detect and respond to VBS malware attacks.

The primary objective of this survey is this survey is to find out the basic knowledge and characteristics of VBS technology. Afterward, we analyze the latest attack cases using Windows VBS malware and derive the attack techniques used. The derived attack technique uses the MITER ATT&CK Framework to perform a formalization process. Finally, we investigate defense techniques against VBS malware attacks. The defense techniques investigated include studies on detection methods for malware using VBS. Related research in this survey referred to papers provided on the Google Scholar website. In this survey, VBS technology and VBS attack cases were referenced from malware reports or projects provided by security-specialized companies.

The structure of this paper is as follows. In Sect. 2, the scope of the survey is explained. Section 3 presents the main characteristics of VBS. Section 4 provides information about VBS malware attack cases. Section 5 examines research related to methods for detecting malware using VBS. Section 6 discusses research on countermeasures against VBS malware attacks. Section 7 concludes by explaining the conclusions of this survey.

## 2   Survey Scope and Screening Process

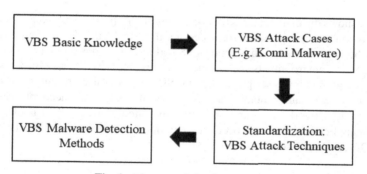

**Fig. 1.** Literature Selection Process.

The literature selection process is shown in Fig. 1. First, VBS-related technical reports published by security-specialized companies were selected as literature on basic knowledge of VBS technology. In addition, we referred to the MITER ATT&CK Framework [5], a security framework targeting Windows systems that classifies information on various attack techniques. For VBS attack cases, only VBS malware attack cases that occurred between March 2024 and May 2024 were selected to ensure the novelty of this survey. The attack cases were chosen from analysis reports on malware attack cases using VBS technology based on data released by a security company specializing in malware detection and analysis. Literature related to VBS malware detection methods was provided by Google Scholar and Web Science websites, and papers published between June 2021 and May 2024 were examined. First, papers that mention VBS technology are selected. This is relevant if a brief description of the VBS technology exists in the paper. Second, we choose papers that describe the VBS attack detection method. This paper is about detecting attacks based on the characteristics of VBS technology.

## 3 Visual Basic Script

VBS is a lightweight active script language based on Visual Basic developed by Microsoft [3]. VBS is basically written in a Function/EndFunction configuration and uses scripting techniques that use Microsoft Component Object Model (COM) objects to access elements of the running environment.

**Table 1.** Key Attribute of VBS.

| Attribute | Description |
|---|---|
| Purpose | Task automation |
| Operation System | Windows (E.g. IE, IIS, WSH) |
| Function | E.g. Change network configuration, System backup and account management, Document program macro |
| Reconnaissance | E.g. Disguised as legitimate emails or downloaded files |

Table 1 shows the main features of VBS, including its purpose of use, execution environment, reconnaissance method for accessing the attack surface, and main functions. The VBS function is built into Windows 98 and later versions and can be run mainly in Windows host environments such as Internet Explorer (IE), Internet Information Services (IIS), and Windows Scripting Host (WSH) [6]. It is used to automate repetitive tasks in the system management area such as system backup and account management when changing network configuration in the environment. Recently, it is often used as a macro in applications that support documentation functions, such as HWP, PDF files, and MS Office's Word and Excel [7].

**Table 2.** Key Vulnerabilities and Obfuscation Techniques of VBS.

| Attribute | Techniques |
|---|---|
| Vulnerabilities | E.g. Allow remote/arbitrary code execution, VBS code injection, Personal information theft |
| Obfuscation | E.g. Wscript.Shell, Base64, XOR |

Table 2 shows frequently used vulnerabilities and obfuscation techniques to perform attacks that exploit vulnerabilities in VBS main functions. First, in the attack reconnaissance phase, a method of disguising a file containing a malicious VBS as a legitimate email or download file and then distributing it is often used [8]. Afterward, various VBS vulnerabilities are exploited to achieve the attack goal. There are 102 VBS vulnerabilities based on Common Vulnerabilities and Exposures (CVE), a list of publicly known security vulnerabilities [9]. Major vulnerabilities exploited in attacks include allowing remote and arbitrary code execution, VBS code injection, and personal information theft. When writing attack code containing the vulnerability, various obfuscation techniques such as Wscript, Shell, Base64, and XOR encoding bypass attack detection, and multiple obfuscation is possible [10].

## 4 VBS Malware Attack Cases

Until recently, various malware attacks exploiting VBS have occurred. This session, cases of VBS malware attacks targeting Windows systems will be investigated and explained.

### 4.1 Konni APT Malware

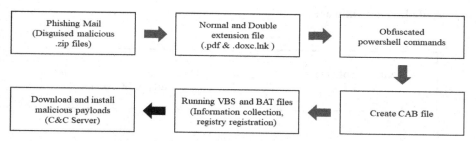

**Fig. 2.** Konni APT Malware Flow Chart.

In March 2024, the 'attachment.zip' malicious file was distributed targeting Korean companies through an attack by an APT group believed to be North Korea's Konni [3]. As shown in Fig. 2, the file consists of a total of two subfiles. It includes LNK files and normal PDF files, each with two extensions. The LNK (shortcut) file is a malicious file that carries out the attack. This exploits a double extension vulnerability and is disguised as a Microsoft Word DOCX document. The malicious file contains obfuscated PowerShell commands, and when executed, it checks the entire length of the shortcut, 0x16EF7F1A. The DOCX file is created with the same name and path as the original, and a Windows CAB file named 'UHCYbG.cab' is created in the public folder path. When the CAB file is unzipped, 'start.vbs' and several BAT files are created, as shown in Table 3. As the BAT file specified in the 'start.vbs' script is executed, user information is collected and leaked, additional malicious files are installed, and additional malicious files are installed. It performs malicious tasks such as obtaining persistence through registry registration.

Table 3 is the 'start.vbs' code that runs a specific file in the file path through the Windows Component Object Model (COM). First, create a new COM object, 'obj' based

**Table 3.** start.vbs code.

| Row | CMD Commands |
|---|---|
| 1 | set obj = GetObject("new:9BA05972-F6A8-11CF-A442-00A0C90A8F39") |
| 2 | set itemObj = obj.Item() |
| 3 | jHxescZHDcebgaNZ = Left(WScript.ScriptFullName, InstrRev(WScript.ScriptFullName, "\") - 1) |
| 4 | itemObj.Document.Application.ShellExecute jHxescZHDcebgaNZ & "\" & "09402649" & ".b" & "at", Null, jHxescZHDcebgaNZ, Null, 0 |
| 5 | set obj = Nothing |

on the GUID, and then search for items in 'obj.' Calculates the currently executing directory path for search purposes. You can check the full path of the script through 'WScript.ScriptFullName' and find the directory by checking the '\' location. Then, run the '09402649.bat' file in the same location as the script. Finally, we free the 'obj' object.

## 4.2 Ande Loader Malware

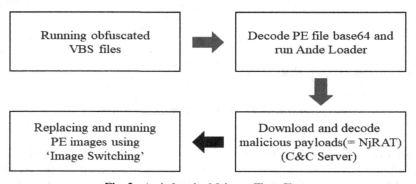

**Fig. 3.** Ande Loader Malware Flow Chart.

In April 2024, Ande Loader malware was distributed targeting North American manufacturing companies [4]. The malware is a VBS containing a Base64-encoded PE file. It is decoded with PowerShell to call a function, pass parameters containing C&C server address information, and directly call the 'VAI' method that can execute the PE file. Afterward, it connects to the C&C server to download and decode the 'NjRAT' malware, which is the final payload encoded in Base64. Image switching technique is used to execute the 'NjRAT' malware. Table 4 shows the process-related functions used in the image-switching technique (Fig. 3).

In Table 4, the processes that comprise the.NET framework are randomly selected first. Afterward, use the 'ZwUnmapViewOf-Section' API, which creates a process and unmaps the code of a normal process from memory. A malicious PE image to be replaced

**Table 4.** Process-related functions used for image-switching.

| Function Name | Description |
|---|---|
| CreateProcess | Process creation |
| WriteProcessMemory | Copy (write) data from the specified buffer of the current process to the address range of the specified process |
| SetThreadContext | Set the context of the specified thread, After loading the context for the execution address, modify and set it |
| ResumeThread | Starting or restarting a thread |

is inserted into the released area, the execution address of the thread is set to the Entry Point of the inserted PE image, and the thread is started. After image switching, the 'NjRAT' malware is executed disguised as a previously randomly selected normal process name, collects system keylogging data, stores it in the registry, and uploads it to the C&C server.

### 4.3 Remcos RAT Malware

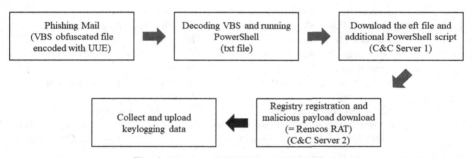

**Fig. 4.** Remcos RAT Malware Flow Chart.

In June 2024, the Remcos RAT malware downloader was distributed through a VBS obfuscated file encoded with Unix-to-Unix Encode (UUE) as a phishing email forged with a quotation, etc. [11]. UUE is a method of encoding binary data in ASCII text format and is believed to have been applied to bypass detection by anti-virus programs. By decoding the UUE file, you can check the obfuscated VBS. The VBS script is executed after saving PowerShell with the file name 'Talehmmedes.txt' in the "C:\Users\Users\AppData\Local\Temp" path. The TXT file contains a 'Haartop-pens.Eft' file that performs the PowerShell script execution function in the "C:\Users\User\AppData" path and a C&C server string for downloading additional PowerShell scripts. An additional PowerShell script registers the registry to achieve persistence and ultimately connects to another C&C server to download and execute the Remcos RAT malware. Remcos RAT malware collects keylogging data from the system, stores it in the "C:\Users\User\AppData" path, and uploads it to the C&C server (Fig. 4).

### 4.4 Standardization of Attack Techniques Used in VBS Malware Attack Cases

As shown in Table 5, attack techniques using VBS malware used in three cases from 4.1 to 4.3 were derived and standardized by mapping them to the attack techniques of the MITER ATT&CK framework. The MITER ATT&CK framework is a security framework that classifies information about various attack techniques developed by MITER Corporation [6]. Based on actual cyber-attack cases, attackers' actions can be categorized and standardized into various tactics and techniques. As a result of standardizing the derived attack techniques, it was confirmed that the attack techniques used by Konni APT and Remcos RAT malware were similar to each other. In the case of Ande Loader malware, it can be seen that the proportion of process-related attack techniques, such as using process image switching techniques, is high.

**Table 5.** Standardization of Attack Techniques.

| Attack Cases | Description | MITRE ATT&CK Techniques |
|---|---|---|
| Konni APT | Spear phishing<br>Execute user's double extension files<br>Running PowerShell and VBS<br>PowerShell obfuscation<br>Securing continuity through registry registration<br>Collection of user information through keylogging<br>C2 server communication<br>(downloading malicious payload and uploading keylogging information) | T1566(Phishing)<br>T1204(User Execution)<br>T1059(Command and Scripting Interpreter)<br>T1027(Obfuscated Files or Information)<br>T1547(Boot or Logon Autostart Execution)<br>T1056(Input Capture)<br>T1071(Application Layer Protocol) & T1041(Exfiltration Over C2 Channel) |
| Ande Loader | Running PowerShell and VBS<br>Base64 obfuscation of 'NjRAT' malware<br>Use 'ZwUnmapViewOfSection' API (image switching)<br>Disguises itself as a normal process name and executes malicious code<br>Collection of user information through keylogging<br>C2 server communication<br>(downloading malicious payload and uploading keylogging information) | T1059(Command and Scripting Interpreter)<br>T1027(Obfuscated Files or Information)<br>T1055(Process Injection)<br>T1574.002(DLL Search Order Hijacking)<br>T1056(Input Capture)<br>T1071(Application Layer Protocol) & T1041(Exfiltration Over C2 Channel) |

*(continued)*

**Table 5.** (*continued*)

| Attack Cases | Description | MITRE ATT&CK Techniques |
|---|---|---|
| Remcos RAT | Phishing emails containing forged quotations, etc<br>User executes forged file<br>Run VBS and PowerShell scripts<br>Obfuscation through UUE encoding<br>Securing continuity through registry registration<br>Collection of user information through keylogging<br>C2 server communication (downloading malicious payload and uploading keylogging information) | T1566(Phishing)<br>T1204(User Execution)<br>T1059(Command and Scripting Interpreter)<br>T1027(Obfuscated Files or Information)<br>T1547(Boot or Logon Autostart Execution)<br>T1056(Input Capture)<br>T1071(Application Layer Protocol) & T1041(Exfiltration Over C2 Channel) |

## 5   VBS Malware Detection Methods

Barr-Smith, Frederick, et al. [12] proposed an Exorcist system that detects the insertion of malicious functions into supply chains through differential analysis of binaries to detect VBS attacks used in evasive malware targeting supply chains. The proposed system was evaluated through experiments analyzing 12 APT campaigns (DarkSide, Not-Petya, Ewon, etc.). However, because the Exorcist system only detects PE files in Windows operating systems, it cannot detect attacks on Linux or Mac systems.

TAI, Dang Quy, et al. [13] proposed activating the Microsoft Antimalware Scan Interface (AMSI) to detect Visual Basic for Application (VBA) and VBS macro malware running on Microsoft Excel. Because ASMI connects to Office applications through user-level DLLs, it can detect malicious activity caused by macro scripts in the applications.

Xiong, Chunlin, et al. [14] defined obfuscation based on the difference in impact on the abstract syntax trees of PowerShell scripts to detect Windows PowerShell attacks using VBS and proposed a new emulation-based recovery technique. They designed a semantic-aware PowerShell attack detection system that utilizes an objective-oriented association algorithm and newly identifies 31 semantic signatures. Experiments on 2342 benign samples and 4141 malicious samples showed that the proposed deobfuscation method took less than 0.5 s on average and increased the similarity between the obfuscated script and the original script from 0.5% to 93.2%. Additionally, an average detection rate of 96.7% was confirmed.

Ongun, Talha, et al. [15] studied a method of expressing command line text using the word-embedding technique and designed an ensemble boosting classifier to distinguish malicious samples from normal samples based on the embedding expression. An average F1 score of 96% was achieved, but the focus was on classifying malware that used VBS technology rather than on how to defend against VBS attacks.

## 6 Discussion

This session, we explain ways to protect against VBS malware attacks and describe analysis using real-time monitoring and Windows log analysis.

### 6.1 Detection Through Real-Time Monitoring

VBS malware files must be detected and automatically stopped or deleted before creation or execution. In the previous attack case, a double extension vulnerability was exploited to induce the user to execute the LNK file directly. Therefore, file detection and deletion for double extension file creation is necessary. Table 6 shows the environment for implementing and verifying the function and blocking the normal operation of malicious code. I installed the Windows 7 and 10 operating systems in the VM virtual machine, installed the Python package, and wrote the source code.

**Table 6.** Implementation and Verification Environment

| Function Name | Description |
|---|---|
| Virtual Machine | VMWare Workstation 16 Pro |
| Operating System | Windows 7, 10 |
| Programming Language | Python |
| Source Code Editing Tools | Visual Studio Code |

Python Watchdog is a file monitoring module that monitors file system events in a specified file path. Table 7 implements the code that uses Python Watchdog to perform monitoring to detect double extension files.

**Table 7.** Implementation and Verification Environment

| Class | Main Code |
|---|---|
| Watcher | DIRECTORY_TO_WATCH = " file_path " |
| | def __init__(self): |
| | self.observer = Observer() |
| Handler | parts = file_name.split('.') |
| | if len(parts) > 2: |
| | try: |
| | os.remove(file_path) |
| | print(f"Complete: {file_path}") |
| | except Exception as e: |
| | print(f"Faie: {file_path}") |

Watchdog is divided into Watcher and Handler, and Watcher specifies the file path to be monitored and creates an Observer object to perform real-time monitoring. In the handler, the detected files were automatically deleted after setting the double extension string detection conditions. After executing the written code and adding a monitoring process, a Konni APT malware file was created. As a result, double extension files with two or more '.' strings were successfully detected and automatically deleted. Meanwhile, many document-type malware creates malicious VBS files in the %temp%, %AppData%, and %Public% paths. Since these file paths are frequently abused as paths to store malicious files, deletion, and execution must be blocked by setting the path in the Watcher and filtering additional VBS and BAT extension files (Fig. 5).

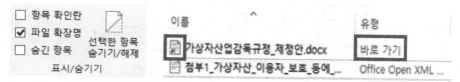

**Fig. 5.** Activating File Extensions and LNK File Types.

Additionally, the user must check the file extension by activating the file extension setting as shown in Fig. 1. The LNK extension is a shortcut file type and has an arrow image on the file icon as shown in Fig. 2, so be careful when running it.

## 6.2 Analyze Windows Log

In the case of Windows, you must use the Windows Event Viewer (eventvwr.msc) function, which can check event logs that occur in the system [16] to check, audit, and track logs and block any abnormal behavior if it is detected. As shown in Fig. 6, when the object access audit function is executed in the Windows Event Viewer, a security log is saved, and the ID saved is different depending on the event's content. Therefore, when an attack occurs or after an attack, the recorded security log must be checked, and the contents corresponding to each event ID must be analyzed to detect and block the attack. The security log consists of the Event ID, Event Type, Event Category of the event that occurred, and Event Message Text, which outputs the event's details. Since Konni APT malware uses PowerShell, Windows PowerShell events were checked and analyzed. First, event ID 400 indicates PowerShell start, ID 403 indicates PowerShell stop, and ID 600 indicates PowerShell code execution event. As a result of analysis in XML format, PowerShell command argument values that create 'UHCYbG.cab' and 'start.vbs' files were detected when creating malicious code.

In addition, because the attacker uses a C&C server connection to download additional payloads, the network is newly configured, so you must check if the network configuration changes. Generally, blocks must be deleted after monitoring to see if non-executing or unrecognized processes are created.

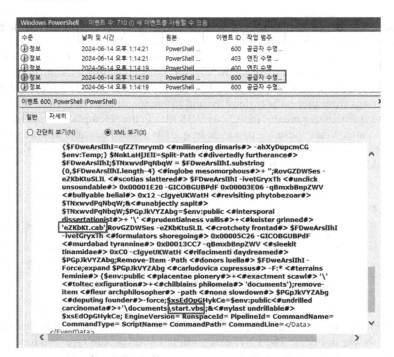

**Fig. 6.** Windows Event Viewer, Konni APT Malware Analysis Results.

## 7 Conclusions

Data such as cyber threat reports indicate that damage caused by VBS malware continues. In this survey, analysis and defense techniques for VBS malware attacks were investigated. Data on the definition and vulnerabilities of VBS were presented. In addition, the latest attack cases regarding VBS malware attack trends are briefly presented and summarized. As for VBS malware detection, research on detecting malware in PE files, macros, and PowerShell containing VBS using data sets was confirmed. In response to VBS malware attacks, real-time monitoring, blocking, and automatic deletion of double-extension files were implemented based on Python Watchdog. In addition, we analyzed file paths frequently used in VBS attacks and proposed VBS file filtering. In addition, we proposed detecting VBS malware through event ID and XML-based Windows PowerShell log analysis in Windows Event Viewer and blocking and deleting processes by checking whether the network configuration has been changed.

**Acknowledgements.** This work was supported by Institute of Information & communications Technology Planning & Evaluation (IITP) grant funded by the Korea government(MSIT) (No. 2021-0-00493, 5G Massive Next Generation Cyber Attack Deception Technology Development, 50%) and Institute of Information & communications Technology Planning & Evaluation (IITP) grant funded by the Korea government(MSIT) (No. RS-2024-00354169, Technology Development of Threat Model/XAI-based Network Abnormality Detection, Response and Cyber Threat Prediction, 50%).

# References

1. Khushali, V.: A review on fileless malware analysis techniques. Int. J. Eng. Res. Technol. (IJERT) **9**(05) (2020)
2. Boannews: VB scripts, which attackers have been using instead of MS Office macros, will soon disappear (2023). https://m.boannews.com/html/detail.html?idx=122647. Accessed 25 Jun 2024
3. Genians: Hacking damage warning due to rapid rise in Bitcoin price (2024). https://www.genians.co.kr/blog/threat_intelligence/bitcoin. Accessed 25 Jun 2024
4. INCA Internet: Ande Loader using image switching (2024). https://isarc.tachyonlab.com/5628. Accessed 25 Jun 2024
5. MITRE: MITRE ATT&CK. https://attack.mitre.org/. Accessed 25 Jun 2024
6. tutorialspoint: VBScript – Overview. https://www.tutorialspoint.com/vbscript/vbscript_overview.htm. Accessed 25 Jun 2024
7. RoleCatcher: VBScript: The Complete Skill Guide (2023). https://rolecatcher.com/en/skills/knowledge/information-and-communication-technologies/software-and-applications-development-and-analysis/vbscript/. Accessed 25 Jun 2024
8. MITRE: Command and Scripting Interpreter: Visual Basic. https://attack.mitre.org/techniques/T1059/005/. Accessed 25 Jun 2024
9. CVE. https://cve.mitre.org/index.html. Accessed 25 Jun 2024
10. Koutsokostas, V., et al.: Invoice# 31415 attached: automated analysis of malicious microsoft office documents. Comput. Secur. **114**, 102582 (2022)
11. ASEC: Remcos RAT Distributed as UUEncoding (UUE) File (2024). https://asec.ahnlab.com/en/66463/. Accessed 25 Jun 2024
12. Barr-Smith, F., et al.: Exorcist: automated differential analysis to detect compromises in closed-source software supply chains. In: Proceedings of the 2022 ACM Workshop on Software Supply Chain Offensive Research and Ecosystem Defenses, pp. 51–61 (2022)
13. Tai, D.Q., Gallus, P., Františ, P.: Macro malware development issues. In: 2023 International Conference on Military Technologies (ICMT), pp. 1–6. IEEE (2023)
14. Xiong, C., et al.: Generic, efficient, and effective deobfuscation and semantic-aware attack detection for PowerShell scripts. Front. Inf. Technol. Electron. Eng. **23**(3), 361–381 (2022)
15. Ongun, T., et al.: Living-off-the-land command detection using active learning. In: Proceedings of the 24th International Symposium on Research in Attacks, Intrusions and Defenses, pp. 442–455 (2021)
16. Microsoft. https://learn.microsoft.com/en-us/host-integration-server/core/msdrdaservice-event-logs. Accessed 25 Jun 2024

# Software Security

# Adversarial Manhole: Challenging Monocular Depth Estimation and Semantic Segmentation Models with Patch Attack

Naufal Suryanto[1]([⊠])[iD], Andro Aprila Adiputra[1][iD],
Ahmada Yusril Kadiptya[1][iD], Yongsu Kim[1,2][iD], and Howon Kim[1,2][iD]

[1] Pusan National University, Busan, South Korea
naufalsuryanto@gmail.com
[2] SmartM2M, Busan, South Korea

**Abstract.** Monocular depth estimation (MDE) and semantic segmentation (SS) are crucial for the navigation and environmental interpretation of many autonomous driving systems. However, their vulnerability to practical adversarial attacks is a significant concern. This paper presents a novel adversarial attack using practical patches that mimic manhole covers to deceive MDE and SS models. The goal is to cause these systems to misinterpret scenes, leading to false detections of near obstacles or non-passable objects. We use Depth Planar Mapping to precisely position these patches on road surfaces, enhancing the attack's effectiveness. Our experiments show that these adversarial patches cause a 43% relative error in MDE and achieve a 96% attack success rate in SS. These patches create affected error regions over twice their size in MDE and approximately equal to their size in SS. Our studies also confirm the patch's effectiveness in physical simulations, the adaptability of the patches across different target models, and the effectiveness of our proposed modules, highlighting their practical implications.

**Keywords:** Adversarial Attack · Adversarial Patch · Monocular Depth Estimation · Semantic Segmentation · Autonomous Driving

## 1 Introduction

Self-driving cars rely on complex algorithms and are equipped with sensing devices such as cameras to navigate intricate environments. The core of a camera-based self-driving system utilizes computer vision techniques and deep learning to perceive objects around the car and make decisions. These cars must be constantly aware of their surroundings to ensure a safe driving environment.

Deep learning-based computer vision technologies used in self-driving cars include Monocular Depth Estimation (MDE) and Semantic Segmentation (SS).

This research was supported by the MSIT (Ministry of Science and ICT), Korea, under the Convergence security core talent training business (Pusan National University) support program (RS-2022-II221201) supervised by the IITP (Institute for Information & Communications Technology Planning & Evaluation).

MDE calculates object distances by extracting depth information from camera images, which is crucial for determining the distance ahead of the car. However, the impact of compromised MDE on autonomous driving tasks remains largely unknown [3]. If MDE provides inaccurate depth information, it can increase the risk of collisions during split-second decisions.

Semantic Segmentation (SS), on the other hand, helps identify traffic objects such as vehicles, pedestrians, and traffic signs, which is vital for safe driving [11]. If SS fails to accurately recognize these objects, it can lead to dangerous driving decisions and result in severe accidents.

Ensuring the robustness of MDE and SS methods is crucial to prevent critical failures. Adversarial attacks, which deceive models into producing incorrect outputs, pose a significant threat [13]. These attacks often use methods like adversarial patches to manipulate predictions [3,6,7,9,16]. However, the practical implementation of such attacks is often overlooked. This work addresses this gap by focusing on realistic patch-based attacks targeting MDE and SS models with patches that resemble road manholes. Manholes, with their diverse designs, are ideal attack vectors. By using manhole-like patches, we highlight the real-world applicability and implications of our approach.

Our contributions can be summarized as follows:

- We present the Adversarial Manhole, a practical adversarial attack targeting MDE and SS in autonomous driving scenarios. To our knowledge, this is the first approach to attack both models simultaneously.
- We propose a Depth Planar Mapping technique that utilizes depth information to accurately position adversarial patches on the road surface, going beyond simple perspective transformations.
- Our framework generates a stealthy adversarial patch designed as a manhole cover, which can be deployed anywhere on the road, exploiting vulnerabilities in autonomous driving systems.
- We conduct an extensive evaluation to assess the robustness of adversarial manholes across various scenarios, including physical simulations, applicability to different models, and ablation studies to analyze the effectiveness of our proposed modules.

## 2    Related Works

### 2.1    Monocular Depth Estimation (MDE)

Monocular Depth Estimation (MDE) can be achieved through various methods. Unsupervised methods, addressing labeling costs, treat MDE as a reconstruction problem using dense correspondence between stereo images. Self-supervised learning enhances this by extracting ego-motion, improving accuracy through automated pixel masking and projection error calculation [5]. Another method sharpens depth representation for thin and close objects by enhancing photometric cues [15]. Techniques addressing inconsistencies between viewpoints, pose estimation, and cost volume loss further improve depth estimation accuracy [14].

## 2.2    Semantic Segmentation (SS)

Semantic Segmentation (SS) assigns semantic labels to each pixel in an image, categorizing them into classes such as vehicles, pedestrians, roads, and buildings.

Deep learning, particularly convolutional neural networks, has significantly advanced image segmentation. PSPNet [19] uses a Pyramid Pooling Module to capture rich contextual information but struggles with real-time performance. ICNet [18] achieves real-time speed (30 FPS) with 70% accuracy using an image cascade network. DDRNet [10] improves upon this with dual-resolution networks, achieving 77.4% mIoU at 102 FPS by using a novel DAPPM module to extract and merge multi-scale context information.

## 2.3    Patch-Based Adversarial Attacks

Research on physical adversarial attacks targeting MDE includes generating noticeable adversarial patches [16], printable stealthy patches with distance limitations [3], and adaptive patches that sacrifice stealthiness for effectiveness [6]. Another approach introduced stealthy patches resilient to transformations but limited to MDE [7]. Our work aims to target both MDE and SS.

Adversarial attacks methods on SS, like the Fast Gradient Sign Method (FGSM) have been explored but is impractical in real-world scenarios as they modify the entire pixel space [1]. Other approaches optimized adversarial patches using cross-entropy loss on pre-trained models, showing effectiveness in digital simulations but reduced performance in real-world applications [9].

Table 1 compares existing adversarial patch methods targeting MDE and SS with the proposed Adversarial Manhole. The comparison focuses on stealth capabilities, victim tasks, and patch projection methods. Our approach supports stealth features, pioneering simultaneous attacks in MDE and SS, and introducing Depth Planar Mapping for optimized road patch projection.

**Table 1.** Comparison of proposed and existing patch-based adversarial attacks.

| Method | Stealthy | Victim Task | Patch Projection |
|---|---|---|---|
| Adversarial Patch [16] | No | MDE | Perspective Transformation |
| SemSegAdvPatch [9] | No | SS | Perspective Transformation |
| OAP [3] | Yes | MDE | Spatial Transformation |
| APARATE [6] | No | MDE | Spatial Transformation |
| SAAM [7] | Yes | MDE | Perspective Transformation |
| Adversarial Manhole (Ours) | Yes | MDE, SS | Depth Planar Mapping |

# 3    Methodology

## 3.1    Problem Definition

The primary objective of our proposed method is to create an adversarial manhole that, when placed on the road, causes monocular depth estimation (MDE) and semantic segmentation (SS) systems to misinterpret the scene. This misinterpretation should lead the vehicle to falsely detect a near obstacle or non-passable object, potentially causing it to stop or choose an alternate path.

Consider a benign input image $x$. In a patch-based adversarial attack, the goal is to alter the image by introducing an adversarial patch $\theta$, creating an adversarial example $x'$. To ensure realism, the patch is applied to the target surface using a patch mapping function $P$. The adversarial example with the patch is formulated as:

$$x' = P(x, \theta, t_o, t_s) = x \odot (1 - m(t_o, t_s)) + M(\theta, t_o, t_s) \odot m(t_o, t_s), \qquad (1)$$

where $M$ maps the patch to the desired texture offset $t_o$ and texture scale $t_s$, $m$ provides a mask indicating where the patch is applied, and $\odot$ denotes element-wise multiplication.

For the MDE model, $D(\cdot)$, the input image $x$ is used to estimate the depth $d$. To manipulate the depth prediction towards a target depth $d_{\text{target}}$ using an adversarial patch $\theta$, we define a loss function $L_d$. The optimization problem is:

$$\arg\min_{\theta} L_d \left( D(P(x, \theta, t_o, t_s)), d_{\text{target}} \right). \qquad (2)$$

For the SS model, $S(\cdot)$, the input image $x$ is used to output the label $y$ for each pixel. We design a loss function $L_{ua}$ for an untargeted attack to predict an incorrect label $y' \neq y$, and $L_{ta}$ for a targeted attack to predict a desired label $y_{\text{target}}$. The optimization problem is:

$$\arg\min_{\theta} \begin{cases} L_{ua} \left( S(P(x, \theta, t_o, t_s)), y \right), & \text{if untargeted} \\ L_{ta} \left( S(P(x, \theta, t_o, t_s)), y_{\text{target}} \right). & \text{if targeted} \end{cases} \qquad (3)$$

To simultaneously attack both $D(\cdot)$ and $S(\cdot)$, we combine the losses and apply Expectation over Transformation (EOT) [2] to enhance the robustness of the patch $\theta$ over different transformations $T$ and background images $X$. The combined optimization problem is:

$$\arg\min_{\theta} \mathbb{E}_{t \in T, x \in X} \Big[ \alpha \cdot L_d \left( D(P(x, \theta, t_o, t_s)), d_{\text{target}} \right)$$
$$+ \beta_{ua} \cdot L_{ua} \left( S(P(x, \theta, t_o, t_s)), y \right)$$
$$+ \beta_{ta} \cdot L_{ta} \left( S(P(x, \theta, t_o, t_s)), y_{\text{target}} \right) \Big], \qquad (4)$$

where $\alpha$, $\beta_{ua}$, and $\beta_{ta}$ are hyperparameters controlling the influence of each loss.

## 3.2   Adversarial Manhole

We propose the Adversarial Manhole Framework (Fig. 1) to address these issues. The framework uses differentiable components and losses to optimize the adversarial manhole $\theta$ through gradient-based methods.

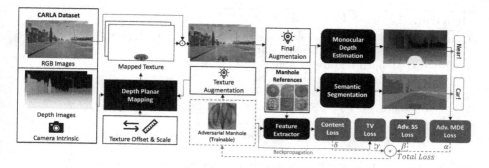

**Fig. 1.** Our proposed framework for generating adversarial manhole.

**Depth Planar Mapping.** We propose Depth Planar Mapping to accurately map adversarial textures onto target surfaces, considering texture offset and scale as defined in Eq. 1. Inspired by [12], our approach uses depth information and camera intrinsics from the corresponding RGB image to calculate local surface coordinates and map the texture accordingly. Unlike their tri-planar mapping, we use single-planar (z-plane) mapping due to the upward normal of road surfaces. This method achieves more accurate texture mapping than typical perspective transformations in patch-based attacks. The detailed is described in Algorithm 1.

**Texture and Final Augmentation.** To enhance the robustness of the adversarial manhole, we apply digital augmentations as in the EOT method [2]. These include random brightness and contrast adjustments for various lighting conditions, and random flips and rotations for texture robustness. We formalize our Texture Augmentation ($A_t$) and Final Augmentation ($A_f$) as follows:

$$\theta_t = A_t(\theta, t_T), \tag{5}$$

$$x'_t = A_f(x', t_F), \tag{6}$$

where $t_T$ represents texture augmentation variables, and $t_F$ represents final augmentation variables.

**Adversarial MDE Loss.** One goal of our adversarial manhole is to deceive the MDE model into detecting a near object in front of the vehicle. The MDE model typically outputs a disparity map, which is the inverse of depth: higher disparity values correspond to closer objects. We design the Adv. MDE Loss ($L_d$) to minimize Eq. 2 by enforcing zero distance predictions in the manhole area ($m$). The loss function is:

$$L_d(x', m) = -\log(D_{disp}(x')) \odot m. \tag{7}$$

This maximizes the disparity in the manhole area, making the perceived distance close to zero.

**Adversarial SS Loss.** The adversarial manhole aims to trick the SS model into detecting an obstacle or non-passable object. For untargeted attacks, we

---

**Algorithm 1.** Depth Planar Mapping (DPM) Algorithm

---

1: **Input:** Depth image $d$, Camera intrinsics $(c_x, c_y, f_x, f_y)$, Texture $\theta$, Texture scales $t_s$, Texture offsets $t_o$, Texture resolution $t_{res}$
2: **Output:** Mapped texture $M$ and Texture masks $m$
3: Calculate surface coordinates $SC_x, SC_y, SC_z$
4: **for** each pixel $(u, v)$ in depth image $d$ **do**
5:     $SC_x = d(u, v) \cdot \frac{u - c_x}{f_x}$, $SC_y = d(u, v) \cdot \frac{v - c_y}{f_y}$, $SC_z = d(u, v)$
6: **end for**
7: Form surface coordinates tensor (z-upward, x-forward): $SC = \{SC_z, SC_x, SC_y\}$
8: Adjust and normalize coordinates: $SC_{norm} = ((SC - t_o) \bmod t_s)/t_s$
9: Compute UV indices: $UV = \max(0, \min(\text{round}(SC_{norm} \cdot t_{res}), t_{res} - 1))$
10: Map texture to surface using z-plane: $M = \theta[UV_x, UV_y]$
11: Calculate bounds for masking:
12:     $x_{min} = t_{o_x}$, $x_{max} = t_{o_x} + t_s$, $y_{min} = t_{o_y}$, $y_{max} = t_{o_y} + t_s$
13: Create texture mask:
14:     $m = (SC_x > x_{min}) \& (SC_x < x_{max}) \& (SC_y > y_{min}) \& (SC_y < y_{max})$
15: **return** Mapped texture $M$ and Texture masks $m$

---

use $L_{ua}$ to force predictions other than the road class, and for targeted attacks, $L_{ta}$ to achieve a desired class. The losses are:

$$L_{ua}(x', m) = -\log(1 - S_{road}(x')) \odot m \tag{8}$$

$$L_{ta}(x', m) = -\log(\max_{c \in C} S_c(x')) \odot m. \tag{9}$$

These losses adjust the probabilities of the road class and target classes ($c \in C$) in the manhole area.

**Total Variation Loss.** To ensure the adversarial manhole texture is smooth, we use Total Variation (TV) Loss [8], which minimizes abrupt color changes that are unrealistic in printed and captured images. The TV Loss ($L_{tv}$) is:

$$L_{tv}(\theta) = \frac{1}{N} \sum_{i,j}^{N} |\theta_{i,j} - \theta_{i,j+1}| + |\theta_{i,j} - \theta_{i+1,j}|, \tag{10}$$

where $\theta_{i,j}$ is the pixel at index $(i, j)$. This loss smooths the texture by minimizing differences between neighboring pixels.

**Content Loss.** To make the adversarial manhole appear natural and more stealthy, we use Content Loss ($L_c$) [3], formulated as:

$$L_c(\theta) = \min_{r \in R} |F_l(\theta) - F_l(r)|, \tag{11}$$

where $F_l$ is the CNN feature extractor output at layer $l$, and $R$ is the set of reference manhole images. This loss minimizes the feature differences between the adversarial and reference images, ensuring visual similarity.

**Algorithm 2.** Adversarial Manhole Generation

---

1: **Input:** RGB Image $X$, Depth image $D$, Camera intrinsics $C$, Texture resolution $t_{res}$, Depth Planar Mapping $DPM$, Texture Augmentation $A_t$, Final Augmentation $A_f$, Random function $R$, Texture scales $t_S$, Texture offsets $t_O$, Texture transformations $t_T$, Final transformations $t_F$
2: **Output:** Adversarial Manhole $\theta$
3: Initialize $\theta$ with random values: $\theta = R(0,1)$
4: **for** each iteration **do**
5:     Select a minibatch sample of data: $x \in X$, $d \in D$, $c \in C$
6:     Initialize random transformations: $t_s \in t_S$, $t_o \in t_O$, $t_t \in t_T$, $t_f \in t_F$
7:     Augment the manhole texture with $A_t$: $\theta_t = A_t(\theta, t_t)$                    ▷ Eq. 5
8:     Output the mapped texture $M$ and texture mask $m$ using $DPM$:
9:     $M, m = DPM(d, c, \theta_t, t_s, t_o, t_{res})$                    ▷ Algorithm 1
10:     Combine the RGB image and mapped texture: $x' = x \odot (1 - m) + M \odot m$
11:     Augment the final image: $x'_t = A_f(x', t_f)$                    ▷ Eq. 6
12:     Calculate losses: $L_d(x'_t, m)$, $L_{ua}(x'_t, m)$, $L_{ta}(x'_t, m)$, $L_{tv}(\theta)$, $L_c(\theta)$   ▷ Eq. 7–11
13:     Update $\theta$ to minimize the total loss $L_{total}$ via backpropagation   ▷ Eq. 12
14: **end for**
15: **return** Adversarial Manhole $\theta$

---

**Adversarial Manhole Generation.** We initialize $\theta$ with random values and generate an adversarial manhole using our framework. We iteratively update the texture to minimize the final loss ($L_{total}$):

$$L_{total}(x', m, \theta) = \alpha \cdot L_d(x', m) + \beta_{ua} \cdot L_{ua}(x', m) + \beta_{ta} \cdot L_{ta}(x', m) + \gamma \cdot L_{tv}(\theta) + \delta \cdot L_c(\theta), \tag{12}$$

where $\alpha$, $\beta_{ua}$, $\beta_{ta}$, $\gamma$, and $\delta$ are hyperparameters. The detailed is in Algorithm 2.

## 4  Experiments

### 4.1  Implementation Details

**Datasets.** We generate autonomous driving scene datasets using CARLA [4] including RGBs, depths, and camera intrinsics as described in Fig. 1. We randomly selected positions from seven towns and captured the datasets resulting in 2,656 images. Each data has $1024 \times 780$ resolution from a 1-meter height camera. We split the dataset into train/val/test with a 60/20/20 ratio.

**Frameworks.** We implemented our framework using PyTorch[1], with MonoDepth2 [5] as the target MDE model and DDRNet [10] as the SS model. For adversarial manhole generation, we use the Adam optimizer with a learning rate of 0.01, batch size of 8, and 25 epochs. We set $T_{O_x} \in [0.0, 0.4]$ to randomly map the texture between 1.8 - 2.6 m from the camera, and $T_{O_y} \in [-0.4, 0.4]$ to randomly map the texture between -0.8 m and 0.8 m from the center of the camera.

---

[1] Code and datasets: https://github.com/naufalso/adversarial-manhole.

For $t_F$ and $t_T$, we use 0.2 for random brightness and 0.1 for random contrast. The total loss hyperparameters are $\alpha = 2.0$, $\beta_{ua} = 0.5$, $\beta_{ta} = 0.5$, $\gamma = 1.0$, and $\delta = 0.5$. For targeted attacks, we set the target label to non-walkable categories, such as buildings, walls, fences, poles, persons, and vehicles.

**Evaluation Metrics.** To evaluate patch performance against the MDE model, we introduce the relative error distance ($Rel.\ Ed$) and region-affected error distance ($Ra_{Ed}$) metrics:

$$Rel.\ Ed = \frac{\sum (|d - d'|/d) \odot m_{patch}}{\sum m_{patch}}, \tag{13}$$

$$Ra_{Ed} = \frac{\sum B((|d - d'|/d) > Rel.\ Ed_{thres}) \odot m_{road}}{\sum m_{patch}}. \tag{14}$$

Here, $d$ and $d'$ are the distance predictions for clean and adversarial images, $m_{patch}$ is the patch mask, $m_{road}$ is the road mask, $B()$ returns 1 if the condition is met, and $Rel.\ Ed_{thres}$ is the threshold for the affected area set to 0.25. $Rel.\ Ed$ measures the mean error caused by the adversarial patch, while $Ra_{Ed}$ gauges the ratio of affected road regions relative to the mask area. These metrics refine $E_d$ and $R_a$ from prior MDE patch attacks [3,6,7].

To evaluate patch performance against the SS model, we use the Attack Success Rate ($ASR$) for untargeted ($ASR_{ua}$) and targeted ($ASR_{ta}$) attacks:

$$ASR = \begin{cases} ASR_{ua} = \frac{\sum B(s' \neq s_{road}) \odot m_{patch} \odot s_{road}}{\sum m_{patch} \odot s_{road}}, & \text{if untargeted} \\ ASR_{ta} = \frac{\sum B(s' = c \in C) \odot m_{patch} \odot s_{road}}{\sum m_{patch} \odot s_{road}}, & \text{if targeted} \end{cases} \tag{15}$$

Here, $s'$ is the semantic prediction of the adversarial image, $s_{road}$ is the road prediction of the original image, and $c$ represents target labels for targeted attacks. Multiplying $m_{patch}$ by $s_{road}$ ensures evaluation only on valid road predictions within patch areas.

Finally, we adapt the $Ra$ metric for the SS model to measure the ratio of affected error regions in the road area relative to the mask area:

$$Ra_{ss} = \begin{cases} Ra_{ua} = \frac{\sum B(s' \neq s_{road}) \odot s_{road}}{\sum m_{patch}}, & \text{if untargeted} \\ Ra_{ta} = \frac{\sum B(s' = c \in C) \odot s_{road}}{\sum m_{patch}}. & \text{if targeted} \end{cases} \tag{16}$$

Unlike $ASR$, $Ra$ also considers the error outside the patch area.

## 4.2   Experiment Results

**Patch Effectiveness.** We evaluate our generated adversarial manhole on test sets, comparing it to baselines like naive, artistic, and random pattern manholes. We also compare it to related work, such as Adversarial Patch [16] and Sem-SegAdvPatch [9], using their official code but with our settings. As shown in Table 2 and Fig. 2, the models are robust against the baselines, correctly predicting depth and segmentation as normal roads. While Adversarial Patch and

**Table 2.** Evaluation results of patches effectiveness in our test sets.

| Evaluated Patches | MonoDepth2 [5] (MDE) | | DDRNet [10] (SS) | | | |
|---|---|---|---|---|---|---|
| | Rel. Ed | $Ra_{Ed}$ | $ASR_{ua}$ | $ASR_{ta}$ | $Ra_{ua}$ | $Ra_{ta}$ |
| Naïve Manhole | 0.03 | 0.02 | 0.00 | 0.00 | 0.00 | 0.00 |
| Artistic Manhole | 0.04 | 0.04 | 0.00 | 0.00 | 0.00 | 0.00 |
| Random Patch | 0.03 | 0.01 | 0.00 | 0.00 | 0.00 | 0.00 |
| Adversarial Patch [16] | 0.35 | 1.62 | 0.00 | 0.00 | 0.00 | 0.00 |
| Ours MDE ($L_d+L_{tv}+L_c$) | **0.43** | **2.39** | 0.00 | 0.00 | 0.00 | 0.00 |
| SemSegAdvPatch [9] | 0.06 | 0.04 | 0.40 | 0.04 | 0.95 | 0.09 |
| Ours SS ($L_{ua}+L_{ta}+L_{tv}+L_c$) | 0.05 | 0.05 | **0.96** | 0.95 | **1.08** | 0.96 |
| **Ours All** ($L_{total}$) | **0.43** | 2.34 | **0.96** | **0.96** | 1.02 | **0.98** |

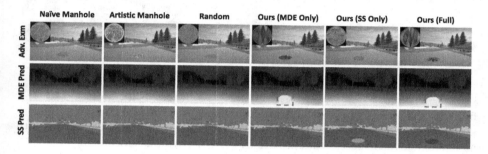

**Fig. 2.** Qualitative results of our patch effectiveness: The results illustrate that naïve, artistic, and random manholes do not affect the model predictions, while our methods successfully fool the models. Zoom for details.

SemSegAdvPatch disturb MDE and SS models, their performance declines due to uncovered manhole orientation during optimization. Note that SemSegAdv-Patch supports only untargeted attacks, and we used the EOT variant since the manhole location isn't fixed. Our adversarial manholes, however, can effectively fool the models based on the applied adversarial loss. If $L_d$ is applied, the adversarial manhole causes an average relative error distance of 43% to the MDE model. When $L_{ua}$ and $L_{ta}$ are applied, it achieves a 96% attack success rate in fooling segmentation. Combining all adversarial losses, the manhole effectively attacks both MDE and SS with similar impact. Notably, the adversarial manhole can cause an error to MDE larger than the patch size, affecting a region 239% relative to the patch size, despite the loss focusing only on the patch area.

**Patch Robustness.** To evaluate the robustness of our adversarial manhole against different placements on the road surface, we conducted experiments across various offsets. As summarized in Fig. 3, our patch remains robust regardless of location but performs best when centrally located and near the camera. For MDE metrics, the relative error distance decreases linearly as the patch is placed further away, from 48% relative error to 25%. However, the region-affected error for MDE shows optimal performance when the patch is 2.8 m from the camera's center. We observe this because the affected error region extends

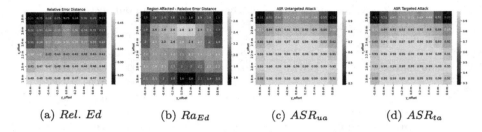

(a) *Rel. Ed*          (b) *$Ra_{Ed}$*          (c) *$ASR_{ua}$*          (d) *$ASR_{ta}$*

**Fig. 3.** Robustness evaluation against different placements. Zoom for details.

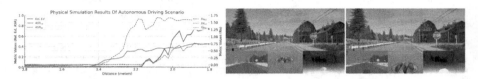

**Fig. 4.** Physical simulation of approaching car in CARLA. Zoom for details.

from the patch region to the bottom of the image. In contrast, the patch demonstrates a more robust performance on the SS model regardless of position, with an average attack success rate of 98% except for edge placements.

**Physical Simulation.** We perform physical evaluation by applying the adversarial patch as a manhole cover in the CARLA simulator. We capture video of an approaching car to mimic an autonomous driving scenario. As illustrated in Fig. 4, the adversarial manhole begins affecting the MDE model from a distance of 2.4 m and the SS model from 2.2 m. The attack's effectiveness increases as the camera approaches the manhole, reaching a peak performance of 45% relative error distance and 166% affected region for MDE, and a 75% attack success rate with a 78% affected region for SS. These results highlight the substantial impact of the adversarial patch in a more realistic setting.

**Table 3.** Evaluation results of targeting different models.

| Target MDE Model | Target SS Model | MDE Metrics | | SS Metrics | | | |
|---|---|---|---|---|---|---|---|
| | | *Rel. Ed* | *$Ra_{Ed}$* | *$ASR_{ua}$* | *$ASR_{ta}$* | *$Ra_{ua}$* | *$Ra_{ta}$* |
| MonoDepth2 [5] | DDRNet [10] | **0.43** | **2.34** | 0.96 | 0.96 | 1.02 | 0.98 |
| DepthHint [15] | DDRNet [10] | 0.33 | 0.83 | 0.97 | 0.97 | 1.01 | 0.98 |
| ManyDepth [14] | DDRNet [10] | 0.28 | 1.51 | 0.96 | 0.96 | 1.02 | 0.97 |
| MonoDepth2 [5] | PSPNet [19] | 0.40 | 2.03 | <u>0.94</u> | <u>0.93</u> | 1.00 | <u>0.95</u> |
| DepthHint [15] | PSPNet [19] | <u>0.24</u> | <u>0.53</u> | <u>0.94</u> | 0.94 | <u>0.98</u> | <u>0.95</u> |
| ManyDepth [14] | PSPNet [19] | 0.25 | 1.32 | <u>0.94</u> | <u>0.93</u> | 1.00 | <u>0.95</u> |
| MonoDepth2 [5] | ICNet [18] | 0.42 | 2.32 | **0.99** | **0.99** | 2.65 | 2.59 |
| DepthHint [15] | ICNet [18] | 0.31 | 0.76 | **0.99** | **0.99** | 2.98 | 2.92 |
| ManyDepth [14] | ICNet [18] | 0.29 | 1.67 | **0.99** | **0.99** | **3.13** | **3.09** |

**Table 4.** Ablation studies with the full baseline under random distortion during evaluation. Values in parentheses indicate the difference from the full baseline.

| Modules | MonoDepth2 [5] (MDE) | | DDRNet [10] (SS) | | | |
|---|---|---|---|---|---|---|
| | $Rel.\ Ed$ | $Ra_{Ed}$ | $ASR_{ua}$ | $ASR_{ta}$ | $Ra_{ua}$ | $Ra_{ta}$ |
| full | 0.42 | 2.18 | 0.97 | 0.96 | 1.01 | 0.98 |
| fixed $t_O$ | 0.19 (−0.24) | 0.51 (−1.68) | 0.27 (−0.69) | 0.26 (−0.71) | 0.24 (−0.78) | 0.20 (−0.78) |
| *no $DPM$ | 0.25 (−0.17) | 0.93 (−1.25) | 0.01 (−0.95) | 0.00 (−0.96) | 0.02 (−0.99) | 0.00 (−0.98) |
| no $A_t$ | 0.26 (−0.16) | 1.12 (−1.06) | 0.41 (−0.55) | 0.40 (−0.56) | 0.45 (−0.56) | 0.42 (−0.56) |
| no $A_f$ | 0.42 (0.00) | 2.13 (−0.05) | 0.90 (−0.07) | 0.90 (−0.07) | 0.96 (−0.05) | 0.93 (−0.05) |
| no $L_{tv}$ | 0.42 (0.00) | 2.13 (−0.06) | 0.91 (−0.05) | 0.91 (−0.05) | 0.94 (−0.07) | 0.91 (−0.07) |
| no $L_c$ | **0.49 (0.06)** | **2.72 (0.53)** | **0.98 (0.02)** | **0.98 (0.02)** | **1.07 (0.06)** | **1.02 (0.04)** |

**Applicability to Different Models.** We regenerated adversarial manholes with different target models to assess their applicability against various MDE and SS models. As summarized in Table 3, our patch has the highest overall impact when targeting MonoDepth2 with DDRNet for MDE metrics (43% relative error distance with 2× affected regions) and ManyDepth with ICNet for SS metrics (99% attack success rate with 3× affected regions). However, the lowest overall impact is observed when targeting DepthHint and PSPNet (24% relative error distance with 53% affected regions for MDE and 94% attack success rate with 95% affected regions for SS), indicating that these models are more robust.

**Ablation Studies.** We performed ablation studies by removing each proposed module, regenerating the patch, and applying random brightness and contrast adjustments to test robustness. As shown in Table 4, removing any module decreased performance, except for content loss ($L_c$), which trades off stealthiness and effectiveness. Optimizing the patch at a fixed offset ($t_O$) reduced robustness against varied placements. Replacing DPM with random spatial and perspective transformations (*no $DPM$) from previous works [3,6,7,9,16] significantly impaired performance in the manhole setting. These findings emphasize the need to cover expected transformations during optimization, as noted in EOT [2].

## 5  Conclusion

We presented a novel adversarial attack using practical patches that mimic manhole covers to deceive MDE and SS models in autonomous driving systems. Our patches achieved a 43% relative error in MDE and a 96% attack success rate in SS. Physical simulations validated the effectiveness of our adversarial patches in an autonomous driving scenario. Ablation studies confirmed the critical role of our proposed modules and highlighted the applicability of patches in different models. Our work underscores the vulnerability and emphasizes the need for robust defense mechanisms, such as certified defense against patch attacks [17].

## References

1. Arnab, A., Miksik, O., Torr, P.H.: On the robustness of semantic segmentation models to adversarial attacks. In: 2018 IEEE/CVF Conference on Computer Vision and Pattern Recognition, pp. 888–897. IEEE, Salt Lake City (2018)

2. Athalye, A., Engstrom, L., Ilyas, A., Kwok, K.: Synthesizing robust adversarial examples. In: International Conference on Machine Learning, pp. 284–293. PMLR (2018)
3. Cheng, Z., et al.: Physical attack on monocular depth estimation with optimal adversarial patches (2022). arXiv:2207.04718
4. Dosovitskiy, A., Ros, G., Codevilla, F., Lopez, A., Koltun, V.: CARLA: an open urban driving simulator. In: Proceedings of the 1st Annual Conference on Robot Learning, pp. 1–16 (2017)
5. Godard, C., Mac Aodha, O., Firman, M., Brostow, G.J.: Digging into self-supervised monocular depth prediction (2019)
6. Guesmi, A., Hanif, M.A., Alouani, I., Shafique, M.: APARATE: adaptive adversarial patch for CNN-based monocular depth estimation for autonomous navigation (2023). arXiv:2303.01351
7. Guesmi, A., Hanif, M.A., Ouni, B., Shafique, M.: SAAM: stealthy adversarial attack on monocular depth estimation. IEEE Access **12**, 13571–13585 (2024)
8. Mahendran, A., Vedaldi, A.: Understanding deep image representations by inverting them. In: Proceedings of the IEEE Conference on Computer Vision and Pattern Recognition, pp. 5188–5196 (2015)
9. Nesti, F., Rossolini, G., Nair, S., Biondi, A., Buttazzo, G.: Evaluating the robustness of semantic segmentation for autonomous driving against real-world adversarial patch attacks. In: 2022 IEEE/CVF Winter Conference on Applications of Computer Vision (WACV), pp. 2826–2835. IEEE, Waikoloa (2022)
10. Pan, H., Hong, Y., Sun, W., Jia, Y.: Deep dual-resolution networks for real-time and accurate semantic segmentation of traffic scenes. IEEE Trans. Intell. Transp. Syst. (2022)
11. Schwonberg, M., et al.: Survey on unsupervised domain adaptation for semantic segmentation for visual perception in automated driving. IEEE Access **11**, 54296–54336 (2023)
12. Suryanto, N., et al.: ACTIVE: towards highly transferable 3D physical camouflage for universal and robust vehicle evasion. In: Proceedings of the IEEE/CVF International Conference on Computer Vision (ICCV), pp. 4305–4314 (2023)
13. Wang, D., Yao, W., Jiang, T., Tang, G., Chen, X.: A survey on physical adversarial attack in computer vision (2023)
14. Watson, J., Aodha, O.M., Prisacariu, V., Brostow, G., Firman, M.: The temporal opportunist: self-supervised multi-frame monocular depth (2021)
15. Watson, J., Firman, M., Brostow, G.J., Turmukhambetov, D.: Self-supervised monocular depth hints (2019)
16. Yamanaka, K., Matsumoto, R., Takahashi, K., Fujii, T.: Adversarial patch attacks on monocular depth estimation networks. IEEE Access **8**, 179094–179104 (2020)
17. Yatsura, M., Sakmann, K., Hua, N.G., Hein, M., Metzen, J.H.: Certified defences against adversarial patch attacks on semantic segmentation. In: The Eleventh International Conference on Learning Representations (2023)
18. Zhao, H., Qi, X., Shen, X., Shi, J., Jia, J.: ICNet for real-time semantic segmentation on high-resolution images. In: Ferrari, V., Hebert, M., Sminchisescu, C., Weiss, Y. (eds.) Computer Vision - ECCV 2018, vol. 11207, pp. 418–434. Springer International Publishing, Cham (2018)
19. Zhao, H., Shi, J., Qi, X., Wang, X., Jia, J.: Pyramid scene parsing network. In: 2017 IEEE Conference on Computer Vision and Pattern Recognition (CVPR), pp. 6230–6239. IEEE, Honolulu (2017)

# Plotting OSS-Based Supply Chain Attack Strategies and the Defense Failure

Arpita Dinesh Sarang[1]⬤, Sang-Hoon Choi[2]⬤, and Ki-Woong Park[3]([⊠])⬤

[1] SysCore Lab, Department of Information Security, and Convergence Engineering for Intelligent Drone, Sejong University, Seoul 05006, South Korea
arpita.sarang@sju.ac.kr
[2] SysCore Lab, Sejong University, Seoul 05006, South Korea
[3] Department of Information Security, and Convergence Engineering for Intelligent Drone, Sejong University, Seoul 05006, South Korea
woongbak@sejong.ac.kr

**Abstract.** The supply chain attack, which targets open-source software, is currently the most discussed cyberattack. This is due to the recent open-source XZ utils and PyPI projects based attacks where the attackers employed similar strategies. A backdoor was injected in the libraries developed by these projects for future exploitation when software users installed them on systems. These attacks were executed by the trusted developers of these projects and influenced by unknown promoters. Therefore, there is a need to scrutinize Open Source Software (OSS) Security to protect the legacy of Open Software development for the future. This paper provides an overview of these two attack strategies through their case studies, which aid in the creation of a generic attack framework for supply chain attacks on OSS. We present the existing detection methods for OSS security in this work and their lacunas taking into account at various stages of a supply chain attack. This makes it necessary to build platforms that allow the current OSS security detection modules to be utilized in sequence. Therefore, we introduce an OSS security Detection platform that does not completely address the limitations of the detection technique, but when combined, they can maximize the effectiveness of an OSS security quality check.

**Keywords:** Supply Chain Attack · Linux distribution · Cyber Security · Supply Chain Attack as a Service (SCAaaS) · Open Source Software (OSS) Security · Software Bill of Materials (SBOM)

## 1 Introduction

A software-based supply chain attack is a cyber-attack that distributes software or its library with a backdoor that can exploit the critical data on systems they get installed on [1]. These backdoors are injected during the development process of the software or its library. They are induced by the developers with malicious intent so strategically that they remain undetected even after distribution. This cyber-attack has been in action since the first "Ken Thompson Hack" in 1984, which warned about the upcoming attacks through the great speech on" Reflections on Trusting Trust" [2]. Such attacks have been planned meticulously for many years and malicious code for them is induced periodically to the software. A global report highlighted that a total of 210,031 software packages were affected by supply chain attacks over the past two years [3]. The number of supply chain incidents on open-source software surged to 245,032 in 2023-a 178% increase from 2022 [4].

Open Source Software (OSS) is the potential target for the software-based supply chain attack. These software are widely consumed by the technical community due to the benefits they provide such as free license, customizability, availability, and so on. Also, the software developers take great interest in developing these software projects by contributing valuable suggestions through comments and code fixes on the software project development open discussions and support emails. The core project developers and maintainers consider the suggestions and notice the valuable contributions to OSS development. In this development process the core developer, maintainers or the developers outside the project comment or promote fixes cannot be trusted as they may have malicious intent. A little ignorance in evaluating development due to trust in these entities can lead to a Supply Chain Attack through OSS. An enhanced taxonomy for Open source software-based supply chain attacks (OSSCAs) that listed some affected vectors, include users, systems, project maintainers, and root nodes [5]. A multi-year social engineering initiative, the XZ Util attack on February 24, 2024 [6], and PyPI attack for extraction of the web browser and cryptocurrency data on March 29, 2024 were well-known OSS security breaches for the first half of the year. Due to the prolonged and organised nature of attacks, they are challenging to detect. Attackers typically introduce backdoors by embedding granular program blocks. By the time exploitation is discovered, it is often too late for the victims.

In this paper, we discuss the two famous OSS-based Supply Chain attacks i.e., the XZ Util and the PyPI Project attack with relevant case studies. These recent attacks on the OSS supply chain allowed us to study their attack strategies closely and draw a generic attack framework for OSS-based Supply Chain Attacks. With the advantage of this attack framework built based on the current attack strategies, we were motivated to study the existing OSS security mechanisms for the detection and their lacunas for such attacks. This assists in understanding why these existing defense mechanisms failed and where is the necessity for upgrade them.

The remainder of this paper is as follows: Sect. 2, provide insight based on previous detection techniques for OSS based Supply Chain Attack. Section 3, describe the OSS-based Supply Chain Attacks in detailed case studies. Section 4, conveys the Generic framework based recent attacks. Section 5, discusses the prevention and detection strategies and their lackings. Finally, Sect. 6, concludes our Learnings and future works.

## 2   Related Work

OSS projects are the most targeted entity for the software-based supply chain attack. Developers are welcomed to the software development environment of these projects based on their development skills, not their good or bad intentions. This allows the malware developer to participate in the development process easily. This is a cyber-security challenge that OSS development projects began to face due to rising supply chain attacks. This victimizes all the OSS users trusting and utilizing the software. When it comes to OSS the well-known ones are downloaded from trusted sites as they are free and can be more customised to use. For studies conducted on OSS security. Detection of supply chain attacks on such software needs to be reviewed thoroughly.

**Table 1.** OSS Supply Chain Attack Detection Techniques

| Related Work | Technique Type | Limitations |
|---|---|---|
| [16] | Query-based detection | It is dependent on source data integrity, normal queries with malicious arguments will be ignored, cannot detect the behavior of queries outside database |
| [17,18] | Library-based detection | Some resource might ignore the less vulnerable packages |
| [19–22] | Vulnerability-based detection | It can prove a package to be less vulnerable due to low vulnerability detected when compared with datasets available even though it is critically malicious |
| [23] | Combination of different detection modules | Combining different modules for detection makes this technique type accurate can differ, third party contracts for different applications are risky due to delayed updates |
| [24,25] | Third party based detection | It depends on application detection capability and compatibility with OSS not causing delays |
| [26–28] | Stakeholder-based detection | It is a quality analysis therefore, cannot be measured and trusted |
| [29] | Network-based detection | This detection fails detect malicious packets when network traffic use encryption techniques, or the malicious traffic trigger not passed |

Table 1 summarizes the types of detection techniques introduced by the previous study. These studies have limitations and can fail in cases mentioned in Sect. 3. The Detection techniques are based on various aspects of the OSS code as discussed. The Query-based detection type performs a scan on OSS code

for malicious queries and performs a match malicious query database [16]. In
[17] and [18], the library-based detection type scan the OSS project dependency
libraries if they are outdated or malicious. Whereas, in [14,19,20] and [22] the
Vulnerability-based detection type detects and matches with the Vulnerability
database for flaws in OSS. For, instance SBOM is majorly consumed by vulnerability assessment tools. These three types of detection techniques depend
majorly on data resource integrity. In [23], combination of different detection
module types is to combine different detection tools available for attack-based
malware detection. Third-party-based detection in [24,25] is implementing the
monitoring, protocol-based authentication techniques for security of OSS project
development. While the Stakeholder-based detection in [28] is trying the detect
the developer's intentions in the project. The Network-based detection in [29]
of malicious packages or activity during network communication with other
resources. Due to unpredictable patterns and the non-generalized design of Supply chain attacks, the detection techniques are not well defined. They depend
on previous attack analysis outcomes and fail to detect new attacks that are
polymorphic in nature and should be detected before distribution of the OSS
stage.

## 3    Case Studies

We conducted these case studies based on various analysis and resources to
outline their attack strategies.

### 3.1    XZ Utils Project Attack

**XZ Utils Project (Backdoor Target):** In 2005, Lasse Collin launched
Project LZMA Utils with a small team of engineers. The goal of the project
was to create a library for data compression that would support the Linux operating system. This library uses the Lempel-Ziv-Markov chain algorithm (LZMA)
for compression and decompression. The xz and lzma file formats can be compressed and decompressed using it. Other software also utilised this library to
compress data. Later on, the project became known as XZ utils. Many developers and programming experts contributed to this project, since it's open source,
by offering their insightful comments and useful code snippets. Lasse Collins had
the authority to approve and merge the code blocks to the project since he was
its primary developer and maintainer. Under Lasse Collin's guidance, several
iterations of the XZ Utils were introduced throughout the year. These included
the compromised versions 5.6.1, which was issued on March 9, 2024, and 5.6.0,
which was released on February 24, 2024 [8]. The malicious file was present in
these version's release tarballs. Through this version's backdoor, an attacker can
command the system of the victim with administrator rights. Version 5.4.6 is
presently the most stable version of this project that is available.

**Malicious Actors:** For years, a number of players worked their part to create this backdoor in the data compression library of the Linux distribution. Some made significant contributions by changing code blocks. While others applied pressure to have the backdoor code added. In this analysis, we attempt to arrange the attack's chronology in order to obtain the event sequence for the supply chain attack carried out on the Linux distribution's XZ Utils project. Major elements of this attack are contributed by the attack contributors mentioned above. We draw a timeline for the attack events (see Fig. 1).

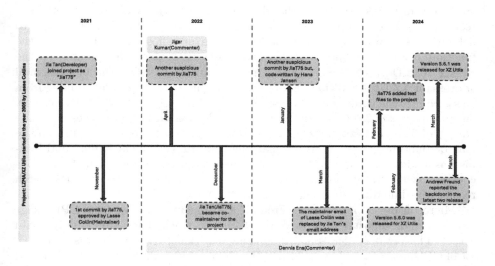

**Fig. 1.** Attack activity timeline for XZ Utils project

Jia Tan (with developer ID JiaT75) joined the XZ Utils project in 2021 and had a significant role in creating this backdoor for supply chain attacks in the XZ Utils library [9]. He provided Lasse Collin with various code blocks for XZ Util development that contained ignorant or obfuscated malicious code that initially was approved and integrated into the main project. Everything maintained on GitHub, including the "xz.tukaani.org" subdomain, was accessible to him. Lasse Collin was the only one with access to the main "tukaani.org" page [10]. JiaTan contributed a number of code blocks to the error-fixing and update of the XZ util project. In November 2021, JiaT75's first commit to xz utils was accepted and merged by Lasse Collin. There was a suspicious code edit in this commit that altered the secure "safe_fprintf()" to the "fprintf()" that code_1 indicated. This was done by employing an insecure function to perform a format string attack. An attacker may run arbitrary programs on the server, read variables off the stack, and cause segmentation faults or application crashes if they supply a format string made up of "fprintf()" conversion characters like %f, %p, %n, etc. as parameter values.

Later, JiaT75 contributed a second suspicious commit to XZ Utils in code_2 in April 2022. The code that ignored the memory and CPU use indication was hardware-related. This was done with the goal of not notifying XZ Util's consumers about any CPU or memory-related issues. By December 2022, Lasse Collin designated JiaT75 as a reliable co-maintainer for the XZ util project. JiaT75 committed a third controversial code commit on January 7, 2023. The code block that was merged was originally composed by Hans Jansen, another developer, rather than JiaT75. This commit carried out an IFUNC()-based exploit using glibc. In order to safeguard the offset tables and procedure linkage tables, the glibc feature known as IFUNC (GNU indirect function) acts as a resolver, helping to replace the function addresses to default at startup. Since these tables can be modified at startup time, the function from the external library was used to replace the pointer to the RSA_Public_Decrypt. JiaT75 gained greater authority when the official email address for XZ Utils code for component testing infrastructure was updated from "lasse.collin@tukaani.org" to "jiat0218@gmail.com" in March 2023. Eventually, on February 23, 2024, he added the test files "good-large_compressed.lzma" and "bad-3-corrupt_lzma2.xz". These two malicious files are executed when the macro "build-to-host.m4". Additional small contributors Jigar Kumar and Dennis Ens made contributions to the project by pressuring the inclusion of malicious code as essential functionality and by causing pointless conflicts with the patch release schedule during the years 2022 to 2024 [11].

Microsoft developer "Andres Freund"'s suspicion on the unusual CPU usage patterns and Valgrind failures enabled him to track down this supply chain attack. This curious Microsoft engineer saw that the SSHD process was utilising a lot of CPU power, which was causing the Debian Linux distribution's SSH-based login to function slowly. This gave Andres the opportunity to investigate the reason for the delay, conduct the necessary analysis based on his expertise, and report the issue to the relevant Linux distribution authorities i.e., oss-security via mail on 29 March 2024 [7]. He notified them with the high-level dynamics of the attack that he had discovered during his analytical process. He discovered that the XZ utils package contained a backdoor committed to the open source linux distribution package code. The backdoor was archived in the download package known as the tarballs and targeted the x86-64 linux.

### 3.2 PyPI Project Attack

**Pytoileur (Backdoor Target):** The supply chain attack's target programme is the PYPI project and its users, through introducing the package pytoileur. The purpose of this package is to automate and manage tasks in Python projects. It mostly automates the work of repetitive development. By offering a streamlined workflow for routine operations like configuring development environments, handling dependencies, and conducting tests, it improves productivity. Include linting and testing tools in your code to guarantee quality. Automate the deployment procedures. This package was actually trojonised with malicious code. That targeted at the user's crypto-based application data and web browser data.

**Malicious Actors:** On May 25, 2024, a developer named "PhilipsPY" joined the PYPI (Python Package Index) project. PYPI is an open source library that allows Python developers to reuse code; there are a lot of packages available for download and installation. He uploaded the malicious code-encoded in Pytoileur package. After joining the open community discussion on stackoverflow, "EstAYA G" (promoter) began responding to other users' questions about Python development. By responding to questions on stackoverflow, he promoted the installation of the pytoileur package as solution to their problems.

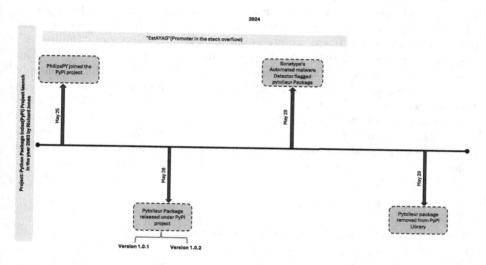

**Fig. 2.** Attack activity timeline for PyPI project

The Project PYPI, included a package Pytoileur version 1.0.1 and version 1.0.2. This package was published on the same day by the author PhilipsPy in the PYPI library on 28 May 2024. We draw a timeline for the attack events (see Fig. 2). It had a total number of 264 downloads This package setup.py included a hidden malicous code. In its metadata, the package calls itself a "Cool package." The HTML webpage description refers to the package as a "API Management tool written in Python." The package is also trying to typosquat users of legitimate packages like "Pyston," as evidenced by the code's reference to "pystob," a now-defunct package (more on that later). The setup.py was injected with whitespaces after the print() statement in its code which can be avoided by the text editors those use the wordwrap. The whitespaces actually was hiding the code that executed the base64-encoded that connected to the remote server. Its payload stated that it connected "http: 51.11.140.144:8086/dl/runtime". Connecting to this external server it retrieved the windows binary called "runtime.exe". This file was undetected by the file scanning software and firewall. The "runtime.exe" was executed using the powershell and vbscript of the system. Once the execution of the "runtime.exe" is performed it dropped more suspicious file that modify the windows registry settings and deploy harmful payloads. This leads to the execution of the main.exe file which gathers information from the web browsers and the crypto currency services. webbrowsers such as Brave, firefox, google etc. and well known crypto currency services such as the Coinbase, Binance, Paysafecard, crypto.com, exodus etc. data were retrieved by this execution. Sonatype's automated malware detection engine for sonatype repository firewall detected and flagged the pytoileur package in PYPI repository on 28 May 2024. The Sonatype security researcher Jeff Thornhill noticed the line 17 whitespaces in the setup.py of the pytoileur package was hiding a code. This allowed him to further analyse this backdoor and track the issue as "SONATYPE-2024-1783" [12]. Later raised an alert to the PYPI admins and declared it a software based supply chain attack. The developer "PhilipsPY" and the promoter ID "EstAYA G" for pytoileur package were discontinued from development community [13]. Sonatype is a business that specialises in supply chain management software. The Sonatype company's automatic malware detection tool was one of their tools that assisted us in finding the backdoor in the earlier mentioned Python programme. This business develops tools and services for identification and the fixing of vulnerabilities in OSS with a focus on security of the OSS's weakness and danger. They support the creation of software security policies. They encourage community engagement and tool enhancement.

## 4    Generic Framework

These days, supply chain attacks based on software have become commodified. On the dark web, configurations, and portions of code for exploiting software vulnerabilities during development are offered for sale. This commodification is majorly known as a Supply chain attack as a service (SCAaaS). Since supply chain attacks are becoming more accessible and commercialized, they can be easily replicated by targeting software development environments and taking advantage of the update process. Software libraries, pirated or open-source development tools, and their distribution networks are its primary targets. As a result, the frequency of attacks increased, having a widespread impact and making the process of detection and attribution more difficult. Based on the case studies this is a preliminary analysis.

**Fig. 3.** OSS-based Supply Chain Attack strategy

There are two primary objectives of a supply chain attack: embed malicious code into software and to promote its use and distribution. As a result, there are two types of criminals involved in a supply chain attack: those who create and insert malicious code and those who promote or encourage on download of software that contains harmful code. These attackers work together to gain access to the target software project, deploy the backdoor code, encourage the software distribution of that project that includes the backdoor and finally exploit the backdoor to gain access to the system and the data (as shown in Fig. 3).

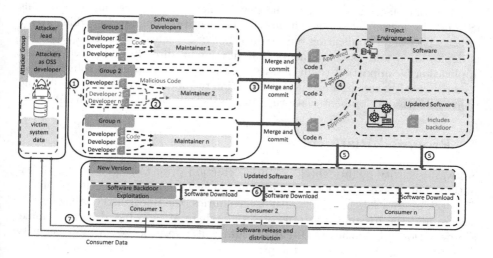

**Fig. 4.** OSS-based Supply Chain Attack framework

We provide a generic architecture for supply chain attacks that are OSS-based (see Fig. 4). This figure clarifies the trade-off that exists between the attacker, the vulnerability, and the exploitation of it. The attacking group's developers attempt to get associated with one of the targeted software's core development projects. The malicious developers begin injecting malicious code into the program's code as soon as they have access to it as authorized developers. The malicious code can be an argument, single-line code or a dependent executable file. To prevent being discovered, this code has been encoded or obfuscated. It is also possible to hide or remove logs produced by this type of programming. During development, the attacker group's developer deactivates alerts for administrative commands, memory utilization, or intrusion detectors. This is accomplished over a longer period by gradually incorporating the malicious code while remaining undetected by other legitimate developers or maintenance leads. Even if any potentially harmful code is discovered, the promoters defend it so well that others are led to believe that the code is necessary and urgent for the project. Since the maintainer or project lead must take the demands of the public into account, they approve the code because they think the developer is legitimate and has good intentions. Once the code is deployed into the software with all its dependencies satisfied, it becomes a backdoor for that software. Later when the software is released by the project authors on their official websites. The promoters working with the malicious developer and team initiate discussions suggesting to download and install the software as solution for most of the queries of users. The users of the OSS then start downloading and installing the dependent packages or software. Finally, when the package or the software is in use the injected backdoor gets executed on the user's system. This backdoor allows exploitation of user data by exposing it to the attacker groups.

To avoid OSS-based attacks, the development of software bill of materials (SBOM) for instance has made it possible to identify dependencies, which aren't directly part of an application but are installed or launched when the application is deployed as well as components that developers directly integrated into an application by importing them into its source code as a potential solution [15]. As a result, after researching current detection techniques, we suggest combining their use with development platforms during the software development lifecycle.

## 5   Proposed Platform

Software security quality checks require detection prior to OSS software distribution. This makes the OSS development Lifecycle require a Security platform. The lack of data labeling for malicious semantics, the uncertainty of the attack design, and the irregular patterns of supply chain attacks based on OSS make the detection approaches in Table 1 insufficient. We propose an OSS Security Quality testing platform using the prior study-based detection approach type in Table 5. This platform will provide software is secure quality tests based on all the detection approaches based on current standards by incorporating the best modules available. Module 1, The Stakeholder-based detection provides their rightful intent, background verifications, and control. Module 2, Third-party-based detection allows authentication, and control privileges and monitors the

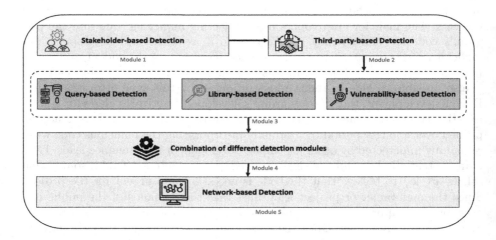

**Fig. 5.** OSS-Security Quality testing Platform

stakeholder's activity once they are part of the project. Module 3, is a combination of three different detection approaches Query-based, Library-based, and Vulnerability-based detection as they all focus on OSS semantics, dependency, and logic. After Semantic and logic check the OSS should go through Module 4, Combinations of different detection modules based on components of the OSS. For instance, if the OSS Utilizes outside resources the connectivity, data transfer and infrastructures should be analyzed well with security tools that are developed resource-based for security. Finally, Module 5, Network-based detection, scans for malicious package exchange by providing different combinations of benign and malicious parameters.

By using the OSS-Security Quality Testing Platform with the best detection techniques for each module, OSS development, and utilization, organizations can improve the security of their software and systems and increase their capacity for identifying and thwarting supply chain attacks on OSS.

## 6    Conclusion

The XZ Utils and PyPI Project attacks were multiyear strategized attacks. They followed the common attack strategy. This motivated us to create the Generic framework for the OSS-based Supply Chain Attack. These attacks remained undetected throughout the development and release process of the packages. The study detection strategies during the development process and after the release of the software is crucial which assisted us in finding the lacunas in these defences. The most critical lacuna for this strategy is ignorance based on trust. Protocols and Standards should be followed strictly to reduce the possibility of such attacks. Our proposed OSS Security Quality Testing platform is an attempt towards securing OSS. For Future works we plan to propose more detailed combinations of the modules in the platform and its feasibility as potential solution for OSS Security.

**Acknowledgment.** This work was supported by the Institute of Information & Communications Technology Planning & Evaluation (IITP) (Project No. 2022-0-00701, 10%; Project No. RS-2023-00228996, 10%, Project No. RS-2022-00165794, 10%), the ICT R&D Program of MSIT/IITP (Project No. 2021-0-01816, 10%), and a National Research Foundation of Korea (NRF) grant funded by the Korean Government (Project No. RS2023-00208460, 60%).

## References

1. Ladisa, P., Plate, H., Martinez, M., Barais, O.: Taxonomy of attacks on open-source software supply chains. arXiv preprint arXiv:2204.04008 (2022)
2. Thompson, K.: Reflections on trusting trust. Commun. ACM **27**(8), 761–3 (1984)
3. Statista Homepage. https://www.statista.com/statistics/1375128/supply-chain-attacks-software-packages-affected-global/
4. Statista Homepage. https://www.statista.com/statistics/1268934/worldwide-open-source-supply-chain-attacks/

5. Ladisa, P., Plate, H., Martinez, M., Barais, O.: SoK: taxonomy of attacks on open-source software supply chains. In: 2023 IEEE Symposium on Security and Privacy (SP), pp. 1509–1526. IEEE (2023)
6. Seah, J.: Sliced cables and cyber-attacks: how safe is our internet? News Weekly **3164**, 22–3 (2024)
7. Openwall Homepage. https://www.openwall.com/lists/oss-security/2024/03/29/4
8. Security Week: Supply Chain Attack: Major Linux Distributions Impacted by XZ Utils Backdoor. https://www.securityweek.com/supply-chain-attack-major-linux-distributions-impacted-by-xz-utils-backdoor/
9. Lins, M., Mayrhofer, R., Roland, M., Hofer, D., Schwaighofer, M.: On the critical path to implant backdoors and the effectiveness of potential mitigation techniques: early learnings from XZ. arXiv preprint arXiv:2404.08987 (2024)
10. The Tukaani Project. https://tukaani.org/xz-backdoor/
11. Evan Boehs. https://boehs.org/node/everything-i-know-about-the-xz-backdoor
12. Sonatype. https://www.sonatype.com/blog/pypi-crypto-stealer-targets-windows-users-revives-malware-campaign
13. Black Hat Ethical Hacking. https://www.blackhatethicalhacking.com/news/
14. SNYK Security Database. https://security.snyk.io
15. America's Cyber Defense Agency. https://www.cisa.gov/sbom
16. Andreoli, A., Lounis, A., Debbabi, M., Hanna, A.: On the prevalence of software supply chain attacks: empirical study and investigative framework. Forensic Sci. Int. Digit. Invest. **1**(44), 301508 (2023)
17. Malka, J.: Increasing trust in the open source supply chain with reproducible builds and functional package management. In: 46th International Conference on Software Engineering (ICSE 2024)-Doctoral Symposium (DS) Track (2024)
18. Nahum, M., et al.: Ossintegrity: Collaborative Open Source Code Integrity Verification. Available at SSRN 4711134
19. Singla, T., Anandayuvaraj, D., Kalu, K.G., Schorlemmer, T.R., Davis, J.C.: An empirical study on using large language models to analyze software supply chain security failures. In: Proceedings of the 2023 Workshop on Software Supply Chain Offensive Research and Ecosystem Defenses, pp. 5–15 (2023)
20. O'Donoghue, E., Reinhold, A.M., Izurieta, C.: Assessing security risks of software supply chains using software bill of materials. In: 2nd International Workshop on Mining Software Repositories for Privacy and Security, MSR4P&S (SANER 2024), Rovaniemi, Finland (2024)
21. Haque, B.M.: An Analysis of SBOM in the Context of Software Supply-chain Risk Management (Master's thesis)
22. Mirakhorli, M., et al.: A Landscape Study of Open Source and Proprietary Tools for Software Bill of Materials (SBOM). arXiv preprint arXiv:2402.11151 (2024)
23. Gokkaya, B., Karafili, E., Aniello, L., Halak, B.: Global supply chains security: a comparative analysis of emerging threats and traceability solutions. Benchmarking Int. J. (2024)
24. Younis, A.A., Hu, Y., Abdunabi, R.: Analyzing software supply chain security risks in industrial control system protocols: an OpenSSF scorecard approach. In: 2023 10th International Conference on Dependable Systems and Their Applications (DSA), pp. 302–311. IEEE (2023)
25. Nygård, A.R., Katsikas, S.K.: Ethical hardware reverse engineering for securing the digital supply chain in critical infrastructure. Inf. Comput. Secur. (2024)
26. Vashisth, M., Verma, S.K.: State of the art different security challenges, solutions on supply chain: a review. In: 2023 International Conference on Innovative

Data Communication Technologies and Application (ICIDCA), pp. 427–431. IEEE (2023)

27. Turksonmez, H., Ozcanhan, M.H.: Enhancing security of RFID-enabled IoT supply chain. Malays. J. Comput. Sci. **36**(3), 289–307 (2023)

28. Boughton, L., Miller, C., Acar, Y., Wermke, D., Kästner, C.: Decomposing and measuring trust in open-source software supply chains. In: Proceedings of the 2024 ACM/IEEE 44th International Conference on Software Engineering: New Ideas and Emerging Results, pp. 57–61 (2024)

29. Chauhdary, S.H., Alkatheiri, M.S., Alqarni, M.A., Saleem, S.: An efficient evolutionary deep learning-based attack prediction in supply chain management systems. Comput. Electr. Eng. **1**(109), 108768 (2023)

# A Proposal of a Supply Chain Security Model for Generative AI

Keun Young Lee[1]([✉]) and Jiyeon Yoo[2]

[1] Financial Security Institute, 143 Uisadang-Daero, Yeongdeungpo-Gu, Seoul,
Republic of Korea
kylee@fsec.or.kr
[2] Sangmyung University, 20 Hongjimun 2-Gil, Jongrogu, Seoul, Republic of Korea
yooo@smu.ac.kr

**Abstract.** As technology continues to evolve and integrate into every aspect of our lives, effective technology management is becoming increasingly critical. Among the latest significant topics in this field is supply chain security management. The growing complexity of technology and the expansion of open-source platforms, cloud services, and other technologies have amplified the roles and authorizations of various third parties involved in the technology supply chain. This has led to a rise in supply chain attacks leveraging these third parties, as such attacks are relatively accessible for attackers and highly efficient; a single successful attack can compromise similar systems.

Generative AI systems are particularly vulnerable to supply chain attacks due to their complex and interconnected nature. These systems comprise various elements such as data, models, and infrastructure that continuously evolve, forming a dynamic system ecosystem. As a result, compromising even a minor component of the generative AI system ecosystem can jeopardize the entire system.

In this paper, we emphasize the importance of supply chain security for generative AI. We define supply chain security for generative AI through an analysis of the structure of these systems and propose a security model for managing supply chain security. This model is based on a comprehensive examination of major security standards and guidelines related to generative AI.

We conceptualize generative AI supply chain security as the implementation of strategies, processes, and controls to secure the entire lifecycle of a generative AI system—from source, design, and development to deployment and maintenance. Our aim is to protect data preprocessing, source code, learning algorithms, third-party libraries, and related components such as prompts and infrastructure from potential vulnerabilities, threats, and attacks. This includes securing the AI system development process, ensuring the reliability of service providers, and implementing continuous surveillance and vulnerability management techniques, and more.

**Keywords:** AI(Artificial Intelligence) · Generative AI · Adversarial Machine Learning · AI Security · Cyber Supply Chain Security

# 1  Instruction

Starting with the launch of ChatGPT (Generative Pre-trained Transformer) ( '22.10), the spread and development of many services based on generative AI, including the launch of various Large Language Models (LLM) mainly by overseas big tech companies, With the popularization of AI, it is having a significant impact on our way of life.

Generative AI has the characteristics of collecting large amounts of data, training through this, and creating text, images, codes, and videos, but reliability and safety issues, hallucinations, jailbreaks, and deepfakes that arise from the use of the algorithm. Concerns about the adverse effects of generative AI, including social and ethical issues, are increasing. The World Economic Forum (WEF, '23.1.) report mentioned both the advantages and risks of generative AI, and stated that the impact of this technology must be carefully managed [1].

Recently, security researchers on the Huntr bug bounty platform discovered important vulnerabilities in famous platforms such as Hugging Face, MLflow, and ClearML, raising concerns about the security of AI solutions used in various industries [2]. This vulnerability can manipulate data sets through remote code execution and read sensitive files, which can pose a serious risk to the entire service. The uses of generative AI are diverse, including publicly generative AI applications and web services, publicly generative AI APIs, cloud solutions, and in-house development. In general, the resources of AI systems are highly dependent on third-party IT infrastructure and data supply chain. In these cases, the data cannot be easily controlled, and tracking the data being used in the model is also very difficult. And vulnerabilities in supply resources can lead not only to the integrity of training data, models, and deployment platforms, but also to biased results in AI model training, security breaches, or even overall system failures. As such, supply chain security, including potential risks related to various suppliers related to AI systems, their data, and the processing of data, is very important.

In terms of the learning and creativity characteristics of generative AI, generative AI systems create models through collecting and learning a large amount of data from unverified sources such as the Internet, and products utilizing the algorithm may have problems with bias and errors inherited from pre-learned data. This can lead to reliability and safety issues in AI systems. Therefore, the security risks of generative AI begin with data and occur during each step of the model improvement process, such as the use of the foundation model and fine tuning, as well as distribution and operation. There is a need for discussion on ways to strengthen risk management.

Accordingly, in order to strengthen the security of generative AI, specific security considerations are required throughout the data and models that make up the generative AI system, as well as the resources, design, development, deployment, operation, and management processes. In this paper, we conceptualize how to define supply chain security for generative AI and propose a security model for generative AI for supply chain security management through analysis of major security standards and guidelines related to generative AI. Through this model, we present specific security considerations to strengthen the security of generative AI.

## 2  Theoretical Background

### 2.1  Concept and Structure of Generative AI

Generative AI is a subset of AI consisting of a model that can generate new content by responding to prompts based on training data [3]. The representative model of generative AI is the foundation model, a concept that first appeared in a Stanford University paper [4]. It is a general-purpose AI model that is pre-trained on a wide range of datasets and can be applied to various use cases, including Transformer Model, LLM, diffusion model, etc. It was analyzed that neural networks constitute an important category called foundation models. Generative AI models are largely divided into foundation models that use pre-trained models as is, and fine-tuned models such as fine tuning, which trains again and adjusts pre-trained models for new data sets, depending on the data training method.

### 2.2  Concept and Structure of ICT Supply Chain Security

As ICT (Information and Communication Technology) is applied to the supply chain and interconnectivity increases in the hyper-connected era, the supply chain is becoming more complex. As the resources and service providers required when building a system in a company are complexly connected, security management becomes more difficult and important in the process of outsourcing and re-entrusting the design, development, production, operation, maintenance, and disposal of products and services.

According to NIST SP 800-161r1 [5], supply chain elements include organizations, entities, and tools used in the research and design, development, manufacture, purchase, distribution, integration, operation, and maintenance or disposal of systems and components. A supply chain refers to a set of resources and processes linked between multiple levels of an enterprise, each beginning with the sourcing of products and services and extending through the product and service life cycle. Supply chain-wide cybersecurity risk refers to the potential for damage or damage to a supplier, its supply chain, products or services.

## 3  Supply Chain Security Model of Generative AI

### 3.1  Supply Chain Security Issues and Components of Generative AI

We derived four major issues that should be considered in the supply chain security of generative AI and the most important components of the generative AI supply chain security model.

First, as an issue of generative AI supply chain security, it is necessary to consider generative AI security at the supply chain level.

In the ICT supply chain, the share of open-source software in recent software development is rapidly increasing, so to ensure transparency and reliability of the SW supply chain, we focus on SW components, create A software bill of materials (SBOM) at each stage of the SW supply chain, and build on this. Ways to build a SW supply chain security management system are being explored. SBOM declares the inventory of components used to build a software artifact such as a software application. The U.S. National Telecommunications and Information Administration (NTIA) It was announced [6] that as the minimum SBOM components, the data fields must include seven items: Supplier Name, Component Name, Version of Component, Other Unique IDs, Dependency Relationship, Author of SBOM Data, and Timestamp. The components of the ICT supply chain include hardware, operating systems, commercial software, binaries, intellectual property rights, embedded software, and open-source software, etc., so it is important to secure visibility based on the characteristics of each component, which is important throughout the entire supply chain process. It must be controlled and managed. The supply chain of generative AI includes the resources, technologies, and other elements involved in the process of developing and maintaining products and services. As generative AI providers may seek to integrate software, data, models and/or remote services provided by third parties into their own systems, traceability of the resources that make up the system becomes more difficult. The recent emergence of various open source-based LLMs and their increased use, as well as the high dependence of resources forming AI systems on third-party IT infrastructure and data supply chains, are forming an increasingly complex supply chain. Therefore, considering the characteristics of open-source models and high data dependency compared to existing software, we must consider strategies, processes, and controls for security management in the complex supply chain of generative AI.

Second, technical security issues must be considered from the perspective of generative AI operating principles.

Data selection and curation are essential to developing and deploying trustworthy generative AI models. Because models may reproduce inaccurate or incorrect information in the training data, it is also important for model developers to consider the representativeness or accuracy of the data in the dataset and to assess whether the data contains personal information or bias [3]. Training data poisoning is a problem that occurs across AI, but in generative AI, training data can be supplied from a variety of sources that can be difficult to control, such as the Internet, making it more vulnerable to such attacks, and external training data published on the Internet. There is a risk that bias may be inherited or lead to sensitive training data output. In addition, generative AI models that use foundation models as they are or undergo fine-tuning may be at increased risk of such attacks through the use of transfer learning, a model optimization method that uses a pre-learned AI model for one task and applies it to other similar problems when the pre-learned model is manipulated. Therefore, generative AI has the main characteristic of starting from data and having a training stage of the model, and technical security issues that arise during this process must be considered.

Third, it is necessary to consider generative AI risk issues according to the training process.

OWASP presents the top 10 vulnerabilities of LLM applications, including Prompt Injection, which manipulates LLM through crafted input to execute the attacker's intention; Supply Chain Vulnerabilities, which compromise the security of the model, training data, and ML models and deployment platforms, causing biased results, security breaches, or complete system failures; and Insecure Plugin Design, which causes harmful results such as data leakage, remote code execution, and privilege escalation due to insufficient access control and improper input validation [7]. Generative AI is vulnerable to a variety of attacks and is segmented into the three most common AI-related attacks: poisoning attacks, evasion attacks, and privacy attacks [8]. Abuse attacks of generative AI systems include attacks that involve hate speech, promoting discrimination, and specific attacks. Images, text, or malicious code, such as inciting group violence, are created and used for attacks. Adversarial Attack [9], a major type of AI attack, is an attack using adversarial examples that causes the AI model to produce incorrect results by adding small-sized perturbations to the data that cannot be distinguished with the naked eye. Types of hostile attacks are divided into Poisoning Attack, Evasion Attack, and Exploratory Attack. Representative examples of Exploratory Attack include Model Inversion, Membership Inference, and Model Extraction via APIs [10]. The main attack details are as shown in Table 1.

**Table 1.** Adversarial Attack Types of Generative AI Risks.

| category | Main Content |
|---|---|
| Poisoning Attack | • During the training phase, an attacker changes the data or model to cause the AI algorithm to malfunction [11]<br>• The attack goal is to cause maximum malfunction by using poison data, which is malicious data that is trained to lead to incorrect results of the training model [12] |
| Evasion Attack | • An attacker interferes with the normal operation of the model by causing a small perturbation to the input data of the trained AI model [10, 12]<br>• It is an attack that deceives AI by manipulating input data at the application stage after training, and has a wide range of applications [10, 12] |
| Model Inversion | • An attack that leaks input values from the output values of the AI model [11–13] |
| Membership Inference Attack | • The attacker infers whether the data he or she has is used to train the AI model [11–13] |
| Model Extraction Attack | • An attack in which the attacker repeatedly queries the AI model to extract the entire model based on the input and output values [14] |

Poisoning attacks occur during the training stage, and evasion attacks and model inversions occur during the utilization stage after training is completed [11, 13]. The attacks in Table 1 do not occur only at specific stages of the AI lifecycle, but occur at multiple stages. It can appear throughout.

Generative AI risks continue to develop into various types of attacks, such as using Adversarial Machine Learning to intervene in the training and inference process to produce unintended results or to bias certain results.

Attacks based on the training stage of the generative AI system, including the pre-training stage of the foundation model and the fine-tuning stage of the AI model, can be classified into ① Training-time Attack and ② Inference-time Attack [15]. In the case of training time attacks, the foundation model is vulnerable to poisoning attacks where the attacker controls a subset of the training data, usually by scraping data from public sources. During the AI model fine-tuning stage, it may be vulnerable to poisoning attacks depending on the attacker's knowledge and capabilities. In the case of inference time attacks, LLM and RAG (Retrieval-Augmented Generation) applications do not provide separate channels for data and instructions, so inference time attacks using data channels are possible.

Therefore, Adversarial Machine Learning continues to develop into various types of attacks, such as interfering in the training and reasoning process to produce unintended results or biased adjustments to specific results, making it possible to mitigate generative AI risks that occur at each stage of the machine learning process. A solution is needed.

Fourth, specific technical and managerial security considerations are needed throughout the supply chain of generative AI.

Research on real-world security vulnerabilities for machine learning suggests that security is best addressed comprehensively, including software, data and model supply chains, networks, and storage systems [15]. The supply chain is vulnerable and can impact the integrity of training data, machine learning models, and deployment platforms. These vulnerabilities can lead to biased results, security breaches, or complete system failures. Machine learning is expanded through pre-trained models and training data provided by third parties, which are vulnerable to tampering and poisoning attacks [7]. Due to this scalability, if connected to a vulnerable service, risks of internal information leakage and model malfunction may occur, so generative AI supply chain security must be considered throughout the system.

OECD (oecd.ai) presented five comprehensive basic principles (① Inclusive and sustainable growth and well-being ② Human rights and democratic values, including fairness and privacy ③ Transparency and Explainability ④ Robustness, Security and Safety ⑤ Accountability) for trustworthy AI in the "AI Recommendation ('19.5.)" unanimously adopted by member countries through national AI policy analysis, and traditional Security considerations for AI systems were presented with a focus on declarative considerations, such as reviewing ethical issues to satisfy reliability requirements.

However, in order to secure the supply chain of generative AI, it is necessary to present specific security requirements for each core component regarding technical security issues, reflecting the structure and operating principles of the generative AI system as well as reliability requirements. Therefore, if some security threats in the generative AI supply chain are considered to have a ripple effect on the entire process, from the preparation of data required for training to the results returned when using the AI system, security issues should be considered at all stages rather than at specific processing stages.

Finally, the life cycle of a generative AI system compared to a traditional AI system of prediction and judgment is as shown in Table 2. When mapping the life cycle stages of a generative AI system to the dimensions of the system's main components, the technical elements of data, models, and systems, as well as the management elements of business understanding, risk management, governance, and compliance, are derived. In particular, the components called 'data' and 'model' are different from the SDLC

(Software Development Lifecycle) process of ISO/IEC 12207: Requirement Analysis → Design → Implement → Testing → Evolution. Therefore, it is important to apply security considerations to the main components that make up the generative AI system.

**Table 2.** The Main Components of a Generative AI System.

| Lifecycle of traditional AI systems | | | | Lifecycle of Generative AI systems | | Component | | |
|---|---|---|---|---|---|---|---|---|
| OECD[16][17] | | NIST (AI RMF 1.0) | EU ENISA[18] | | | Technical | | Manage |
| Planning and Design | | Planning and Design | Business Goals | Planning | | | | |
| Data Collection and Processing | De-sign, Data and Model | Data Collection and Processing | Data Collection | Data Collection and preparation | | → Data | | Understanding of business, Risk Management and Gorvernance, Compliance |
| | | | Data Exploration | | | | System | |
| | | | Data Preprocessing | Data management and operations | | | | |
| | | | Feature Selection | | | | | |
| Model Building and Use | | Model Building and Use | Model Selection and Build | Design and development | Model selection | Model | | |
| | | | Model Training | | Training and fine-tuning | | | |
| Verification and Validation | | Verification and Validation | Model Optimization | | | | | |
| | | | Model Application | | Inference and evaluation → | | | |
| Deployment | | Deployment and Use | Model Deployment | | | | | |
| Operation and Monitoring | | Operation and Monitoring | Model Maintenance | Operation and management | | | | |
| | | Use or Impact | Business Understanding | | | | | |

## 3.2  Supply Chain Security Framework of Generative AI

Supply chain security of generative AI can be defined as security involved in the process of supplying, designing, developing, modifying, deploying, and operating components, with data and models learned from data forming the generative AI system as core components. By considering the four security issues derived for generative AI supply chain security and analyzing the components of generative AI supply chain security, we will apply the generative AI supply chain security framework as follows.

First, in order to construct a supply chain security model for generative AI, some of the framework that applies the concept of supply chain elements such as systems and components and process steps for cybersecurity management are borrowed according to the definition of the ICT supply chain, but the supply chain of generative AI is Reflects security specialties.

The components of the generative AI supply chain are derived from mapping the generative AI lifecycle stages to the main component dimensions of the AI system, as shown in Table 2. The core components are technical (data, models, systems) and managerial (business understanding, risk management and governance, compliance) elements.

In the complex generative AI supply chain, security considerations are important to secure visibility based on the characteristics of the supply chain components, and as in ICT supply chain security, source and processing for each component that makes up the generative AI system for the entire AI system life cycle. Risks occurring at each stage of the process must be considered. For example, as the sharing and distribution of generative AI models becomes common, attackers can maliciously distribute or change AI models, and if developed using a modified model, it is possible to cause serious security problems for the entire AI system. Additionally, because AI systems evolve through data-based training, changes to AI models over time may require frequent maintenance and response to new risks. Accordingly, from the perspective of the operation principle of generative AI, technical security matters and generative AI security risk response measures according to the training process are reflected.

Therefore, the supply chain security model for generative AI should be created to include the process from source and design/development to distribution/operation management for the components of generative AI. Finally, we will present specific security considerations throughout the entire supply chain of generative AI through this model.

**Table 3.** Supply chain security model of generative AI.

| component | | Process | | |
|---|---|---|---|---|
| | | Source | Design and Development | Deployment and Operations Management |
| Technical | Data | • Data source and information [20, 24, 25, 27]<br>※ Example of a data card template: Data subject, source, version, privacy and security handling, collection method, appropriate/inappropriate use cases, etc<br>• Privacy and security [27]<br>• Maintaining supply chain integrity [15, 19, 27] | • Design of collection pipeline architecture [24, 27]<br>• Data minimization, personal and sensitive information processing [21, 24, 26, 27]<br>• Data preprocessing, removal of duplicate/similar data [21–24, 28] | • Data information documentation and management [24, 27]<br>• AI data privacy and security management [19, 21, 22, 27]<br>• Manage service-generated data [19, 21]<br>• Establish data leak prevention and security measures [22] |

(*continued*)

**Table 3.** (*continued*)

| component | Process | | |
|---|---|---|---|
| | Source | Design and Development | Deployment and Operations Management |
| Model | • Model source and information [25, 28]<br>✳ Example of a model card template: Model version, training data and methodology, performance metrics, privacy and bias or restrictions, etc<br>• Supply chain AI deployment assurance practices [15, 28]<br>✳ Supply chain assurance practices: Adoption of secure model persistence formats, cryptographic hashing as integrity check for web-scale data, and immunization of images to prevent manipulation by models | • Model design and architecture decision [22, 24, 25, 27]<br>• SbD (Security by Design), PbD (Privacy by Design) design [25, 26]<br>• Review of model security, such as model cards and risk cards, and supply chain security evaluation [15, 24, 28]<br>• Development of training and fine-tuning processes [22, 24, 27]<br>• Fine-tuning and ensuring model safety through human feedback such as RLHF (Reinforcement Learning from Human Feedback)[3][15][26]<br>• Prompt Engineering [15, 24, 27]<br>• Perform model and prompt documentation [25, 27]<br>• Improved learning efficiency and performance, output optimization, and learning pipeline security [27, 28]<br>• Model bias, fairness, and safety [23, 27] | • Strengthening security and responsible AI launch through AI Red Team [15, 25, 28]<br>• Deploy DevOps, CI/CD, utilize release assurance practices, manage model versions and information, deploy and maintain [14, 22, 27, 28]<br>• Manage model and input/output security, secure AI plugins [21, 22, 25, 27]<br>• Evaluate and validate prompts, evaluate and monitor model performance, and maintain quality standards [22, 24, 27]<br>• Maintain appropriate human participation in automated processes (Human-In-The Loop) and strengthen supervision [24] |
| System | | • Check infrastructure and quality requirements [25, 27]<br>• System Security measures [23]<br>• Clear interface design and user education about risks [24, 25] | • Manage identity and access [21, 27]<br>• Manage system security and performance [21, 22]<br>• System operation, input monitoring [21, 24, 25] |

(*continued*)

**Table 3.** (*continued*)

| component | | Process | | |
|---|---|---|---|---|
| | | Source | Design and Development | Deployment and Operations Management |
| Manage | Understanding of business | | • Establishing a business case for AI adoption [28]<br>• Supply chain security assessment, requiring suppliers to comply with standards [25]<br>• AI operation continuity management, accident prevention and response procedure development [23, 25, 26, 28]<br>• Technical Debt Management [25, 28] | |
| | Risk Management and Gorvernance | | • Identifying and listing AI assets [20, 24, 25, 28]<br>• Performing risk management of risk assessment and selection/implementation of protective measures [20]<br>• Establishing governance, assigning organizational roles and responsibilities [20, 28] | • RMF Operation, TEVV Verification [20, 28]<br>＊Test, Evaluation, Verification, and Validation<br>• Security and Privacy Protection Mechanism Operation [20, 24]<br>• Third party, supply chain monitoring [20, 25]<br>• AI Security / Privacy Protection Education, Awareness Raising [20, 28] |
| | Compliance | | • Reviewing compliance with legal requirements and regulatory compliance [20, 21, 23, 28]<br>• Verifying SLAs, reviewing contracts and insurance [20, 23, 28] | |

## 3.3 Supply Chain Security Model of Generative AI

The supply chain security model of generative AI consists of the processes of source, design and development, deployment, and operation management by component in Table 3, and proposes security considerations to protect the entire life cycle of generative AI systems. Through this model, we aim to protect generative AI-related components from potential vulnerabilities, threats, and attacks through security control that considers the overall ripple effect from the perspective of the technical operation principle of data learning and the model improvement process such as fine-tuning of generative AI for the complex generative AI supply chain.

Through this model, we aim to protect the components of generative AI systems from potential vulnerabilities, threats, and attacks through security control that considers the overall ripple effect from the perspective of the technical operation principle of data learning and the model improvement process such as fine-tuning of generative AI, as well as security management for complex generative AI supply chains.

Security considerations through this model include documents from standards and standards organizations on the security of foreign generative AI on supply chain security issues of generative AI [15, 19, 20], and domestic guidelines for the introduction and use of generative AI [21, 22], security guidelines for generative AI from foreign government agencies [23–26], and security and governance reports for generative AI from other major organizations [27, 28]. It was analyzed and presented thoroughly. If security considerations overlap for each component process step, they will be presented first in the steps that must take precedence or be important.

## 4 Conclusion

Supply chain attacks, which are easy to attack but have high impact, are expanding to repository platforms used for developing and sharing generative AI. Given the characteristics of generative AI's open-source model and high dependency on data, supply chain security management for generative AI is an important issue. In addition, generative AI starts from training data and goes through a model improvement process such as fine tuning, so this process can lead to overall system errors and serious security risks, such as unintended or biased results. Accordingly, a plan to strengthen risk management is needed to eliminate these risks in advance and secure reliability.

In this paper, we conceptualize how important supply chain security is and how to define generative AI supply chain security through structural analysis of generative AI systems, and generative AI for supply chain security management through analysis of major security standards and guidelines related to generative AI. A security model was designed and proposed.

Generative AI's supply chain security model was proposed by analyzing the structural characteristics and security risks of generative AI and approaching it from a new perspective of supply chain security by reflecting the special characteristics of the process for data and models, which are core components of generative AI. In addition, the significance of this study lies in the inclusion of specific security considerations by approaching it from a multi-faceted perspective by responding to each process of the generative AI system components through the model. We believe that this will be meaningful research that will help implement a practical and effective risk management and governance system for generative AI in the future.

## References

1. AI TIMES: Generative AI is a game changer, necessary for societal level (2023)
2. Daily Secu: Beware of critical security vulnerabilities in open source AI platforms such as MLflow and ClearML (2024)

3. OECD: AI language models technological, socio-economic and policy considerations. OECD Digital Economy Papers, No.352 (2023)
4. Center for Research on Foundation Models (CRFM), Stanford Institute for Human-Centered Artificial Intelligence (HAI), Stanford University. On the opportunities and risks of foundation models. arXiv:2108.07258 (2021)
5. NIST: Cybersecurity supply chain risk management practices for systems and organizations", NIST SP 800–161, r1 (2022)
6. National Telecommunications and Information Administration: Framing software component transparency: establish a common software bill of materials(SBOM) (2021)
7. OWASP: OWASP TOP 10 for LLM Application, Ver 1.1 (2023)
8. Federal Office for Information Security: Generative AI models, opportunities and risk for industry and authorities. Ver.1.1 (2024)
9. Ian, J., et al.: Explaining and harnessing adversarial examples. arXiv:1412.6572 (2015)
10. Aniban, C., et al.: Adversarial attacks and defenses: a survey. arXiv:1810.00069 (2018)
11. ENISA: Securing machine learning algorithms (2021)
12. Park, S., Choi, D.S.: Artificial intelligence security issues. Rev. KIISC **27**(3) (2017)
13. Kim, M.J., Lee, S.K.: Cyber threats and countermeasures due to the development of artificial intelligence technology. Inf. Commun. Mag. **39**(12) (2022)
14. Tramer, F., et al.: Stealing machine learning models via prediction APIs. arXiv:1609.02943 (2016)
15. NIST: Adversarial machine learning, adversarial machine learning, a taxonomy and technology of attack and mitigations. AI 100–2e2023 (2024)
16. OECD: Scoping the OECD AI principles. OECD Digital Economy papers, No.291 (2019)
17. OECD: Framework for the Classification of AI Systems. Digital Economy Papers, No, 323 (2022)
18. ENISA: AI Cybersecurity Challenges-Threat Landscape for Artificial Intelligence (2020)
19. ETSI: Securing Artificial Intelligence (SAI); Data Supply Chain Security. Group Report SAI 002 V1.1.1 (2021)
20. NIST: Artificial Intelligence Risk Management Framework: Generative Artificial Intelligence Profile. NIST AI 600–1 Initial Public Draft (2024)
21. National Intelligence Service, National Security Technology Research Institute: Security guidelines for using generative AI such as Chat GPT (2023)
22. Digital Platform Government Committee, NIA: Guidelines for introducing and utilizing large-scale AI in the public sector (2023)
23. Japan Ministry of Internal Affairs and Communications Ministry of Economy, Trade and Industry: AI Guidelines for Business ver 1.0 (2024)
24. Central Digital and Data Office: Generative AI framework for HM Government. ver.1.0 (2024)
25. US CISA, UK NCSC: Guidelines for Secure AI System Development (2024)
26. Singapore Infocomm Media Development Authority, AI Verify Foundation: Proposed model AI governance framework for generative AI (2024)
27. EY: Generative AI Risk and Governance, Way towards a responsible and trusted AI (2024)
28. OWASP: LLM AI Cybersecurity & Governance Checklist (2024)

# Emerging Topic

# Privacy Enhanced P2P Power Trading Using DID-Based Identity Verification in a Microgrid

Taeyang Lee[✉]

Department of Computer and Information Security and Convergence Engineering for Intelligent Drone, Sejong University, Seoul, Republic of Korea
taeyang@pel.sejong.ac.kr

**Abstract.** Smart meters play a crucial role in accurately measuring power usage and distribution data in microgrids. However, fine-grained data collection raises significant privacy concerns. To address this, it is essential to develop a distributed power trading system that is both trustworthy and privacy-preserving. In this paper, we propose a peer-to-peer power trading mechanism that ensures privacy through identity verification based on decentralized identifiers, zero-knowledge proofs, and pseudonyms. Besides, we introduce an efficient claims verification scheme with Boneh-Lynn-Shacham aggregate signature. We also validate the security of our proposed mechanism through the Real-or-Random model.

**Keywords:** DID · ZKP · Privacy Enhancing · Smart Metering

## 1 Introduction

Conventional grids suffer from environmental pollution, resource shortages, and regional imbalances in power distribution, degrading end-user Quality of Service (QoS) and Quality of Experience (QoE) [1]. Distributed Energy Resource (DER) systems, which are small-scale generators, typically ranging from 3kW to 10,000kW, such as solar panels and small wind turbines, are being used to overcome these limitations [2]. It has led to the emergence of microgrids, which group power generation, storage, and load locally and generate power from such renewable energy sources as solar, wind, and biomass. Therefore, they can help address environmental pollution and resource shortages. They also resolve the regional power distribution imbalances by allowing end-users to generate and use their own energy and distribute surplus power. This is where the concept of prosumers, end consumers who can produce, consume, and sell power, in microgrids emerged. They are capable of distributed power trading with end consumers. Particularly through Information and Communications Technology (ICT), it is possible to measure and monitor data in real-time in microgrids. This enables Demand-Side Management (DSM), which controls power production and distribution to more accurately reflect the energy supply and demand

© The Author(s), under exclusive license to Springer Nature Singapore Pte Ltd. 2025
J.-H. Lee et al. (Eds.): WISA 2024, LNCS 15499, pp. 339–351, 2025.
https://doi.org/10.1007/978-981-96-1624-4_26

in a region, enabling efficient power distribution control and dynamic pricing [3]. Smart meters play a major role in enabling distributed power trading by precisely measuring the energy supply and demand status at the end-users side. However, fine-grained data collection in real-time raises privacy concerns. Suppose the data is collected and analyzed over a long period of time. In that case, it is possible to identify the behavior patterns of end-users, like when the users get up, when they come back from work, their power purchase/sale volume and price, etc. The disclosure of such information could have adverse consequences for users, potentially leading to a breach of privacy [4].

In this paper, we design a microgrid based on a permissioned blockchain to prevent service interruption caused by a Single Point Of Failure (SPOF). The proposal also aims to protect privacy by controlling the participation of nodes in the network and regulating access to data based on their authorities. Additionally, we utilize pseudonyms in communications so that the real identity of the other party cannot revealed even if data is exchanged between the parties for a long period of time. A Self-Sovereign Identity (SSI) model is designed based on a Decentralized Identifier (DID) which allows data subjects to control the scope of information required for identity verification. In the SSI model, we utilize Boneh-Lynn-Shacham (BLS) aggregate signature to improve verification efficiency for multiple claims. Privacy is enhanced by using Verifiable Presentation (VP) with Zero-Knowledge Proof (ZKP) in the model.

This paper is organized as follows. Section 2 discusses related works and briefly describes a signature algorithm and ZKP as preliminaries to the proposal. Section 3 presents a microgrid system based on a permissioned blockchain and describes an identity verification protocol for auction-based Peer-to-Peer (P2P) power trading. Section 4 shows the results of the security analysis of the proposed protocol. Finally, Sect. 5 concludes this paper.

## 2 Preliminaries

### 2.1 Existing Works for Enhancing Privacy in Power Trading

Diao et al. [4] proposed a Privacy-preserving Smart Metering scheme using Linkable Anonymous Credential (PSMLAC), which is an anonymous credential protocol based on the Camenisch-Lysyanskaya (CL) signature. It can provide identity anonymity, message authentication, and traceability to failed smart meters. However, it only addresses privacy issues in smart metering and not in P2P power trading. Xie et al. [5] proposed a privacy-preserving distributed power trading framework, namely the Private Energy Market (PEM). Under the theory of secure Multi-Party Computation (MPC), it is possible to allocate energy transactions and calculate prices without revealing private data by performing all computations using a novel cryptographic protocol based on homomorphic ciphers. However, they do not consider identity verification and authentication mechanisms. Hassan et al. [3] proposed a blockchain-based power auction method, namely the Differentially private Energy Auction for bLockchain-based microgrid systems (DEAL), which utilizes a consortium blockchain for the efficiency of the system. Differential privacy technique was utilized to ensure privacy in this system. However, it does not consider mutual authentication in the process of P2P power trading.

## 2.2 BLS Aggregate Signature

The Boneh-Lynn-Shacham (BLS) signature algorithm based on bilinear mapping is one of the digital signature algorithms. Let $G_1$, $G_2$, and $G_T$ each be a multiplicative cyclic group composed of a large prime number $p$. Then, $e : G_1 \times G_2 \rightarrow G_T$ satisfies the following three properties.

- Bilinear: $e\left(aU, bV\right) = e\left(U, V\right)^{ab}$ for all $U \in G_1$, $V \in G_2$, and $a, b \in Z_p^*$.
- Non-degeneracy: There exists $U \in G_1$ and $V \in G_2$, such that $e\left(U, V\right) \neq 1$. That is the map does not send all pairs into the identity in $G_T$.
- Computability: For all $U \in G_1$ and $V \in G_2$, the polynomial-time algorithm calculation can be found.

The BLS signature algorithm operates in four steps: initialization, key pair generation, aggregated signature generation, and verification. In the initialization step, system parameters $(G_1, G_2, G_T, e, g_1, g_2, p, H)$ are set, where $g_1$ and $g_2$ are generators, and $H : 0, 1^* \rightarrow G_2$ is a hash function. A random number $x \in Z_p$ is chosen, and $v = g_1^x \in G_1$ is computed to generate a key pair. Let $sk = x$, which is a private key, and $pk = v$, which is a public key. A message $m$ and $sk$ are given as inputs to generate a BLS signature. A hash value $h$ for $m$ can be obtained through a hash function, and then $h^{sk} \in G_2$ is calculated to generate a signature $\sigma$. The inputs used are $m$, $pk$, and $\sigma$ to verify the signature. After hashing $m$ as $h$, $c = e(pk, h)$ and $c' = (g_1, \sigma)$ are computed. If $c' = c$, Accept is returned. Otherwise, Reject is returned as a verification result.

This algorithm can aggregate signatures into a single signature. When the number of users $u_i \in U$ is $k$, each $u_i$ generates an individual signature $\sigma_i$ for a different message $m_i \in \{0, 1\}^*$. The multiple $\sigma_i$ $(i = 1, 2, 3, \ldots, k)$ are used as inputs to generate an aggregated signature $\sigma_{agg} \in G_2$ by computing $\sigma_{agg} = \prod_{i=1}^{k} \sigma_i$. When verifying $\sigma_{agg}$, it requires multiple $pk_i$, $m_i$, and $\sigma_i$ $(i = 1, 2, 3, \ldots, k)$ as inputs to calculate $c = \prod_{i=1}^{k} e\left(pk_i, H\left(m_i\right)\right)$ and $c' = e\left(g_1, \sigma_{agg}\right)$. If $c' = c$, Accept is returned. Otherwise, Reject is returned as a verification result [6].

BLS signatures can increase the efficiency of signature verification by aggregating multiple signatures into a single signature. Taking advantage of this feature, this paper aims to improve the efficiency of identity verification by generating aggregated signatures for multiple claims contained in VCs.

## 2.3 Non-interactive Zero-Knowledge Proofs

ZKP is a cryptographic technique used to prove that a statement is true without revealing any additional information beyond the validity of the statement itself.

As such, ZKP can be used where user privacy is important, as they allow the prover to prove his claim without revealing information relevant to his claim. Therefore, in this paper, we aim to enhance privacy by applying ZKP to the claims contained in VPs in the SSI model.

There are two types of ZKP: interactive and non-interactive. In this paper, we use a non-interactive ZKP called Zero-Knowledge Succinct and Non-Interactive Arguments of Knowledge (zk-SNARK), which can verify proofs within a few milliseconds. zk-SNARK works through the *Setup*, *Prove*, and *Verify* algorithms. To describe the algorithms, let $u \in \mathcal{L}$ be a statement known to both a prover and verifier. Then, for any $u$, if there exists a witness $w$ known only to the prover, then $(u, w)$ belongs to a polynomial-time decidable binary relation $\mathcal{R}$ (i.e., $(u, w) \in \mathcal{R}$) [7].

- $pk, vk \leftarrow Setup(\mathcal{R})$: A trusted party generates a proving key $pk$ and verifying key $vk$ with a given $\mathcal{R}$.
- $\pi \leftarrow Prove(\mathcal{R}, pk, u, w)$: A prover generates a proof $\pi$ by multiplying $u$ and $w$ by some polynomials.
- $0/1 \leftarrow Verify(\mathcal{R}, vk, u, \pi)$: A verifier utilizes $vk$ to verify $\pi$ when $u$ is given. The verifier approves the proof (1), if the equation of the three pairings holds. Otherwise, the proof is rejected (0).

## 3   Privacy Enhanced P2P Power Trading

### 3.1   System Model

The proposed decentralized microgrid consists of three layers: physical layer, blockchain layer, and application layer.

**Physical Layer.** This layer may consist of Utility Service Providers (USPs), DERs, power management equipment, transmission systems, and end-consumers. The elements that are relevant to P2P power trading are the USP, smart meters, and end-consumers. The USPs provide P2P power trading services. Smart meters measure power-related data on the end-user side. There are two types of end-consumers: prosumers and general consumers. Prosumers can generate and consume power themselves, as well as sell surplus energy. Typical consumers do not have the ability to generate power, but they can purchase energy from prosumers through auctions and consume it.

**Blockchain Layer.** This layer is made up of blockchain functions. P2P communication takes place over the P2P network. Consensus algorithms are utilized to process transactions and agree on block generation. Smart contracts support auction automation. Decentralized ledger records various data and is also used as a Verifiable Data Registry (VDR) to manage data related to identity verification.

**Application Layer.** This layer consists of supporting services for P2P power trading. An automated auction-based P2P power trading service is provided to assist users in selecting a suitable counterparty using smart contracts. An identity verification service based on an SSI model is provided to ensure reliable and secure transactions. In the SSI model, a USP acts as an issuer and a Certificate Authority (CA) issuing Verifiable Credentials (VCs) to holders. A holder requests the issuer to issue a VC and submits a VP containing the necessary claims to prove its identity to a verifier, who verifies the VP. In the proposed model, each smart meter acts as both a holder and a verifier, i.e., it acts as a holder when it needs to prove its identity and as a verifier when it needs to verify the identity of the other party. The identity verification data is recorded in the VDR. Figure 1 shows the proposed SSI model for P2P power trading.

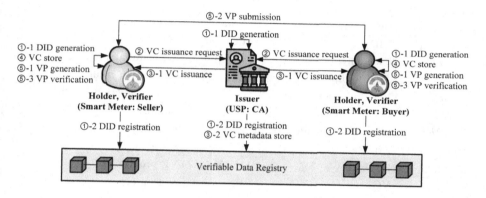

**Fig. 1.** Proposed SSI Model for P2P Power Trading

## 3.2 Assumptions

This section establishes the following assumptions for the supported SSI model to perform secure and reliable P2P power trading in a decentralized microgrid.

- During the registration, each party communicates through a secure channel.
- All parties fully trust USP and adversarial intervention by the USP is impossible.
- Verifiers must be able to identify USP through a trust issuer list.
- As an issuer, USP must define and register VC schemas in VDR, which verifiers can use to verify the holder's VC.
- USP installs smart meters in each household in advance and manages the relevant information (e.g., owner, installed location, etc.). Therefore, the USP can identify the smart meters and issue VCs for each smart meter.
- Smart meters must be mutually authenticated each time to participate in the auction, even if authentication has previously taken place between the same smart meters.

## 3.3  Proposed P2P Power Trading Mechanism

In the proposed system, P2P power trading is performed in three phases: registration, auction initiation, and bid submission. Before executing the three phases, the proposed system needs to set the system parameters. The USP and each smart meter should then generate their DIDs for identification and key pairs for message signing. The DIDs are resolved through DID documents containing public keys, metadata for identifiers, etc. The DID documents are recorded in the VDR. The key pairs are generated using the BLS key pair generation algorithm. The notations used to describe the specific operations of the proposed system are shown in Table 1.

**Table 1.** Notations

| Notations | Descriptions | Notations | Descriptions |
|---|---|---|---|
| $DID_A$ | DID | $VCproof_A$ | VC proof field |
| $PID_A$ | Pseudonym | $VC_A^{meta}$ | VC metadata |
| $T_A$ | Timestamp | $VR_A$ | Verification result |
| $Req_{VC}$ | VC issuance request | $auc$ | A set of auction conditions |
| $Ddoc_A$ | DID document | $bid_A$ | Bidding |
| $IPFS$ | Interplanetary file system | $ZVP_A$ | ZKP VP |
| $K_A^s$ | Private key | $VPID_A$ | VP identifier |
| $K_A^p$ | Public key | $VPproof_A$ | VP proof field |
| $VC_A$ | VC | $SK_{A-B}$ | Session key |
| $VCID_A$ | VC identifier | $EM_A$ | Encrypted message |

**Registration Phase.** In this phase, smart meters are registered in the system. This is done by issuing VCs for the smart meters. For example, if a VC is issued for one smart meter $SM_i$, the interaction between $SM_i$ and USP is as follows, where $SM_i$ functions as both a buyer and a seller of electricity. Figure 2 presents the detailed process.

1. $SM_i$ constructs a message $M_{SM_i}$ with $Req_{VC}$, $DID_{SM_i}$, $PID_{SM_i}$, and $T_1$, and sends $M_1 = \{M_{SM_i}, \sigma_{M_{SM_i}}\}$ to $USP$.
2. $USP$ first checks $|T_1 - T_1^*| \leq_\Delta T$ and then queries $Ddoc_{SM_i}$ in $VDR$ using $DID_{SM_i}$. $VDR$ returns $Ddoc_{SM_i}$ by sending $M_2$. $USP$ then checks $\sigma_{M_{SM_i}}$ with $M_{SM_i}$ and $K_{SM_i}^s$. If $\sigma_{M_{SM_i}}$ is valid, $USP$ sends $M_3$ to store $DID_{SM_i}$ and $PID_{SM_i}$ in $IPFS$. Next, $USP$ queries $SM_i$'s claims in $IPFS$, and $IPFS$ returns a set of claims $C_{SM_i} = \{claim_1, claim_2, claim_3, \ldots, claim_n\}$ via $M_4$. Afterward, $USP$ generates a set of signatures $S$ for $\{claim_i\}_{i=1}^n$ using $K_{USP}^s$ with the BLS signature algorithm. It also generates a signature $\sigma_{C_{SM_i}'}$ for $C_{SM_i}'$, derived by concatenating $\{claim_i\}_{i=1}^n$, and constructs

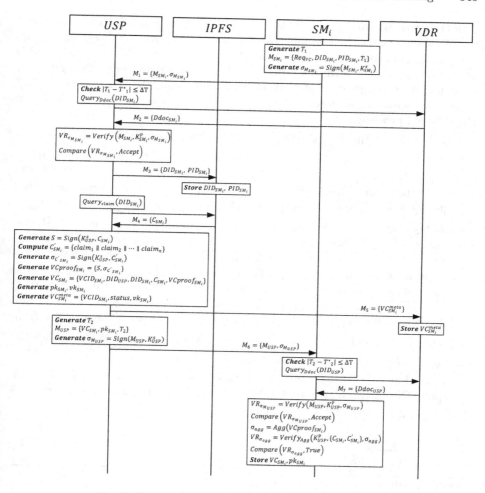

**Fig. 2.** Sequence Diagram of the Registration Phase

$VCproof_{SM_i} = \{S, \sigma_{C'_{SM_i}}\}$ for a VC. Finally, $USP$ can obtain $VC_{SM_i} = \{VCID_{SM_i}, DID_{USP}, DID_{SM_i}, C_{SM_i}, VCproof_{SM_i}\}$ of $SM_i$. $USP$ and then generates $pk_{SM_i}$ and $vk_{SM_i}$ and constructs $VC_{SM_i}^{meta} = \{VCID_{SM_i},\ status,\ vk_{SM_i}\}$ and stores it in $VDR$ via $M_5$. $USP$ also generates $T_2$, and then signs $M_{USP} = \{VC_{SM_i}, pk_{SM_i}, T_2\}$ with $K_{USP}^s$. $M_6 = \{M_{USP}, \sigma_{M_{USP}}\}$ is then sent to $SM_i$.

3. When $SM_i$ receives $M_6$ from $USP$, it checks $|T_2 - T_2^*| \leq \Delta T$ and queries $Ddoc_{USP}$ in $IPFS$ with $DID_{USP}$. $IPFS$ then returns $Ddoc_{USP}$ via $M_7$. Afterward, $SM_i$ checks $\sigma_{M_{USP}}$ using $K_{USP}^p$ obtained in $Ddoc_{USP}$ and $M_{USP}$. If $\sigma_{M_{USP}}$ is valid, it generates $\sigma_{agg}$ with $VCproof_{SM_i}$ for verifying $VC_{SM_i}$. $SM_i$ then verifies $\sigma_{agg}$ using $K_{USP}^p$, $C_{SM_i}$, and $C'_{SM_i}$, if the result is $True$, it stores $VC_{SM_i}$ and $pk_{SM_i}$.

**Auction Initiation Phase.** This is the phase where $SM_i^p$, a party that wants to sell power, starts the auction. The auction starts with $SM_i^p$ setting auction conditions and propagating them to nearby smart meters. $SM_i^p$ and $SM_j^b$ that is willing to participate in the auction to purchase power must verify the legitimacy of each other through identity verification. For example, the process of one $SM_i^p$ interacting with one or more $SM_j^b$ for an auction is as follows. Figure 3 illustrates the detailed process.

1. $SM_i^p$ selects claims $C'_{SM_i^p} = \{claim_j\}_{j=1}^m$, which is required to prove its identity from $C_{SM_i^p} = \{claim_j\}_{j=1}^n$ in its VC. $SM_i^p$ then generates $W_{SM_i^p} = \{C'_{SM_i^p}, S'_{SM_i^p}\}$ with $C'_{SM_i^p}$ and $S'_{SM_i^p} = \{\sigma_{claim_j}\}_{j=1}^m$, a set of signatures for selected each $\{claim_j\}_{j=1}^m$. $W_{SM_i^p}$ corresponds to a set of witnesses that only $SM_i^p$ knows for the ZKP. $SM_i^p$ then generates $VC'_{SM_i^p} = \{VCID_{SM_i^p}, DID_{USP}, U_{SM_i^p}\}$, where $U_{SM_i^p}$ is a set of statements to be proven. It also generates $VPproof_{SM_i^p}$ using inputs $\mathcal{R}$, $pk_{SM_i^p}$, $U_{SM_i^p}$, and $W_{SM_i^p}$ and creates $ZVP_{SM_i^p} = \{VPID_{SM_i^p}, VC'_{SM_i^p}, VPproof_{SM_i^p}\}$, random value $p_i$ to compute secret value $P_i = p_i \times G$, and $auc$ including power volume, minimum bid, auction time, etc. Afterward, $SM_i^p$ starts auction by propagating $M_8 = \{PID_{SM_i^p}, auc, ZVP_{SM_i^p}, P_i, T_3\}$ to near one or more $SM_j^b$.

2. Each $SM_j^b$ checks $|T_3 - T_3^*| \leq_\Delta T$ and $auc$ and retrieves the $VC_{SM_i^p}^{meta}$ from $VDR$. $VDR$ sends $M_9$ to return $VC_{SM_i^p}^{meta}$. Afterward, each $SM_j^b$ verifies the status value $status$ contained in $VC_{SM_i^p}^{meta}$ to check the status of $VC'_{SM_i^p}$ included in $ZVP_{SM_i^p}$. If the status is valid, each $SM_j^b$ verifies $ZVP_{SM_i^p}$ using inputs $\mathcal{R}$, $vk_{SM_i^p}$, $U_{SM_i^p}$, and $VPproof_{SM_i^p}$. When the result is returned as $Accept$, it means $SM_i^p$ is legitimate.

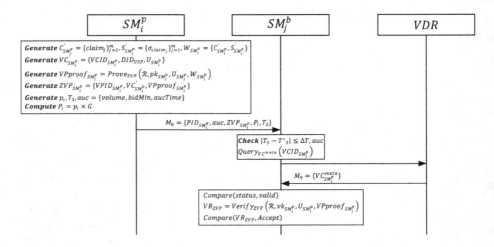

**Fig. 3.** Sequence Diagram of the Auction Initiation

**Bid Submission Phase.** This is the phase where each $SM_j^b$ places bids. Each $SM_j^b$ interacts with $SM_i^p$ by presenting its ZKP-based VP required to prove its identity and bid. For example, the process of one $SM_j^b$ presenting its VP and bidding to $SM_i^p$ is as follows. Figure 4 depicts the detailed process.

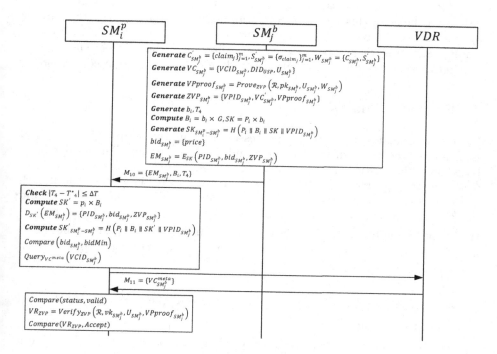

**Fig. 4.** Sequence Diagram of the Bidding

1. $SM_j^b$ generates $ZVP_{SM_j^b}$ to participate in auction by proving its identity. The $ZVP_{SM_j^b}$ generation process is the similar to that of $SM_i^p$. After creating $ZVP_{SM_j^b}$, $SM_j^b$ generates random number $b_i$ and $T_4$ and then computes secret values $B_i = b_i \times G$ and $SK = P_i \times b_i$. Afterward, it generates $SK_{SM_i^p - SM_j^b} = H\left(P_i \parallel B_i \parallel SK \parallel VPID_{SM_j^b}\right)$. It sets $bid_{SM_j^b}$ and encrypts $PID_{SM_j^b}$, $bid_{SM_j^b}$, and $ZVP_{SM_j^b}$ with $SK$ to form $EM_{SM_j^b}$. After that, $SM_j^b$ then places a bid for power purchase by sending $M_{10} = \{EM_{SM_j^b}, B_i, T_4\}$ to $SM_i^p$.

2. When $SM_i^p$ receives $M_{10}$, it checks $|T_4 - T_4^*| \leq \triangle\, T$ and then derives $SK' = p_i \times B_i$. Then, $SM_i^p$ decrypts $EM_{SM_j^b}$ using derived $SK'$ and computes $SK'_{SM_i^p - SM_j^b} = H\left(P_i \parallel B_i \parallel SK' \parallel VPID_{SM_j^b}\right)$. After that, $SM_i^p$ checks whether the $SM_j^b$'s $bid_{SM_j^b}$ is at least $bidMin$, a crucial threshold in the

matching counterparty process, and verifies $ZVP_{SM_j^b}$ if the $bid_{SM_j^b}$ meets $auc$. The verification process for $SM_j^b$ is the same as for $SM_j^b$ verifying $ZVP_{SM_i^p}$. If the result of $ZVP_{SM_j^b}$ verification is $Accept$, it means that $SM_j^b$ is legitimate.

$SM_i^p$ can perform identity verification for multiple $SM_j^b$ by receiving VPs and bids from them. In this scenario, $SM_i^p$ can determine the best trading partner by considering the bids submitted by one or more $SM_j^b$ to perform P2P power trading. Sein et al. [8] proposed the power trading algorithm. The specific process of determining an auction destination based on bids can be adopted from [8].

## 4   Security Analysis

In this section, the security of the session key in the proposed mechanism is demonstrated through the Real-or-Random (RoR) model. The RoR model, based on probabilistic game theory, is widely used to prove the semantic security of session key agreements [9]. In the model, an adversary $\mathcal{A}$ interacts with the $t$-th instance of the participants in execution. Specifically, the instances of $SM_i^p$ and $SM_j^b$ participating in P2P power trading are defined as $\mathcal{P}_{SM_i^p}^{t1}$ and $\mathcal{P}_{SM_j^b}^{t1}$, respectively. Additionally, the RoR model considers four queries that assume the actual attacks of the adversary: $Execute\left(\mathcal{P}_{SM_i^p}^t, \mathcal{P}_{SM_j^b}^t\right)$, $Send\left(\mathcal{P}^t, M\right)$, $Reveal\left(\mathcal{P}^t\right)$, $Test\left(\mathcal{P}^t\right)$.

- $Execute\left(\mathcal{P}_{SM_i^p}^t, \mathcal{P}_{SM_j^b}^t\right)$: $\mathcal{A}$ can eavesdrop on the messages exchanged between $\mathcal{P}_{SM_i^p}^{t1}$ and $\mathcal{P}_{SM_j^b}^{t1}$.
- $Send\left(\mathcal{P}^t, M\right)$: $\mathcal{A}$ can send a message $M$ to the instance $\mathcal{P}^t$ and receive a response message from $\mathcal{P}^t$.
- $Reveal\left(\mathcal{P}^t\right)$: $\mathcal{A}$ can obtain the current session key between $\mathcal{P}^t$ and its communication partner.
- $Test\left(\mathcal{P}^t\right)$: $\mathcal{A}$ can request the session key from $\mathcal{P}^t$ and obtain it, with the result being a probabilistic response based on the outcome of an unbiased coin flip $c$. If $c = 1$, $\mathcal{P}^t$ returns the session key, and if $c = 0$, returns a random number. Otherwise, null ($\perp$) is returned.

Additionally, the collision-resistant one-way hash function $Hash$ is utilized as a random oracle, allowing access to all parties and $\mathcal{A}$.

**Theorem 1.** *When $\mathcal{A}$ attempts to break the semantic security of the proposed protocol, $\mathcal{A}$ can query $Hash$ up to $q_{hash}$ times. The length of the hash output is denoted as $|Hash|$. When $\mathcal{A}$ attempts to break the Elliptic Curve Computational Diffie-Hellman Problem (ECCDHP), $\mathcal{A}$'s advantage is denoted as $Adv_{\mathcal{A}}^{ECCDHP}(t)$. Thus, the advantage of $\mathcal{A}$ in breaking the session key security in the proposed protocol can be estimated as $Adv_{\mathcal{A}}(t) \leq \frac{q_{hash}^2}{|Hash|} + 2Adv_{\mathcal{A}}^{ECCDHP}(t)$.*

*Proof.* Following games $G_i$ ($i = [0, 3)$) are considered to prove the semantic security of the session key in the proposed protocol. The advantage of $\mathcal{A}$ winning in each $G_i$ is denoted as $Pr[Succ_{G_i}]$. The process of each game is as follows.

– $G_0$: In this game, the actual attack by $\mathcal{A}$ is modeled while the proposed protocol is in operation. At this point, $\mathcal{A}$ does not perform any queries and cannot obtain any information. Therefore, since $c$ is chosen randomly, the advantage of $\mathcal{A}$ follows the following Eq. (1).

$$Adv_{\mathcal{A}}(t) = |2Pr[Succ_{G_0}] - 1| \tag{1}$$

– $G_1$: In this game, $\mathcal{A}$ is modeled as performing an eavesdropping attack. $\mathcal{A}$ $Execute\left(\mathcal{P}^t_{SM^p_i}, \mathcal{P}^t_{SM^b_j}\right)$ to obtain $M_8 = \{PID_{SM^p_i}, auc, ZVP_{SM^p_i}, P_i, T_3\}$ and $M_{10} = \{EM_{SM^b_j}, B_i, T_4\}$. Afterward, to ascertain whether the derived $SK_{SM^p_i - SM^b_j}$ is the actual key or a random key, $\mathcal{A}$ invokes $Reveal(\mathcal{P}^t)$ and $Test(\mathcal{P}^t)$. For $\mathcal{A}$ to correctly derive $SK_{SM^p_i - SM^b_j}$, the short-term secret values $p_i$ and $b_i$ are required. However, $\mathcal{A}$ cannot determine these values from the obtained messages. Therefore, since $M_8$ and $M_{10}$ do not help $\mathcal{A}$ increase the probability of a successful attack, $\mathcal{A}$'s advantage in $G_1$ is similar to that in $G_0$ and is derived as shown in Eq. (2).

$$Pr[Succ_{G_1}] = Pr[Succ_{G_0}] \tag{2}$$

– $G_2$: In this game, $\mathcal{A}$ uses $M_8$ and $M_{10}$ to compute $SK_{SM^p_i - SM^b_j}$ by executing *Hash* and *Send* queries. However, the eavesdropped $M_8$ and $M_{10}$ are protected by a one-way hash function. Additionally, $\mathcal{A}$ attempts to derive $SK_{SM^p_i - SM^b_j}$, which requires solving the ECCDHP within polynomial time $t$ to find $SK = b_i \times P_i = b_i \times (p_i \times G) = p_i \times (b_i \times G) = p_i \times B_i$. However, this is computationally infeasible due to the birthday paradox and the ECCDHP. Therefore, according to the birthday paradox and the hardness of the ECCDHP, the attacker's advantage in $G_2$ is determined as shown in Eq. (3).

$$|Pr[Succ_{G_1}] - Pr[Succ_{G_2}]| \leq \frac{q^2_{hash}}{2|Hash|} + Adv^{ECCDHP}_{\mathcal{A}}(t) \tag{3}$$

After all the games are done, $\mathcal{A}$ guesses a correct $c$, leading to Eq. (4).

$$Pr[Succ_{G_2}] = \frac{1}{2} \tag{4}$$

By using Eqs. (1) and (2), we can derive Eq. (5).

$$\frac{1}{2}Adv_{\mathcal{A}}(t) = \left|Pr[Succ_{G_0}] - \frac{1}{2}\right| = \left|Pr[Succ_{G_1}] - \frac{1}{2}\right| \tag{5}$$

Next, using Eqs. (3), (4), and (5), we can derive Eq. (6).

$$\frac{1}{2}Adv_{\mathcal{A}}(t) = |Pr[Succ_{G_1}] - Pr[Succ_{G_2}]| \leq \frac{q^2_{hash}}{2|Hash|} + Adv^{ECCDHP}_{\mathcal{A}}(t) \tag{6}$$

Finally, by multiplying both sides of Eq. (6), we obtain the predetermined $Adv_{\mathcal{A}}(t)$ as shown in Eq. (7). This corresponds to a negligible value.

$$Adv_{\mathcal{A}}(t) \leq \frac{q_{hash}^2}{|Hash|} + 2Adv_{\mathcal{A}}^{ECCDHP}(t) \tag{7}$$

## 5    Conclusion

This paper addresses privacy issues in microgrids during decentralized power trading, where smart meters collect fine-grained real-time data. We proposed a decentralized microgrid system using a permissioned blockchain to protect privacy and introduced an identity verification mechanism based on DID-based SSI, which enhances privacy through VP using ZKP. The P2P power trading mechanism utilizes pseudonyms during message exchanges to protect participants' identities. Additionally, leveraging VC based on the BLS signature algorithm enables efficient aggregate signature verification. However, BLS signatures are less efficient for individual signature tasks compared to the elliptic curve digital signature algorithm, indicating the need for further research. The security of the proposed mechanism was validated using the RoR model, ensuring the semantic security of session keys.

**Acknowledgments.** This work was supported by Korea Internet & Security Agency (KISA) grant funded by the Korea government(PIPC) *(2780000004, Development of Standards for Personal Information Protection in the Blockchain Environment)*. The author would like to express sincere gratitude to Prof. Jong-Hyouk Lee for his invaluable guidance and support throughout the research and writing of this paper.

## References

1. Aggarwal, S., Kumar, N.: PETS: P2P energy trading scheduling scheme for electric vehicles in smart grid systems. IEEE Trans. Intell. Transp. Syst. **23**(9), 14361–14374 (2022)
2. Fang, X., Misra, S., Xue, G., Yang, D.: Smart grid-The new and improved power grid: a survey. IEEE Commun. Surv. Tutor. **14**(4), 944–980 (2011)
3. Hassan, M.U., Rehmani, M.H., Chen, J.: DEAL: differentially private auction for blockchain-based microgrids energy trading. IEEE Trans. Serv. Comput. **13**(2), 263–275 (2019)
4. Diao, F., Zhang, F., Cheng, X.: A privacy-preserving smart metering scheme using linkable anonymous credential. IEEE Trans. Smart Grid **6**(1), 461–467 (2014)
5. Xie, S., Wang, H., Hong, Y., Thai, M.: Privacy preserving distributed energy trading. In: 2020 IEEE 40th International Conference on Distributed Computing Systems, ICDCS, pp. 322–332 (2020)
6. Liu, X., Feng, J.: Trusted blockchain oracle scheme based on aggregate signature. J. Comput. Commun. **9**(3), 95–109 (2021)
7. Salleras, X., Daza, V.: ZPiE: zero-knowledge proofs in embedded systems. Mathematics **9**(20), 2569 (2021)

8. Myung, S., Lee, J.H.: Ethereum smart contract-based automated power trading algorithm in a microgrid environment. J. Supercomput. **76**(7), 4904–4914 (2020)
9. Thakur, G., Kumar, P., Jangirala, S., Das, A.K., Park, Y.: An effective privacy-preserving blockchain-assisted security protocol for cloud-based digital twin environment. IEEE Access **11**, 26877–26892 (2023)

# Quantum Implementation of LSH

Yujin Oh, Kyungbae Jang, and Hwajeong Seo[✉]

Hansung University, Seoul 02876, South Korea
hwajeong84@gmail.com

**Abstract.** As quantum computing progresses, the assessment of cryptographic algorithm resilience against quantum attack gains significance interests in the field of cryptanalysis. Consequently, this paper proposes the depth-optimized quantum circuit of Korean hash function (i.e., LSH) and estimates its quantum attack cost in quantum circuits. By utilizing an optimized quantum adder and employing parallelization techniques, the proposed quantum circuit achieves a 78.8% improvement in full depth and a 79.1% improvement in Toffoli depth compared to previous the-state-of art works. In conclusion, based on the proposed quantum circuit, we estimate the resources required for a Grover collision attack and evaluate the post-quantum security of LSH algorithms.

**Keywords:** Quantum circuit · Quantum collision attack · LSH

## 1 Introduction

The advancement of quantum computing presents new challenges and opportunities in cryptography. The parallel processing capability of quantum computers can exponentially enhance the speed of breaking many traditional cryptographic systems. Particularly, it enables finding solutions to classical hard problems such as large-scale factorization and discrete logarithm problems at a much faster rate.

Moreover, the development in quantum computing allows for the discovery and application of new quantum algorithms. These algorithms can be employed to uncover vulnerabilities in currently used classical cryptographic systems. For instance, Shor's algorithm [16] demonstrated the ability to factorize large numbers efficiently, leading to the collapse of security in public-key cryptography schemes such as RSA. Grover's algorithm [7], on the other hand, reduces the time complexity of cryptographic functions such as symmetric key encryption and hash functions.

As quantum computing technology progresses further, there is numerous research underway to assess the security of current cryptographic systems. These studies involve implementing cryptographic systems as quantum circuits and estimating quantum attack costs to assess security strength. Accordingly, the National Institute of Standards and Technology (NIST) is actively hosting a competition for post-quantum cryptography (PQC) and has established quantum security levels that span from 1 to 5 [13,14]. Levels 1, 3, and 5 correspond

© The Author(s), under exclusive license to Springer Nature Singapore Pte Ltd. 2025
J.-H. Lee et al. (Eds.): WISA 2024, LNCS 15499, pp. 352–363, 2025.
https://doi.org/10.1007/978-981-96-1624-4_27

to the cost of a Grover's key attack on AES-128, AES-192, and AES-256 quantum circuits, respectively. Levels 2 and 4 pertain to the collision attack cost on SHA-2 and SHA-3 hash function quantum circuits, which have not yet been defined (with only classical costs reported). In the future, all post-quantum hash functions will be required to estimate the cost of collision attacks to align with Levels 2 and 4.

In this paper, we propose a depth-optimized quantum circuit of Lightweight Secure Hash (LSH) [11], which is a hash function included as validation subjects in the Korean Cryptographic Module Validation Program (KCMVP). Additionally, based on the quantum circuit, we estimate the cost of collision attack using Grover algorithm for LSH.

## 2  Background

### 2.1  Quantum Gates

In this section, we explain the quantum gates to implement our quantum circuit. The Hadamard gate creates superposition states of qubits. The X gate, also known as the Pauli-X gate, operates on a single qubit. It can invert the state of a qubit, transforming $|0\rangle$ state to $|1\rangle$ and $|1\rangle$ state to $|0\rangle$. This operation is similar to the classical NOT gate in traditional computing. The CNOT (Controlled-NOT) gate uses two qubits and performs a NOT operation on the target qubit if the control qubit is in the state $|1\rangle$. If the control qubit is in the $|0\rangle$ state, the target qubit remains unchanged. The Toffoli gate, also known as the CCNOT gate (Controlled-Controlled-NOT), uses two control qubits and one target qubit. The Toffoli gate performs a NOT operation on the target qubit only if both control qubits are in the state $|1\rangle$. Thus, it is similar to the classical AND operation. The Toffoli gate can be decomposed into a combination of gates such as H, CNOT and T gates (Fig. 1).

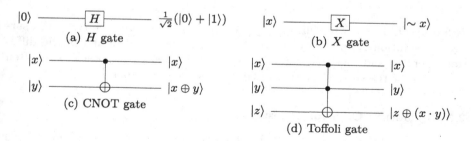

Fig. 1. Quantum gates

## 2.2 The Grover Algorithm

The Grover algorithm can find a solution for the $n$-qubit data (in a superposition state) with a complexity of $O(\sqrt{2^n})$ (i.e., a square root speedup compared to classical search of $O(2^n)$). As such, Grover's algorithm has an advantage in solving problems with high search complexity. Notably, extensive research has been conducted on Grover's algorithm for block ciphers and hash functions [8, 10, 15]. We explain Grover's algorithm through its use in pre-image attacks for hash functions. Grover's algorithm consists of three major processes; *Input setting, Oracle, Diffusion operator.*

*Input Setting.* $H$ gates are used to prepare an $n$-qubit in a superposition state ($|\psi\rangle$). As a result, an $n$-qubit input with a superposition state can represents $2^n$ cases as probabilities.

$$H^{\otimes n}|0\rangle^{\otimes n} = |\psi\rangle = \left(\frac{|0\rangle + |1\rangle}{\sqrt{2}}\right) = \frac{1}{2^{n/2}} \sum_{x=0}^{2^n-1} |x\rangle \qquad (1)$$

*Oracle.* The target function (e.g., block ciphers or hash functions) is placed in the oracle and returns the solution using the superposition state of input. To accomplish this, the target function should be implemented using quantum gates (i.e., a quantum circuit). If the quantum circuit finds a solution for the target function (i.e., if $f(x) = 1$), the amplitude of the specific input in a superposition state changes negatively (see Eq. 3).

$$f(x) = \begin{cases} 1 \text{ if } \text{Hash}(x) = \text{target output} \\ 0 \text{ if } \text{Hash}(x) \neq \text{target output} \end{cases} \qquad (2)$$

$$U_f(|\psi\rangle|-\rangle) = \frac{1}{2^{n/2}} \sum_{x=0}^{2^n-1} (-1)^{f(x)}|x\rangle|-\rangle \qquad (3)$$

*Diffusion Operator.* The diffusion operator enhance the probability for measuring the solution returned by the oracle. Due to the fixed design of the diffusion operator and relatively low complexity compared to the oracle, it is often neglected for the cost estimation in Grover's search [6, 8, 10, 12].

## 2.3 Quantum Collision Search

Grover's search for an $n$-bit key of block ciphers or a pre-image of an $n$-bit hash output for hash functions can be approached straightforwardly, as the complexity of $O(n)$ in classical computing is reduced to $O(\sqrt{n})$ in quantum computing. However, quantum collision search for hash functions is more complicated and can be approached in various ways.

There are various quantum collision attack algorithms using Grover's algorithm. Among them, the BHT algorithm [2] has a query complexity of $O(2^{n/3})$.

However, this algorithm demands a notably large quantum memory, $O(2^{2n/3})$. Also, Bernstein pointed out in [1] that this algorithm is controversial. Considering these aspects, we employ the CNS algorithm [3], which has a query complexity of $O(2^{2n/5})$ and requires only $O(2^{n/5})$ classical memory. Note that the CNS algorithm can be parallelized to reduce the search complexity of $O(2^{n/5})$. By utilizing $2^s$ quantum instances in parallel, the search complexity for finding collisions is reduced to $O(2^{\frac{2n}{5}-\frac{3s}{5}})$, with $s \leq \frac{n}{4}$. In [9], the authors defined a parallelization strength of $s = n/6$ to estimate the required quantum resources for finding a collision in the SHA-2 and SHA-3 hash functions. Following this approach, we also define a parallelization strength of $s = n/6$ for finding a collision in the LSH hash functions.

## 2.4  Description of LSH Hash Function

LSH is a Korean cryptographic hash algorithm included among the validation subjects of the KCMVP. LSH consists of LSH-256-224, LSH-256-256, LSH-512-224, LSH-512-256. LSH-512-384 and LSH-512-512. LSH-256-n operates based on a 32-bit word and LSH-512-n operates based on a 64-bit word. LSH operates in three stages: *Initialization, Compression*, and *Finalization*.

**Initaillization.** During the *initialization* process, a given input message undergoes one-zero padding. Following this, the padded input message is divided into 32-bit word array messages. Additionally, in the initialization, the 16-bit word array hash chaining variables $(CV^{(i)})$ are set as an initialization vector.

**Compression.** The *compression* function consists of MsgExp and Step (MsgAdd, Mix, and WordPerm) functions. The MsgExp function converts a 32-bit word array message into a 16-bit word array. The MsgExp function process is as follows in Eq. 4. The permutation function $\tau$ in Eq. 4 is defined in Table 1.

$$
\begin{aligned}
&\mathbf{M}_0^{(i)} \leftarrow (M^{(i)}[0], ..., M^{(i)}[15]), \mathbf{M}_1^{(i)} \leftarrow (M^{(i)}[16], ..., M^{(i)}[31]) \\
&\mathbf{M}_j^{(i)} \leftarrow (M_j^{(i)}[0], ..., M_j^{(i)}[15])_{j=2}^{N_s} \\
&M_j^{(i)}[l] \leftarrow M_{j-1}^{(i)}[l] \boxplus M_{j-2}^{(i)}[\tau(l)] \; for \; 0 \leq l \leq 16
\end{aligned}
\tag{4}
$$

**Step Function.** The *step* function is composed of MsgAdd, Mix, and WordPerm functions. The MsgAdd inputs are $CV^{(i)} = T[0], ..., T[15]$ and $M_j^{(i)} = (M_j^{(i)}[0], ..., M_j^{(i)}[15])_{j=2}^{N_s}$. The MsgAdd process is MSGADD(T,M) $\leftarrow (T[0] \oplus M[0], ..., T[15] \oplus M[15])$. The Mix function updates the 16-bit word $T = T[0], ..., T[15]$. In this function, the 16-bit word array $T$ is split into upper eight words and lower eight words, which are then used as input. The operation of the Mix function involves modular addition, XOR, and left rotation. The process of the Mix function is shown in Fig. 2 and the the bit rotational amounts using in Mix function $(\alpha_j, \beta_j$ and $\gamma_l)$ are shown in Table 2. The WordPerm function is defined as follows : $X = (X[0], ...X[15]) \leftarrow (X[\sigma(0)], ...X[\sigma(15)])$, where $\sigma$ is defined by Table 1.

**Table 1.** The permutation $\tau$ and $\sigma$

| 1 | 0 | 1 | 2 | 3 | 4 | 5 | 6 | 7 | 8 | 9 | 10 | 11 | 12 | 13 | 14 | 15 |
|---|---|---|---|---|---|---|---|---|---|---|----|----|----|----|----|----|
| $\tau(l)$ | 3 | 2 | 0 | 1 | 7 | 4 | 5 | 6 | 11 | 10 | 8 | 9 | 15 | 12 | 13 | 14 |
| $\sigma(l)$ | 6 | 4 | 5 | 7 | 12 | 15 | 14 | 13 | 2 | 0 | 1 | 3 | 8 | 11 | 10 | 9 |

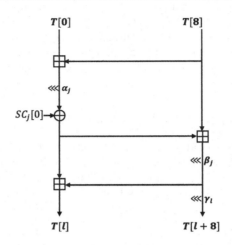

**Fig. 2.** Mix function

***Finallization.*** The finalization function produces an $n$-bit hash value, denoted as $h$, obtained from the final chaining variable. The finalization process is as follows:

$$\mathbf{h} \leftarrow (CV^t[0] \oplus CV^t[8], ..., CV^t[7] \oplus CV^t[15])$$
$$\mathbf{h} = (h[0] \,||\, ... \,||\, h[w-1]) \tag{5}$$
$$h \leftarrow (h[0] \,||\, ... \,||\, h[w-1])_{[0:n-1]}$$

## 3 Quantum Circuit Implementation of LSH

This section describe our quantum circuit implementation of LSH. Our main focus is to optimize the circuit depth for the efficiency of the Grover collision attack. For the sake of simplicity, we primarily focus on explaining LSH-256-256. We set the input length to be equal to the hash length for implementation.

### 3.1 Quantum Adder for Optimizing the Depth

To implement the MsgExp function and Mix function, we use a quantum adder. Quantum adders can indeed be designed in various ways, and the choice depends on optimization techniques. Commonly used types of quantum adders include the ripple-carry adder (RCA) and the carry-lookahead adder (CLA).

The RCA adder operates in a sequential manner, where it calculates the carry-out from the previous stage before proceeding with the addition in the

**Table 2.** Bit rotation amounts: $\alpha_j$, $\beta_j$ and $\gamma_l$

| Algorithm | $j$ | $\alpha_j$ | $\beta_j$ | $\gamma_0$ | $\gamma_1$ | $\gamma_2$ | $\gamma_3$ | $\gamma_4$ | $\gamma_5$ | $\gamma_6$ | $\gamma_7$ |
|---|---|---|---|---|---|---|---|---|---|---|---|
| LSH-256-n | even | 29 | 1 | 0 | 8 | 16 | 24 | 24 | 16 | 8 | 0 |
|  | odd | 5 | 17 | | | | | | | | |
| LSH-512-n | even | 23 | 59 | 0 | 16 | 32 | 48 | 8 | 24 | 40 | 56 |
|  | odd | 7 | 3 | | | | | | | | |

next stage. This sequential operation leads to a high depth of the adder, as each stage depends on the carry-out from the previous stage.

On the contrary, the CLA adder accelerates addition by pre-computing carry values for each stage. It adds extra circuits to calculate carry values in advance, determining whether a carry will occur at each stage. This pre-calculation is processed in parallel, speeding up the overall addition process and reducing the depth of the quantum circuit.

A previous work used a Cuccaro adder [4], an improved ripple-carry adder. This adder is implemented in-place operation and requires only one ancilla qubit, $(2n - 3)$ Toffoli gates, $(5n - 7)$ CNOT gates, and achieves a circuit depth of $(2n + 2)$.

In our case, we utilize a Draper adder [5], which is a carry-lookahead adder. This adder can be implemented both in-place and out-of-place. Table 3 compares the resource estimation for 32-bit adders used in LSH-256-n application. Table 3 shows that the out-of-place Draper adder has about half the depth compared to the in-place adder but requires 32-bit output qubits for each adder. With a total of 1024 adders, 32,768 ($1024 \times 32$) qubits are garbage qubits. Hence, to avoid this inefficiency, we opt for the in-place adder, which slightly increases the depth but significantly reduces the number of qubits required. By using Draper in-place adders, we can reuse all ancilla qubits (53 qubits) except for the input and output qubits in other operations. Although it involves a higher depth than the out-of-place adder, we compensate for this drawback by using adders in parallel within each function(described in Sect. 3.2 and Sect. 3.3). This allows us to conserve 32,768 qubits instead of allowing for a higher depth of about 4,134.

## 3.2    Parallel Addition of MsgExp and Mix Functions

In the MsgExp function, 16 adders are needed to update $\mathbf{M}_j^{(i)}$. According to Sect. 3.1, we can initially allocate 53 ancilla qubits and reuse them throughout. However, in this scenario, the adders are executed sequentially, increasing the depth of the circuit. To optimize the circuit depth which is our purpose, we employ addition in parallel by allocating more ancilla qubits. To process 16 adders in parallel in the MsgExp function, 848 ($16 \times 53$) ancilla qubits are required.

Similarly, in the Mix function, 24 ($8 \times 3$) adders are used and 8 out of the 24 adders can be operated simultaneously. In other words, 8 adders can be

**Table 3.** Comparison of quantum resources required for adder (32-bit).

| Adder | Operation | #CNOT | #Toffoli | Toffoli depth | #Qubit (reuse) | Depth |
|---|---|---|---|---|---|---|
| Cuccaro [4] | in-place | 153 | 61 | 61 | 65 (1) | 66 |
| Draper [5] | in-place | 123 | 254 | 22 | 117 (53) | 28 |
| | out-of-place | 94 | 127 | 11 | 118 (22) | 14 |

※: Estimation of undecomposed resources

**Table 4.** Comparison of quantum resources required for each component.

| Function | Operation | #CNOT | #Toffoli | Toffoli depth | #Qubit | Depth |
|---|---|---|---|---|---|---|
| MsgExp | Sequential | 1,968 | 4,064 | 352 | 1,077 | 433 |
| | Parallel | 1,968 | 4,064 | **22** | 1,872 | **28** |
| Mix | Sequential | 2,952 | 6,096 | 528 | 565 | 649 |
| | Parallel | 2,952 | 6,096 | **66** | 936 | **84** |

※: Estimation of undecomposed resources

processed in parallel, and this parallel addition is repeated a total of 3 times. In this scenario, the ancilla qubits used in the MsgExp function can be reused. Therefore, there is no need to allocate additional ancilla qubits for the adders in the Mix function. As a result, 848 ancilla qubits are initially allocated at once. However, due to the reuse of qubits, the depth may increase (the description continues in Sect. 3.3).

Table 4 shows the comparison of quantum resources required for MsgExp and Mix function. The parallel operations greatly reduce the toffoli depth and full detph compared to the sequential operations.

### 3.3   Combined Architecture of Compress Function

Within the Compression function, the MsgExp function, and the Mix function can operate independently. However, due to the ancilla qubit reuse in the Mix function, these functions cannot operate independently. While this architecture can reduce the number of qubits, it increases the circuit depth due to the sequential operations of high complexity. To optimize the circuit depth, we execute the MsgExp function and Mix function in parallel by allocating additional ancilla qubits as shown in Fig. 3. This parallel execution method allows us to effectively reduce the overall circuit depth, improving efficiency.

In previous work [17], Song et al. conducted sequential operations in the Compression function as shown in Fig. 4. In contrast, our proposed circuit reduces the depth compared to previous work by allocating additional ancilla qubits and implementing the Mix and MsgExp functions in parallel. Specifically, the $i$-th Mix function and the $i + 1$-th MsgExp function can execute in parallel,

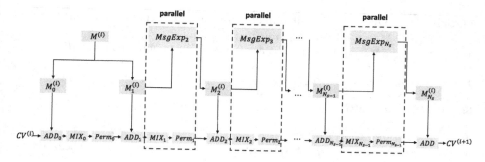

**Fig. 3.** Parallel process of Compression function

effectively reducing the circuit depth. Figure 5 shows our proposed Compression function. To enable this parallel process, we additionally allocate 424 (8 × 53) ancilla qubits for Mix function. Thus, we initially allocate 1,272 ancilla qubits at once and reuse them each round. Algorithm 1 represents the overall process of Compress function. By allocating two sets of ancilla qubits, we can parallelize the even-round Mix function with the odd-round MsgExp function, and the odd-round Mix function with the even-round MsgExp function.

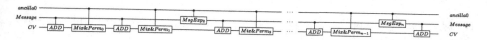

**Fig. 4.** Compression function in [17] using a sequential process

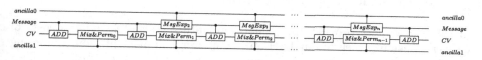

**Fig. 5.** Proposed parallel Compression function architecture

Table 5 shows the comparision of quantum resources required for Compression function. In parallel process, only the depths of the Mix functions are estimated because they have a higher depth compared to the MsgExp functions. Consequently, the process of the Compression and the Mix functions in parallel demonstrates lower depth compared to processing them sequentially.

---

**Algorithm 1.** Quantum circuit implementation of Compress function.

**Input:** $M_{even}$, $M_{odd}$ $CV$, $\alpha$, $\beta$, $SC$, $ancilla_0$, $ancilla_1$
**Output:** $M_{even}$, $M_{odd}$, $CV$, 424 qubit array-$ancilla_0$, 848 qubit array-$ancilla_1$

1: $CV \leftarrow \text{MsgAdd}(M_{even}, CV)$
2: $CV \leftarrow \text{Mix}(CV, \alpha_{even}, \beta_{even}, SC, ancilla_0)$
3: $CV \leftarrow \text{WordPerm}(CV)$

4: $CV \leftarrow \text{MsgAdd}(M_{odd}, CV)$
5: $CV \leftarrow \text{Mix}(CV, \alpha_{odd}, \beta_{odd}, SC, ancilla_0)$                    ▷ Parallelization 1
6: $CV \leftarrow \text{WordPerm}(CV)$

7: **for** $1 \leq i \leq 13$ **do**
8:     $M_{even} \leftarrow \text{MsgExp}(M_{even}, M_{odd}, ancilla_1)$                    ▷ Parallelization 1
9:     $CV \leftarrow \text{MsgAdd}(M_{even}, CV)$
10:    $CV \leftarrow \text{Mix}(CV, \alpha_{even}, \beta_{even}, SC, ancilla_0)$           ▷ Parallelization 2
11:    $CV \leftarrow \text{WordPerm}(CV)$

12:    $M_{odd} \leftarrow \text{MsgExp}(M_{even}, M_{odd}, ancilla_1)$                     ▷ Parallelization 2
13:    $CV \leftarrow \text{MsgAdd}(M_{odd}, CV)$
14:    $CV \leftarrow \text{Mix}(CV, \alpha_{odd}, \beta_{odd}, SC, ancilla_0)$            ▷ Parallelization 1
15:    $CV \leftarrow \text{WordPerm}(CV)$
16: **end for**

17: $M_{even} \leftarrow \text{MsgExp}(M_{even}, M_{odd}, ancilla_1)$                       ▷ Parallelization 1
18: $CV \leftarrow \text{MsgAdd}(M_{even}, CV)$

19: **return** $CV$

---

## 4    Performance and Evaluation

In this section, we provide an estimated quantum resources and the costs of Grover collision attack of our LSH quantum circuit implementation comparing the previous work. We utilized ProjectQ as our quantum programming tool for circuit implementation and simulation. Our implementation was verified using the `ClassicalSimulator` library, and we analyzed the quantum resource using the `ResourceCounter`. For LSH-256-n, the only differences lie in the constant value and the hash length, while the overall operation remains identical. Therefore, all estimated resources, excluding X gates, remain the identical. Similarly, the same applies to LSH-512-n. Thus, we will only compare LSH-256-256 and LSH-512-512.

Table 6 shows the comparison of the decomposed quantum resources required for implementations of LSH. In [17], the decomposed quantum resources were not provided, so we estimate the quantum resources based on the undecomposed resources provided in the paper.

As shown in Table 6, we can observe that our implementation, which applies Cuccaro adders (the same adder as [17]) and parallelization method utilizes 8

**Table 5.** Comparison of quantum resources required for the Compression function.

| Function | Operation | #CNOT | #Toffoli | Toffoli depth | #Qubit | Depth |
|---|---|---|---|---|---|---|
| Compression | Sequential | 139,776 | 260,096 | 2,266 | 2,384 | 2,873 |
| | Parallel | 139,776 | 260,096 | **1,716** | 2,808 | **2,198** |

※: Estimation of undecomposed resources

more qubits compared to [17]. However, it reduces the full depth by approximately 12,000. Additionally, applying the Draper adder further increases the qubit usage, but it significantly reduces the full depth. To assess the trade-off between qubits and depth, we provide metrics $TD\text{-}M$, $FD\text{-}M$, $TD^2\text{-}M$ and $FD^2\text{-}M$. As a result, our proposed quantum circuit achieves the optimized performance across all trade-off metrics.

Based on the estimated resources of the LSH quantum circuit, we can estimate the cost of collision attacks on LSH. To estimate the collision attack cost for LSH, we adopt the CNS algorithm described in Sect. 2.3. The CNS algorithm has the complexity of $O(2^{\frac{2n}{5}-\frac{3s}{5}})$ $(s \leq \frac{n}{4})$. According to [9], they set $s = \frac{n}{6}$ to define suitable criteria for NIST post-quantum security levels, and we follow that approach. Furthermore, since most of the quantum resources are used in implementing the target cipher in the quantum circuit, the overhead of the diffusion operator can be considered negligible compared to the oracle. Additionally, the Grover oracle consists of LSH quantum circuit twice consecutively. The first constructs the encryption circuit, and the second operates the encryption circuit in reverse to return to the state before encryption. As a result, the oracle necessitates twice the cost of implementing the quantum circuit, excluding qubits. Consequently, the cost of Grover's search for LSH is approximately $2 \times 2^{(\frac{2n}{5}-\frac{3s}{5})} \times$ Table 6, as shown in Table 7. Since the cost of collision attacks varies depending on the input and output lengths, we present the resource costs for all LSH parameters.

**Table 6.** Quantum resources required for implementations of LSH.

| Cipher | Source | #CNOT | #1qCliff | #T | Toffoli depth (TD) | #Qubit (M) | Full depth (FD) | TD-M | FD-M | TD²-M | FD²-M |
|---|---|---|---|---|---|---|---|---|---|---|---|
| LSH-256-256 | [17] | 545,536 | 187,813 | 437,248 | 6,283 | 1,552 | 50,758 | $1.16 \cdot 2^{23}$ | $1.17 \cdot 2^{26}$ | $1.78 \cdot 2^{35}$ | $1.82 \cdot 2^{41}$ |
| | Ours-CDKM | 545,536 | 187813 | 437,248 | 4,758 | 1,560 | **38,483** | $1.77 \cdot 2^{22}$ | $1.79 \cdot 2^{25}$ | $1.03 \cdot 2^{35}$ | $1.05 \cdot 2^{41}$ |
| | Ours-Draper | 1,700,608 | 306,947 | 1,820,672 | 1,716 | 2,808 | **13,647** | $1.15 \cdot 2^{22}$ | $1.14 \cdot 2^{25}$ | $1.93 \cdot 2^{32}$ | $1.90 \cdot 2^{38}$ |
| LSH-512-512 | [17] | 1,203,760 | 418,369 | 966,000 | 13,875 | 3,088 | 111,532 | $1.28 \cdot 2^{25}$ | $1.28 \cdot 2^{28}$ | $1.08 \cdot 2^{39}$ | $1.09 \cdot 2^{45}$ |
| | Ours-CDKM | 1,203,760 | 418,369 | 966,000 | 10,500 | 3,096 | **84,451** | $1.94 \cdot 2^{24}$ | $1.95 \cdot 2^{27}$ | $1.24 \cdot 2^{38}$ | $1.26 \cdot 2^{44}$ |
| | Ours-Draper | 4,030,000 | 736,569 | 2,614,473 | 2,028 | 5,832 | **17,385** | $1.41 \cdot 2^{23}$ | $1.51 \cdot 2^{26}$ | $1.40 \cdot 2^{34}$ | $1.60 \cdot 2^{40}$ |

Table 7. Costs of the Grover's collision search for LSH.

| Cipher | #Gate (G) | Full depth (FD) | T-depth (Td) | #Qubit (M) | G-FD | FD-M | Td-M | FD²-M | Td²-M |
|---|---|---|---|---|---|---|---|---|---|
| LSH-256-224 | $1.65 \cdot 2^{89}$ | $1.5 \cdot 2^{81}$ | $1.51 \cdot 2^{80}$ | $1.72 \cdot 2^{48}$ | $\mathbf{1.23 \cdot 2^{171}}$ | $1.29 \cdot 2^{130}$ | $1.3 \cdot 2^{129}$ | $1.95 \cdot 2^{211}$ | $1.97 \cdot 2^{209}$ |
| LSH-256-256 | $1.25 \cdot 2^{99}$ | $1.13 \cdot 2^{91}$ | $1.14 \cdot 2^{90}$ | $1.08 \cdot 2^{54}$ | $\mathbf{1.42 \cdot 2^{190}}$ | $1.23 \cdot 2^{145}$ | $1.24 \cdot 2^{144}$ | $1.41 \cdot 2^{236}$ | $1.42 \cdot 2^{234}$ |
| LSH-512-224 | $1.96 \cdot 2^{90}$ | $1.91 \cdot 2^{81}$ | $1.78 \cdot 2^{80}$ | $1.79 \cdot 2^{49}$ | $\mathbf{1.87 \cdot 2^{172}}$ | $1.71 \cdot 2^{131}$ | $1.6 \cdot 2^{130}$ | $1.64 \cdot 2^{213}$ | $1.43 \cdot 2^{211}$ |
| LSH-512-256 | $1.49 \cdot 2^{100}$ | $1.45 \cdot 2^{91}$ | $1.35 \cdot 2^{90}$ | $1.13 \cdot 2^{55}$ | $\mathbf{1.07 \cdot 2^{192}}$ | $1.64 \cdot 2^{146}$ | $1.53 \cdot 2^{145}$ | $1.18 \cdot 2^{238}$ | $1.03 \cdot 2^{236}$ |
| LSH-512-384 | $1.96 \cdot 2^{138}$ | $1.91 \cdot 2^{129}$ | $1.78 \cdot 2^{128}$ | $1.42 \cdot 2^{76}$ | $\mathbf{1.87 \cdot 2^{268}}$ | $1.36 \cdot 2^{206}$ | $1.27 \cdot 2^{205}$ | $1.3 \cdot 2^{336}$ | $1.13 \cdot 2^{334}$ |
| LSH-512-512 | $1.29 \cdot 2^{177}$ | $1.26 \cdot 2^{168}$ | $1.17 \cdot 2^{167}$ | $1.79 \cdot 2^{97}$ | $\mathbf{1.63 \cdot 2^{345}}$ | $1.13 \cdot 2^{266}$ | $1.05 \cdot 2^{265}$ | $1.43 \cdot 2^{434}$ | $1.24 \cdot 2^{432}$ |

# 5    Conclusion

In this work, we focused on optimizing the depth of quantum circuits for the Korean cryptographic hash function LSH. To optimize the depth, we use optimized quantum adders and parallelization. Our quantum circuit implementation of LSH achieves a significant improvement in depth over 78.8% compared to the approach presented in [17]. Additionally, the Toffoli depth sees an enhancement of more than 79.1%.

Through the depth-optimized implementation, we also obtain the optimized quantum resources of Grover collision attack for LSH. Although NIST provide the post-quantum security level and quantum attack costs for symmetric key ciphers, they do not provide the specific quantum cost for hash functions. If NIST defines criteria for hash functions, we will compare our results with those criteria.

**Acknowledgment.** This work was supported by the National Research Foundation of Korea (NRF) grant funded by the Korea government (MSIT). (No. RS-2023-00277994, Quantum Circuit Depth Optimization for ARIA, SEED, LEA, HIGHT, and LSH of KCMVP Domestic Cryptographic Algorithms, 90%) and this work was supported by Institute for Information & communications Technology Planning & Evaluation (IITP) grant funded by the Korea government(MSIT) (<Q|Crypton>, No. 2019-0-00033, Study on Quantum Security Evaluation of Cryptography based on Computational Quantum Complexity, 10%)

# References

1. Bernstein, D.J.: Cost analysis of hash collisions: will quantum computers make SHARCS obsolete. SHARCS **9**, 105 (2009)
2. Brassard, G., Hoyer, P., Tapp, A.: Quantum algorithm for the collision problem. arXiv preprint quant-ph/9705002 (1997)
3. Chailloux, A., Naya-Plasencia, M., Schrottenloher, A.: An efficient quantum collision search algorithm and implications on symmetric cryptography. In: Takagi, T., Peyrin, T. (eds.) ASIACRYPT 2017. LNCS, vol. 10625, pp. 211–240. Springer, Cham (2017). https://doi.org/10.1007/978-3-319-70697-9_8
4. Cuccaro, S., Draper, T., Kutin, S., Moulton, D.: A new quantum ripple-carry addition circuit. arXiv (2008). https://arxiv.org/pdf/quant-ph/0410184.pdf

5. Draper, T.G., Kutin, S.A., Rains, E.M., Svore, K.M.: A logarithmic-depth quantum carry-lookahead adder. arXiv preprint quant-ph/0406142 (2004)
6. Grassl, M., Langenberg, B., Roetteler, M., Steinwandt, R.: Applying Grover's algorithm to AES: Quantum resource estimates. In: Takagi, T. (ed.) Post-Quantum Cryptography, pp. 29–43. Springer, Cham (2016)
7. Grover, L.K.: A fast quantum mechanical algorithm for database search. In: Proceedings of the Twenty-Eighth Annual ACM Symposium on Theory of Computing, pp. 212–219 (1996)
8. Jang, K., Baksi, A., Kim, H., Song, G., Seo, H., Chattopadhyay, A.: Quantum analysis of AES. Cryptology ePrint Archive, Paper 2022/683 (2022). https://eprint.iacr.org/2022/683
9. Jang, K., et al.: Quantum implementation and analysis of sha-2 and sha-3. Cryptology ePrint Archive (2024)
10. Jaques, S., Naehrig, M., Roetteler, M., Virdia, F.: Implementing grover oracles for quantum key search on AES and LowMC. In: Canteaut, A., Ishai, Y. (eds.) EUROCRYPT 2020. LNCS, vol. 12106, pp. 280–310. Springer, Cham (2020). https://doi.org/10.1007/978-3-030-45724-2_10
11. Kim, D.C., Hong, D., Lee, J.K., Kim, W.H., Kwon, D.: Lsh: a new fast secure hash function family. In: Information Security and Cryptology-ICISC 2014: 17th International Conference, Seoul, South Korea, December 3-5, 2014, Revised Selected Papers 17, pp. 286–313. Springer (2015)
12. Liu, Q., Preneel, B., Zhao, Z., Wang, M.: Improved quantum circuits for AES: reducing the depth and the number of qubits. Cryptology ePrint Archive, Paper 2023/1417 (2023). https://eprint.iacr.org/2023/1417
13. NIST.: Submission requirements and evaluation criteria for the post-quantum cryptography standardization process (2016). https://csrc.nist.gov/CSRC/media/Projects/Post-Quantum-Cryptography/documents/call-for-proposals-final-dec-2016.pdf
14. NIST.: Call for additional digital signature schemes for the post-quantum cryptography standardization process (2022). https://csrc.nist.gov/csrc/media/Projects/pqc-dig-sig/documents/call-for-proposals-dig-sig-sept-2022.pdf
15. Rahman, M., Paul, G.: Grover on katan: quantum resource estimation. IEEE Trans. Quant. Eng. 3, 1–9 (2022)
16. Shor, P.W.: Algorithms for quantum computation: discrete logarithms and factoring. In: Proceedings 35th Annual Symposium on Foundations of Computer Science, pp. 124–134. IEEE (1994)
17. Song, G., Jang, K., Kim, H., Seo, H.: A parallel quantum circuit implementations of LSH hash function for use with Grover's algorithm. Appl. Sci. 12(21), 10891 (2022)

# Who Ruins the Game?: Unveiling Cheating Players in the "Battlefield" Game

Dong Young Kim and Huy Kang Kim[✉]

School of Cybersecurity, Korea University, Seoul, Republic of Korea
{klgh1256,cenda}@korea.ac.kr

**Abstract.** The "Battlefield" online game is well-known for its large-scale multiplayer capabilities and unique gaming features, including various vehicle controls. However, these features make the game a major target for cheating, significantly detracting from the gaming experience. This study analyzes user behavior in cheating play in the popular online game, the "Battlefield", using statistical methods. We aim to provide comprehensive insights into cheating players through an extensive analysis of over 44,000 reported cheating incidents collected via the "Game-tools API". Our methodology includes detailed statistical analyses such as calculating basic statistics of key variables, correlation analysis, and visualizations using histograms, box plots, and scatter plots. Our findings emphasize the importance of adaptive, data-driven approaches to prevent cheating plays in online games.

**Keywords:** Cheating Play Detection · Online Game ·
The Battlefield · Statistical Method · Correlation Analysis ·
Visualization

## 1 Introduction

The Battlefield game [3] (operated by Electronic Arts Inc.) is a large-scale team multiplayer online game. It is also well-known for its unique gaming features, such as enabling various vehicle controls (*e.g.*, Tank, Armored Personnel Carrier, Infantry Fighting Vehicle, Fighter Jet, and Attack Helicopter) by game players. Such an aspect distinguishes it from other First-Person Shooters (FPS) games, attracting gamers worldwide. As the same as the real-world battlefield, the vehicle's ability is too strong enough to eliminate the opponent player's infantry troops. To leverage vehicles' ability, some players use game cheating programs that are regarded as unfair gameplay.

Cheating play is an axis of evil in online gaming. If game companies fail to detect cheating play in time, the game users quit and leave the game because they can feel unfair. Consequently, cheating play detection is a critical success factor in preventing a game company's financial damage and managing the user's loyalty.

J.-H. Lee et al. (Eds.): WISA 2024, LNCS 15499, pp. 364–375, 2025.
https://doi.org/10.1007/978-981-96-1624-4_28

**Fig. 1.** The BattleField in-game cheating play example [13]

Not only in the Battlefield game, but cheating programs such as Aimbot, Wallhack, Speedhack, Weaponhack, and EXP hack have also been widely used in FPS games for several decades [5].

Thus, like the other FPS games, the Battlefield game has many users complaining about the cheating play. Figure 1 shows a cheating player use the Wallhack and ESP cheating tool during the battle. In response, the latest version, the Battlefield 2042, deploys an Anti-Cheat program on the client-side. However, detecting cheating on the client-side may diminish user experience due to program errors and vulnerabilities. Detecting cheating over the network is practically impossible, as it requires real-time monitoring of all users' communications, which could degrade the overall gaming experience due to the real-time nature of FPS games. Server-side detection demands significant resources from game servers. It is practically impossible for game companies to monitor all users' logs, which could increase the game's latency, which is critical in FPS games. Thus, the existing cheating detection methods used in other game genres (*e.g.*, frequently used data mining or machine learning methods in MMORPG genre [4].) are not easily applicable in FPS games.

Therefore, this paper aims to provide insights for discovering users who use cheating tools without consuming resources from the game servers and clients, based on statistical analysis and visualization.

Our research method employs fundamental statistical analysis, which can effectively distinguish cheating players' behaviors. The main contributions of this study can be summarized as follows.

– Unlike existing cheating detection methods in FPS games, our approach does not need to be deployed in-game client-side. The current countermeasures deployed in the game client-side can harm the overall gaming experience because of the overhead (*i.e.*, typical usability vs. security problem)

– To the best of our knowledge, it is the first approach for cheating play user detection by lightweight statistical analysis of kill-log in the Battlefield game. We discovered features that can distinguish cheating players' behaviors successfully.

## 2   Background

### 2.1   How to Play the Battlefield Games?

The Battlefield game provides specialized game modes. For instance, some modes focus on the number of infantry kills to win, while others modes focus on the score based on the result of capturing specific areas during the combat. Among various modes, one of the most representative modes is the 'Conquest mode'. Conquest mode involves 64 or 128 players, where participants are divided into several classes, such as Assault, Support, Ammunition, and Recon. Each class has specialized equipment. For example, the Support class users, one of the infantry solder classes in the game, carry a medical kit to heal their wounded teammates, or they carry a defibrillator to revive soldiers who have been downed.

Depending on the map size and scale, these soldiers can control various vehicles. These vehicles include Tanks, Armored Personnel Carriers, Infantry Fighting Vehicles, Anti-Aircraft Vehicles, Fighter Jets, and Attack Helicopters. There are land, water, and air vehicles that players can use from the initial starting point or specific points on the map. The amount of damage dealt by the weapons on these vehicles is significantly higher than that of infantry weapons. Consequently, vehicles can massacre infantry, or infantry may find themselves hiding from the vehicles.

Conquest mode involves infantry using vehicles to capture specific points. Capturing a point occurs when there are more allied soldiers than enemies at a location for a certain period, and it happens faster with more allies present.

The Conquest mode is the most preferable play mode, but cheating play exists in all modes, not only the Conquest mode.

### 2.2   Definition and Types of Cheating in the Game

The well-known cheating plays in FPS are Aimbot, Damage Modify, Gadget Modify, Wallhack, Stealth, and Magical Bullet. 'Aimbot' is a program that artificially enhances a player's shooting accuracy by automatically targeting opponents' critical areas (*e.g.*, headshot), enabling precise shooting. This type of cheating elevates a player's shooting abilities, and eventually disrupting the game's balance seriously. 'Damage Modify' is cheating that manipulates a player's weapon to cause more damage than usual, allowing players to overpower enemies with fewer bullets. 'Gadget Modify' alters or enhances the functions of the equipment or gadgets players use. For example, it could increase the blast radius of explosives or reduce the cooldown period of gadgets. 'Wallhack' makes walls or other obstacles transparent or allows players to see the outlines of enemies through them. It provides a significant tactical advantage by predicting the location and movements of concealed enemies. 'Stealth' renders players invisible to enemy sights or detection systems, granting the ability to move covertly and disrupt game balance. 'Magical Bullet' includes features that allow players' bullets to penetrate obstacles or automatically target enemies at unrealistically long distances, ignoring ballistics and physical laws, resulting in highly unfair gameplay.

## 2.3  Why Cheating Detection in FPS is Important?

Why is it necessary to prevent cheating in FPS games? First, it is essential to maintain fairness. Ensuring the game's fairness allows all players to compete under equal conditions, making the gaming experience more enjoyable and satisfying. Second, it is to ensure that all users can enjoy the game. One of the main purpose of playing a game is to have fun and feel a sense of accomplishment through challenge. Fun and challenge are key rewards in a game system. If the fun and challenge based reward system is disrupted by some cheating players, then many normal players will quit and leave the game. Third, it disturbs the growth and development of players. Honest players can develop their skills and learn strategies, whereas cheating players skip this developmental process, negatively impacting other players (i.e., contagion) [14]. Thus, if cheating players gain an advantage in the game, honest players are disadvantaged, leading to many players leaving the game. For these reasons, cheating can ruin the game's overall fair-play culture and lead to user churn.

## 3  Related Work

Tekofsky et al. [12] analyzed play styles by age in Battlefield 3. Their study used data from 10,416 users to demonstrate that performance and speed of play decrease with age. May et al. [8] analyzed how the game Battlefield 2042 implements climate crises and environmental challenges. This study investigated how the game's settings and scenarios encourage players to think about ecological issues and reviewed how user-generated content and discussions about the game promote ecological engagement. They demonstrated through data analysis from 13,129 users how these elements stimulate ecological thinking among players.

Various studies have been conducted on detecting cheating in FPS games. Most of these studies use computer vision to detect changes in status or visually apparent cheating patterns. For example, Nie et al. [9] identified cheating patterns such as Aimbots in FPS games using a deep learning vision framework called VADNet. Jonnalagadda et al. [6] proposed a new vision-based approach that captures the final game screen state to detect illegal overlays. They collected data from two FPS games and several cheating software using deep learning models to verify cheat detection performance. Liu et al. [7] detected Aimbots using cosine similarity and statistical methods. Cosine similarity was used to measure the change in aim when players first spot an enemy, calculating the angle between vectors of the player's aiming direction to compare the automatic aiming patterns of Aimbots with those of regular players. Pinto *et al.* [10] proposed a novel approach using deep learning and multivariate time-series analysis to detect cheats in video games. Instead of game data, they analyzed user behavior data such as key inputs and mouse movements, demonstrating high accuracy in cheat detection. Han *et al.* [5] discovered several features (*e.g.*, winrate, headshot-ratio, play counts and play time, etc.) and detection rules to differentiate cheating players in Point Blank, one of the famous FPS games in Asian game market. In this work, the proposed method detected cheating plays based on the analysis of action logs, while our proposed model is based on the analysis of kill-log and stat data.

## 4   Methodology

Figure 2 shows the overall procedure of the proposed method. We aimed to conduct an in-depth analysis of cheating players using statistical analysis. In this process, we calculated basic statistics such as mean, standard deviation, and minimum/maximum values for each variable. Then we extracted meaningful variables based on these calculations. This approach allowed us to understand the overall characteristics of the data and identify key factors.

First, to understand the data distribution, we calculated basic statistics for each variable, including mean, standard deviation, minimum value, maximum value, median, and quartiles. This helped us grasp the central tendency and variability of the data and check for outliers or anomalies.

Second, we analyzed the correlations between variables. Then, we identified the relationships between variables through correlation analysis; and we determined which variables have influence value to others. This provided crucial

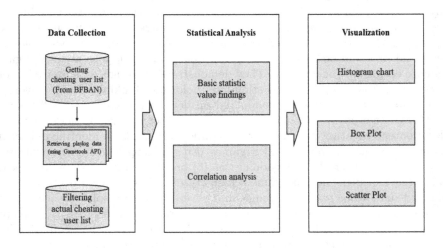

**Fig. 2.** Overall procedure of FPS cheating play detection

information for understanding the interactions between variables. By measuring correlation coefficients, we identified variables that showed significant correlations.

Finally, for the data visualization, we created various graphs such as histograms, box plots, and scatter plots. Histograms allowed us to visually confirm the distribution of each variable, while box plots provided a clear view of the quartiles, median, and outliers. Scatter plots were used for visually expressing the relationships between two variables, making it easier to understand correlations or trends between variables.

By visually representing the results of complex statistical analyses, we could easily identify key characteristics and patterns in the data. Additionally, using various graphs to illuminate different aspects of the data enabled a more comprehensive and in-depth analysis.

# 5 Experiment Result

## 5.1 Dataset

Due to the absence of publicly available datasets for experimenting with the methodology of this paper, we collected the data directly. The dataset was gathered using the "Gametools API" [1] with the Requests [11] library. The "Gametools API" allows us to fetch the list and information of users identified as cheating players from "BFBAN" [2]. "BFBAN" is a site where users can report cheating players and check the status of their bans online. We specifically retrieved the list of users banned by the game company and analyzed their statistics.

The data was collected in two stages. First, we collected the list of cheating players from the "Gametools API". Second, we gathered detailed information about these users' cheating activities using the same API.

The total number of cheating players is 119,569. The data spans from the first reported cheating player on October 27, 2018, to the most recent report on April 29, 2024. However, due to some data being missing during the collection process from the "Gametools API", we were only able to collect data for 44,307 users.

## 5.2 Explanation of Key Variables

The variables *hack_score* and *hack_score_current* indicate the extent of a user's hacking activities. The *hack_score* represents the highest value of either *hack_score_current* or the player's highest historic *hack_score*, while the *hack_score_current* represents the *hack_score* of the player's current stats. Hack Score measures how abnormal and hacker-like a player's stats are. When the *hack_score* is more than 100, that means their stats are highly abnormal and can only be produced by hacks (except rare false positives. Refer to the dataset's description; the false positive ratio is 0.5% in total.). A *hack_Score* from 0–100 is calculated for each weapon the player has used. The *stats.kills* variable represents the number of opponents a user has eliminated in the game. The *stats.kpm* shows how many opponents the user kills per minute in the game. The *stats.rank* indicates the user's level in the game, with higher values showing that the user has gained more experience points. The *unreleased_weapons.kills* represents the number of kills a user has made using weapons that have not yet been officially released, indicating kills made with special or test weapons.

### 5.3  Basic Statistical Analysis

The dataset consists of 44,307 observations and includes various variables. Basic statistics, such as mean, standard deviation, minimum, maximum, median, and quartiles, were calculated for key variables (hack_score, hack_score_current, stats.kills, stats.kpm, stats.rank, unreleased_weapons.kills). These calculations allowed us to understand the central tendency and variability of the data and identify any outliers or anomalies. The whole result of the basic analysis is summarized in Table 1.

**Table 1.** Summary Statistics of Key Variables

| Column | Mean | Std | Min | Q1: 25% | Q2: 50% | Q3: 75% | Max |
|---|---|---|---|---|---|---|---|
| hack_score | 477.45 | 736.96 | 0 | 41.75 | 143.0 | 528.25 | 16667.0 |
| hack_score _current | 473.89 | 732.86 | 0 | 41.75 | 143.0 | 528.25 | 16667.0 |
| stats.kills | 6937.79 | 14906.77 | 0 | 527.25 | 2958.5 | 7826.5 | 781157.0 |
| stats.kpm | 1.13 | 6.74 | 0 | 0.33 | 0.64 | 1.02 | 1488.56 |
| stats.rank | 65.45 | 46.87 | 0 | 22.0 | 61.0 | 109.0 | 154.0 |
| unreleased _weapons. kills | 6937.79 | 14906.77 | 0 | 527.25 | 2958.5 | 7826.5 | 781157.0 |

### 5.4  Correlation Analysis Between Variables

The hack_score and hack_score_current showed a high correlation of 0.996, indicating that users who have cheated once tend to continue cheating. The stats.kills, and stats.rank showed a strong correlation of 0.794, meaning that recording a high number of kills increases the likelihood of reaching higher levels. The hack_score and stats.rank showed a moderate correlation of 0.449, suggesting that the relationship between cheating and level is not significant. This result indicates that low-level users are not necessarily more prone to cheating and high-level users are not guaranteed to refrain from cheating. The stats.kills and unreleased_weapons.kills showed a perfect positive correlation, indicating that users who use unreleased weapons (cheating players) have a 100% probability of recording a high number of kills. This suggests that some cheating players use these cheats to generate high number of kills, adversely affecting innocent opponents. The whole result of the correlation analysis is summarized in Table 2.

**Table 2.** Correlation Matrix between key features

|  | hack_score | hack_score _current | stats.kills | stats.kpm | stats.rank | unreleased _weapons. kills |
|---|---|---|---|---|---|---|
| hack_score | 1.000000 | 0.996151 | 0.385814 | 0.015135 | 0.449039 | 0.385814 |
| hack_score _current | 0.996151 | 1.000000 | 0.379819 | 0.015231 | 0.442342 | 0.379819 |
| stats.kills | 0.385814 | 0.379819 | 1.000000 | 0.004692 | 0.793550 | 1.000000 |
| stats.kpm | 0.015135 | 0.015231 | 0.004692 | 1.000000 | -0.006504 | 0.004692 |
| stats.rank | 0.449039 | 0.442342 | 0.793550 | -0.006504 | 1.000000 | 0.793550 |
| unreleased _weapons. kills | 0.385814 | 0.379819 | 1.000000 | 0.004692 | 0.793550 | 1.000000 |

## 5.5   Data Visualization

We visualized the result using histograms, box plots, and scatter plots.

The histogram chart is used to visually confirm the distribution of variables and identify data concentrated in specific ranges and outliers. The Histogram chart is shown in Fig. 3.

The box Plot is used to visually analyze the median, quartiles, and outliers of the variables to understand the overall data distribution. The Box Plot result is presented in Fig. 4.

The scatter Plot is used to visually express the relationship between hack score and other variables, making it easy to understand correlations and trends between variables. The Scatter Plot result is presented in Fig. 5.

The key findings from the visualization process are as follows.

- Most benign users have lower hack_score than the median value. It indicates that most users do not use cheating programs.
- We observe the hack_score and hack_score_current have a similar distribution. That means a user who does a cheating play tends to keep on doing cheating play continuously.
- We find the cheating player's records do not show a higher kill count (stats.kills). On the one hand, it means the cheating program is not always effective for all opponent users (some high-level human players can still overwhelm the cheating players.) On the other hand, it also mean the cheating tool can limit the kill ratio not to be detected by an in-game monitoring system. The lower kpm value (stats.kpm < 40) supports this point of view. Also, some cheating players use unknown weapons to kill the opponent players.

The proposed method does not require a high-performance computing environment. The simple statistical values can be estimated in near real-time by streaming in-game play logs. In particular, the continuous cheating behavior of users with high hack scores and the perfect correlation between stats.kills and unreleased_weapons.kills can serve as strong indicators for identifying cheating players. These findings can be beneficial for detecting and responding to cheating behavior in real-time within the game.

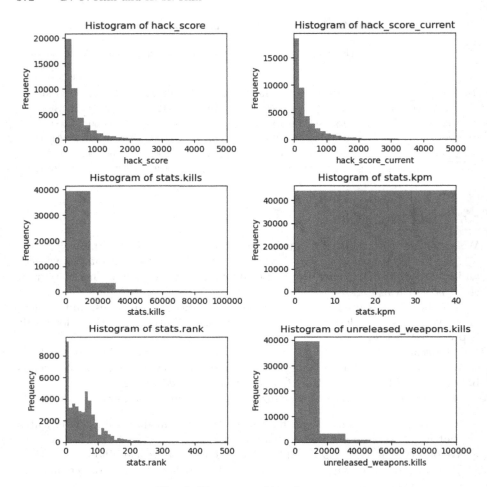

**Fig. 3.** Histogram of key features

## 6  Discussion

We gathered the dataset from the several public sites. and the banned user list can be regarded as reliable. The game company does not provide the official dataset, including banned users, to the public; thus, our approach is the best way so far. However, the dataset does not include a complete cheating player list (*i.e.*, it has a false-negative error) because it relies on the volunteer users' reporting. Also, the dataset can have a false-positive issue when the reporting is intentionally misreported (to dishonor a specific opponent user).

In this study, we adopt simple methods such as correlation analysis and statistical visualization to detect cheating play. As a result, we identified general patterns of cheating players through the correlation analysis between key variables. In the future, we will explore using more statistical techniques for

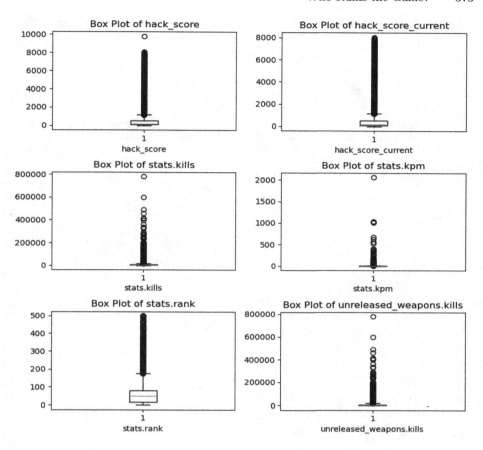

**Fig. 4.** Box Plot of key features

robust and lightweight cheating play detection. We will consider testing other FPS games to get more generalizations of the proposed method. Also, we will research anomaly detection based on malicious and benign user data to overcome the drawbacks of our methods. Due to the difficulty in obtaining data from normal players, there are limitations in creating an anomaly detection model. We plan to implement an anomaly detection model based on the kill-log of abnormal players and explore this topic further.

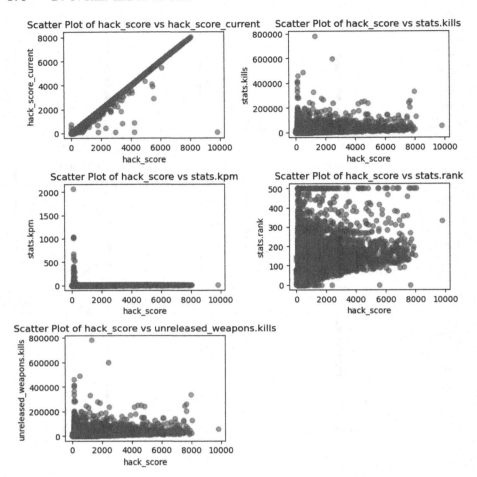

**Fig. 5.** Scatter between hack_score and other variables

## 7    Conclusion

This study proposed a data-driven approach to address the issue of cheating in the Battlefield. To conclude, the main contributions of this study are as follows: First, we confirm the repeatability of cheating behavior. The high correlation (0.996) between hack_score and hack_score_current indicates that users who start cheating tend to continue cheating. This is a significant finding as it shows that cheating behavior is not a one-time occurrence but follows a repetitive pattern. These results emphasize the need for continuous monitoring and response to cheating players in cheating detection systems.

Second, we discovered that the use of specific weapons could be an indicator of cheating behavior. The perfect correlation (1.000) between stats.kills and unreleased_weapons.kills indicates that cheating players tend to record many kills using unreleased weapons. This suggests that monitoring the use of specific weapons can be an important indicator for detecting cheating. Game developers can use this pattern to detect cheating behavior more effectively.

Last, we showed that cheating behavior can occur at all player levels. The moderate correlation (0.449) between hack_score and stats.rank indicates that cheating players are not necessarily concentrated at high levels. This implies that cheating can frequently occur even at lower levels, highlighting the need for cheating detection across all player levels.

**Acknowledgement.** This work was supported by the Institute for Information & Communications Technology Promotion (IITP) grant funded by the Korea government (MSIT). (Grant No. 2020-0-00374, Development of Security Primitives for Unmanned Vehicles).

# References

1. API. https://api.gametools.network/docs/. Accessed 09 Aug 2024
2. BFBAN. https://admin.bfban.com/player. Accessed 09 Aug 2024
3. EA: Battlefield games. https://www.ea.com/ko-kr/games/battlefield. Accessed 09 Aug 2024
4. Han, M.L., Kwak, B.I., Kim, H.K.: Cheating and detection method in massively multiplayer online role-playing game: systematic literature review. IEEE Access **10**, 49050–49063 (2022)
5. Han, M.L., Park, J.K., Kim, H.K.: Online game bot detection in FPS game. In: Handa, H., Ishibuchi, H., Ong, Y.-S., Tan, K.-C. (eds.) Proceedings of the 18th Asia Pacific Symposium on Intelligent and Evolutionary Systems - Volume 2. PALO, vol. 2, pp. 479–491. Springer, Cham (2015). https://doi.org/10.1007/978-3-319-13356-0_38
6. Jonnalagadda, A., Frosio, I., Schneider, S., McGuire, M., Kim, J.: Robust vision-based cheat detection in competitive gaming. In: Proceedings of the ACM on Computer Graphics and Interactive Techniques, vol. 4, no. 1, pp. 1–18 (2021)
7. Liu, D., Gao, X., Zhang, M., Wang, H., Stavrou, A.: Detecting passive cheats in online games via performance-skillfulness inconsistency. In: 2017 47th Annual IEEE/IFIP International Conference on Dependable Systems and Networks (DSN), pp. 615–626. IEEE (2017)
8. May, L., Hall, B.: Thinking ecologically with battlefield 2042. Game Stud. **24**(1) (2024)
9. Nie, B., Ma, B.: Vadnet: visual-based anti-cheating detection network in FPS games. Traitement du Signal **41**(1) (2024)
10. Pinto, J.P., Pimenta, A., Novais, P.: Deep learning and multivariate time series for cheat detection in video games. Mach. Learn. **110**(11), 3037–3057 (2021)
11. Reitz, K.: Requests: HTTP for humans™. https://requests.readthedocs.io/en/latest/. Accessed 09 Aug 2024
12. Tekofsky, S., Spronck, P., Goudbeek, M., Plaat, A., van Den Herik, J.: Past our prime: a study of age and play style development in battlefield 3. IEEE Trans. Comput. Intell. AI Games **7**(3), 292–303 (2015)
13. terDwas: Hurricane loader in the battlefield 2042. https://github.com/terDwas/Battlefield-2042-Hurricane-Cheat. Accessed 09 Aug 2024
14. Woo, J., Kang, S.W., Kim, H.K., Park, J.: Contagion of cheating behaviors in online social networks. IEEE Access **6**, 29098–29108 (2018)

# Author Index

Printed in the United States
by Baker & Taylor Publisher Services